SUBNATIONAL POLITICS

READINGS IN STATE AND LOCAL GOVERNMENT

Edited by **DAVID C. SAFFELL**
and **TERRY GILBRETH**

Ohio Northern University

▲▼ ADDISON-WESLEY PUBLISHING COMPANY

Reading, Massachusetts • Menlo Park, California
London • Amsterdam • Don Mills, Ontario • Sydney

Cover Painting: "County Politics" by Thomas Hart Benton
Copyright © Estate of Thomas Hart Benton 1981
Courtesy Associated American Artists

Library of Congress Cataloging in Publication Data

Main entry under title:
Subnational politics.

  Includes index.
  1. State governments. 2. Local government—United
States. I. Saffell, David C. II. Gilbreth, Terry.
JK2443.S92   320.8'0973   81-8110
ISBN 0-201-06569-X   AACR2

ISBN 0-201-06569-X
ABCDEFGHIJ-AL-8987654321

PREFACE

For decades college and university professors have routinely made use of edited collections of readings in their introductory American national government courses. When done well and used in conjunction with a conventional text, such collections serve at least two purposes: they provide students with a more extensive treatment of particular topics than does the basic text, and they heighten student interest by providing a different perspective and some additional insights into the problems and controversies that beset American national government.

Surprisingly, comparative collections of readings have generally not been available to those of us who teach state and local government. Perhaps in part because of this, state and local government is too often viewed by undergraduates as one of the duller courses in the political science curriculum, something to be suffered through if it cannot be avoided. Such an attitude does, unfortunately, hinder the learning process. Our purpose here is to help the professor combat this attitude by providing an appropriate collection of materials that will do what good national government readers do: stimulate student interest in the subject at hand and offer students some information that is not always available in texts.

We have sought to make this collection compatible with as many state and local government texts as possible by following what seems to us to be a conventional breakdown of chapters. While the order in which they are presented may not be precisely the same as that which the individual instructor finds in his or her favorite text, we believe that the individual chapters in this collection can be readily matched up with those in most current state and local government textbooks. Discussion questions follow each chapter and are designed to stimulate, not control and direct, classroom discussion of the articles. A novel feature of this reader is its index, provided for the convenience of both students and instructors who seek ready access to topics covered by the various readings.

We would like to express our gratitude to Stuart Johnson of Addison-Wesley Publishing Company. At a time when publishers are commonly reluctant to look at anything that does not fit into a conventional, easily defined mode, he not only listened to our ideas but encouraged us to carry them through to completion.

Ada, Ohio   D. C. S.
July 1981   T. G.

CONTENTS

CHAPTER ONE

STATES AND CITIES IN THE FEDERAL SYSTEM

For many years political scientists assumed, and therefore taught their students, that there existed an indestructible, functional boundary between the federal government and state and local governments. If such a "layer cake" image of our federal system of government was ever accurate, and that is doubtful, it certainly is inaccurate today. Instead of dividing up power, federal, state, and local governments share the responsibility for meeting virtually all of the various needs of the American people. This current reality is reflected not only in the two readings in this chapter, but also in those found in most of the other chapters of this book. Virtually all state and local institutions, problems, and policies have by now been affected in one way or another by federal policies and decisions.

The first article in this chapter was originally written by the late Morton Grodzins, but it has been revised by his student Daniel Elazar, himself a major authority on American federalism. The article graphically describes the intergovernmental sharing of functions and the reasons why those functions cannot be separated by means of a decentralization of national responsibilities to state and local governments. It concludes with a very interesting and unusual conception of the American political system—one with which you may disagree. Certainly it is a conception that you should discuss in class.

The second article focuses on federal grants-in-aid and their current impact on state and local autonomy. Grants come in a wide variety of forms, commonly referred to as the "grant system," but essentially they all involve a transfer of money from the federal government to state or local governments. With the partial exception of general revenue sharing, grants are designed to help their recipient governments achieve goals and implement programs that the federal government deems of value to the nation as a whole.

The article is part of a summary of a fourteen-volume study on the grant system that was conducted by the Advisory Commission on Intergovernmental Relations (ACIR). This is a federal agency that paradoxically contains more

1

representatives of state and local governments than of the federal government. There are fourteen state and local representatives, nine federal representatives, and three representatives of the general public. Consequently, the ACIR itself is a good example of the breakdown of divisions between federal, state, and local governments that Grodzins and Elazar discuss.

In the article the ACIR considers the impact of the shift in the grant system toward grant types (notably block grants and general revenue sharing) that are characterized by relatively broad recipient discretion as to how and for what purposes the money shall be spent and away from categorical grants (categoricals), which can be used for only limited purposes and are subject to numerous other federal restrictions. Specifically, the ACIR is concerned here with this question: *Have the changes in the federal grant system of the past decade increased the amount of discretion exercised by state and local governments in the use of grant funds and have they effected a noticeable devolution of authority?* The complexity of the answer the ACIR arrives at reflects the complexity of the grant system itself.

Centralization and Decentralization in the American Federal System*

Morton Grodzins and Daniel Elazar

I. THE MARBLE CAKE OF AMERICAN GOVERNMENT

To put the matter bluntly, government in the United States is chaotic. In addition to the central government and the fifty states, there are something like 18,000 general-purpose municipalities, almost an equal number of general-purpose townships, more than 3,000 counties, and so many special-purpose governments that no one can claim even to have counted them accurately. At an educated guess, there are some 81,000 tax-levying governments in the country. Single citizens may be buried under a whole pyramid of governments. A resident of Park Forest, Illinois, for example, though he may know very little else about them, knows that he pays taxes to eleven governments. The Park Forest citizen enjoys more governments than most people in the United States, but he is by no means unique. Though no one has made the exact calculation, it is not unlikely that a majority of citizens are within the jurisdiction of four or more governments, not counting the state and national ones.

The multitude of governments does not mask any simplicity of activity. There is no neat division of functions among them. If one looks closely, it appears that virtually all governments are involved in virtually all functions. More precisely, there is hardly any activity that does not involve the federal, state, and some local government in important responsibilities. Functions of the American governments are shared. Consider a case that seems least likely to demonstrate the point: the function of providing education. It is widely believed that education is uniquely a local responsibility, the province of

Reprinted from *A Nation of States*, edited by Robert A. Goldwin (Chicago: Rand McNally and Company, 1974). Used by permission of the Public Affairs Conference Center, Kenyon College, Gambier, Ohio.

* This essay was originally prepared by Professor Morton Grodzins. It has been revised for the second edition of this volume by Daniel Elazar.

governments especially created for that purpose. A quarter of all governments in the United States are school districts. Is this a great simplifying fact? Does it indicate a focusing of educational responsibility in the hands of single-purpose local governments?

The answer to both questions is a clear "no." That there exist something like 21,000 school districts in the United States does not indicate that education, even in the elementary and high schools, is in any sense an exclusive function of those districts. In several states, local districts are administrative arms of state departments of education, and the educational function is principally a state responsibility. In all states, to a greater or lesser degree—and the degree tends to be greater—local districts are dependent upon state financial aid, state teacher certification, state prescription of textbooks, and state inspection of performance in areas as diverse as janitorial services and the caliber of Latin instruction. School districts also have intricate and diverse relationships with county and city governments. The latter, for example, often act as tax-levying and tax-collecting agencies for the districts; they are responsible for certifying that standards of health and safety are maintained on school property; they must provide special police protection to students.

Nor does the federal government play an unimportant role. Even prior to the Elementary and Secondary Education Act of 1964, the United States Office of Education provided technical aids of all sorts. Since the passing of that act, the federal role has become even more clear-cut. A federal milk and school-lunch program supplies food and milk at low cost to children in all fifty states. Federal surplus property supplies many essentials of school equipment. Federal aid to vocational and agricultural education programs make possible the employment of special teachers. In many areas "affected" by national government installations, federal funds build and maintain school buildings and contribute to general school support. Federal aid trains high-school teachers of science, mathematics, and foreign languages; contributes equipment and books for instruction in these fields; makes possible testing and guidance programs for the identification of superior students; provides special assistance for schools in poverty areas; and may be used generally to strengthen state departments of education.

All this barely hints at the diverse ways in which the federal government participates in the "local" functioning of primary and secondary education. It does not consider, for example, that employees of the United States Office of Education often serve as officers and leading members of a number of teachers' professional organizations, including the associations whose principal concern is curriculum development in the primary grades. A good portion of the new ideas and new programs that local governments adopt come from these professional groups. A complete catalog of federal aids to education would also have to include the federal government's grants-in-land to states and localities for free public education. This program began in 1785 and, before the public domain was exhausted, supplied some 145 million acres, an area larger than France, for primary and secondary education (excluding the tens of millions of acres recently granted Alaska for the same purposes). So the federal government, through the land grants, was a prime force in making possible the most local of all so-called local functions: free public education.

What is true of education is also true of other functions of American government. Police protection, like education, is considered a uniquely local function. Even more than education, police work involves the continuous collaboration of federal, state, and local authorities, and more recently, formal federal cash grants to aid states and localities in the improvement of law enforcement and criminal justice activities. And the sharing of functions is equally important from the federal perspective. Foreign affairs, national defense, and the development of atomic energy are usually considered to be exclusive responsibilities of the national government. In fact, the state and local governments have extensive responsibilities, directly and indirectly, in each of these fields. The mixture of responsibilities, of course, varies. The federal government, for example, has less to do with fire-fighting than with police protection on the local scene; and the states and localities have less importance in the post office than in atomic energy development. But the larger point is that all areas of American government are involved in all functions.

The federal system is not accurately symbolized by a neat layer cake of three distinct and separate planes. A far more realistic symbol is that of the marble cake. Wherever you slice through it you reveal an inseparable mixture of differently colored ingredients. There is no neat horizontal stratification. Vertical and diagonal lines almost obliterate the horizontal ones, and in some places there are unexpected whirls and an imperceptible merging of colors, so that it is difficult to tell where one ends and the other begins. So it is with federal, state, and local responsibilities in the chaotic marble cake of American government.

II. FEAR OF THE FEDERAL OCTOPUS: DECENTRALIZATION BY ORDER

The federal system has been criticized in recent years from two sides. On the one hand, it is said that the strength of special and local interests (including the strength of state and local governments) frustrates national policy. In Congress, this critique holds, the power of the peripheries makes consistent national leadership impossible. Members of Congress, dependent for reelection on local constituencies rather than on national centers of party power, can with impunity sacrifice national goals for special interests. This argument concludes that an expansion of national powers is essential. On the other hand, it is said that the power of the national government is growing to such an extent that it threatens to efface the state and local governments, reducing them to compliant administrative arms of national offices. The "federal octopus" is held to threaten the very existence of the states and to destroy local initiative.

The two critiques are to a large extent contradictory. Yet reforms of the federal system are often proposed as if one or the other of these complaints were the complete truth. Those concerned about the federal system are uniformly found expressing fear of the federal octopus.

Four attempts have been made since the end of World War II to strengthen the states by devolving upon them functions now performed by the federal government and we may be into a fifth at the present time. The first and second Hoover Commissions devoted a portion of their energy to this end. The Kestnbaum Commission, although extolling federal-state cooperation in a number of fields, nevertheless operated on the false assumption that "the principal tradition is the tradition of separation." The President's Federal-State Action Committee was established in 1957 at the recommendation of President Eisenhower for the specific purpose of bringing about an ordered devolution of functions from the federal government to the states. It is this last that is especially instructive in light of President Nixon's "New Federalism."

Mr. Eisenhower was greatly concerned over increases in federal functions at the expense of the states, which, he felt, transgress "our most cherished principles of government, and tend to undermine the structure so painstakingly built by those who preceded us." "Those who would stay free," he insisted, "must stand eternal watch against excessive concentration of power in government." The president suggested the formation of a committee, composed of high federal and state officials, whose first mission would be "to designate functions which the States are ready and willing to assume and finance that are now performed or financed wholly or in part by the Federal Government." The president also charged the committee "to recommend the Federal and State revenue adjustments required to enable the States to assume such functions." The effort of the committee, in short, would be to take direct steps against the threat of the federal octopus. The committee would recommend federal functions to be turned over to the states, and would further recommend the transfer of federal tax resources to the states so that they could perform with their own funds the new functions they would assume. "I assure you," Mr. Eisenhower told the governors, "that I wouldn't mind being called a lobbyist for such a worthy cause."[1]

The committee established at Mr. Eisenhower's suggestion was a distinguished one. It had as co-chairmen Robert B. Anderson, secretary of the treasury, and Lane Dwinell, governor of New Hampshire. Two additional cabinet members, as well as the director of the Bureau of the Budget and several members of the president's personal staff, from the federal side, and nine additional governors, from the state side, completed the group. The committee had excellent staff assistance and complete presidential support. There were no disagreements on party or regional lines. The group was determined not to write just another report, but rather it wished to live up to its name and produce "action" toward decentralization via devolution and separation of functions and tax sources. It worked hard for more than two years.

Never did good intent, hopes, and labor produce such negligible results. The committee could agree on only two activities from which the federal government should withdraw in favor of complete state responsibility. One was the federal grant for sewage-treatment plants; the other was federal aid for vocational education (including aid for practical-nurse training and for training in fishery trades and industry). These programs represented some $80 million of federal funds in 1957, just over 2 percent of all federal grants for that year. To enable the states to finance these functions, the committee recommended a state offset for a fraction of the federal tax on local telephone calls. It was calculated that the offset tax, plus an equalization grant, would provide each state with at least 40 percent more money than it would spend on the two functions it would assume. Some states would receive twice as much.

Faithful to his pledge, President Eisenhower recommended all aspects of this program to Congress. Opposition developed from those benefiting from the vocational-educational and sewage-plant grants. Many individual mayors, the American Municipal Association, the United States Conference of Mayors, the several professional groups concerned with vocational education, public health and sportsmen's associations, state departments of education, and even a large number of governors were included in the opposition. As modest as the program was and as generous as the financing provisions seemed to be, no part of the recommendations was made law. The entire program died before the end of Eisenhower's presidency. Indeed, both programs have since been expanded substantially.

III. THE FAILURE TO DECENTRALIZE BY ORDER

Why have all attempts to decentralize the federal system failed? Why has it proved impossible to separate federal and state functions by an act of the national government?

History

In the first place, the history of the American governments is a history of shared functions. All nostalgic references to the days of state and local independence are based upon mythical views of the past. There has in fact never been a time when federal, state, and local functions were separate and distinct. Government does more things in 1974 than it did in 1790 or 1861; but in terms of what government did, there was as much sharing of functions then as today. The effort to decentralize government through the ordered separation of functions is contrary to 180 years of experience.[2]

The Nature of American Politics

A second reason for the failure to decentralize government by order is inherent in the nature of American political parties. The political parties of this country are themselves highly decentralized. They respond to directives from bottom to top, rather than from top to bottom. Except during periods of crisis, not even the president of the United States requesting action from a congressman or senator can command the sort of accommodating response that, as a matter of course, follows requests from an individual, an interest group, or a mayor of a city in the legislator's district. The legislator, of course, cannot fully meet all constituent requests; indeed, their very multiplicity, and their frequently conflicting character, are a liberating force, leaving room for individual judgment, discretion, and the expression of conviction. Nevertheless, the orientation of the vast majority of congressmen and senators is toward constituency. Constituency, not party or president, is principally responsible for the legislator's election and reelection. And he feels that accommodation to his constituency, rather than to party leaders, is his principal obligation.

The parties are thus not at all, as they are in other countries, centralizing forces. On the contrary, they act to disperse power. And the significant point here is that they disperse power in favor of state and local governments.

I have described the actual mechanisms in another place.[3] Briefly, the parties can be seen as decentralizers in four ways. (1) They make possible the "multiple crack" attribute of American politics. That is to say, the loose party arrangements provide innumerable access points through which individuals, interest groups, and local and state governments take action to influence the processes of national legislation and administration. (2) The party arrangements are responsible for giving to state governments a role in national programs. What is remarkable in recent history is how consistently the Congress has insisted that the states, and now the localities, share responsibility in programs that, from constitutional and administrative considerations, might easily have been all-national programs. The local orientation of the members of Congress, overriding the desires of national party leaders, is clearly responsible for this phenomenon. (3) The party system also makes possible the widespread, institutionalized interference of members of Congress in national administrative programs on behalf of local constituents (again including the state and local governments). This, on The Hill, is called "case work." The bureaucracy in the United States is subject to an hour-by-hour scrutiny by members of the Congress. No aspect of procedure and no point of policy is free from inquiry. Any administrative decision made in a national agency that is contrary, for example, to the desire of a mayor or governor is immediately subject to congressional inquiry which, if not satisfactorily answered, can in the end produce a meeting in a cabinet member's office, or a full-scale congressional investigation, or a threat of reprisal through the appropriation or legislative process. (4) Finally, the loose national parties, since they cannot themselves supply the political support needed by administrators of national agencies, force administrators to seek their own support in Congress. This support must come from locally oriented members of the Congress. The result is that national administrative policies must be made with great sensitivity to the desires of state and local governments and other local interests.

What does this have to do with decentralization by order? There can be no such decentralization as long as the president cannot control a majority of the Congress, and he can rarely exercise this control, as long as the parties remain in their decentralized state. The decentralization of parties indicates a decentralization of power that is strong enough to prevent a presidentially sponsored decentralization of government. States and localities, working through the parties, can assume that they will have an important role in many national programs; that is to say, there will be few domestic all-federal programs. The parties also give the peripheral governments significant influence in the administration of national programs, including those in which they have no formal role.

Influence of the federal government in state and local operations, made possible by its purse power and exercised through grants-in-aid, is more than balanced by the political power of the peripheral units, exercised through the multiple crack, the localism of legislators, their "case work," and the political role of federal administrators. Politics here are stronger than the purse, in part because the locally oriented Congress is also the final arbiter of federal expenditures. The states and localities are more influential in federal affairs than the federal government is in theirs. And this influence must be a part of the equation when balancing the strength of state and local governments against the national government. State and local officials, whatever their verbally expressed opposition to centralization, do not in fact find federal activities a threat to their position because of their substantial control over those activities.

In sum, the nation's politics, misunderstood by those advocating decentralization by order, accounts in large part for the failure to achieve that sort of decentralization.

The Difficulty of Dividing Functions: The Issue of "Closeness"

History and politics are two reasons for the failure of decentralization by order. A third, related, reason is the sheer difficulty of dividing functions between central and peripheral units without the division resulting in further centralization.

It is often claimed that local or state governments are "closer" to the people than the federal government, and are therefore the preferred instrument for public action. If one carefully examines this statement, it proves to be quite meaningless.

"Closeness" when applied to governments means many things. One meaning is the provision of services directly to the people. Another meaning is participation. A third is control: to say that local governments are closer to the people than the federal government is to say that citizens can control the former more easily and more completely than the latter. A fourth meaning is understanding, a fifth communication, a sixth identification. Thorough analysis of "closeness" would have to compare local, state, and federal governments with respect to all these, as well as other, meanings of the term.

Such an analysis reveals that in few, if any, of these meanings are the state and local units "closer" to the people than the federal governments. The big differences are between rural or small urban communities on the one hand and the big cities on the other: citizens in the former are "closer" (in many, but not all, meanings) to both the local and federal governments than are residents of big urban areas.

Consider, for example, "closeness" as the provision of services. All governments in the American system operate in direct contact with people at their places of residence and work, and in important activities the units operate collaboratively. It cannot even be said that the local units provide the most important local services. The important services are those of shared responsibility. Where it is possible to recognize primary responsibilities, the greater importance of local government does not at all emerge.

Where in the American system is the government closest to the people as a provider of services? The answer is clearly neither the local nor federal government in urban areas and not even local government in rural areas. Rather it is the federal government in rural areas that is closest to the people (as a provider of services). As a consumer of services the farmer has more governmental wares to choose from than any other citizen. They are largely federal or federally sponsored wares, and they cover virtually all aspects of his personal and economic life.

If he wished to take full advantage of what was offered, an individual farmer could assemble a veritable convention of government helpers in his home and fields. He could have a soil-conservation technician make a survey of his property, prepare plans for conservation practices and watershed protection, and give advice on crops, growing practices, wood-lot plantings, and wild-life maintenance. A Forest Service officer collaboratively with a state forester would provide low-cost tree stock. Extension workers would aid the farmer's wife on all aspects of home management, including gardening, cooking, and sewing; instruct the children with respect to a whole range of health, recreational, and agricultural problems; provide the farmer himself with demonstrations and information aimed at reducing costs, increasing income, and adjust production to market demands, and give the entire family instruction with respect to "social relations, adjustments and cultural values." An officer of the Agricultural Conservation Program would arrange federal grants for part of the costs of his soil and conservation practices, including ditching and building ponds. (Another official would provide a supply of fish at little or no cost with which to stock the pond.) A Commodity Stabilization Service worker would arrange for loans on some crops, for government purchase of others, and for special incentive payments on still a third category: he would also pay the farmer for constructing crop-storage facilities. Another officer from the same agency would arrange cash payments to the farmer under the soil-bank program, if he takes out of production acres devoted to designated basic crops (the "acreage reserve") or puts general cropland to conservation use (the "conservation reserve"). An official of the Farmers Home Administration, if credit is not elsewhere available, will make loans to the farmer for the operation, improvement, and enlargement of his property, and (to maximize repayment possibilities) will "service" the farmer-borrower by providing him with comprehensive and continuous technical advice on how to make his operation as profitable as possible. All this just begins the list.

It can be concluded that the farm sector of the population receives a wider range of governmental services than any other population group. These services are largely inspired by federal legislation and largely financed with federal funds. From the point of view of services rendered, the federal government is clearly "closest" to the farm population and closer to it than any other American government is to the population it serves. Outside of institutionalized persons and those dependent upon relief, the American farmer receives at first hand more governmental services than any other American. And while he receives these services as the consequence of collaboration among all governments, the federal government plays the key role.

Local rural governments (but not local urban ones) show to better advantage when closeness as participation is considered. Only if participation is measured in terms of voting do the local rural units rank low. Elections for national offices almost invariably turn out a larger fraction of the eligible voters than local elections. And rural local elections attract proportionately fewer voters than urban local elections. Voting aside, participation in rural, local governments possesses an intensity and personal quality that is, on the whole, unmatched for other governments. In part, this participation is the consequence of simple arithmetic. Where relatively many governments serve relatively few people, participation of citizens in some ways must increase. Pure statistical chance will produce a large fraction of rural residents—and their relatives, neighbors, and friends—who are elected or appointed to public office. Governmental services become hand tooled under such circumstances. Recipients of services personally share in the decisions of government, and the services themselves become personalized. A father, for example, will deliver his son to jail, explaining to his neighbor, the chief of police, that the lad has been drinking and that the family would appreciate the courtesy of allowing him to spend a few days in safety behind bars. Poor relief is granted when a doctor telephones a county supervisor who then walks across the street to talk to the welfare officer. A farmer can appear personally before his neighbors on the township or county board to argue that an old road near his place should be scraped or a new one built. A township meeting may be adjourned so that a person arguing his case for a new drainage ditch can go home to his chores before dark. I have visited a mayor being consulted in his hardware store by parents complaining about a dangerous school crossing; and I have attended traffic court in the blueberry patch of the justice of the peace.

This sort of community government—of neighbors serving neighbors in a neighborly fashion—has not been (and perhaps cannot be) duplicated in the big cities (although urban surrogates are sought and achieved in some measure by political organizations and, more recently, by community action groups stimulated by federal and anti-poverty programs). The federal government in rural areas—through its extensive network of local units—is in many ways similar to rural local governments in these marks of closeness via participation. So are some suburban governments. But no big city government as presently structured can achieve the attributes of neighborly participation found widely in the rural areas. If "closeness" is participation, therefore, rural local governments—followed by rural federal government in its several forms—achieve levels and styles of closeness unattainable in urban areas. The important partial exception for rural local governments is participation in voting.

Closeness as participation should not be confused with closeness as control. Indeed, maximum citizen participation may be combined with maximum control in the hands of a minority. In general there is no evidence that residents of rural areas direct the affairs of their local governments to a greater extent than the big-city dwellers. In several significant ways, they have less control over the governments serving them.

Rural local governments are probably more frequently boss-controlled than any other American governments. Roscoe C. Martin has said flatly that local rural government is "too small to be truly democratic."[4] He referred particularly to the fact that these governments did not excite or stimulate citizens and that the scope of rural governments was "too picayune, too narrow in outlook, too limited in horizon, too self-centered in interests. . . ." Beyond such considerations, in small communities homogeneity of outlook may be combined with gross inequality of power. A small group of farmers or businessmen, a single politician, or a rich family of old settlers can frequently control the entire politics of a rural community. The control may contain attributes of beneficence, and it may be wielded silently. It nevertheless represents an effective monopolization of power over those things that the rural government does and refuses to do. The small size of the community means that minority groups find difficulty in organizing opposition, a difficulty that is compounded by the wide range of personal, social, and economic penalties that may be exacted by the ruling group. The widespread sharing of influence is not impossible in the small community; but possibilities of clique and one-man rule are maximized, ideal images of small-town democracy notwithstanding.[5]

A system of shared governmental functions by its very nature rarely allows a single government to exercise complete control over a given activity. All officers of government in the United States consequently experience what may be called "frustration of scope of action." This is the frustration produced by the inability of decision-makers in one government to produce action at their own discretion: other governments must also be moved. Limited scope of discretion is felt universally, by the largest as well as the smallest governments, but it is felt most keenly by the rural local governments.

The smaller the government, the more limited the span of control. Hardly any function of the small rural government does not involve other governments. A farmer may gain full support from local officers with respect to where a road should go through his land, but he sees the road go elsewhere because the basic decisions are not made by his friends in the local government but by the combined efforts of local, county, state, and federal officials. Decisions of rural governments with respect to most other matters are similarly conditioned by decision-makers elsewhere. Frustration of scope of control, a universal of the American system, is nevertheless felt most acutely in the small local governments of rural America.

Channels exist by which local populations can bring effective pressure to bear upon officers of the state and federal governments. Sharing by local groups in the decisions of those governments is characteristic. But this sort of influence is not the consequence of the opportunity of rural citizens to participate actively and directly in their governments. Rather it is the consequence of the form and operation of American political parties. Similarly, the considerable rural control of federal agricultural programs is not the result of farmer participation in the many federally sponsored local governments. In this case, direct participation at the grass roots may be only a shadow of genuine power and may indeed be a device of others to implement their own programs. We are discovering that this is equally true in the big city anti-poverty programs with all their emphasis on citizen participation. Unremitting civic participation is more characteristic of totalitarianism than of democracy, and the greater participation of rural over urban citizens in the affairs of local governments cannot be equated with the citizen control of those governments.

The full analysis of all meanings of closeness would not establish that local governments are in significant ways "closest" to the people. Only a portion of the analysis has been presented here. Incomplete as it is, it is sufficient to demonstrate that the criteria of closeness cannot serve to give more functions to local governments.

The Difficulty of Dividing Functions: Issues of Logic

Nor does it help, on grounds of logic, to attempt a divison of federal and state (or local) functions. Indeed, such a division would probably result in putting virtually all functions in the hands of the national government.

The logical difficulty of dividing functions can be seen in the Federal-State Action Committee's recommendation for turning over all responsibility for constructing sewage plants to the states and localities. The committee's reason for recommending this program, rather than others, was only a simple affirmation:

> *The Joint Federal-State Action Committee holds that local waste-treatment facilities are primarily a local concern and their construction should be primarily a local or State financial responsibility. . . . There is no evidence to demonstrate the continuing need for the present Federal subsidy of an essentially local responsibility.*[6]

This sort of language was necessary because no more reasoned argument was possible. There is no way to distinguish, for example, the "localness" of sewage-treatment plants from the "nationalness" of, say, grants for public health. Both programs are equally aimed at increasing public health and safety. Where there are no adequate plants, the untreated sewage creates health hazards, including higher infant-mortality rates. This sewage, when dumped into streams (the usual practice), creates in many cases interstate hazards to health and safety. Every indicator of "localness" attributed to sewage-treatment plants can also be attributed to public-health programs. And every attribute of "nationalness" in one is also found in the other. Barely ten years after the committee's report, it was difficult to find any knowledgeable people who were prepared to argue that sewage-treatment was simply a local matter.

Why did the committee choose sewage plants—rather than public-health grants, or federal old-age assistance, or the federal school-milk program—to transfer to states and localities? Clearly not because one program is more "local" than the other. The real basis of choice can be easily guessed. The federal sewage-plant program was relatively new, and it did not have as many direct recipients of aid as the other programs. The political risk to the governors of recommending local responsibility for sewage-treatment plants was relatively small. To recommend federal withdrawal from public health, or old-age assistance, or the school-lunch program would have aroused the wrath of numerous individuals and interest groups. Governors cannot alienate such groups and still remain governors. The choice of sewage-treatment plants as "primarily a local concern" had little or nothing to do with genuine distinctions between local and national functions.

A detailed analysis would show that any division of functions, on the line of their "local" or "national" character, would leave precious few activities in the local category. In 1963, automobile safety, for example, was almost exclusively a state and local (and private) responsibility. Although automobile deaths approached 40,000 annually, the injuries exceeded 1,500,000. If the number of deaths due to road accidents in even a small state were the result of an airplane crash, several teams of federal officers, operating under a number of federal statutes, would have been combing the area in order to prevent further deaths. But there were no federal officers on the scene to prevent further auto deaths, not even if some fatalities in California were caused by drivers licensed in New York. In a division of responsibilities, assuming that they have to be all federal or all state-local, would automobile safety have remained in the state-local category? As it was, only a few years later, in response to certain public pressures, the federal government did enter the auto-mobile safety field with serious intent but it did so in a manner that reflected the federal nature of the body politics, assuming major direct responsibilities for setting the safety standards of vehicles while requiring (and bribing) the states to enforce minimum federal standards (or better) on the road themselves. There are still no federal officers at each crash scene but the problem itself is being treated "federally."

This sort of analysis can be applied to a number of fields in which states and localities have important, if not exclusive, responsibility. It is hard to find any areas in which the states and localities would remain in control, if a firm division of functions were to take place. Not even education would be an exception. Pseudo-historical considerations, outworn conceptions of "close-ness," and fears of an American brand of totalitarianism would argue for an exclusive state-local control of primary and secondary education. But inequities of state resources, disparities in educational facilities and results, the gap between actual and potential educational services, and, above all, the adverse national consequences that might follow long-term inadequacies of state-local control would almost certainly, if the choice had to be made, establish education as the exclusive concern of the national government.

The clear conclusion is that widespread separation of functions would reduce states and localities to institutions of utter unimportance. They can no longer sustain the claim that they are closer to the people. Their strength has never been a strength of isolation. Their future depends upon their continued ability to assume important roles in the widening scope of public service and regulation. Their future, in short, depends upon the continuation of shared responsibilities in the American federal system.

IV. DECENTRALIZATION VIA STRENGTHENING OF STATE GOVERNMENTS

The strength of state governments is not often measured in terms of the states' influence on national programs. Rather the strength of the states is most frequently discussed as state independence, or at least as fiscal and administra-tive power sufficient to carry out their own functions. It is often held that federal programs follow the failure of states to meet their own responsibilities. "By using their power to strengthen their own governments and those of their subdivisons," the Kestnbaum Commission said, "the States can relieve much of the pressure for, and generate a strong counterpressure against, improper expansion of National action."[7] A distinguished scholar of American politics, V. O. Key, has expressed the same point, although somewhat more guardedly. He considers deficiencies of representation in state legislatures, constitutional restrictions on state power, and state political systems as a "centralizing factor in the federal system."

> *Evidently the organization of state politics builds into the governmental system a more or less purely political factor that contributes to federal centralization. The combination of party system and the structure of representation in most of the states incapacitates the states and diverts demands for political action to Washington.*[8]

The argument's simplicity is persuasive. But what it accurately describes is insignificant, and for larger events it is wrong. The inability of state legislatures and executives to plan a national airport program undoubtedly led to federal grants in that field. But could the states, even if endowed with ideal constitutions, legislatures, and political parties, be expected to design and finance such a program? The same sort of question could be asked with respect to housing and urban renewal, the second conspicuous federal-local program of the postwar era. (In both fields, incidentally, the states are given the chance to assume important responsibilities and an increasing number do so.) The great expansion of federal domestic programs came during the depression. Certainly it can be said that the federal government went into the business of welfare on a wholesale scale because the states were unable to do the job. Was state inability the result of the ineffectiveness of state political parties, inequities of legislative representation, and outmoded constitutions? Or was the states' inability the result of a catastrophic depression? The first factors may have had some effect, but they are picayune compared with the devastating impact of the depression on state income. And the depression would have demanded action from the federal government (with its virtually unlimited borrowing power) in new fields whatever the status of the states' political parties or the modernity of their constitutional arrangement.

Furthermore, expansion of national programs has not only followed the *failure* of state programs; the nation has also assumed responsibility upon demonstration of the *success* of state programs. Thus requirements for health and safety in mining and manufacturing, the maintenance of minimum wages, unemployment compensation, aid to the aged and blind, and even the building of roads, were all undertaken, more or less successfully, by some or even most states before they were assumed as national functions. So the states can lose exclusive functions both ways. The national government steps in as an emulator when the states produce useful innovations, making national programs of state successes; and it steps in when crisis is created as the consequence of state failure, making national programs of state inadequacies.

The role of the national government as an emulator is fostered by the nationwide communication network and the nationwide political process which produce public demands for national minimum standards. The achievement of such standards in some states raises the issue of reaching them in all. Many reasons exist for this tendency: for example, the citizens of the active states feel that with their higher tax rates they are pricing themselves out of the market. Those in the laggard states can find specific points of comparison to demonstrate that their services are unsatisfactory. National fiscal aid may be essential for the economically disadvantaged states. State legislatures may be less congenial to a given program than the national Congress. Combinations of these and other causes mean that national programs will continue to come into being although, and even because, some states carry out those programs with high standards. The only way to avoid this sort of expansion by the national government would be if all fifty states were politically, fiscally, and administratively able to undertake, more or less simultaneously, a given program at acceptable national standards. This is not likely to happen. Even if it were, those in states less likely to undertake the program are certain to raise public demands for the national government to take responsibility for it.

If both state failures and state successes produce national programs, it must be added that neither of those mechanisms is the important cause for the expansion of the central government. This expansion, in largest part, has been produced by the dangers of the twentieth century. (War, defense, and related items constitute more than 70 percent of the federal budget, and federal increases of nondefense activities lag far behind expenditure increases by the states and localities.) National-security items aside, the free votes of a free people have sustained federal programs in such areas as public welfare, highway, airports, hospitals and public health, agriculture, schools, and housing and urban redevelopment, to name only some of the largest grant-in-aid programs. The plain fact is that large population groups are better represented in the constituencies of the president and Congress than they are in the constituencies of governors and state legislatures. No realistic program of erasing inequities of representation in state legislatures—not even action consequent to the Supreme Court's reapportionment decision—will significantly alter this fact in the foreseeable future. Only those who hold that "the federal government is something to be feared" (to use the words of Senator Morse, in his minority criticism of the Kestnbaum Commission Report) would wish to make the federal government unresponsive to those national needs expressed through the democratic process, needs which by their very nature will not, and cannot, be met by state action.

In sum, strong as well as weak states turn "demands for political action to Washington." More important, the ability of the national government to meet citizen needs that cannot be met by either strong or weak states, whatever those adjectives mean, also accounts for the expansion (as well as for the very existence) of the federal government. Strengthening states, in the sense of building more effective parties and of providing legislatures and executives who have a readiness and capacity for action, may indeed prevent an occasional program from being taken up by the federal government. The total possible effect can only be insignificant. The only way to produce a significant decline in federal programs, new and old, would be to induce citizens to demand fewer activities from all governments. (The cry, "Strengthen the states," in many cases only means, "Decrease all governmental activity.") This is an unlikely development in an age of universal literacy, quick communications, and heightened sensitivities to material factors in the good life, as well as to the political appeals of an alternative political system. One can conclude that strengthening the states so that they can perform independent functions and thereby prevent federal expansion is a project that cannot succeed.

Historical trend lines, the impetus of technology, and the demands of citizenry are all in the direction of central action. The wonder is not that the central government has done so much, but rather that it has done so little. The parties, reflecting the nation's social structure, have at once slowed up centralization and given the states (and localities) important responsibilities in central government programs. Furthermore, political strength is no fixed quantum. Increasing one institution's power need not decrease the power of another in the same system. Indeed, the centralization that has taken place in the United States has also strengthened the states—with respect to personnel practices, budgeting, the governors' power, citizen's interest, and the scope of state action—as every impartial study of federal aid has shown.[9] The states remain strong and active forces in the federal system. The important reason that state institutions should be further strengthened is so that they may become more effective innovators and even stronger partners in a governmental system of shared responsibilities.

V. TWO KINDS OF DECENTRALIZATION

If I have not proved, I hope I have at least given reasonable grounds for believing: First, the American federal system is principally characterized by a federal-state-local sharing of responsibilities for virtually all functions. Second, our history and politics in largest part account for this sharing. Third, there is no reasonable possibility of dividing functions between the federal government, on the one hand, and states and localities, on the other, without drastically reducing the importance of the latter. Fourth, no "strengthening" of state or local (or neighborhood) governments will materially reduce the present functions of the federal government; nor will it have any marked effect on the rate of acquisition of new federal functions.

A final point may now be made. Those who attempt to decentralize by order are far more likely to produce centralization by order. In so doing they will destroy the decentralization already existing in the United States. Therein lies much of the paradox of Mr. Nixon's recent proposals to "improve" the operation of the federal system, which, to date, have led to an expansion of the federal role rather than its contraction in any respect.

The circumstances making possible a decentralization by a decision of central officials are simple to specify. What is principally needed is a president and a congressional majority of the same party, the president consistently able to command a majority of the Congress through the control of his party. With such an arrangement, a recommendation by a committee of cabinet members and governors or some other body to devolve functions to the states and localities if strongly backed by the president, could be readily implemented. Party control of the central government and the president's control of Congress through his party are the essentials. In other words, party *centralization* must precede governmental *decentralization by order*.

But a centralized party pledged to decentralization — to minimizing central government activities — can hardly be or remain a majority party in the twentieth century. The power to decentralize by order must, by its very nature, also be the power to centralize by order. Centralized majority parties are far more likely to choose in favor of centralization than decentralization.

Decentralization by order must be contrasted with another sort of decentralization. This is the decentralization that exists as the result of independent centers of power and that operates through the chaos of American political processes and political institutions. It may be called decentralization by mild chaos. It is less tidy and noisier than an ordered decentralization. But it is not dependent upon action of central bodies, and its existence is not at the mercy of changing parties or of changing party policy.

If decentralization is a desirable end, decentralization by mild chaos is far preferable to decentralization by order. The former is built upon genuine points of political strength. It is more permanent. And, most important, it is a decentralization of genuinely shared power, as well as of shared functions. Decentralization by order might maintain a sharing of functions, but it cannot, because of its nature, maintain a sharing of political power. An ordered decentralization depends upon a central power which, by the very act of ordering decentralization, must drastically diminish, if not obliterate, the political power of the peripheral units of government.

A president of the United States at present does not have consistent control of his Congress. The power of the president is often contested by the power of individuals, interest groups, and states and localities, made manifest through the undisciplined parties. And the president is not always the winner. President Eisenhower was not the winner in his proposals to devolve federal functions to the states. (His situation was complicated by the fact that his party was a minority of the Congress, but the results would almost certainly have been the same if he had had a majority.) He lost because his proposals were contested by many governors, many mayors, their professional organizations, and a number of other groups. The party system allowed these protests to be elevated over the decision of the president. Today Mr. Nixon is in an extraordinarily similar position.

Thus the strength of states and localities in the federal system is evidenced in the failure to decentralize by order. Successful decentralization by order would mean the decline of state and local power and the death of America's undisciplined parties. It could only follow profound changes in the nation's political style and supporting social structure.

The rhetoric of state and national power becomes easily and falsely a rhetoric of conflict. It erroneously conceives states and localities, on one side, and the central government, on the other, as adversaries. There are undoubtedly occasions when the advantage of a locality, state, or region is a disadvantage to the nation as a whole. But in most circumstances at most times compatibility rather than conflict of interests is characteristic. There are sufficient, if often overlooked, reasons for this compatibility. The nation's diversities exist within a larger unity. Voters at local, state, and national elections are the same voters. A congressman in one role is a local citizen in another. Professional workers in education, welfare, health, road-building and other fields adhere to the same standards of achievement, regardless of which government pays their salaries. Federal, state, and local officials are not adversaries. They are colleagues. The sharing of functions and powers is impossible without a whole. The American system is best conceived as one government serving one people.

NOTES

1. President Eisenhower's address was delivered before the Governors' Conference on June 24, 1957. For the complete text see Joint Federal-State Action Committee, *Progress Report No. 1* (Washington: U.S. Government Printing Office, 1957), pp. 17-22.
2. See Daniel J. Elazar, *The American Partnership: Intergovernmental Cooperation in the Nineteenth Century United States* (Chicago: University of Chicago Press, 1962).
3. "American Political Parties and the American System," *Western Political Quarterly*, Vol. XIII (December, 1960), pp. 974-98.
4. *Grass Roots* (University: University of Alabama Press, 1957), p. 92.
5. A prime example of a rural political boss emerges from the pages of Arthur J. Vidich and Joseph Bensman, *Small Town in Mass Society* (Princeton: Princeton University Press, 1958).
6. *Progress Report No. 1* (December, 1957), p. 6.
7. The Commission on Intergovernmental Relations, *A Report to the President* (Washington: Government Printing Office, 1955), p. 56.
8. *American State Politics* (New York: Alfred A. Knopf, 1956), pp. 81, 266-67.
9. See, for example, *The Impact of Federal Grants-in-Aid on the Structure and Functions of State and Local Governments* (a study covering 25 states submitted to the Commission on Intergovernmental Relations), by the Governmental Affairs Institute (Washington, 1955); and the report of the New York Temporary Commission on the Fiscal Affairs of State Government (the Bird Commission) (Albany, 1955), especially Vol. II, pp. 431-672.

Devolution

Advisory Committee on Intergovernmental Relations

On the face of it, the issue of whether there has been a devolution of authority to states and localities as a result of the establishment of a tripartite grant system seems fairly obvious, considering the portion of federal grants now represented by general revenue sharing and block grants and the essential nature of these two assistance mechanisms. With respect to the first point, the following figures tell the story:

Percentage of federal grant dollars by grant type, FY 1966 and FY 1975

	FY 1966	FY 1975
Categoricals	99.5%	76.0%
Block grants	0.5	10.0
General revenue sharing	0.0	14.0

Regarding the nature of GRS and block grants, a useful summary is the typology of federal grant forms presented in the introduction to this study.[1] The typology distinguishes among the three grant forms on the basis of three factors: the degree of administrative discretion exercised by federal grant administrators; the range of limitations on grantees in choosing activities to be covered by the federal assistance; and type, number, detail and scope of conditions attached to the grant program. Application of these characteristics to the

Excerpted from *Summary and Concluding Observation: The Intergovernmental Grant System: An Assessment and Proposed Policies*, Advisory Commission on Intergovernmental Relations, Report A-62 (Washington, D.C.: Government Printing Office, June 1978), pp. 34-43.

three principal types of federal grant assistance produces a continuum, with certain categorical grants at the extreme of limited recipient discretion and "no strings" general revenue sharing at the other extreme of broad recipient discretion.

Putting these two sets of information together leads to the clear conclusion that there has been a decided devolution of authority to state and local governments via the evolution of the tripartite federal grant system in the past decade.

The hitch, of course, is the degree to which the three types of grant mechanism conform to the model set forth in the typology. Has the shift to block grants and general revenue sharing in the past ten years really constituted as much of an increase in state and local discretion in the expenditure of grant funds as is indicated by the grant characteristics identified in the typology and the rise from 0.5% to 24% in the share of grant dollars attributable to revenue sharing and block grants? To answer this question requires a closer examination of what has actually happened along the entire grant-in-aid front. It also calls for a look at the issue of fungibility.

GENERAL REVENUE SHARING

The general revenue sharing program is completely an entitlement program—federal administrators have no discretion in determining who shall get money and in what amounts. From this perspective alone, general revenue sharing represents a substantial movement—in excess of $6 billion in FY 1976—in the direction of increased state and local authority.

Local recipients' discretion in spending the funds was limited in the original 1972 legislation by the attachment of nine specific conditions, in addition to certain fiscal and accounting requirements for all recipients. These conditions covered functional limitations on the expenditure by local governments of GRS funds for operating and maintenance purposes, use of funds as the nonfederal share of federal grants, maintenance of the level of state aid to their localities, filing of reports on the planned and actual use of GRS funds, compliance with recipients' own laws and procedures in spending of revenue sharing money, nondiscrimination in employment, compliance with Davis-Bacon minimum wage requirements, by contractors and subcontractors, payments of not less than prevailing wages to the jurisdiction's own employees, and use of GRS funds within a reasonable period of time.

Yet despite these conditions, the ACIR concluded in its 1974 report, "state and local policymakers have enjoyed wide discretion in the use of the dollars."[2] Three reasons were cited for this wide latitude. First, there was a lack of revenue and expenditure maintenance requirements and it was virtually impossible to distinguish revenue sharing dollars from the recipient jurisdiction's own dollars. Second, Congress clearly intended to provide wide discretion in the use of revenue sharing dollars. Third, states and localities received various assurances, from President Nixon on down, that in implementing the law, the administration would not dictate how the money should be spent.[3]

The 1976 legislation extending the GRS statute eased up on some of the conditions and stiffened others.[4] It eliminated the functional limitations on local operating and maintenance expenditures and the prohibition on use of funds for the nonfederal share of matching grants. Requirements for reporting the use of funds were made more specific regarding the amounts appropriated, spent and obligated but required publication of only a planned-use report and dispensed with the actual-use report. More detailed publication requirements were specified to accommodate public convenience. Separate public hearings were mandated on the use of the revenue sharing funds and on a recipient jurisdiction's entire budget. The nondiscrimination provisions were broadened, including adding prohibitions against discrimination for age, handicapped status, and religion. In addition, the legislation provided for an "independent" financial and compliance audit at least every three years for all governments receiving $25,000 or more a year. The Secretary of the Treasury was given authority to waive this requirement if a recipient demonstrated it was making "substantial progress" to establish acceptable auditing and accounting procedures.

A further word is needed about the nondiscrimination and Davis-Bacon provisions, which are the only so-called "across-the-board" requirements applicable to GRS.[5] The nondiscrimination provision applies to all programs and activities of recipient governments, but its coverage is limited to the direct use of shared revenue. In effect if a recipient government "demonstrates by clear and convincing evidence" that shared revenue was used in a specific program area, the nondiscrimination provision does not apply to other programs or activities in that government, even though these programs may be indirectly affected, as in cases where shared revenue simply substitutes for funds that otherwise would have been used for these programs. The Davis-Bacon "prevailing wage" conditions apply only to construction projects for which more than 25% of the cost was paid out of revenue sharing.

Apart from the presence or absence of conditions on assistance recipients, there is another aspect of the federal grant relationship involved in the issue of devolution. This is the matter of eligibility and the "reach" of the program.

Since the GRS legislation makes all general purpose units eligible, and excludes only special purpose units, including school districts, it has brought into contact with federal grant programs many units of local government that had never had that experience previously.[6] As the Brookings Institution stated:

> Though firm evidence is not readily available, it seems likely that only a minor fraction of all the local jurisdictions that now receive shared revenue had ever before received grant funds directly from the federal government.[7]

Thus while many cities and some counties and other jurisdictions which had been familiar with the categorical grant system from past exposure felt that the general revenue sharing program was relatively free of federal conditions, jurisdictions having their first experience with the federal government in the aid relationship found themselves now subject to federal conditions, however minimal relatively, which they had never previously experienced. The way in which some of the conditions were applied, moreover, meant that the federal government was intruding not only into their decisions and practices in regard to general revenue sharing funds but all moneys received and spent by those jurisdictions. Thus hearings must be held on the relationship of the proposed use of revenue sharing funds to the recipient jurisdiction's entire budget. The original legislation also gave the Secretary of the Treasury broad power to prescribe necessary accounting and auditing procedures to assure compliance with the law, and empowered the Comptroller General to conduct necessary reviews. The Secretary's power was considerably reduced in the 1976 extension but the Comptroller General's was untouched.

Thus the general revenue sharing program is bringing the federal presence to the local level much more extensively than had been the case with categorical grants in the past. Where it applies federal requirements to the gamut of local expenditures, moreover, it probably extends the federal presence far beyond the expectations of those who originally supported the general revenue sharing legislation as a move toward devolution and as a lightening of the federal hand.

Brookings Study

The Brookings monitoring study addressed the issue of devolution indirectly. The study looked at the degree to which the revenue sharing program appeared to increase public interest and participation in decisionmaking. Where a positive result was found it was taken to reflect a strengthening of the recipient governments and hence a flow of influence to them relative to the grantor federal government.

Examination of the decisionmaking process was centered on the budget process. Major concern was over the degree to which the budget process for handling general revenue sharing funds was set up separately from the established procedure for handling other state and local funds.

Brookings made preliminary findings on this issue in its first monitoring report.[8] It found that one-third of the jurisdictions in its survey sample showed some degree of separate handling of the revenue sharing funds, which seemed to involve increased public and interest group participation. Another nine jurisdictions indicated no separate treatment of the GRS funds but did display a changed behavior in local groups' participation in the budget process. The authors emphasized the importance of local conditions as important factors explaining differences among the budget processes of the several jurisdictions. However, they did feel that there was some evidence of change in the degree of local interest and participation in the budget process affected by GRS.

In its second monitoring report,[9] Brookings found that for about one-fifth of the sampled jurisdictions, revenue sharing was associated with either a shift in political influence among the generalists (especially local legislative bodies) or with a relatively competitive decisionmaking process in allocating these funds. Elsewhere a less pronounced impact was found but the study felt that the overall effect was not politically neutral. Their conclusion was that there was no dramatic change in the politics of state and local governments as a consequence of receiving GRS moneys, but there was some shifting in broadening the political influence and strengthening of the generalist officials. The second monitoring review concluded that the long-run effect was hard to predict at that point.

BLOCK GRANTS

The ACIR's examination of the four block grant programs concluded that, while they had a mixed impact on the sharing of authority between the federal government and state and local governments, on the whole, they served to broaden the scope of the activities aided and to decentralize decisionmaking.[10] To understand the range of differences implied by the word "mixed," it is necessary to look at the individual block grants.

Partnership for Health

Under the Partnership for Health (PHA) grant,* expansion of the functional scope covered by the grant was partly illusory. The functions performed under the grant were largely those that had been performed previously by state health departments under the covered-in categorical grant programs. In addition, following establishment of the program, Congress specified particular health problems to be addressed by the block grant, and enacted numerous new categorical programs that could have been covered under PHA.

The failure to expand the program's functional coverage was due in large part to the fact that, contrary to original expectations, Congress did not gradually increase the amount of appropriations for this block grant. The relative tightfistedness of federal funding also served to circumscribe the degree of discretion exercised by state health departments in identifying needs and developing public health programs to deal with them. Hence while discretion was increased under PHA, as a practical matter it was used as a filler of small gaps not covered by larger federally aided and state-supported specialized servicing efforts.

The intrusiveness of the federal government in imposing performance and procedural conditions declined over the life of the PHA. The early years of uncertainty over balancing national and state concerns witnessed a number of controversies over state program content, reflecting federal officials' habitua-

---

* *Editors' note:* This grant was created by the Partnership in Health Act of 1966, which consolidated more than a dozen categorical grants for disease control.

tion to the categorical mode of operations and their concern about accountability to Congress. As time passed, HEW assumed a more hands-off approach, responding to the low-level funding of the program. Congress's growing tendency to enact separate new health categoricals, and the administration's emphasis on administrative simplification and recipient discretion.

Safe Streets

In some respects, the *Safe Streets Act** was more effective than the health block grant in decentralizing authority. In the first place, the program covered a broad scope of law enforcement activities. Second, substantial discretion was given to the states in identifying problems and designing programs to deal with them. The states were called on to prepare statewide plans, review and approve applications from state agencies, regional planning units, and local governments, coordinate implementation efforts, and monitor and evaluate recipient performance. State planning agencies (SPAs) were created to do these things.

Yet limits were placed on states' discretion. A certain amount of funds had to be set aside for corrections expenditures and the level of expenditures had to be maintained for juvenile justice purposes. Judicial planning committees were required to prepare plans and set priorities for court improvement. In addition, variable matching was mandated for different functions, limits were placed on the amount of funding to be allocated to personal service expenses, and an annual comprehensive plan was required for federal review and approval. These restrictions apply specifically to the state government, which was the key unit in the administration of the program. In passing funds to local jurisdictions, moreover, four-fifths of the state governments narrowed the scope of localities' use of the pass-through funds.

Just how serious these limits on recipient discretion were is difficult to measure. Some local officials, receiving Safe Streets money through the double filter of the federal and state governments, saw little difference between the block grant and categorical grants in the limits on local discretion. On the other hand, SPA directors felt that they had a "great" amount of discretion, despite the various federally imposed limitations.

Performance and procedural requirements imposed by LEAA administrators constituted additional limitations on recipients' freedom of action.† Such conditions applied to the timing of application approval, limited the areas to

---

* *Editors' note:* Passed in 1968, the Omnibus Crime Control and Safe Streets Act established the first federal block grant program.

† *Editors' note:* The Law Enforcement Assistance Administration (LEAA) is the federal agency that awards grants to state and local agencies under the terms of the Safe Streets Act.

be covered by Part C action funds, and specified requirements for development of the annual criminal justice plan. Administrative guidelines, especially in the financial reporting area, were criticized as restrictive, repetitive and overly detailed. Finally, federal administrators' categorization of Part C grants further limited recipient discretion.

In short, the crime control block grant does not necessarily minimize federal strings.

CETA

General application of the term "hybrid" to the CETA block grant reflects in part a mixed record in meeting the block grant criterion of providing broad discretion to state and local jurisdictions.* In the first place, the block grant appropriation represented only one-third of the total appropriations for the CETA act, and only one-fifth of the total of federal financial assistance for employment and training. In addition, it was surrounded by a cluster of 47 categorical grants in the manpower area administered by ten separate departments and agencies.

The CETA program fell somewhere between GRS and categorical grants with respect to recipient discretion in identifying and prioritizing needs and allocating resources. Prime sponsors were given latitude in determining the mix and beneficiaries for a variety of purposes, so long as they directed adequate attention to specified target groups. In the first year, many sponsors did not fully use their discretion, but rather relied on previously existing categorical programs in deciding on target groups to be served as service providers. Yet some changes were made, particularly as national economic and local unemployment conditions became more acute. These changes then sometimes induced federal administrators to try to restrain prime sponsors' use of discretion; as, for example, when the sponsors turned away from contracting with the state employment service for services traditionally provided by those agencies.

With respect to establishing program conditions, CETA presents a mixed picture. In its first year, the Employment and Training Administration (ETA) was far from intrusive, giving the impression to some observers that it was leaning over backward in favor of local autonomy. Responding to criticism on this score, there was indication that in the second year, ETA was moving more toward a categorical mode of federal oversight and technical assistance.

---

* *Editors' note:* The Comprehensive Employment and Training Act (CETA) replaced a number of categorical manpower training grants with a more decentralized system under the control of state and local governments (prime sponsors). However, it also created or continued other categorical manpower training grants. Hence the ACIR's use of the term "hybrid."

Community Development

Like CETA, the Community Development Block Grant does not cover a substantial portion of federal outlays for its broad legislative purpose. Recipient jurisdictions may pursue any of 13 eligible activities covered by the block grant. Yet two major HUD programs were not folded in—the Section 312 Rehabilitation Loan program and the Section 701 Comprehensive Planning and Management Assistance program. Also, although a linkage between housing and community development was established by requiring applicants to submit a housing assistance plan in order to qualify for community development funds, direct block grant expenditures for housing subsidies were abandoned and housing assistance was covered in other titles of the act. Finally, the block grant did not cover several other federal community development related programs that were not under HUD or authorized by the Congressional committees that produced the grant merger.

Recipients are, in general, given a high degree of flexibility in decision-making, but there are certain limitations on the types of activities eligible for aid. Thus public service projects are limited to those that meet a five-part test in the act. Public facilities may be funded only when they serve neighborhoods, except that, by HUD regulation, sewage treatment facilities are eligible in areas where other community development related activities are not underway.

In its first year of operations, HUD, like ETA, took a general hands-off attitude in monitoring performance and procedural requirements such as those that apply to application and planning processes. It received some criticism for this posture and responded with regulations and guidelines delineating minimum federal requirements in certain areas. It was still too early to discern the effect of these actions on the block grant.

*   *   *

To sum up the extent of devolution of decisionmaking under the four block grants, as measured by the degree of latitude provided for determining the scope of activities, by the discretion allowed in setting goals and program priorities, and by the measure of freedom from performance and procedural conditions imposed by the federal government—while all devolved to some extent, all fell short (in varying degrees) of what might be considered the norm for this feature of the prototype block grant. All these programs are hybrids to a varying degree, surrounded by a number of related categorical aids or subdivided by new categories of assistance or earmarked funds within the framework of the block grant itself. Further they have been subjected to administrative categorization as the programs have matured. Yet the shortfall of devolution through the block grant, varying as it does among the four programs, seems like an essential characteristic of a grant form that is designed to strike a balance between the achievement of national objectives and the meeting of recipient needs.

MIDDLE RANGE REFORM EFFORTS

In the discussion of the Partnership for Health block grant, the administration's emphasis on administrative simplification was cited as one of the reasons that HEW assumed more of a hands-off attitude toward monitoring implementation of that program. Administrative simplification was one of the key objectives of the entire gamut of middle range reform efforts of the past decade, aimed at improving grants management short of grant consolidation. The way in which that effort relates to the devolution of decisionmaking deserves further elaboration.

Among the middle range reform measures, two types of actions tended to enhance the decisionmaking discretion of grant recipients. The first are those measures which tend to impose restraints on the actions of federal grant administrators in their relations with grantees. Such restraints, in a sense, draw lines beyond which the grantor agencies may not venture in imposing conditions, either procedural or performance, upon their grantee associates. Included in this class are the various management circulars and other administrative mechanisms directed toward simplifying and standardizing grant administration procedures. The effectiveness of these measures as constraints, of course, depends upon the care with which they are observed by federal agencies upon whom they are imposed, and as was pointed out in another volume in this series, observation of these management requirements has not been uniformly adequate.[11]

The other type of middle range reform measure tending to devolve power to state and local governments are those which "free up" the recipients in exercising their authority over the spending of grant funds. Among these were the integrated grants administration demonstration and its successor, the *Joint Funding Act*. Their central objective was, and is, to simplify the process by which state and local grantees can identify, apply for, and administer funds from several federal assistance programs to carry out a single project. Other administrative reform efforts with freeing up spillovers were the Chief Executives Review and Comment (CERC) and Annual Arrangements initiatives, which laid the groundwork for the Community Development Block Grant. The former gave chief executives in selected cities the right to review and comment on all grant applications affecting their jurisdictions. The latter was a negotiated agreement between HUD and a local community to bring about better coordination of the department's separate categorical grant programs. It was geared to simplify federal procedures and expand the authority of local elected officials.

Like the measures that impose constraints upon federal administrators, this latter group has had only limited success. However the jury is still out, for the *Joint Funding Simplification Act* is still in process of development, and the Community Development Block Grant is in the early stages of "proving out" the concepts of CERC and Annual Arrangements.

With some justification one might also add to the freeing up group the entire series of efforts to improve intergovernmental communications and consultation. These included the Regional Management Information System (RMIS), the Grant Tracking Information Subsystem (REGIS), Treasury Circular 1082 requiring federal grantor agencies to inform states of grant awards made within their jurisdictions, the *Catalog of Federal Domestic Assistance* (an indispensable source of information despite continuing complaints about inadequacies and imperfections), the Federal Outlays report providing information on past expenditures, and the OMB Circular A-85 procedure for consultation with elected chief executives of state and local general purpose governments in advance of the issuance of new regulations. To the extent that this range of procedural reforms made it easier for state and local officials to administer federal grant programs, their time and energies were released for strengthening their internal policy and resource management.

COUNTERCYCLICAL AID

Nothing in the recent past has affected the federal grant system as much in dollar terms as the countercyclical programs of 1976 and 1977. Initiated with Titles I and II of the *Public Works Employment Act of 1976*, this economic stimulus package allocated almost $13.9 billion to states and localities from November 1976 through November 1977. The $13.9 billion amounted to almost 7% of state and local governments' own-source revenue of $200.6 billion in 1975-76.

For FY 1978, the administration requested countercyclical assistance of almost $10 billion, or 12.1% of estimated federal outlays to state and local governments. This total was distributed as indicated in the table below.

With the stimulation of economic recovery through the creation of additional jobs as the overall objective, these funds were intended to be quickly injected into the economy. Three paths were chosen: public works projects (the local public works of the *Public Works Employment Act*), maintenance of basic state and local public services (antirecession provisions),

Countercyclical Program	1978 Revised Budget (in millions)
Public Works Employment Act of 1976 amended	
Title I—Local Public Works	$2,789
Title II—Antirecession Fiscal Assistance	1,550
CETA Act of 1973 amended	
Title II—Employment and Training Assistance	672
Title VI—Temporary Employment Assistance	4,872

and public service employment (CETA Titles II and VI). Fund distribution in each case is geared to rates of unemployment in the areas aided. Recipients are given the broadest spending discretion through the antirecession program, which was essentially an extension of GRS. Payments are to be used for the "maintenance of basic services." The local public works program provides for 100% federal project grants, with few limits on the Secretary of Commerce's discretion apart from consideration of certain factors reflecting unemployment levels. Recipients have wide latitude in choice of projects on which to use the money—"construction, renovation, repair, or other improvement of local public works projects." The CETA Titles II and VI programs offer prime sponsor recipients less discretion than they have under the CETA Title I block grant program inasmuch as the grants are limited to use for providing transitional employment and related training in jobs involving needed public services. Yet the choice of possibilities within the public service jobs category is itself broad, so that these programs can be regarded as extending considerable discretion to recipient jurisdictions. Overall, therefore, the package of four countercyclical programs represents a substantial devolution of spending authority to state and particularly local governments.

INTRUSIVENESS: GENERALLY APPLICABLE NATIONAL POLICY REQUIREMENTS

The earlier section on general revenue sharing indicated that recipients of GRS funds are subject to civil rights and Davis-Bacon requirements. These are only two of some 31 requirements, enacted by the Congress to carry out national policy objectives, which apply more or less across the board to all grant programs. In addition to nondiscrimination and labor and procurement standards, they impose conditions under environmental protection, planning and project coordination, relocation and real property acquisition, public employee standards, and access to government information and decision processes. These requirements came into being largely in the 1960s and 1970s and the number applicable to grant programs continues to grow year by year. Current indications are that grant programs may become subject to additional guidelines in conserving energy, curbing inflation, and reducing unemployment.[12]

The consequence of this Congressional approach to achievement of national policy objectives is an encroachment on state and local discretion of a much wider and deeper magnitude than is indicated by looking only at the conditions that apply to individual grants. Any conclusion that the entire grant system has moved in the direction of providing greater discretion to state and local recipients as a consequence of the enactment during the past ten years of block grants and general revenue sharing, therefore, must be carefully weighed against the counter effect of the 31-odd, so-called, across-the-board, national policy objectives as conditions of receipt of federal financial assistance and the fact that general revenue sharing . . .

establishes a direct and continuing fiscal relationship between the national government and all 38,000 units of local government, 90% of whom (the units under 10,000 people) have had little or nothing to do with the federal government in the past.[13]

THE ISSUE OF FUNGIBILITY

A frequently cited explanation for Congress's heavy reliance on categorical grants is that they are effective instruments for Congress to influence state and local recipients to do certain things, involving expenditure of money. In other words, a leading objective of the grants is to stimulate state and local recipients to spend more money on specific activities identified in the categorical grant.

An analysis of legislative intent conducted by ACIR staff tends to confirm this reading of Congressional motivations. For its study of categorical grants, the Commission staff perused the law and legislative history behind formula-based or project grants. Exercising considerable subjective judgment in examining the record, the staff estimated that about 50% of the 146 formula-based grants and about 63% of the 296 project grants were in whole or part intended to be stimulative at the time they were enacted by Congress. In other words, 259 or 59% of the total of 442 categorical grants in 1975 had at least a partially stimulative purpose when passed by Congress.[14]

Local Officials' Views

Local officials surveyed by ACIR showed that there was little doubt in their minds about the effect of categorical grants. Two-thirds of the city officials and four-fifths of the county respondents believed that they would allocate federal grant funds differently if they had a chance. More than three-fourths of both groups thought that the reallocation would be moderate or substantial. Clearly, as seen by these officials, federal categorical grants tend to skew local decision-making, both in the use of federal funds and in the local match.[15] The skewing effect represents the stimulus of the federal categorical grants.

In response to parallel questions regarding block grants, local officials seemed to feel that categoricals tend to skew local priorities more than the two block grants examined (Safe Streets and Partnership for Health).[16] This supports the theory that block grants allow recipients greater discretion in the use of funds.

Considering then, Congressional intent, the perceptions of local officials, and the nature of block grants, one might expect that any shift in the composition of the total grant structure away from categorical grants and toward block grants and general revenue sharing would alter the fiscal impact of that system. There would be less federal influence in determining recipient priorities—in other words, more devolution of decisionmaking. Is this what has actually happened? The issue gets down to a question of whether the system has become more or less stimulative or substitutional.

ACIR-Syracuse Analysis

An ACIR-Syracuse University study examined the issue of stimulation vs. substitution in an analysis of the effect of federal grants on state and local expenditures, employment levels, and wage rates.[17] This study looked at state-local expenditures in the aggregate, rather than individual grant programs or functional sections of the total grant package. It concluded that all federal grants tend to call for additional state-local own-source expenditures, but that this result is greater for some types of grants than for others. Both project and formula grants were found to generally stimulate state-local expenditures. The overall degree of stimulation was somewhat higher for project grants than for formula grants, suggesting that project grants tend to be more in line with state-local expenditure preferences and reflect a greater degree of voluntarism than formula grants.

The study divided federal grants into high, low, and no state-local matching, with a high state-local match defined as 50% or more. As might be expected, the greatest degree of expenditure stimulus was associated with high matching grants.*

In sum, the ACIR-Syracuse study found that the federal aid system in aggregate stimulated new expenditures among state and local recipients; that the stimulation was greater through project grants than formula grants; and that it was highest in the high-match grants. The fact that the study was focused on grant aggregates left unanswered the issue of whether specific grants or grants in specific functional areas have a stimulative or substitutive effect.

The Fungibility of Specific Grants

In its analysis of cost sharing arrangements in another volume of this series, the ACIR drew conclusions from a study of the literature on grants stimulation or substitution and its own analysis of the issue.[18] The analysis concluded that a number of factors may influence whether a particular grant program is stimulative or substitutive. The principal factor is the recipient's taste for the aided activity in preference to other competing uses of funds. Other factors are the size and servicing range of the recipient government, the number and variety of grant programs in which it participates, the timing and size of the grant relative to the ongoing recipient spending for the aided activity, the type of grant, and the grant's fiscal requirements. Taste and a recipient's fiscal and servicing condition provide the motivation for using federal funds to substitute for nonfederal funds. What makes fungibility practical is the size of the grant,

---

* *Editors' note:* Many federal grants require the grant recipient to "match" federal dollars with some of their own. Matching requirements vary greatly among grants. A 50 percent match would require that half of the expenditures come from state-local resources.

the number of grant programs, and presence or absence of local political pressure.

The Brookings Institution study of general revenue sharing for the one-year period ending June 30, 1974—a period during which expenditures for operating and maintenance purposes by local governments were restricted to certain "priority expenditure categories"—endeavored to identify the extent to which recipients used the revenue sharing funds as their actual-use reports indicated. For that period, the study found that local jurisdictions' officially reported expenditures of shared revenue for law enforcement were four times greater than new spending for such purposes actually identified by the Brookings field research. The report concluded:

> *The differences revealed by this special study of the programmatic impact of revenue sharing clearly indicate that revenue sharing funds have not gone for new public safety and law enforcement programs in anything like the amounts suggested by the ORS (Office of Revenue Sharing) actual-use data. This is not to say that the Treasury data are wrong, only that public safety and law enforcement are areas in which official designations for general revenue sharing uses reflect especially high substitution effects as opposed to the new spending effects.*[19]

The Brookings authors argue that in attempting to differentiate among different federal grants as to their effect on recipient governments' expenditure decisions, the fungible or substitutive nature of these funds must be carefully considered. They assert that all forms of federal aid to state and localities are fungible, no matter how ingenious the conditions placed on the use of grant moneys. Thus, they contend, fungibility is an issue not only in noncategorical grants, such as revenue sharing, but also in categorical grants, where the allocational impact is "ultimately determined by the preferences that recipient governments have for the particular public goods and services at which such grants are aimed; for these types of grants, fungibility is also a very real issue."[20]

The Brookings study derived several grant points about substitution vs. new spending effects that arise from many studies made of the issue of fungibility:

> 1. *The older the grant, the greater will be its substitution or displacement effects.*
>
> 2. *Project grants can be expected to have greater new spending effects than formula grants.*
>
> 3. *The higher the matching ratio, the greater will be the ratio of substitution to new spending effects.*
>
> 4. *Grants made to special purpose jurisdictions (such as school districts and housing and urban renewal districts) will have greater new spending effects than grants made to general purpose units of state and local governments.*

5. *Overall, the broader the permissible uses and the fewer restrictions on the federal grants, the greater will be the substitution effects.*[21]

Part of the reason for Congress's decision to authorize general revenue sharing and block grants is the desire to permit greater state and local discretion in the expenditure of assistance funds. This contrasts with their reason for choosing the categorical instrument, namely, their desire to specify the use and the conditions under which those funds may be spent. Yet research studies to date, admittedly inconclusive, suggest that, while categorical grants as a type are less fungible than block grants and GRS, in certain circumstances they are likely to be highly fungible. These include situations where the recipient receives a multitude of intergovernmental fiscal transfers, has a number of independent revenue sources, and provides an expanding or broad range of public services. If this analysis is correct, to the extent that such circumstances become more common among grant recipients, the recipients are exercising a greater degree of discretion in the use of categorical grant funds. To that extent, moreover, the shift from categorical grants to block grants and general revenue sharing becomes less significant as a factor in increasing recipient discretion in the spending of federal funds. Of more significance is the growing size of the aid flows, the increasing number of programs, and the rate of recipient participation. All this is not to say that GRS and block grants have not enhanced recipient fiscal discretion. They have, but so has the continued and expanded reliance on categoricals, especially in combination with the newer forms of funds transfer.

The question raised about fungibility also casts doubt about the long-standing allegations by state and local officials, fortified by the survey findings cited earlier, that federal grants have a heavy skewing effect, at least at this point, on local budget priorities.

SUMMARY

By definition almost, the shift to the tripartite grant system has seemed to effect a notable devolution of decisionmaking to the state and local levels of government. This change has been abetted by two trends in the middle range efforts to reform grants management—the imposition of limits on federal grant administrators' freedom to impose conditions on grantees, and the freeing up of local recipients in their administration of grants. In the past two years, moreover, the infusion of some $14 billion in countercyclical aid has tended to tilt the grant system further in the direction of increased recipient discretion.

While in theory GRS and block grants are biased toward the devolution of authority to state and local recipients, in practice their influence has not been entirely this way. GRS imposes some conditions upon recipients, notably in regard to budgeting, reporting and auditing. Most significantly, for the first time it brings the federal aid presence to a multitude of smaller jurisdictions that previously were not exposed to that presence.

The four block grants examined are hybrids in varying degree, in the sense that they depart from the model block grant. They are surrounded by categoricals, constitute only a part of the total federal funds applied to their functional areas, and are subject to varying numbers and complexity of procedural and performance requirements.

All grants are subject in some degree to special requirements established by Congress for the attainment of certain national objectives. This includes GRS, which is subject to nondiscrimination and Davis-Bacon wage rate conditions. The nondiscrimination requirements, in fact, are more demanding under GRS than under other programs. All the across-the-board requirements represent a substantive and growing means of increasing federal intrusiveness into the conduct of state and local government, heightened in the case of GRS by its near universal coverage of all general purpose units.

The issue of the degree to which the switch from categorical grants to GRS and block grants has liberated decisionmaking at the recipient level depends to some extent on the degree to which categorical grants are fungible. Evidence, while not conclusive, is sufficient to suggest that fungibility, although most pronounced in GRS and block grants, exists among all types of grants, including categoricals, and is dependent upon factors other than the type of grant—particularly the number of separate grants and the total cash flow. Hence the switch from a monolithic categorical grant system to one in which categoricals make up only 75% of the grant dollars means that there has been some increase in the decisionmaking flexibility of grant recipients. While much of it is due to the introduction of block grants and GRS, much is also attributable to the expansion in the number and dollar magnitude of categorical grants.

NOTES

1. See ACIR, *Categorical Grants: Their Role and Design* (Report A-52), Washington, DC, U.S. Government Printing Office, May 1978.
2. See ACIR, *General Revenue Sharing: An ACIR Reevaluation* (Report A-48), Washington, DC, U.S. Government Printing Office, October 1974, p. 2.
3. *Ibid.*, p. 2.
4. P. L. 94-488.
5. The Civil Service Commission attempted to make the *Hatch Act* also apply to revenue sharing but the Attorney General eventually ruled in favor of excluding the *Hatch Act* provisions from application. For further reference to the "across-the-board" requirements in grant programs generally, see the discussion on "intrusiveness."
6. In 1975 the Office of Revenue Sharing stated that revenue sharing payments were being made to more than 38,000 of the eligible 38,861 local governments. Department of the Treasury, *Second Annual Report of the Office of Revenue Sharing*, Washington, DC, U.S. Government Printing Office, March 1, 1975, p. 7.
7. Richard P. Nathan, Allen D. Manvel, Susannah E. Calkins, and Associates, *Monitoring Revenue Sharing*, Washington, DC, The Brookings Institution, 1975, p. 281.

8. *Ibid.*, pp. 263-278.
9. Richard P. Nathan, Charles F. Adams, Jr., and Associates, *Revenue Sharing: The Second Round*, Washington, DC, The Brookings Institution, 1977, pp. 108-132.
10. See ACIR, *Block Grants: A Comparative Analysis* (Report A-60), Washington, DC, U.S. Government Printing Office, November 1977.
11. See ACIR, *Improving Federal Grants Management* (Report A-53), Washington, DC, U.S. Government Printing Office, February 1977.
12. For an in-depth analysis of this development, see ACIR (Report A-52), *op cit.*, Chap. VIII.
13. Thomas J. Anton, Institute of Policy Studies, University of Michigan, quoted in Neal R. Peirce, "Fiscal Federalism: Sharing Revenue is Not Enough," *Publius*, Philadelphia, PA, Center for the Study of Federalism, Fall 1976, p. 181.
14. See ACIR (Report A-52), *op cit.*, Chap. V.
15. The existence of skewing is, of course, widely accepted as an effect of categorical grants. See for example, U.S. General Accounting Office, *Revenue Sharing and Local Government Modernization: A Conference Report*, Washington, DC, U.S. GAO, April 17, 1975, p. 10.
16. See ACIR, *The Intergovernmental Grant System as Seen by Local, State, and Federal Officials* (Report A-54), Washington, DC, U.S. Government Printing Office, May 1977, p. 24.
17. See ACIR, *Federal Grants: Their Effects on State-Local Expenditures, Employment Levels, and Wage Rates* (Report A-61), Washington, DC, U.S. Government Printing Office, February 1977.
18. ACIR (A-52), *op cit.*, Chap. VI.
19. *Ibid.*, p. 78.
20. *Ibid.*, p. 79. For other testimony regarding the fungibility of GRS, see U.S. Congress, Senate Committee on Finance, *General Revenue Sharing Hearings*, 94th Congress, 1st Sess., Washington, DC, U.S. Government Printing Office, April 16 and 17, and May 21 and 22, 1975, especially that of the Comptroller General, pp. 125 ff.; also U.S. General Accounting Office, *Revenue Sharing: Its Use by and Impact on State Governments*, Washington, DC, U.S. GAO, August 2, 1973, p. 2.
21. *Ibid.*, p. 80.

Discussion Questions

1. Grodzins and Elazar assert that the majority of American citizens "are within the jurisdiction of four or more governments, not counting the state and national ones," and that there is "no neat division of functions among them." Do you find this to be true in your own case?

2. Do you agree with Grodzins and Elazar that we cannot separate federal functions from state and local functions? Why or why not?

3. Grodzins and Elazar argue that "the American system is best conceived as one government serving one people." Do you agree?

4. In brief, how would you summarize the ACIR's findings about changes in the grant system and the devolution of authority to states and localities?

5. Do the ACIR's findings prove that, as Grodzins and Elazar argue, the system is indivisible, or do they suggest that we just might be able to separate federal from state and local responsibilities?

6. Do you feel that the federal government ought to continue its efforts to devolve authority to state and local governments or that it ought to provide more policy direction by a renewed reliance on categoricals?

CHAPTER TWO

POLITICAL PARTIES
AND INTEREST GROUPS

American political parties are typically described in textbooks as decentralized, fragmented, and nonideological. As a result, the center of power for parties most often is located at the county or city level. Power tends to flow from the local level to the state level. State central committees usually lack a strong organizational base and the means to control the activities (including the nomination of candidates) of local party groups.

Although they never were typical of all cities, political machines flourished in many American cities in the late nineteenth and early twentieth centuries. They were organized around strong precinct and ward leaders who reported to the city "boss." Party workers offered the poor jobs, recognition, and financial help at a time when government welfare programs were nearly nonexistent. To a large extent political machines were victims of their own success. As the poor and the first-generation immigrants became better educated and acquired better jobs they had less reason to turn to machines for help. Federal and state welfare programs replaced party assistance. Better-educated residents valued their vote more and were less willing to accept graft and corruption as a way of political life. However, remnants of several urban machines remain in the 1980s, and machines continue to leave their mark on the operation and structure of many local party organizations.

Whether reformed or unreformed (machine oriented), political parties face the difficult task of finding volunteers to staff a host of party offices, as well as to perform many routine tasks of party management. Of course, the need for workers is even greater in election years. In some instances party posts go unfilled and most party organizations find themselves short of volunteer workers. While parties offer a variety of rewards and incentives, only a very small percentage of Americans (less than 10 percent) ever become members of a party organization.

However, a larger number of people are members of interest groups. A wide variety of business, labor, and ideological groups are active in state and local government. Interest groups tend to be strongest in states with weak party organizations. In a sense, they move into a political vacuum and provide many of the representational functions performed by political parties.

Social scientists continue to debate the role of interest groups and whether or not some elite groups of like-minded citizens (typically downtown business-persons) are able to dominate and direct the course of political action in cities. While some accept the elite model of control, others, called pluralists, contend that power is more evenly distributed among a variety of groups.

The first article in this chapter, by Raymond Wolfinger, discusses some of the reasons why city political machines have *not* disappeared. As noted earlier, changing conditions in twentieth-century America have taken their toll on many urban political machines. Yet as Wolfinger points out, many of the factors that created a constituency for the early machines still exist to support contemporary machines. Patronage is still available as a political resource. The growth of government programs has created more opportunities for political favoritism. Growing levels of bureaucracy provide greater need for the machine's services as an ombudsman to help citizens deal with governmental red tape and confusion. In some cases political leaders have been able to use these resources effectively to perpetuate machines. In many other cases this potential political power has not been utilized and machines have withered away.

In the second article in this chapter, political scientist Frank Sorauf reviews the incentives that parties use to induce workers to devote long hours of hard work, without pay, to the party cause. As Sorauf notes, an increasing number of people are working for parties because they believe strongly in a policy issue and want to see positive government action. This, of course, contrasts with the more traditional incentive of economic self-interest.

In the last article Edward Banfield and James Wilson examine the role of businesspeople as a political force in large cities. Clearly, businesspeople operate as powerful interest groups in many cities. However, Banfield and Wilson conclude that they are unlikely to function as a "power elite."

Why Political Machines Have Not Withered Away

Raymond E. Wolfinger

The conventional wisdom in American social science interprets machine politics as a product of the social needs and political techniques of a bygone era. Advocates of this position attempt to explain both the past existence of machines and their supposed current demise in terms of the functions that the machines performed.[1] In analyzing the functions —now supposedly obsolete— that machine politics served, it is useful to consider four questions:

1. Did political machines actually perform these functions in the past?

2. Do machines still perform them?

3. Has the need for the functions diminished?

4. Is machine politics found wherever these needs exist?

It is commonly argued that various historical trends have crucially diminished the natural constituencies of machines—people who provided votes or other political support in return for the machine's services. The essential machine constituency is thought to have been the poor in general and immigrants in particular. The decline of machine politics then is due to rising prosperity and education, which have reduced the number of people to whom the rewards of machine politics are attractive or necessary. These trends have also, as Thomas R. Dye puts it, spread "middle class values about honesty, efficiency, and good government, which inhibit party organizations in purchases, contracts, and vote-buying, and other cruder forms of municipal corruption. The more successful machine [sic] today, like Daley's in Chicago, have had to reform themselves in order to maintain a good public image."[2]

Reprinted from "Why Political Machines Have Not Withered Away and Other Revisionist Thoughts," *Journal of Politics* 34 (May 1972): 383-398.

One function that machines performed was furnishing needy people with food, clothing, and other *direct material assistance* —those legendary Christmas turkeys, buckets of coal, summer outings, and so on. There is no way of knowing just how much of this kind of help machines gave, but it seems to have been an important means of gleaning votes. From the time of the New Deal, government has assumed the burden of providing for the minimal physical needs of the poor, thus supposedly preempting a major source of the machine's appeal. The growth of the welfare state undeniably has limited politicians' opportunities to use charity as a means of incurring obligations that could be discharged by political support. Some political clubs still carry on the old traditions, however, including the distribution of free turkeys to needy families at Christmas time.[3]

Machines supposedly provided other tangible rewards, and the need for these has not been met by alternative institutions. The most obvious of these benefits is employment. The welfare state does not guarantee everyone a job and so the power to hire is still an important power resource. It has been argued, most ably by Frank J. Sorauf, that patronage jobs, mainly at the bottom of the pay scale, are not very attractive to most people.[4] But these positions are attractive to enough people to maintain an ample demand for them, and thus they still are a useful incentive.

A second major constituent service supplied by machine politics was *helping poor and unacculturated people deal with the bureaucratic demands of* urban government. Describing this function, some writers emphasized its affective dimension. Robert K. Merton put it this way: "the precinct captain is ever a friend in need. In our increasingly impersonal society, the machine, through its local agents, performs the important social *function of humanizing and personalizing all manner of assistance* to those in need.[5] In Dye's view, the machine "personalized government. With keen social intuition, the machine recognized the voter as a man, generally living in a neighborhood, who had specific personal problems and wants."[6] William F. Whyte saw a more cognitive element in politicians' services to the common man: "the uninitiated do not understand the complex organization of government and do not know how to find the channels through which they can obtain action."[7] Whyte's view of the relation between the citizen and his "friend in need" the precinct captain is a great deal less innocent than Merton's: "Everyone recognizes that when a politician does a favor for a constituent, the constituent becomes obligated to the politician."[8]

If machine politics were a response to "our increasingly impersonal society," it would seem to follow that continuing growth in the scope, complexity, and impersonality of institutional life would produce *greater* need for politicians to mediate between individuals and their government. The growth of the welfare state therefore has not diminished this need but increased it and presumably offers the machine politician new opportunities for helping citizens get what they want from the government. Describing the advent of New Deal social services in a poor Boston neighborhood, Whyte made it clear that the new welfare policies did not so much subvert machine politics as rearrange the channels of access while presenting some politicians with a new opportunity to accumulate obligations. Whyte quotes the wife of a state senator: "If you're qualified, you can get on [WPA] without going to a politician. But it will be four weeks before you get certified, and I can push things through so that you get on in a week. And I can see that you get a better job . . ."[9]

As far as local politicians are concerned, new public services may be new prizes that covetous or needy citizens can more easily obtain with political help. Writing a generation after Whyte, Harold Kaplan reported that in Newark "a public housing tenant, therefore, may find it easier to secure a public housing unit, prevent eviction from a project, secure a unit in a better project, or have NHA [Newark Housing Authority] reconsider his rent, if he has the right sponsor at City Hall."[10] There is no necessary connection, then, between expanded public services and a decline in the advantages of political help or in the number of people who want to use it. While the expansion and institutionalization of welfare may have ended "the party's monopoly of welfare services,"[11] they have vastly expanded the need for information, guidance, and emotional support in relations between citizens and government officials, and thus there is no shortage of services that machines can provide the poor and unassimilated, who are still with us.[12]

There is no doubt that in the past 50 years income levels have risen and the flow of foreign immigrants has dwindled considerably. But there are plenty of poor people in the cities, the middle classes have been moving to the suburbs for the past two generations, and the European immigrants have been succeeded by blacks, Puerto Ricans, Mexicans, and poor rural whites.[13] Moreover, about two and a half million people came to this country as immigrants in the decade from 1950 to 1960. The argument that affluence and assimilation have choked machine politics at the roots, one familiar to scholars for decades, may now look a bit more threadbare. Yet the recent rediscovery of poverty and cultural deprivation has not had a major effect on thinking about trends in the viability of machine politics.

Along with the new interest in the urban poor has come a realization that existing institutions do not meet their needs. Among these inadequate institutions is the political machine, which, in the traditional view, should be expected to do for today's blacks, Chicanos, Puerto Ricans, and poor whites just what it is supposed to have done for yesterday's immigrants. But even in cities with flourishing machine politics there has been a tremendous development of all kinds of community action groups for advice, information exchange, and the representation of individual and neighborhood interests—precisely the functions that the machines are said to have performed. The gap between the disoriented poor and the public institutions serving them seems to be present equally in cities like Chicago, generally thought to be political anachronisms, and in places like Los Angeles that have never experienced machine politics. This leads to an important point: most American cities have had the social conditions that are said to give rise to machine politics, but many of these cities have not had machine politics for a generation or more.

This fact and the evident failure of existing machines to perform their functions cast doubt on the conventional ways of explaining both the functions of machines in their supposed heyday and the causes of their "decline." One conclusion is that the decline is real, but that the principal causes of the decline do not lie in affluence and assimilation. A second possibility is that the machines persist, but have abandoned the beneficient functions they used to perform. A third is that they are still "humanizing and personalizing all manner of assistance to those in need," but cannot cope with a massive increase in the needs of their clienteles. And a fourth alternative is that the extent to which they ever performed these functions has been exaggerated.

It does seem that a whole generation of scholarship has been adversely affected by overreaction to the older judgmental style of describing machine politics. Until a decade or two ago most work on machines was moralistic and pejorative, dwelling on the seamy side of the subject and concerning itself largely with exposure and denunciation.[14] More contemporary social scientists have diverged from this tradition in two respects. One, apparently a reaction to the highly normative style of the old reformers, is a tendency to gloss over the very real evils they described. The other, addressed to the major problem of explaining the durability of machine politics, is the search for "functions": acculturating immigrants and giving them a channel of social mobility, providing a link between citizen and city hall, and coordinating formally fragmented government agencies. Some writers suggest that urban political organizations were a rudimentary form of the welfare state. While the tone of these later works has been realistic, some of them leaned toward idealizing their subject, perhaps in reaction to the earlier moralism or because functionalism has not been accompanied by an inclination to confront the sordid details. Thus the development of a more dispassionate social science has produced, on the descriptive level, a retreat from realism. The functionalists seem to have been somewhat overcredulous: "the precinct captain is ever a friend in need."

This innocence may explain the popularity in recent textbooks of a pious declaration by a celebrated and unsavory ward boss in Boston: " 'I think,' said Martin Lomasny [sic], 'that there's got to be in every ward somebody that any bloke can come to—no matter what he's done—and get help. Help, you understand; none of your law and your justice, but help.' "[15] The kind of "help" that could be expected is suggested by the remarks of another local leader in Boston that convey, I think, a more realistic sense of the priorities in machine politics:

> *When people wanted help from the organization, they would come right up here to the office [of the political club]. Matt [the boss] would be in here every morning from nine to eleven, and if you couldn't see him then, you could find him in the ward almost any other time. If a man came in to ask Matt for a job, Matt would listen to him and then tell him*

he'd see what he could do; he should come back in a couple of days. That
would give Matt time to get in touch with the precinct captain and find
out all about the man. If he didn't vote in the last election, he was out.
Matt wouldn't do anything for him—that is, unless he could show that
he was so sick he couldn't get to the polls.[16]

"Helping" citizens deal with government is, in this context, usually thought
to be a matter of advice about where to go, whom to see, and what to say. The
poor undeniably need this service more than people whose schooling and
experience equip them to cope with bureaucratic institutions and procedures.
But in some local political cultures advice to citizens is often accompanied by
pressure on officials. The machine politician's goal is to incur the maximum
obligation from his constituents, and merely providing information is not as
big a favor as helping bring about the desired outcome. Thus *"help" shades*
into "pull."

Now there is no reason why the advantages of political influence appeal
only to the poor. In places where the political culture supports expectations
that official discretion will be exercised in accordance with political considerations, the constituency for machine politics extends across the socio-economic
spectrum. People whose interests are affected by governmental decisions can
include those who want to sell to the government, as well as those whose
economic or social activities may be subject to public regulation.

Favoritism animates machine politics, favoritism not just in filling pick-
and-shovel jobs, but in a vast array of public decisions. The welfare state has
little to do with the potential demand for favoritism, except to expand opportunities for its exercise. The New Deal did not abolish the contractor's natural
desire to minimize the risks of competitive bidding, or the landlord's equally
natural desire to avoid the burdens of the housing code. It is all very well to
talk about "middle-class values of efficiency and honesty," but the thousands
of lawyers whose political connections enable them to benefit from the billion-
dollar-a-year case load of the Manhattan Surrogates' Court are surely not
members of the working class.

While "help" in dealing with the government may be primarily appealing
to people baffled by the complexities of modern society and too poor to hire
lawyers, "pull" is useful in proportion to the size of one's dealings with government. Certain kinds of business and professional men are *more* likely to have
interests requiring repeated and complicated relations with public agencies,
and thus are potentially a *stronger* constituency for machine politics than the
working classes. The conventional wisdom that the middle classes are hostile
to machine politics rests on several types of evidence: (1) The undeniable fact
that reform candidates almost always run better in well-to-do neighborhoods.
(2) The equally undeniable fact that machine politics provides, in patronage
and petty favors, a kind of reward for political participation that is not
available in other incentive systems. (3) The less validated proposition that
middle-class people think that governments should be run with impartial,

impersonal honesty in accordance with abstract principles, while the working classes are more sympathetic to favoritism and particularistic criteria. These characterizations may be true in the aggregate for two diverse such categories as "the middle class" and "the working class" (although that has not yet been established), but even if these generalizations are true, they would still leave room for the existence of a sizable subcategory of the middle class who, in some political cultures, benefits from and endorses machine politics.

Textbook interpretations recognize these middle-class interests in machine politics, but generally relegate them to an hypothesized earlier stage in urban history. This was the era when America changed from a rural to an urban society, a shift that created a vast need in the new cities for municipal facilities and services: streetcars, electricity, paved streets, and so on. These needs were met by businessmen who corrupted officials wholesale in their eagerness to get franchises. Since the businessmen wanted action, they profited from political machines that could organize power to get things done by centralizing the formally fragmented agencies of government. Thus machine politics served the needs not just of poor immigrants, but also of the generation of businessmen who exploited the foundation of urban America. But after the first great rush of city building, the essential facilities and utilities had been supplied and business interest in local government declined. Machine politics no longer performed a coordinating function for the franchise seekers and hence lost an important constituency.

While this may be an accurate description of relations between business greed and governmental corruption in the Gilded Age, it has a number of deficiencies as an explanation of the rise and fall of machine politics. Three of these flaws have already been discussed in other contexts: (1) Like poverty, urban growth is not a bygone phenomenon, but continues to this day. (2) Machine politics does not occur wherever cities have experienced sudden and massive needs for municipal services. (3) This explanation confuses patronage and centralization of party organizations at the city level, two phenomena that may not be found together.

There are other difficulties with this line of thought. First, uncoordinated public agencies and jurisdictions continue to proliferate. If machine politics were a response to the formal decentralization of government, one would think that it, too, would increase, and that party organizations would grow stronger rather than weaker. It may be that one or more unstated intermediary conditions are preventing these latter trends from occurring; if so, no writer has, to my knowledge, shown what this interactive relation is.

If it were true that "the key structural function of the Boss is to organize, centralize, and maintain in good working condition the 'scattered fragments of power'" typical of American local government, one would expect to find a positive relation between the prevalence of machine politics and municipal institutions that maximize fragmentation. "Strong-mayor" cities should be least ridden by patronage, and commission and council-manager cities should have the most. There is no systematic evidence available about these relations, but what data there are do not support the propositions. (They are also not supported by another piece of conventional wisdom, which associates city managers with reformism.) Machine politics seems to be far more common on the East Coast than in the West, but so are cities with elected mayors. Cities with mayors and cities with managers are equally likely to have merit systems for their employees, which could be considered an index of the weakness of machine politics.[17]

Finally, political centralization may not be conducive to the interests of businessmen who want prompt and affirmative action from local government. Whether centralized power is preferable depends on what the businessman wants. If he wants a license or franchise to sell goods or services, or to buy something belonging to the government, it may be in his interests to deal with an autonomous official or agency, not with a government-wide hierarchy. John A. Gardiner's study of the notoriously corrupt city of "Wincanton" provides evidence for the proposition that decentralized political systems are *more* corruptible, because the potential corrupter needs to influence only a segment of the government, and because in a fragmented system there are fewer centralized forces and agencies to enforce honesty. The "Wincanton" political system is formally and informally fragmented; neither parties nor interest groups (including the criminal syndicate) exercise overall coordination. The ample patronage and outright graft in "Wincanton" are not used as a means of centralization.[18] Indeed, governmental coordination clearly would not be in the interests of the private citizens there who benefit from corruption, or of the officials who take bribes. Attempts by reformers to stop graft or patronage often founder on the city's commission form of government, which is both the apotheosis of local governmental fragmentation and an hospitable environment for machine politics.

The conventional wisdom also holds that the machines' electioneering techniques are as obsolete as the social functions they used to perform. According to this interpretation, "the old politics" based its campaigns on divisible promises and interpersonal persuasion, and these methods have been outdated by the mass media—particularly television, the growing importance of candidates' personalities, and the electorate's craving for ideological or at least programmatic promises.[19]

Like the other explanations of the machines' demise, this argument has serious factual and logical deficiencies. As we have seen, machine politics is an effective way of raising money for political purposes. There is no reason why the money "maced" from public employees or extracted from government contractors cannot be spent on motivational research, advertising copywriters, television spots, and all the other manifestations of mass media campaigns.

Similarly, there is no inconsistency between machine politics and outstanding candidates. Just as machine politicians can spend their money on public relations, so can they bestow their support on inspirational leaders who exude integrity and vitality. Many of the most famous "idealistic" politicians in American history owe their success to the sponsorship of machine politicians. Woodrow Wilson made his first venture into electoral politics as the gubernatorial candidate of an unsavory Democratic organization in New Jersey. (Once elected governor, Wilson promptly betrayed his sponsors.) In more recent times, such exemplars of dedicated public spirit as the elder Adlai Stevenson, Paul H. Douglas, and Chester Bowles were nominated for office as the candidates of the patronage-based party organizations in their several states.[20]

Sayre and Kaufman explain this organization willingness to support blue-ribbon candidates: "They [machine politicians] have also learned the lesson of what retailers call the loss leader—that is, the item that may lose money for the storekeeper but which lures customers in and thereby leads to increases in purchases of profitable merchandise."[21] Generally, party regulars turn to blue-ribbon "loss leaders" when they think that their popularity is necessary to carry the ticket to victory. Otherwise, machine politicians eschew candidates with independent popular appeal, since popularity is an important bargaining resource in intraparty negotiating. Without it, an elected official is more dependent on organization politicians.

"The new politics" is an ambiguous term. It is used to describe increasing campaign emphasis on the mass media and professional public relations, and also is applied to popular participation in party affairs and direct contact with the voters by campaign workers. In the 1968 election "the new politics" was associated with peace advocates and the young enthusiasts who gave so much tone to Eugene McCarthy's presidential bid. Except for the age of the activists, there was little to distinguish this aspect of McCarthy's campaign from the idealistic appeal of such previous and diverse presidential candidates as Adlai Stevenson and Barry Goldwater, both of whom projected to some people an image of altruism and reform that attracted legions of dedicated workers. "The new politics" seems to be one of those recurring features of American politics that political writers are always rediscovering. The trademark of "the new politics" is intense precinct work, one-to-one conversations with citizens, the same interpersonal style that machines have relied on for generations. As a Democratic organization politician in New York observed: "If the new politics teaches anything, it's that the old politics was pretty good. The McCarthy kids in New Hampshire rang doorbells, made the telephone calls, made the personal contact that people associate with the old-style machine."[22]

Both kinds of "new politics" have at least one thing in common: they tend to be found in elections that draw a great deal of attention and arouse strong emotions. State and local elections and party primaries (except presidential ones) rarely attain much visibility. Candidates for the city council, the state legislature, or the city or state under-ticket seldom attract much public attention. Even paid media advertising in such elections is not feasible because the voting jurisdiction for a single candidacy generally includes only a fraction of the reading or viewing audience of the most widely used media. An occasional mayoral or gubernatorial race may get a good deal of media space and arouse popular enthusiasm, but otherwise these elections do not present a high profile in most voters' perspectives. This is particularly true for local elections, which generally are not concurrent with national campaigns, as well as for party primaries and campaigns for any state office except the governorship. These low-salience contests are particularly amenable to the resources typical of machine politics. A New York state senator explained this point bluntly: "My best captains, in the primary, are the ones who are on the payroll. You can't get the average voter excited about who's going to be an Assemblyman or State Senator. I've got two dozen people who are going to work so much harder, because if I lose, they lose."[23] It is in elections of this type, where neither the mass media nor idealistic amateurs are likely to participate, that most of the spoils of machine politics are at stake. Since precinct work is effective in inverse relation to the salience of the election,[24] "old fashioned machines" do not seem very seriously threatened by either form of "the new politics."

CONCLUSIONS AND SUGGESTIONS

To sum up my argument: Since an increasing proportion of urban populations is poor and uneducated, it is not persuasive to argue that growing prosperity and education are diminishing the constituency for machine politics. While governments now assume responsibility for a minimal level of welfare, other contemporary trends are not so inhospitable to machine politics. Various kinds of patronage still seem to be in reasonable supply, and are as attractive as ever to those people—by no means all poor—who benefit from them. The proliferation of government programs provides more opportunities for the exercise of favoritism. The continuing bureaucratization of modern government gives more scope for the machine's putative function of serving as a link between the citizen and the state.

These trends would seem to have expanded the need for the services the machines supposedly performed for the poor. Yet surviving machines apparently are not performing these functions, and machine politics has not flourished in many cities where the alleged need for these functions is just as great.

The potential constituency for political favoritism is not limited to the poor; many kinds of business and professional men can benefit from machine politics. They do in some cities but not in others. Again, it appears that the hypothesized conditions for machine politics are found in many places where machines are enfeebled or absent.

Real and imaginary changes in campaign techniques are not inconsistent with machines' capacities. In short, machines have not withered away because the conditions that supposedly gave rise to them are still present. The problem with this answer is that the conditions are found in many places where machine politics does not exist.

Attempts to explain the growth and alleged decline of machine politics usually emphasize the importance of immigrants as a constituency for machines.[25] Yet many cities with large immigrant populations have never been dominated by machine politics, or were freed of this dominance generations ago.[26] Machine politics continues to flourish in some states like Indiana, where foreign-stock voters are relatively scarce. In other states, like Pennsylvania and Connecticut, machines seem to have been as successful with old stock American constituents as with immigrants.[27]

Far more interesting than differences in ethnicity or social class are regional or subregional variations in the practices of machine politics and in attitudes toward them.[28] Public acceptance of patronage, for example, appears to vary a good deal from place to place in patterns that are not explained by differences in population characteristics such as education, occupation, and ethnicity. Although systematic data on this subject are not available, it does seem that voters in parts of the East, the Ohio Valley, and the South are tolerant of practices that would scandalize most people in, say, the Pacific Coast states or the Upper Midwest. The residents of Indiana, for example, seem to accept calmly the remarkable mingling of public business and party profits in that state. One researcher notes that these practices have "not been an issue in recent campaigns."[29] Another student of midwestern politics reports that "Indiana is the only state studied where the governor and other important state officials described quite frankly and in detail the sources of the campaign funds. They were disarmingly frank because they saw nothing wrong in the techniques employed to raise funds, and neither did the opposing political party nor the press nor, presumably, the citizenry."[30]

California provides a particularly useful contrast to the East Coast states and Indiana. While California has a cosmopolitan population and an urban, industrial economy, it also displays virtually no signs of machine politics. The Governor has about as many patronage jobs at his disposal as the Mayor of New Haven. Californians who worked in John F. Kennedy's presidential campaign report the bemusement of Kennedy organizers from the East who came to the state with thoughts of building their campaign organization around public employees. These and other practices that are widely accepted in the East are abhorred on the West Coast. Paying precinct workers is commonplace in eastern cities. But when Jess Unruh, a prominent California Democratic leader, hired some canvassers in the 1962 election, he was roundly denounced from all points of the political spectrum for importing such a sordid practice. The president of the California Democratic Council said that Unruh's action "smacked of ward politics" ("ward politics" is a common pejorative in California) and sternly announced, "I am firmly convinced that the expansion and development of the use of paid workers is unhealthy for the Democratic party in California."[31]

The reasons for these marked geographical variations in political style are not easily found, but looking for them is a more promising approach to explaining the incidence of machine politics than the search for functions supposedly rooted in the socio-economic composition of urban populations.[32]

NOTES

1. For a cautious, qualified synthesis of the orthodox position, see Fred I. Greenstein, "The Changing Pattern of Urban Party Politics," *The Annals*, 353 (May 1964), 2-13. Another presentation of the conventional wisdom, with fewer caveats, may be found in Thomas R. Dye, *Politics in States and Communities* (Englewood Cliffs, N.J.: Prentice-Hall, Inc., 1969), 256-272.

2. Dye, *Politics*, 276.

3. Tolchin and Tolchin, " 'Honest Graft'—Playing the Patronage Game," *New York Magazine*, March 22, 1971, 42.

4. See especially his "Patronage and Party," *Midwest Journal of Political Science*, 3 (May 1959), 115-126. In this and other articles Sorauf has argued not only that patronage is unattractive, but that it is inefficiently exploited by party leaders. His direct observations are limited to his study of the consequences of the 1954 Democratic gubernatorial victory for the highway maintenance crew in one rural county in Pennsylvania. Sorauf is more persuasive about the ineffectuality of Democratic leaders in Centre County than about the generalizability of his findings. He concludes, moreover, that "the parties need the strength of patronage, however minor and irregular it may be . . ." (*ibid.*, 126).

5. Robert K. Merton, *Social Theory and Social Structure* (revised edition; Glencoe, Ill.: The Free Press, 1957), 74 (emphasis in original).

6. Dye, *Politics*, 257.

7. William F. Whyte, *Street Corner Society* (enlarged edition; Chicago: University of Chicago Press, 1955), 241.

8. *Ibid.*, 240.

9. *Ibid.*, 197.

10. Harold Kaplan, *Urban Renewal Politics* (New York: Columbia University Press, 1963), 42-43.

11. Dye, *Politics*, 271.

12. Some contemporary political organizations do give advice and legal aid, mediate disputes, and serve as clearinghouses for information. See James Q. Wilson, *The Amateur Democrat* (Chicago: University of Chicago Press, 1962), 176; and Tolchin and Tolchin, " 'Honest Graft,' " 42.

13. As many writers are now beginning to realize, the acculturation and assimilation of the European immigrants is far from complete. See my "The Development and Persistence of Ethnic Voting," *American Political Science Review*, 59 (December 1965), 896-908; and *The Politics of Progress* (Englewood Cliffs, N.J.: Prentice-Hall, 1973), chap. 3.

14. For a description of trends in the study of city politics see Wallace S. Sayre and Nelson W. Polsby, "American Political Science and the Study of Urbanization," in *The Study of Urbanization*, ed. by Philip M. Hauser and Leo F. Schnore (New York: John Wiley & Sons, Inc., 1965), 115-156.

15. Originally quoted in *The Autobiography of Lincoln Steffens* (New York: Harcourt, Brace and Company, 1931), 618.

16. Quoted in Whyte, *Street Corner Society*, 194.
17. Raymond E. Wolfinger and John Osgood Field, "Political Ethos and the Structure of City Government," *American Political Science Review*, 60 (June 1966), 314-316.
18. John A. Gardiner, *The Politics of Corruption* (New York: Russell Sage Foundation, 1970), 8-12.
19. Interviewing a number of party officials in New Jersey, Richard T. Frost found that "old-fashioned" techniques like door-to-door canvassing were considered more effective, and used more frequently, than newer methods like television advertising. See his "Stability and Change in Local Party Politics," *Public Opinion Quarterly*, 25 (Summer 1961), 221-235.
20. Bowles is sometimes depicted as a high-minded victim of crasser and smaller men in the Connecticut Democratic party. The principal event presented as evidence for this viewpoint is his defeat by Thomas J. Dodd for the senatorial nomination at the 1958 state Democratic convention. Dodd had long been an opponent of the regular Democratic organization headed by then-Governor Abraham A. Ribicoff and state chairman John Bailey. Bowles, on the other hand, had been the organization's winning gubernatorial candidate in 1950. After his defeat for the senatorial nomination in 1958, he accepted the organization's offer of a congressional nomination and was elected to Congress in the fall. Ribicoff and Bailey thought that Bowles's popularity would help win the seat, then held by a Republican, and brushed aside the claims of the announced candidates for the Democratic nomination, who "voluntarily" withdrew their names from consideration by the convention.

   One of the seconding speeches in support of Bowles's unsuccessful try for the senatorial nomination was by Arthur T. Barbieri, the New Haven town chairman (and later a close ally of Dodd's). It was devoted to praising Bowles's willingness, when governor, to accede to the party's wishes in matters involving patronage. The disciplined New Haven delegation voted unanimously for Bowles, a Yankee patrician. Dodd, an Irish Catholic, was the sentimental favorite of many delegates, but almost all of them were city employees or otherwise financially dependent on city hall.
21. Wallace S. Sayre and Herbert Kaufman, *Governing New York City* (New York: Russell Sage Foundation, 1960), 155.
22. Quoted in the *New York Times*, June 1, 1970, 27.
23. Quoted in the *New York Times*, June 17, 1968, 30.
24. Raymond E. Wolfinger, "The Influence of Precinct Work on Voting Behavior," *Public Opinion Quarterly*, 27 (Fall 1963), 387-398. Turnout in the primary to select the Democratic candidate for the Manhattan Surrogates Court rarely reaches 100,000 voters and thus the outcome is more easily influenced by party organizations.
25. For a good statement of this position, see Elmer E. Cornwell, Jr., "Bosses, Machines, and Ethnic Groups," *The Annals*, 353 (May 1964), 27-39.
26. This is most obviously true of the large cities of the West Coast: San Francisco (44 percent foreign stock in 1960), Los Angeles (33 percent), and Seattle (31 percent). These cities are equally or more ethnic than eastern and midwestern cities characterized by machine politics, e.g., Chicago (36 percent), Philadelphia (29 percent), and St. Louis (14 percent).
27. See the works by Frank J. Sorauf cited in notes 4 and 30 and Duane Lockard, *New England State Politics* (Princeton: Princeton University Press, 1959), 245-251.

28. Several studies show major regional or subregional variations in political prefer-
ences that cannot be accounted for by varying demographic characteristics. See,
e.g., Irving Crespi, "The Structural Basis for Right-Wing Conservatism: The Gold-
water Case," *Public Opinion Quarterly*, 29 (Winter 1965), 523-542; James W.
Prothro and Charles M. Grigg, "Fundamental Principles of Democracy: Bases of
Agreement and Disagreement," *Journal of Politics*, 22 (Spring 1960), 276-294; and
Raymond E. Wolfinger and Fred I. Greenstein, "Comparing Political Regions: The
Case of California," *American Political Science Review*, 63 (March 1969), 74-86.

29. Robert J. McNeill, *Democratic Campaign Financing in Indiana, 1964* (Bloomington,
Ind., and Princeton, N.J.: Institute of Public Administration, Indiana University
and Citizens' Research Foundation, 1966), 39.

30. John H. Fenton, *Midwest Politics* (New York: Holt, Rinehart and Winston, 1966), 7.
For an account of public acceptance of patronage in bucolic, native-stock Centre
County, Pennsylvania, see Frank J. Sorauf, "Chairman and Superintendent," in
Cases in State and Local Government, ed. by Richard T. Frost (Englewood Cliffs,
N.J.: Prentice-Hall, Inc., 1961), 109-119.

31. *San Francisco Chronicle*, December 17, 1962, 10; and *CDC Newsletter*, December
1962.

32. The study of regional variations in American political perspectives is still in its
infancy. For a general discussion and survey of the literature see Samuel C. Patter-
son, "The Political Cultures of the American States," *Journal of Politics*, 30
(February 1968), 187-209.

For an interesting typology of three American political value systems that
encompasses the regional differences concerning machine politics discussed here see
Daniel J. Elazar, *American Federalism: A View from the States* (New York: Thomas
Y. Crowell Company, 1966).

The System of Incentives
for Party Activists

Frank J. Sorauf

The American political parties have never operated primarily in a cash economy. They have rarely bought or hired the millions of man-hours of labor they need. Even today paid staffs are small or nonexistent in most party organizations, and it is a rare party chairman who draws a substantial salary from the party organization. The great number of Americans active in the parties receive no cash in return for their considerable time and skills. Even the earthy old custom of paying precinct workers on election day is vanishing. What is it, then, that induces party workers to lavish their hours and efforts on the affairs of the parties? If the parties' payments are not made in cash, in which coin are they made?[1]

PATRONAGE

Patronage, the use of appointive governmental positions to reward past party work and induce future labors, is hardly unique to the American political parties.[2] Even today the municipal services of the Italian cities swarm with the partisans in power. But very probably no other party system over its history has relied as systematically on patronage as the American. The easy confidence of the Jacksonians that no public task was so complex that it demanded experience and their matching conviction that "to the victors go the spoils" set the ethic early in the nineteenth century. From then to the present a vast array of public jobholders—from elevator operators and charwomen in city hall to American ambassadors in foreign capitals—have owed their appointment to political worthiness and the right political sponsorship.

Despite the explosive growth of government bureaucracy in this century, the amount of patronage available to the parties has declined precipitously. The expansion of civil service and merit systems has been the chief reason. What was once a flourishing federal patronage—historians write of the hordes of ill-mannered job seekers overrunning presidential inaugurations—has by now dwindled to well below 1 percent of the federal establishment. There still remain the United States marshals and attorneys, the collectors of customs, and the rural mail carriers, to mention a few of the classic federal patronage posts, but theirs is a shrinking roster.

Similar declines have come, albeit more slowly, to the states and localities. Any number of states, counties, and cities—the great majority probably— have virtually abolished patronage, moving to merit systems of some sort. In a number of states the governor has no patronage available beyond his own immediate staff. Patronage does, of course, continue to flourish in a minority of states. New York, for example, has some 40,000 positions available for party patronage. But in recent years even some of the vaunted centers of patronage have seen the merit principle make new and severe inroads. Kentucky legislation in 1960 reduced the number of year-round jobs available for patronage from 16,000 to 4000, about 75 percent of them on the highway maintenance crews.[3] Pennsylvania, which had almost 50,000 patronage positions as late as 1970, lost a sizable number in collective bargaining. In 1971 some 17,500 workers, most of them also with the highway crews, negotiated a contract in which the state agreed not to discriminate against any employee on the basis of political affiliations. The contract also forbids the state to require workers to make political contributions or to engage in political activity. Furthermore, in 1976 the U.S. Supreme Court held that patronage dismissals violated the Constitution of the United States. That is, a majority of the justices thought that the dismissal of an otherwise satisfactory employee for political reasons— especially those having to do with a change in parties in power—violated the employee's freedoms of political belief and association.[4]

The unavailability of patronage is, however, only a part of the parties' problem. There are administrative problems as well. A recent survey of county chairmen in Ohio finds that they achieve only a partial return in party work or contributions from their patronage appointees.[5] The problems the parties encounter in using the available patronage jobs are legion. Patronage seekers may not meet the skill requirements of the job; heavy-equipment operators are hard enough to find without adding a set of political credentials. Also, the politics of patronage has always worked best among the depressed and disadvantaged; most patronage positions do not tempt the educated, "respected" middle-class leadership the parties would like to attract. Furthermore, elected executives may use patronage to build their own political followings rather than the party apparatus. Finally, the parties may not be able to use the patronage available to them. Especially when they win power after years of failure, they do not have the necessary administrative machinery or an adequate list of job seekers.[6]

At the same time pressures have understandably grown for patronage with which to reward the educated, middle-class activists in the parties and campaigns. One solution is the "political non-job."

> *Happily, political leaders have devised ways to bestow the status symbols of high office without the job itself. At Democratic national headquarters in Washington, where many such split-level appointments are routinely requisitioned and cleared, the new institution is known as "the honorary." Elsewhere it has been dubbed the patronage non-job, and it can range from nomination to a White House advisory committee to an invitation to be an honored member of an Air Force civic inspection tour of California, arranged at the behest of your local Congressman.*[7]

But chief executives who make appointments to administrative positions, boards, commissions, legal staffs, and judgeships also find themselves pressed to use these positions for patronage purposes. They can and do so use them, but the political considerations must often be tempered by or balanced against important considerations of ability and professional experience. In any event, the positions are not all that plentiful, and they often go—when used for patronage purposes—to reward workers in the campaigns of the appointing official rather than the workers of the party organization.

POLITICAL CAREER

Elective political office has the income, responsibility, prestige, and excitement —not to mention the power—that most patronage positions do not. And since the political party offers an efficient, and in some cases the only, avenue to elective office, it is inevitable that the possibility of an elective political career should recruit new party activists or sustain activity after other incentives have worn off. Robert Huckshorn, for instance, finds that between 1962 and 1972 one-third of all the state party chairmen were candidates for elective office after serving as chairman. The offices they sought, moreover, were often important ones: governorships, other statewide office, and seats in the United States Congress.[8]

There are party organizations with such disciplined control over their primaries that they can and do "give" public office, especially at the state and local level, to loyal party workers. If the party dominates the politics of the area, control of the primaries makes public offices an "elective patronage." The candidate is offered the chance to run and then does little more as the party organization runs up the necessary majorities. That degree of control over nomination and election to office is, however, vanishing along with patronage. The party must increasingly look for candidates with some appeal and qualities beyond their service to the party. The candidates know that, useful though the advantage of party support may be, it is rarely sufficient by itself.

What then does the candidate get from the support of the party? He needs advice, know-how, manpower, and money, and in most parts of the country the party still remains a likely source of them. Service in the party, then, yields the skill, experience, connections, approval, and resources that any candidate needs. It is, of course, possible for the candidate without party ties to seek election, but for every one who does, there are dozens of successful office seekers who have party ties. And for the partisan who already holds office there is no easier way to ensure reelection or to move to a more attractive office than by work in the party. So sedulous are the party's officeholders in currying the support of the party organizations that speculation over their ambitions and "moves" remains a favorite intraparty recreation.

PREFERMENTS

The tangible, material rewards of politics may take forms other than appointive or elective office. The active partisan or the financial "fat cat" may, for example, seek preference in the awarding of public contracts. In this respect, it is no accident that the leaders of the construction industry are so active politically in the states and localities that spend millions every year on roads and public buildings. Preference may take other forms: a tolerant or haphazard application of regulatory or inspection politics, unusually prompt or efficient public services (snow and garbage removal, for example), a forgiving instrument of the law (e.g., the fixed traffic ticket), or the granting of a scarce public service (admission to crowded mental hospitals, for instance). It may also involve the granting of scarce "opportunities" such as liquor licenses or franchises. By "preferment," in other words, one means special treatment or advantage, and it is dependent usually on the party's holding the decision-making positions in government. It is partly in this sense that parties talk of "controlling" city hall, the county courthouse, or the state capitol.

One particularly unappealing form is the "preferment" given activities that operate on the shady side of the law. It may involve a calculated ignoring of prostitution, bookmaking, the numbers game, or traffic in drugs in return for some form of political support. In other forms it has involved the parties' taking a share of protection money or the proceeds from crime, vice, or the rackets. The prevalence of such an incentive to party effort is understandably difficult to estimate. Perhaps it suffices to say that it is probably less vital than the political cynics think and more important than the Pollyannas admit. The chances are, though, that what nexus there is between organized crime and government goes on through mechanisms other than the political party. And when it touches the party and electoral politics, the influence of crime is probably felt more through campaign contributions than directly in the party organization. In 1960 Alexander Heard estimated ("a guess—that is what it is") that underworld money accounted for 15 percent of the campaign expenditures at state and local levels.[9]

SOCIOECONOMIC MOBILITY

Political activity offers easy publicity (or notoriety) and contacts for those who seek them: young lawyers trying to build a practice, owners of food and watering spots, insurance and real estate brokers, storekeepers, and the socially ambitious. Party activity opens up the contacts that lead to prosperity in a business or profession, to a new job or business opportunity, even to an elevated social status.

Writes one observer of the Philadelphia organization men:

> *One explanation of their motivation would locate the "boys'" essential urge in the factor known as "prestige." The truth is, many intellectuals and many members of the upper class who have come in contact with politicians argue that, for the Irish, Jewish, Italian bright boys who pursue it, politics is a "status-conferring" occupation. The Bill Greens and the Victor Blancs and the Aus Meehans, they point out, could no doubt have earned wealth and even the respect of their fellow-men by selling insurance, practicing law, and the like. But one thing that they could not earn in these ways is "place" in the community. Politics gives them that.[10]*

In the tired American phrase, some people join the active ranks in the parties to "get ahead," whether they define getting ahead in terms of upward social mobility or economic mobility.

SOCIAL AND PSYCHOLOGICAL SATISFACTIONS

The personal, nonmaterial rewards of party activity are not easy to identify and certainly not easy to measure. But one can sense the social rewards of politics in the camaraderie of the gang at party headquarters or the courthouse. It is evident at a party dinner as the workers press around the great and near great of the party, hoping for a word of greeting or a nod of recognition. In the new-style political clubs the attractiveness of the social life and friendship circle is explicit. "Many volunteers are rootless, transient newcomers searching the city for a means of associating with like-minded people." But while the parties' clubs rely on the social incentives, those incentives are probably secondary:

> *Although many clubs in various cities offer their members reduced air fares to Europe on charter flights, a full schedule of social events, forums featuring prestigious speakers, and the opportunity to play the political game, and although some members join simply to find a mate quickly or get to Paris inexpensively, if the clubs should cease to define themselves as organizations devoted to liberalism or reformisn or similar worthy causes, they could not for long sustain the interest of any but the handful who simply enjoy the company of others or like being district leader.[11]*

Perhaps one can say more simply that party politics is a splendid vehicle for gregariousness. Almost all reported research on the motivations of party activists finds that they say they "like people" or that they "like politics."

Social satisfactions merge almost imperceptibly into the psychological. "Like the theater, politics is a great nourisher of egos," writes one observer. "It attracts men who are hungry for attention, for assurance that somebody loves them, for the soul-stirring music of their own voices."[12] Party work may also offer the individual a cause or an enterprise with which to identify, a charismatic leader to follow, a round of activities that can lift him above the personally unrewarding tasks of the workaday world. The party may be a small island of excitement in a sea of routine. It may even offer an occasion for the manipulation or domination of others, a chance to decide or command, even an avenue for the projection of aggressions and hostilities.

IDEOLOGY AND POLICY ISSUES

Even the most casual soundings of party rhetoric indicate an increasing identification of partisans as "liberals" or "conservatives." Behind these phrases lies a potent motivation to party activity: a commitment to clusters of related attitudes about government and politics, especially about the proper role of government in contemporary society. On a more modest and limited scale the spur to activity may be concern for a single issue or interest (tax cuts, the war in Vietnam, abortions, the maintenance of local schools) or a single area of policy concern (foriegn policy, civil rights, local planning). The "cause" may, indeed, be the reform or rehabilitation of the political party itself.

Just as the importance of the immediate, material, personal rewards of politics has recently declined, that of issue and ideology has increased. Even in Manhattan, long the fief of Tammany Hall, the trend is evident:

> There is a "new look" among today's political activists. They are "re-
> spectable," solid middle-class citizens. The party "hack" of fiction, films,
> and the traditional literature is hard to find among the young, well-
> educated, affluent, and socially acceptable committeemen — and
> women — of the nineteen-sixties. Concomitantly, both the nature of
> political motivation and the character of political activity have changed.
> The contemporary politician considers his party organization an
> instrument for effectuating policy rather than a haven of personal
> security. He tends to be more interested in social reform than in catering
> to individual constituents.[13]

In national politics the country in 1964 witnessed the capture of the Republican national party by conservative partisans whose chief criterion for candidate and platform was frankly ideological. And in 1968 and 1972 the ideological left organized around the presidential candidacies of Eugene McCarthy and George McGovern, deeply affecting the presidential politics of the Democrats.

The party activist may also be drawn to the party by a more general civic commitment. A sense of obligation and duty as a citizen, a belief in the democratic values of citizen participation, may impel him. Scholars who have questioned party workers about their motives for service in the party know the familiar answers. They were "asked" to serve, and they assented because it was their civic duty. Often that response, in whatever words it may be couched, merely masks what the respondent feels are less acceptable motives. Often, however, it is an honest reflection of deeply ingrained civic values. Often, too, it may be combined with honest, if vague, commitments to "good government" and political reform.

THE PARTY ITSELF

Two final varieties of incentive, both essentially related to the party per se, must be mentioned. First of all, as a party activist works within the party, the well-being of the party itself becomes an incentive for work. He attaches many of his loyalties and aspirations to the party, and its health becomes an end in itself. The party's wins and losses become issues in and of themselves, and attacks on it are far more than attacks on its policies and activities. Second, it may be, as Robert Salisbury suggests in his study of St. Louis politicians, that large numbers of party activists participate "because they were brought up in a highly politicized atmosphere." The party "participant per family socialization was probably not exposed to involvement in other kinds of organizations, any more than a devout young communicant of the church would necessarily be taught to carry his devotion into other organizational settings."[14] In other words, party workers may gravitate to the party because they are accustomed to it and because through years of socialization they have invested loyalties in it.

No party organization depends on a single incentive, and very few partisans labor in the party for only one. Most party organizations rely on a variety or system of incentives. A residuum of patronage workers may coexist with workers attracted by policy issues or by a middle-class sense of civic responsibility. The mixture of incentives may vary between urban and rural areas, or between different local political cultures. One study suggests that at least in New York's Nassau County, issues and ideologies are a less potent incentive in the majority than in the minority party.[15] The mix may even vary within the same party organization. Eldersveld reports that in Wayne County, Michigan, the precinct chairmen depend heavily on the rewards of social contacts, whereas the party's higher leadership seeks a combination of immediate economic gain and ideological-philosophical rewards.[16]

For all the subtleties of the mix and variety of incentives, however, general comments about their overall frequency are possible. Scholarly evidence on the point comes from sporadic studies of parties in scattered parts of the country, but what evidence there is points to the dominance of ideological or issue incentives. Put very simply, the desire to use the party as a means to achieve policy goals appears to be the major incentive attracting individuals to party work these days.[17] And even though similar data are unavailable for earlier periods, there is ample reason to believe that this generalization was far less true of party workers a generation or two ago.

Indeed, incentives may change even for any individual—that is, the incentive that recruits people to party activity may not sustain them in that activity. Several studies suggest that a shift in incentive takes place in those party activists attracted by the purposive incentives—those who seek to achieve issue, ideological, or other impersonal goals through their party activity. To sustain their involvement in party work, they tend to depend more on incentives of social contact, identification with the party itself, and other personal rewards and satisfactions.[18] Perhaps an electorally pragmatic party— one traditionally committed to the flexibilities necessary to win elections—has difficulty providing the ideological successes to sustain the worker whose incentive remains ideological for any length of time.

NOTES

1. For a somewhat different categorization of incentives, see James Q. Wilson, *Political Organizations* (New York: Basic Books, 1974).
2. The concept of patronage here is, therefore, one of appointment to governmental jobs on the basis of political criteria. Other studies use broader definitions that include at least the two categories of patronage and preferment used here. For example, Martin and Susan Tolchin in *To the Victor . . .* (New York: Random House, 1971) work with a definition of patronage that includes "the allocation of the discretionary favors of government in exchange for political support" (p. 5).
3. Malcolm E. Jewell and Everett W. Cunningham, *Kentucky Politics* (Lexington: University of Kentucky Press, 1968), p. 43.
4. *Elrod* v *Burns*, 427 U.S. 347 (1976). In late 1979 a federal district court judge in Chicago extended the logic of *Elrod* to hold that hiring (as well as firing) for political reasons violated the Constitution in that it discriminated against job applicants without the proper political credentials. As of early 1980 an appeal in the case was pending. [*Editor's note:* In *Branti* v *Finkel* (1980) the Supreme Court held that the First Amendment forbids an officeholder to fire his subordinates from patronage jobs solely on the basis of their political beliefs.]
5. W. Robert Gump, "The Functions of Patronage in American Party Politics: An Empirical Reappraisal," *Midwest Journal of Political Science* 15 (1971): 87-107.
6. On patronage see also Daniel P. Moynihan and James Q. Wilson, "Patronage in New York State, 1955-1959," *American Political Science Review* 58 (1964): 286-301; and Frank J. Sorauf, "State Patronage in a Rural County," *American Political Science Review* 50 (1956): 1046-56.
7. Don Oberdorfer, "The New Political Non-Job," *Harper's* (October 1965), pp. 108ff.
8. Robert J. Huckshorn, *Party Leadership in the States* (Amherst: University of Massachusetts Press, 1976), p. 37.
9. Alexander Heard, *The Costs of Democracy* (Chapel Hill: University of North Carolina Press, 1960), p. 163. Beyond Heard's estimate it is not easy to find a

serious treatment of the relationships between crime and politics. Undoubtedly the subject itself restricts the usual scholarly inquiries. There are broader studies of "corruption" in government and politics, but they often suffer from a broad or imprecise definition of "corruption." A number extend the concept of corruption far beyond mere illegality. For a discussion and bibliography, see John G. Peters and Susan Welch, "Political Corruption in America: A Search for Definitions and a Theory," *American Political Science Review* 72 (1978): 974-84.

10. James Reichley, *The Art of Government: Reform and Organization Politics in Philadephia* (New York: Fund for the Republic, 1959), p. 104.

11. James Q. Wilson, *The Amateur Democrat* (Chicago: University of Chicago Press, 1962), p. 165.

12. John Fischer, "Please Don't Bite the Politicians," *Harper's* (November 1960), p. 16.

13. Robert S. Hirschfield, Bert E. Swanson, and Blanche D. Blank, "A Profile of Political Activists in Manhattan," *Western Political Quarterly* 15 (1962): 505.

14. Robert H. Salisbury, "The Urban Party Organization Member," *Public Opinion Quarterly* 29 (1965-66): 562, 564. For additional intergenerational data see David R. Derge, *Public Leadership in Indiana* (Bloomington: Indiana University Institute of Public Administration, 1969).

15. Dennis S. Ippolito and Lewis Bowman, "Goals and Activities of Party Officials in a Suburban Community," *Western Political Quarterly* 22 (1969): 572-80.

16. Samuel Eldersveld, *Political Parties: A Behavioral Analysis* (Chicago: Rand, McNally, 1964), p. 278; see also all of Chap. 11.

17. Lewis Bowman, Dennis Ippolito, and William Donaldson, "Incentives for the Maintenance of Grassroots Political Activism," *Midwest Journal of Political Science* 13 (1969): 126-39; Charles W. Wiggins and William L. Turk, "State Party Chairmen: A Profile," *Western Political Quarterly* 23 (1970): 321-32.

18. Among others, see M. Margaret Conway and Frank B. Feigert, "Motivation, Incentive Systems, and the Political Organization," *American Political Science Review* 62 (1968): 1159-73.

Businessmen in Politics

Edward C. Banfield and James Q. Wilson

Businessmen (meaning here owners and managers of *large* enterprises) seldom run for local offices. It is possible to suggest several reasons why. Like most prosperous people, they live in suburbs and are therefore ineligible to run in the central city. Holding local office—even being mayor of a large city—may be no more exciting or prestigious than being head of a big business. Politics—so many businessmen seem to think—is both demeaning and frustrating. These factors all tend to keep the businessmen from running, no doubt. But in all probability, the really decisive consideration is that he could not get elected if he tried. If he is an Anglo-Saxon, a Protestant, or a Republican (and he is likely to be all three), he is in effect disqualified for a high elective office in many large cities.

Even though he does not hold office, a businessman may play an important, or even a dominant, part in city affairs. In some cases, the nature of his business virtually requires him to do so. Where this is the case, he is likely to conclude that in order to serve well the interest of his business he must join with others to serve the interest of "business" and also the interest (as he himself defines it) of the "city as a whole." As a rule, neither he nor anyone else can distinguish clearly between his business-serving and his community-serving activity. Since he stands in the midst of most of the city's volunteer civic activity, the last chapter dealt, albeit somewhat obliquely, with the community-serving side of his role. This one deals mainly with its company-serving side.

BUSINESS INTERESTS IN CITY AFFAIRS

The businessmen who are most active in city affairs are those whose companies are most directly affected by what the city government does. These include especially the department stores, utilities, real estate operators, banks, and (a special case to be considered in a later chapter) newspapers.

Typically department stores (especially those without suburban branches) want to increase the volume of trade coming into the central business district. This means that they want to encourage good customers to come there and to discourage "undesirable" ones, that is, people with little money to spend whose presence would make the shopping district less attractive to the good customers. Therefore, they are enthusiastic promoters of urban renewal projects that will displace low-income people, particularly Negroes, from close-in districts and replace them with higher-income (white) customers. They favor construction of expressways to bring suburbanites downtown, underground parking facilities to make it convenient for them to come to their stores, and (sometimes) the subsidization of commuter railroads. If an important new public building is to be built, they want it so placed that the office workers will shop in their stores during lunch time or that it will serve as a barrier against the entry of "undesirables."

Utility companies tend to favor measures to increase the city's population, employment, and income. Because of the large fixed cost of putting down mains and constructing other such facilities, they benefit from steady, predictable growth of the city. If there is a shift of population from one part of the city to another—say from an inner deteriorating area to an outlying fringe—the company is left with excess capacity in the old area and must provide facilities in the new one before there are enough customers there to make doing so profitable. For this reason, utilities are usually strong advocates of city planning and of land-use control. They are also usually in favor of the consolidation of local government units; it is easier for a utility to deal with one local government than with many. Because they are peculiarly subject to regulation (usually by the state, not the city) they tend to be public-relations conscious and anxious to avoid controversy.

The real-estate operators fall into two main groups. One consists of brokers, who arrange sales and purchases, and make their money by turnover; sometimes this tends to make them not only willing backers of sweeping plans of all kinds but also the initiators of such plans. The other group consists of owners and managers of office buildings; these people are much interested in tax and assessment practices and in plans to stabilize or to raise property values. If a public building is to be built, each one wants it placed where it will enhance the value of his property. Architects and contractors have a community of interest with both groups of real estate operators. They too are active promoters of civic centers, industrial parks, urban renewal projects, and monumental undertakings in the name of city beautification.[1]

Banks often own office buildings in choice central-business-district locations. Where this is the case, their interest is to that extent the same as the second group of real estate operators. However, they have a more important, although less direct, interest in the growth and prosperity of the city as a whole, and particularly of those large enterprises (for example, department stores, news-papers, real estate operators, and manufacturers) which are their principal customers. Each of the big banks in a city is the center of a clique of business influence and it is part of the job of the head of the bank to act as leader of the clique and to represent it in its dealings with officialdom. Many banks are prevented by the terms of their charters from doing business outside the city; these banks naturally take a greater interest in local affairs than do those whose charters do not limit them in this way.

Railroads and manufacturing companies are sometimes active in city affairs. Usually, however, they are less so than are the other businesses we have listed. Their holdings lie outside the city for the most part, and therefore their stake in what the city government does is less.

Companies that sell on a regional or national market often take little or no interest in local affairs. Having its headquarters or a plant in a city is not enough to give a business firm an interest in it; usually any city in the same region or postal zone would suit the firm as well. The Ford, Chrysler, and General Motors corporations, for example, are probably less important in the affairs of Detroit than the J. L. Hudson Company department store. (The Ford *family* has done much for Detroit, but that is another matter.) "It makes little difference to us what happens in the city," the president of a great industry headquartered in Philadelphia told an interviewer. "We do not have our homes here; we have no large plants located within the city limits; we have only an office building that we can close at any time that conditions within the city become too oppressive."[2]

In El Paso, Texas, for example, businessmen are the most powerful interest group in the community, and the most powerful members of this group are known locally as the "Kingmakers." But the officers of the biggest corporations in the city—Standard Oil, Texaco, American Smelting and Refining, and Phelps-Dodge—are not considered to be among the Kingmakers because they are national firms with little interest in local politics.

Similarly, absentee-owned companies are less likely than others to partici-pate in local affairs. A manager who expects to be transferred to New York in a few years identifies less fully with the local business community and with the city than does an owner who intends to live out his life in the city.[3] What is more, the manager does not have the owner's freedom and action. The break-up of large fortunes by inheritance and otherwise, and the removal of the heirs from the active management of companies, has therefore tended to reduce business influence in local government. In the South and Southwest, however, absentee ownership of large corporations is less common than elsewhere, and in cities like Atlanta, Dallas, and Houston, business influence is comparatively strong. Furthermore, in any city, when an absentee-owned firm is a public utility, a department store, or some other institution that exists primarily to serve local markets (rather than to produce in local plants goods and services for national markets), it will be more likely to participate in local affairs.

THE MODES OF BUSINESS INFLUENCE

Businessmen have usually had a principal say about the civic agenda and sometimes they have had *the* principal one. The vantage points from which they have spoken and the rhetoric they have used have differed, however, according to time and place. Several generations ago, businessmen occupied most of the elective offices in many cities. Where they did not occupy office, they sometimes bossed political machines.[4] Much more often, however, they stood in the shadows behind the political boss, supporting him and dealing with him as business required. Indeed, as Tom Johnson, the businessman-turned-reformer who was mayor of Cleveland, explained to Lincoln Steffens, it was the businessman—more particularly, the businessman who wanted privileges—who was the root of all evil in local politics.

> *"Oh, I could see," he [Johnson] said, "that you did not know what it was that corrupted politics. First you thought it was bad politicians, who turned out to be pretty good fellows. Then you blamed the bad business men who bribed the good fellows, till you discovered that not all business men bribed and that those who did were pretty good business men. The little business men didn't bribe; so you settled upon, you invented, the phrase 'big business,' and that's as far as you and your kind have got: that it is big business that does all the harm. Hell! Can't you see that it's privileged business that does it? Whether it's a big steam railroad that wants a franchise or a little gambling-house that wants not to be raided, a temperance society that wants a law passed, a poor little prostitute, or a big merchant occupying an alley for storage—it's those who seek privileges who corrupt, it's those who possess privileges that defend our corrupt politics. Can't you see that?"[5]*

Once they got their privileges and had prospered from them, the businessmen who had corrupted politics (or, more likely, their heirs) embraced reform. Being well established themselves, they wanted to prevent others from buying the same privileges and competing with them. They wanted also to keep the cost of government down, and this was something that "good government" promised to do. Further, they wanted a stable, predictable governmental environment, and this could best be provided by a professionalized city bureaucracy. Generally speaking, local businesses were the chief supporters of reform. Manufacturers, wholesalers, and investment houses—in fact, all who depended upon a regional or national market—had not gained from local corruption in the first place and were not threatened by the continuance of it. Accordingly they often took little interest in reform.

Outright bribery of local government officials by the heads of large, well-established businesses is certainly a very rare thing today. The only businessmen who would try to buy favors from local government nowadays are the heads of criminal syndicates (organized gamblers, for example) and, perhaps, of new enterprises trying to break into an established field. These latter — businessmen who are "on the make" — are viewed with pain and disgust (as of course they should be) by the owners and managers of businesses that were created in exactly the same way not many years ago.[6]

Today the respectable (established) businessman is likely to use political influence for purely private purposes only in what may be called defensive actions. He may try his best to prevent some disturbance to the *status quo* that would affect his company adversely, but he is not at all likely to try to upset the *status quo* in order to get a windfall for himself.[7] For example, he may pull wires at City Hall to block a change of assessment practices that would hurt his company but he would not think of soliciting a change to benefit the company. The reason he behaves as he does is perhaps not hard to find. Not being willing to resort to bribery, and dealing with an officialdom that is too large and too professionalized to be bribed, he must limit himself to demands which are in some sense legitimate. In short, defensive action, being easier to justify, is more likely to succeed.

Businessmen whose companies are sensitive to actions by local government — but apparently few others — contribute to local political campaigns. Some businessmen have reason to fear direct reprisals if they do not contribute; a contractor whose business is largely with the city, for example, may suspect that ways will be found of preventing him from bidding successfully if he does not show gratitude for past favors. Some business firms contribute not so much from fear of reprisal as from a sense of obligation to support an administration which has been "good for business" and "good for the city." Some of these contributors are trying to lay up good will in City Hall against a rainy day or to put themselves in line for appointment to an advisory committee of some sort, either for business reasons (the committee may make recommendations touching the interest of the business) or for the sake of personal prestige and the fun of being a civic statesman. Others, however, contribute without even an implied *quid pro quo*. When someone suggested to a group of Chicago businessmen (Republicans) that they attach conditions to their support of Mayor Richard Daley (a Democrat), they replied indignantly that this would be "crooked."

Because of the respect in which they are held by newspapers and middle-class voters, the endorsement of leading businessmen is often worth more to a politician than their money. Businessmen who can be co-opted formally are especially valuable, provided, of course, that their standing in the community is unimpeachable.[8]

In the large cities, whatever support the businessman gives is likely to be at the expense of the Republican party. The great Democratic party strongholds in New York and Chicago, for example, are financed in part by businessmen who are staunch Republicans in state and national politics.

THE BUSINESSMAN AS CIVIC STATESMAN

After the Second World War, the leading businessmen of most large cities organized themselves to prepare ambitious plans for the redevelopment of the central business districts. The Central Area Committee of Chicago, Civic Progress in St. Louis, the Allegheny Conference in Pittsburgh, the Civic Conference in Boston, the Greater Philadelphia Movement—these and many more organizations were formed on the same pattern. The business elite of the city met privately, agreed upon more or less comprehensive plans for the redevelopment of the central city, and presented the plans to the press, the politicians, and the public as their contribution to civic welfare.

The committees were something new in business-government relations. Chambers of Commerce had long represented "business," but they spoke for it frankly as a "special interest," they spoke for small as well as large businesses, and they represented not only the central business district but also outlying districts, whose interest was generally opposed to that of the central area. The new committees were different in that they consisted of a few "big men" whose only concern was with the central business district and who, far from regarding themselves as special interests, insisted that they served "the public interest," often at a considerable sacrifice of private, business interests.

It was the flight of the middle class to the suburbs, the deterioration of the central business districts and, of course, the prospect of getting large grants of federal money for urban renewal that stirred the "big men" to action. They were the owners and managers of the big department stores, banks, and office buildings, and the trustees of colleges, hospitals, and museums, and they could see that unless they acted fast, and acted with the power of government behind them, the central business district was doomed.

To some extent also, the big businessmen's interest in civic improvements reflects a new view of public relations. To seek the advantage of one's own business, or even of "business" in general (as the Chambers of Commerce did), tends, it is now thought, to create an "unfavorable image." "Service to the community," on the other hand, creates a favorable one. As the Vice President for Civic Affairs and Real Estate (*sic*) of a large department store explained to an interviewer,

> Obviously a business of the stature I hope ours has should present a good face to the public . . . should be for constant improvement for the public. All through the years, this business has tried to achieve the feeling among the public that we are just a nice, fine, wonderful organization, and whatever it takes to achieve that, we are interested in.
>
> What it takes is to be just a plain, honest, good citizen—and fostering the kinds of things that are good for everyone.[9]

Another thing that turns the big businessman toward civic statesmanship is his belief that his company has a responsibility to the community which ought to be discharged even at some sacrifice of profits. Corporations have grown steadily more "soulful" as the separation between ownership and control has widened. In a good many cases, however, the talk about the corporation's responsibilities to the community may be mainly rationalization to hide the personal inclinations of managers who are bored with making heavily taxed profits and who find it more "fun" to work up grandiose schemes for civic improvement and to pull strings to get them accepted. The opportunity to do good in the name of the company and to be a civic statesman may be one of the fringe benefits that a large corporation gives its head.[10]

Often, the civic projects advanced by the committees of businessmen have been ill-conceived, overly ambitious, and politically unworkable. Typically a committee has hired consultants to perform some hasty rituals of "research," had an architect make some perspective drawings suitable for newspaper reproduction, and then revealed its vision of the new city in the banquet hall of the best hotel amid fanfares of press releases. Such plans usually call for huge federal expenditures for land clearance and redevelopment, for forcing low-income people out of the central city and attracting upper-income ones into it, and for building freeways, civic centers, exhibition halls, and anything else that might prop up property values and stimulate optimism. On awkward matters of detail—where to put the displaced Negroes, where to find equity capital for rebuilding once sites were cleared, how to raise the larger amounts of taxes that would be needed, and precisely where to put new buildings and highways—they are almost always silent. It is up to the politician, the businessmen think, to work out the details; they have done their part by "providing leadership."

It goes without saying that the politician is often less than enthusiastic about such plans. He is sensitive, even if the businessmen are not, to the many interests that will be disturbed and he knows very well that it will be he, and not the businessmen, who will be responsible if the plan fails. He is skeptical, to say the least, of the businessmen's claim to be serving "the public interest." It is his job to know who will gain and who will lose by public action, and he is well aware that the big businessman, although he may convince himself to the contrary by his after-dinner rhetoric, will be the principal beneficiary of the schemes for civic improvement and that the ordinary taxpayer, and especially the Negro slum dweller, will be adversely affected by it. Knowing all this, the politician, although he may pay glowing tribute to the statesmanship of the business leaders who sponsored the plan, is likely to be slow about endorsing it. In the end, he usually does endorse it, or something like it, however, for he too believes that something must be done to stop the decline of the central business district and his judgment tells him that whatever the leading business-man can agree upon is the most feasible place to begin.

Even if he did not share the businessman's concern about the future of the central business district, the politician would as a rule take their plan seriously. To an increasing extent, he needs their financial and other support in order to be re-elected. He also needs accomplishments—the more visible the better—to point to with pride when addressing the voters. Projects for the rebuilding of the central business districts, even though they make make matters worse for the slum dweller by reducing the amount of housing available to him, can be offered to "liberals" as evidence of his profound concern for the underdog. And of course—a happy feature of the situation indeed—since most of the cost of the undertaking will be paid for by the federal government, he can take credit for having got the city something for nothing. In general, therefore, there exists a solid basis for a three-way alliance between the politician, the business elite, and the "liberal" groups that want the city rebuilt.

*   *   *

TYPES OF INFLUENCE STRUCTURE

The ability of a business elite to win adoption of its proposals for civic improvements depends to some extent upon the general circumstances affecting the ease or difficulty with which action can be concerted. Proposals will be more readily adopted (other things being equal) to the extent that there exist "structures" of control in both the business and the political spheres and to the extent that those who control the business structures have adequate means of influencing those who control the political ones.[11] At the turn of the century, according to Lincoln Steffens, these conditions were met to a high degree in most cities; there was a "boss" who controlled business and another who controlled politics, and the business boss could "buy" the political one.[12]

To Steffens, the most interesting feature of the situation was the illicit character of the inducements by which the structure of influence was maintained. Today outright bribery of politicians by businessmen (or, for that matter, of politicians by politicians) is, as we have said, comparatively rare. Structures of influence remain, however, other inducements having been found to take the place of the illicit ones. Six principal types of structure exist in American cities today:

1. *A high degree of centralization in both the business and the political spheres, and the two spheres controlled directly by the same (business) elite.* Dallas, Texas, provides an example of an influence structure of this type. The Citizens' Council, membership in which is limited to presidents or general managers of business enterprises ("boss men," they are called), speaks authoritatively for business. In the political sphere, there is also considerable centralization: the city has a strong city manager who is backed by a stable council majority.[13] The structure of business control is dominant, not simply because all nine members of the city council are businessmen, but more importantly because businessmen control those things (money, prestige, publicity) which would-be councilmen need to get elected. Another city of the same type may be Atlanta, Georgia. There, according to Floyd Hunter, "men of independent decision" are few and, almost without exception, businessmen.[14]

2. *A high degree of centralization in both spheres, the business elite controlling the political sphere not directly but through control of a political boss.* Many political machines began under these circumstances. A powerful business leader (or coterie of leaders) would create, with their wealth and influence, a political boss who would mobilize for their ends the voters the businessmen either could not or would not mobilize by themselves. Philadelphia in the period when the Republican machine of the Vare brothers was subsidized by Gates and his associates was perhaps the most recent and conspicuous example. Such a relationship, however, is inherently unstable; if the political boss is strong enough to deliver the vote for his business backers, he usually is strong enough to deliver it for himself, making up for any threatened loss in income by the opportunities for corruption within the government which political power affords. What began as an employer-employee relationship often changed into an equal partnership, with both businessman and politician obliged to bargain with the other from positions of comparable strength.

3. *A high degree of centralization in both spheres, with neither the businessman nor politician able to impose his will on the other.* Such a structure of influence emerged in Pittsburgh. There, Richard Mellon, who by virtue of his great personal prestige as well as his ownership of a large share of the city's real estate and industry, was a powerful business leader able to speak authoritatively for other businessmen in negotiating with the equally powerful political leader, David Lawrence, the boss of the city's strong Democratic machine. Neither could command the other but each could commit his followers to whatever bargains were struck between the two.

4. *Moderate centralization in the business sphere but much centralization in the political one, the (relatively many) controllers of business having little influence over the (few) controllers of politics.* In Chicago, for example, the size of the city and the diversity of its business prevent a high degree of centralization of business influence; the Central Area Committee, although comprised of the business elite, lacks the unity and discipline of, say, the Citizens' Council of Dallas. Control over politics, on the other hand, is highly centralized in the hands of the Democratic boss, Mayor Daley. The relatively poorly organized business leaders compete with each other by advancing mutually incompatible proposals; under the circumstances they have little influence on Daley. In a particular matter (although not, perhaps, in *all* matters), he can safely ignore their efforts to influence him.[15]

5. *Much centralization in the business sphere but little in the political one, the business controllers thus being hampered in their efforts to bring about political action.* In Los Angeles, for example, business interests are fairly well-organized, but the political system is highly decentralized. The mayor has little power over the city council, which is not dominated by any single faction. Public questions of even small importance are decided by the voters in referenda. The business controllers therefore have no one with whom they can deal in the political sphere. If they are to get their proposals adopted, they must influence the electorate through the mass media—an expensive and unreliable procedure.

6. *Decentralization in both business and political spheres, and, consequently, minimal influence of business.* None of Boston's many businesses, nor any few of them, is large enough to dominate or "lead" the business community. The political sphere too is characterized by decentralization; the city is nonpartisan, and no politician or possible combination of politicians has enough prestige, or enough organization, to dominate the city. Between the Anglo-Saxon Protestant business elite and the Irish Catholic political elite, there is a long history of mutual hostility. If there existed a business boss and a political boss the two might very possibly come to terms despite this hostility. Given the existing decentralization in both spheres, however, the ethnic cleavage constitutes an additional obstacle to the exercise of business influence.

To sum up: the extent of business influence (and thus the extent to which one can speak of a business-dominated "power elite") in American cities varies with the degree of centralization in the political and economic spheres and with the extent to which economic interests control those resources (money, status, publicity, and legitimacy) which politicians may require in order to win and hold office. Businessmen are most likely to control those resources in relatively homogeneous, middle-class communities where the class basis for machine politics is absent, or in communities where changes in the formal structure of politics (the introduction of such systems as nonpartisanship, the short ballot, at-large elections, and the like) have made it difficult or impossible for politicians to win votes with organizations entirely of their own making.[16] If the class basis of the city or its formal governmental structure (or both) precludes the possibility that politicians will have an independent base of power, then the only thing that can prevent other, nonpolitical groups (usually businessmen) from wielding power will be disagreements among themselves. The larger and more diverse the city's economy, however, the greater the likelihood that such disagreements will arise. And many businessmen— particularly those whose firms are national rather than local in character—will have little interest in local political influence.

Thus at least three conditions are requisite to a high degree of business influence: (1) businessmen must have an interest in wielding local influence; (2) they must have a common set of goals, either because they agree or because they can be made to agree by some centralizing influence in the business community; and (3) they must control those resources valued by politicians and thus control the politicians. So little research has been done in large American cities that no general answer can be given to the question of how influential businessmen are. However, on the basis of what we know of such cities as Chicago, New York, Detroit, St. Louis, Cleveland, and others, we feel safe in surmising that it is the exception rather than the rule for all three conditions to exist in any large, diverse American city, particularly in the industrial North. Special conditions—such as the absence of an immigrant lower class, the preponderance of a few large local industries, and the prevalence of "good government" institutions—may make the incidence of business dominance higher in the large cities of the South and Southwest.

NOTES

1. Prior to the Second World War, when city planning was concerned mainly with zoning and city beautification, real estate men, contractors, and architects were heavily represented on planning commissions. See Robert A. Walker, *The Planning Function in Urban Government* (Chicago: University of Chicago Press, 1950), p. 150.
2. James Reichley, *The Art of Government: Reform and Organization Politics in Philadelphia* (New York: Fund for the Republic, 1959), p. 61.
3. In a Michigan city, Robert O. Schulze found differences between "local businessmen and the managers of absentee-owned firms; the managers were younger, better educated, more mobile socially and geographically, and less involved in civic affairs; they held no public offices and held fewer memberships in voluntary associations. See Schulze's "The Bifurcation of Power in a Satellite City," in Morris Janowitz (ed.), *Community Political Systems* (New York: Free Press of Glencoe, 1961), pp. 19-20. However, students of other cities who employed different research methods found executives of national firms participating fully in local affairs. See Roland J. Pellegrin and Charles H. Coates, "Absentee-Owned Corporations and Community Power Structure," *American Journal of Sociology*, March 1956, pp. 413-419. For reflections on the significance to the community of the growing separation between it and the large corporation, see Norton E. Long, *The Polity* (Chicago: Rand-McNally, 1962), chap. ix.
4. Two thirds of those elected to local office in New Haven in the period 1875-1880 were businessmen. Robert A. Dahl, *Who Governs?* (New Haven: Yale University Press, 1962), p. 37. For a brief account of a businessman-boss, see Constance M. Green, *Holyoke, Massachusetts: A Case Study of the Industrial Revolution in America* (New Haven: Yale University Press, 1939), p. 268.
5. *The Autobiography of Lincoln Steffens* (New York: Harcourt, Brace, 1931), p. 479.
6. Cf. the essay by Daniel Bell on "Crime as an American Way of Life" in his *The End of Ideology* (New York: Free Press of Glencoe, 1959).
7. This point is made and evidence for it supplied in Peter B. Clark, "The Chicago Big Businessman as a Civic Leader" (unpublished dissertation, Department of Political Science, University of Chicago, 1959). Dahl (in *Who Governs?*, pp. 79-84 and 241) concludes that the "economic notables" in New Haven do not receive (and presumably do not seek) special favors; their property seems to be somewhat overassessed.
8. For example: "Graham Aldis, a prominent real estate man generally regarded as a Republican, is heading up the citizens' advisory committee for the Democrat, Assesor Cullerton. As his friends say, Aldis is no fool. Cullerton hailed the committee members for their 'unselfish interest and knowledge' to achieve better assessments." *Chicago Tribune*, March 30, 1959.
9. Personal communication. Whether the community-serving endeavors of a business do in fact rebound to its business advantage is of course open to question. Peter H. Rossi concluded from a study of such activities on the part of the American

Telephone & Telegraph Company in a small city that the general public was indifferent to them or else felt that there were more important things that the company could do (National Opinion Research Center, Report no. 64, *Industry and Community*, October 1957).

10. These developments were remarked by John Maynard Keynes in 1926. See his *Essays in Persuasion* (London: Macmillan, 1931), pp. 314-315. On the "soulful" corporation, see Carl Kaysen, "The Social Significance of the Modern Corporation," *American Economic Review*, vol. XLVII (1957), pp. 311-319. See also Robert A. Gordon, *Business Leadership in the Large Corporation* (Berkeley: University of California Press, 1961), esp. the preface and chap. xiv.

11. The analytical framework of this discussion is from Banfield, *Political Influence* (New York: Free Press of Glencoe, 1961), chap. xi.

12. *Autobiography of Lincoln Steffens*, p. 596.

13. John Bainbridge, *The Super Americans* (New York: Random House, 1962), pp. 145-146.

14. Floyd Hunter, *Community Power Structure* (Chapel Hill: University of North Carolina Press, 1953). We have grave reservations about Hunter's method, but are prepared to accept his substantive findings *as they apply to Atlanta*. Further research suggests to us that Hunter may have been right for the wrong reason.

15. See Banfield, *Political Influence*, chaps. ix and x.

16. Peter H. Rossi comes to essentially the same conclusion in his article, "Power and Community Structure," *Midwest Journal of Political Science*, November 1960, pp. 390-400.

Discussion Questions

1. Discuss the current state of political machines in American cities. Do you believe that any political machines will be resurrected in cities where they have withered away?

2. Discuss the involvement by members of your class in political parties. For those who have been active, what incentives were important to them? What incentives might be offered to increase participation?

3. Try to determine the degree of involvement by business leaders in the political affairs of your community. How does your assessment compare with that of Banfield and Wilson?

CHAPTER THREE

CAMPAIGNS AND ELECTIONS

Participation in American political parties has remained consistently low during the past thirty years. Voter turnout in state and local elections often is well under 50 percent. Still, most of us follow political campaigns with some interest. Especially in presidential election years we find it hard to ignore the barrage of television, newspaper, and billboard advertising.

While interest in more traditional means of political participation has declined in recent years, in the 1960s there was an increase in direct-action politics—demonstrations, sit-ins, and violent protests. In the 1970s direct-action politics continued, but in a less radical manner. Citizens increasingly made use of the initiative in their attempts to secure political goals. The initiative is a procedure whereby voters can propose a law or constitutional amendment. For example, a special-interest group may draft a petition calling for a ban on the construction of nuclear power plants in a state. Typically, to be valid the petition must be signed by 5 to 10 percent of the state's voters. Direct initiatives (as in California) then go straight to the voters. In states and localities that have an indirect initiative, the proposal is first presented to a legislative body and goes on the ballot for voter approval only if acted upon favorably by the legislature. Although there has been an increase in the frequency of initiatives (clearly indicating an increase in political activity for their advocates), evidence is not clear whether or not the presence of an initiative on the ballot increases voter turnout.

Campaigns, whether in support of individual candidates or initiative measures, have become more and more sophisticated and expensive. Statewide races often utilize professional campaign management firms. In urban areas expenses have grown significantly due to the costs of television advertising. Gubernatorial races may involve expenditures of millions of dollars.

Skyrocketing expenditures and the Watergate affair led to new federal guidelines for political finance in the mid-1970s. In turn, most states made major changes in their campaign laws in the second half of the decade. Several states have instituted public financing of campaigns and virtually all states have tightened their restrictions on campaign spending.

The first article in this chapter looks at the increasing use of the initiative during the 1970s. As noted by Michael Nelson, there is a move to create a national initiative. Although many state and local governments permit the use of the initiative, referendum, and recall, none of these "direct democracy" techniques can be used at the national level. As Nelson points out, the initiative has been used by both liberals and conservatives to further their political aims. Although California's Proposition 13 did not spawn a widespread tax revolt in other states, some liberals fear the potential use of the initiative by conservative, single-issue groups.

The second article, by Steven Brams, presents a truly innovative proposal for election reform. Since states have broad control over the conduct of elections (for both federal and state offices), approval voting could be implemented if individual states made relatively minor statutory changes or changes in their constitutions. The presidential candidacy of John Anderson in 1980 may have given more impetus to the proposal. Brams contends that in multicandidate elections (those with three or more candidates) approval voting would increase the likelihood of the strongest candidate winning. As things now stand with plurality voting, a strong argument can often be made that you are "throwing away" your vote if you choose a third-party candidate such as McCarthy or Anderson. Multicandidate elections often occur in primaries, and they occurred twice recently in New York State senate elections (1970 and 1980), where the Liberal and Conservative parties endorse candidates in elections.

In the last article Herbert Alexander, an authority on campaign financing, discusses current state regulations on political finance as well as public financing of state elections and the use of bipartisan election commissions. Alexander concludes with an evaluation of public financing of campaigns and its impact on political parties.

Power to the People:
The Crusade for Direct Democracy

Michael Nelson

Starting sometime next month, we can expect to suffer the usual plague of end-of-the-decade assessments. Judging from the early returns, the verdict on the Seventies seems fairly predictable. The instant historians will tell us that this has been a placid decade, notable mostly for being different from the last one. The Sixties, they will say, were above all a time of direct-action politics—demonstrations, mass participation, plebiscitary rather than representative democracy. By contrast—a constrast that then-and-now pictures of Jerry Rubin, Rennie Davis, and Berkeley's Sproul Plaza will underscore—the Seventies have been apolitical.

Some will mourn the passing of Sixties-style politics, others will rejoice. Both will miss the point. For Americans in the Seventies did not turn away from the politics of direct action, they merely domesticated it, institutionalized it, and embraced it in the bosom of the middle class.

Nothing illustrates this better than the rising use of the initiative, a device by which—in the 23 states and more than 100 cities that allow it—citizens can draft a piece of legislation, place it on the ballot by petition, and have their fellow voters directly decide on election day whether it should become law or not. (Initiatives are different from referendums, which allow voters to accept or reject laws already passed by the legislature.) By the end of 1979, some 175 initiatives will have been voted on at the state level since 1970, almost twice as many as in the 1960s. The rate of initiative use accelerated through the decade, from 10 in 1970 to more than 40 each in 1976 and 1978. Two states and the District of Columbia have added the initiative process to their constitutions, and at least 10 others now are considering doing so. In one of them, New

York, the initiative idea is being pushed by an unlikely coalition of the League of Women Voters, the Conservative Party, the local branch of Ralph Nader's Public Interest Research Group, and an ad hoc organization called V.O.T.E., which is headed by a conservative investment banker who says he hopes to become New York's Howard Jarvis.

Coalitions like this one (which, to confuse matters further, bears the editorial imprimatur of the *New York Times* and *Newsday*, as well as a host of conservative upstate newspapers) make it hard to characterize the rising initiative tide in standard liberal-conservative terms. So does the sponsorship in Congress of the proposed constitutional amendment to allow national initiatives, which ranges from senators like Mark Hatfield on the left to Dennis DeConcini in the middle and Larry Pressler on the right. Among conservative columnists, George F. Will has condemned the initiative, Patrick Buchanan has praised it, and James J. Kilpatrick has been all over the lot. Liberals such as Tom Wicker (pro) and the *New Republic*'s Henry Fairlie (con) can be found on either side.

Most distressing of all to those who like their politics tidy has been the extraordinary range of purposes to which the initiative has been put. Last year, for example, Oregon voters passed an initiative that restored capital punishment, but defeated one to restrict state funding of abortions. (They also decided to break the dentists' monopoly on the sale of false teeth.) Michigan voted to raise the drinking age from 19 to 21, but spurned a conservative educational "voucher" plan that would have subsidized parents' decisions to send their children to private schools. (Californians may be voting on a similar plan next June.) An Alaska initiative to set aside some 30 million acres of land for small homesteaders was approved; another to ban no-deposit bottles failed. Californians turned down an anti-smoking proposal; they also refused to require school boards to fire homosexual teachers. A Montana initiative to place restrictions on nuclear power-plant licensing and operations won. A North Dakota plan to regulate health-care costs lost. Collective-bargaining rights did well in Michigan and Missouri, while casino gambling did poorly in Florida.

The most celebrated initiative of 1978 was, of course, California's Proposition 13, the astonishingly popular proposal by Howard Jarvis and Paul Gann to reduce property taxes in the state by 57 percent. Its success in June quickly triggered a middle-class "tax revolt" that terrified liberals in other states. James Farmer, the erstwhile civil rights leader who now heads a group called the Coalition of American Public Employees, complained that "the tax revolt represents nothing more than the overthrow of equity among taxpayers." Worried commentators predicted that right-wing Jarvis fever would sweep the initiative states in November.

It did not quite turn out that way, however. Although Proposition 13 clones passed in two small states, Idaho and Nevada, they failed in Michigan and Oregon. Four state initiatives to limit increases in government spending passed, but two were turned down. Still others failed to garner enough signatures to get on the ballot. This year Nevada voters repealed the state's 3.5 percent sales tax on food, a reform dear to liberal hearts. And next year a whole host of tax initiatives—liberal, conservative, or both—will come up at the polls. Ohio and Massachusetts proposals would cut property taxes but make up the lost revenues with increased levies on business. Interestingly enough, political scientist Austin Ranney found that in the 33 years prior to 1978, the initiative served as a tool for liberals on tax issues. Their side triumphed 77 percent of the time.

The lack of a clear ideological tilt in the initiative process also is evidenced by the new style of initiative politicians who have led the direct-action efforts of the 1970s. Thus far, arch-conservative Howard Jarvis is the one national celebrity to come out of the initiative movement—he even made *People* magazine's list of "The 25 Most Intriguing People of 1978." But Pat Quinn of Chicago is a more typical wielder of the initiative tool. Quinn is a full-time law student at Northwestern University who, as "a 40-hour-a-week hobby," heads an 8,000 member organization called the Illinois Coalition for Political Honesty. (Members are defined simply as those who pass petitions to get initiatives on the ballot.) Although he got into state politics seven years ago in the traditional way, as an aide to victorious gubernatorial candidate Dan Walker, Quinn's experience in the campaign and in the Walker administration was discouraging. "I became disillusioned in the potential of candidate politics," he says. "You get candidates who either can't deliver on their promises after the election, or don't want to. With initiatives you can address the issues directly."

Illinois has allowed an initiative process since 1970, but neither Quinn nor anybody else had much sense of its potential until his brother Tom came home in 1975 from college in California, where he had gotten involved in a successful campaign to pass a candidate-and-lobbyist-disclosure initiative. "Illinois at that time had around 20 state legislators convicted or under indictment, and the legislature wasn't doing anything about ethics," Pat recalls. "It also had a rule that allowed legislators to draw their whole year's pay on the first day of the session, so even if they were sent to jail in the middle of the year, they still kept the rest of their year's salary. Five of us—me, my brother, and three friends—started a petition drive to get that changed, so at least they'd be paid the same way everybody else is. The issue took off and we got enough signatures to put it on the ballot. Within a month the legislature gave us what we wanted on their own, but we decided to keep the Coalition for Political Honesty going and see what else could be done by initiative."

The coalition's current plan is for a 1980 initiative that, if passed, would overhaul the legislature completely. Presently, Illinois is divided into 59 districts, each of which elects three legislators-at-large. In Quinn's view, the combination of a large number of legislators (177, third highest in the nation) and a small number of districts gives Illinois the worst of both worlds—"too many politicians, but too little representation." His initiative would double the number of districts to 118 and assign one representative to each, thus reducing the membership of the legislature by one third. "A change like this is the kind of thing a legislature would never make by itself," says Quinn, "because it would threaten the jobs of the legislators who would have to make it. They get paid $28,000 a year and for many it's a second job. The initiative is the only tool a citizen has."

Quinn, a young liberal, and Jarvis, an aging conservative, have a good bit more in common than first meets the eye. So do the conservative tax "revolters" in Idaho and the liberal tax "reformers" in Ohio, the conservative pro-voucher people in California and the liberal anti-dentists in Oregon, and other seemingly dissimilar groups of activists. For whatever their political coloration, the greater part of initiative users seem motivated by a basic shared concern: They regard the government itself as just another self-serving interest, one that is all the more threatening because it cannot be reformed except from outside, through direct-action politics.

Looking back over the history of political reform in this century, it is remarkable how many fundamental political changes were hastened by initiative after state legislators balked, reluctant to alter the rules of the game by which they had been elected. Long before Congress and the state legislatures saw the handwriting on the wall, initiatives in several states had already been passed to repeal the poll tax, establish woman suffrage, provide for direct election of United States senators, and institute primary elections. Similarly, the Seventies have been marked by a whole host of ethics, disclosure, and "sunshine-in-government" initiatives, passed by voters after legislatures had turned them down. Austin Ranney finds that historically, the initiative has been used more to alter governmental and political processes than for any other purpose.

In this light, it also seems apparent that the Proposition 13-inspired "tax revolt" has been aimed less at taxes per se than at the ever larger and more prosperous government bureaucracies that are collecting and spending them. In California, for example, powerful government-employee unions, along with their colleagues in the legislature, beat back fairly modest efforts to reduce evermore burdensome property taxes for years, even after the state treasury accumulated a multi-billion-dollar surplus. Finally, things reached the point where the lamentations of public officials simply were not believed. One poll taken on the eve of Proposition 13 found 88 percent of Californians insisting that "if government services were made more efficient, the current level of services could be provided even though budgets were reduced."

This perception of selfish behavior *by* government officials *for* government officials seems to exist among voters everywhere. A nationwide survey commissioned by the *Washington Post* found that three out of four citizens said they too would vote for a Proposition 13-style tax cut if they had the chance. But an even higher percentage also said that it wasn't so much the taxes that bothered them as the way the money was being wasted. Given a choice of low taxes or high taxes that are spent efficiently, two-thirds picked the latter. "Their real concern," the *Post* concluded, "is that it is the bureaucracy, not the public, that benefits from taxes."

Are people correct in attributing many of the ills of government to the self-serving behavior of the governing class of legislators and bureaucrats? It would be surprising if they were not. It is almost an axiom of sociological theory that when organizations grow larger and more powerful—as all levels of governments have in order to meet our demand for a militarily powerful welfare state—they develop interests of their own, different from those they were created to represent. This clearly has happened at the state and local level, where the number of government employees has tripled from four million in 1950 to 12 million today, with their unions vigorously advocating both higher benefits and higher taxes to finance them. But nowhere is the rise of a governing class more evident than in Washington, D.C. "Right now there are two popular clichés about Washington," writes *Washington Post* reporter Nicholas Lemann, "and both of them, like most clichés, have a lot of truth in them. The first is that Washington is a company town, where everything revolves around the federal government and there's always just one topic of conversation. The second is that Washington has become the national capital of affluence as well as of government."

It was inevitable, then, that someone would take the iniative to Washington.

As it turned out, there were two people. John Forster and Roger Telschow, fresh out of college, had spent 1976 working in state initiative campaigns all over the country. "We were really struck at the time by the contrast between the enthusiasm people had about initiatives and the indifference they felt toward the presidential and congressional elections," says Telschow. After the election, the figures bore them out: Though voter turnout had dropped for the fourth straight time since 1960, initiative use reached a postwar high. Deciding that national initiatives on citizen-proposed federal laws were an idea whose time had come, they set off for Washington to try to get Congress to pass a constitutional amendment permitting such an innovation. Here is how the national initiative would work:

Citizens initiating a new law would have 18 months to collect petitions with valid signatures equal in number to 3 percent of the votes cast in the preceding presidential election—at present that would be 2.5 million. The Justice Department would then check the signatures for validity. If it certified them within 120 days of the next national election, the proposed initiative would go on the ballot right away; otherwise it would have to wait two years until the next election.

The initiative, if passed by a simple majority of voters, would become law 30 days after the election. As with any other legislation, it would be subject to judicial review and congressional override, though the latter would require the two-thirds vote of Congress and presidential concurrence. Finally, the initiative could not be used to declare war, call up troops, or propose constitutional amendments.

Initiative America (which is what the two young men named their organization) can be described generously as a shoestring operation; in Washington's constellation of elaborate and well-financed interest groups, it is the equivalent of a lemonade stand in midtown Manhattan. But through sheer energy, will, and talent, Forster and Telschow managed to do everything a shoestring operation can do in politics. In 1977, they persuaded Senator James Abourezk to sponsor their amendment. They then roused interest among press and pollsters—Cambridge Survey Research found three-to-one public support for the idea, for example, and George Gallup included it in a *Reader's Digest* article on the "Six Political Reforms Americans Want Most." Because of this attention, and because Abourezk was a member of the constitutional amendments subcommittee, Senate hearings soon were held on it.

The power of a good idea, of course, can take it only so far through an amendment process that requires the support of two-thirds of each house of Congress and three-fourths of the states—especially an idea whose premise is that Congress has not been representing the people adequately. But Forster and Telschow felt that once Senate hearings rendered the idea respectable, they would be able to rally a coalition of open-government groups like Common Cause behind it.

What followed was a bitterly disappointing experience, one that illustrates yet another sociological axiom: Adversarial organizations end up more alike than different. "We found out that these Washington-based 'people's groups' have become little bureaucracies of their own," recalls Forster. "They see the initiative as a threat to their interests. They thrive on the fact that they can claim to represent people to the government on various issues. If people had an initiative to turn to, two things would happen: One, they could represent themselves, and two, the scene of the action would shift from Washington to the country. That would diminish the public-interest groups' importance. They prefer not to change the rules, even if there doesn't seem to be any chance of winning under the status quo."

Stalled in the Washington community, Initiative America's great hope for the future is that its proposal will be picked up in next year's presidential campaign. This would not be altogether surprising. The governing class's popular standing has been steadily declining. Support for the initiative amendment may prove a constructive way of tapping the public's dissatisfaction. So far, only Jimmy Carter and Howard Baker have brushed off Initiative America, and Jerry Brown, Ronald Reagan, Edward Kennedy, and John Connally are among those who at least have expressed interest. Kennedy, for example, has told Initiative America that he would "like to be with you on this," and Brown's *éminence grise*, Jacques Barzaghi, recently informed board member

David Schmidt that Brown might campaign hard on the proposal, which he already has endorsed.

Although it is far from certain that the 1980s will see the adoption of the national initiative amendment, there are a couple of predictions about the coming decade we can safely make.

The first is that, with the bicentennial of the Constitution looming in 1987, we are going to be hearing more than ever about the "intentions of the framers." In the case of the national initiative amendment, those intentions should be fairly easy to ascertain. Democracy was a dirty word at the Philadelphia convention—speakers used it only to raise the specter of mob rule and demagoguery—and any proposal to allow citizens to initiate and decide laws on their own surely would have been hooted off the floor.

Should we be bound by this? No, and I don't think the Founding Fathers (Warren Harding's phrase, not theirs) would want us to be so bound, any more than they would have when we abolished the poll tax, required direct election of senators, and gave the vote to blacks and women—other proposals that were or would have been dismissed at the Constitutional Convention. The authors of the Constitution were aware that they had no monopoly on truth for the ages. Indeed, their most important intention was that the plan of government they drafted be able to adapt to changing times and new kinds of experience. That is why they defined the nature and powers of its institutions in flexible language and why they included an amendment process.

Changing conditions have already altered the nature of our political system, in ways that make the initiative now seem constitutionally appropriate. "Admittedly," argues Professor Henry Abraham of the University of Virginia, "the Founding Fathers envisaged lawmaking to be the province of the people's representatives in assembled Congress, but as our history has demonstrated, laws—or, if one prefers, policies *cum* laws—are increasingly made and applied not only by Congress but by the Chief Executive; by the host of all-but-uncontrollable civil servants in the executive agencies and bureaus; and by the judiciary. Why not permit another element of our societal structure to enter the legislative realm, namely, the people in their sovereign capacity as the ultimate repositor of power under our system, as envisaged by the letter and the spirit of the Preamble to the Constitution?"

As Abraham suggests, the theories of the framers about how their plan of government really would work out in practice were just that—theories. Seventy-five years of experience with state initiatives (Oregon held the first one in 1904) can be safely said to have demonstrated the groundlessness of their fears. Historically, only about one-fifth of the initiatives filed have gotten enough petition signatures even to reach the ballot. And only about one-third of those that have reached the ballot have been passed by voters. This is hardly the "mobocracy" the framers feared democracy would breed.

The other sure prediction that we can make about the 1980s is that the politics of direct action will become even more widespread. For not only has initiative use been increasing, but also the use of other pressure tactics that lie outside the normal processes of representative democracy—with no sign that the basic dissatisfactions with the governing class that have caused all this are abating. Demonstrations, for example, now seem as American as apple pie. In Washington alone, the National Park Service currently issues a record 750 to 1,000 demonstration permits every year, many of them to groups opposing abortion, Equal Rights Amendment proponents, tractor-driving farmers, and other activists from the middle class. Surveying a wide range of poll data, political scientists Robert Gilmour and Robert Lamb recently concluded that "Mass protest, civil disobedience, and illegal disruption are now a part of the accepted political scene."

The Seventies also saw the rise of forms of direct-action politics that Sixties activists overlooked. The most spectacular recent example is the movement for a constitutional convention to consider a balanced-budget amendment. Presently, 30 states have demanded that Congress issue such a call, only four short of the required two-thirds. So plausible has the idea become that White House adviser Patrick Caddell felt comfortable suggesting to Jimmy Carter that he call for a constitutional convention that would reconsider the whole document. (Caddell made his recommendation in the famous "crisis-of-confidence" memorandum that persuaded Carter to cancel a planned energy speech and retreat to Camp David for two weeks in July.) Carter declined the suggestion, but Jerry Brown has endorsed the effort to bring about a balanced-budget convention.

There is no telling what innovations the Eighties will bring in the way of direct-action politics—in Columbus, Ohio, people are already "participating" in televised local government meetings through their two-way cable television system. But whatever these innovations may be, they probably will make the initiative look good to its current opponents by comparison. The initiative is, after all, a technique of the ballot, not the streets or the living room. This not only makes it close kin to the standard system of representative democracy, but it also seems to strengthen that system in the long run. Thus political scientist Charles Bell recently reported that "half the high [election] turnout states use the initiative while only 14 percent of the low-turnout states use it." A Caddell poll found that 74 percent of the voters said they would be more inclined to vote in candidate elections if they also could vote on issues. And far from weakening state legislatures, initiatives seem to prod them on to better things. Eight of the 10 legislatures ranked highest by the Citizens Conference on State Legislatures are in initiative states.

The assault on the governing class of officials will continue. Whether it will come through the ballot box or some less pleasant route is up to them.

Approval Voting: A Practical Reform for Multicandidate Elections

Steven J. Brams

Approval voting is a system in which a voter may choose or approve of as many candidates as desired in a multicandidate election. For example, a voter might vote for just one candidate, or for several candidates if more than one is found acceptable. However, only one vote may be cast for every approved candidate—that is, votes may not be cumulated and several cast for one candidate. The candidate with the most votes wins.

With approval voting, two or more candidates each could receive the votes of more than 50 percent of the voters, though in a large field of candidates such an outcome would probably be unlikely. Even so, the thought that more than one candidate could be supported by a majority of voters does seem strange. So does the idea of giving voters the opportunity to vote for more than one candidate that can produce this result. Yet, approval voting is not only compatible with most constitutions but it also has several advantages over plurality voting, plurality voting with a runoff (if no candidate receives a majority in the first election), and preferential voting (in which voters can rank candidates). Moreover, it is practical: among other things, it can readily be implemented on existing voting machines, and it is more efficient than holding both a plurality and runoff election.

Here are the main arguments for approval voting:

1. *It is best for the voters.* Approval voting allows citizens to do exactly what they do now—vote for their favorite candidate—but, if they have no clear candidate, it also allows them to express this fact by voting for all candidates that they rank highest. In addition, if a favorite seems to have little chance of winning, the voter can still cast a ballot for that candidate without worrying

From Steven J. Brams, "Approval Voting: A Practical Reform for Multicandidate Elections," *National Civic Review* 68 (November 1979). Reprinted with permission of the National Municipal League.

about "wasting one's vote." This is done by voting for the favorite *and* the candidate considered most acceptable who seems to have a serious chance of winning. This way a voter is able to express a sincere preference and at the same time vote for the candidate who would be preferable if the favorite cannot win.

Apart from the question of wasting one's vote, plurality voting is fundamentally unfair to a voter who may have a hard time deciding who is the best candidate in a crowded field but can choose the two or more candidates considered most acceptable. Approval voting thus provides more flexible options and thereby encourages a truer expression of preferences than does plurality voting.

2. *It elects the strongest candidate.* It is entirely possible in a three-candidate plurality race in which A wins 25 percent of the vote, B 35 percent and C 40 percent that the loser, A, is the strongest candidate who would beat B in a separate two-way contest (because C supporters would vote for A), and would beat C in a separate two-way contest (because B supporters would vote for A). Even a runoff election between the top vote getters (B and C) would not show up this fact. On the other hand, approval voting in all likelihood would reveal A to be the strongest candidate because some B and C supporters—who liked A as much or almost as much—would cast second approval votes for A, who would thereby become the winner.

It is not hard to think of actual elections in which minority candidates triumphed with less than 50 percent of the vote who almost surely would have lost if they had been in contests with just one of their opponents. For example, a liberal, John Lindsay, won the 1969 mayoral election in New York City against two opponents who split the moderate-conservative vote (58 percent of the total); and a conservative, James Buckley, won the 1970 U.S. Senate election in New York against two opponents who split the moderate-liberal vote (61 percent of the total). This problem of a minority candidate's eking out a victory in a crowded field is aggravated the more candidates there are in a race. Moreover, as the examples indicate, the minority-candidate bias of plurality voting is not ideological; it can afflict both liberals and conservatives. Approval voting, by contrast, is biased in favor of the strongest candidate, especially a candidate like A in the earlier example who would defeat each of the others in head-to-head contests.

3. *It is best for the parties.* For reasons just given, approval voting would tend to favor the strongest and most viable candidates in each party. It is unlikely, for example, that Barry Goldwater would have won the Republican presidential nomination in 1964, or George McGovern the Democratic presidential nomination in 1972, if there had been approval voting in the state presidential primaries. Both nominees were probably minority candidates even within their own parties, and both lost decisively in the general election.

4. *It gives minority candidates their proper due.* In 1968, George Wallace dropped from 21 percent support in the polls in September to 14 percent in the actual vote on election day in November. It seems likely that the one-third of Wallace supporters who deserted him in favor of one of the major-party candidates did so because they thought he had no serious chance of winning — the wasted vote phenomenon. But, if there had been approval voting, Wallace would almost surely have retained his original supporters, some of whom would also have voted for Nixon or Humphrey. One of these candidates would have won, probably with more than 50 percent of the vote (Nixon received 43.4 percent in the election; Humphrey, 42.7 percent), but Wallace would have registered much more substantial support than he did. With approval voting, minority candidates would get their proper due, but majority candidates would generally win.

5. *It is insensitive to the number of candidates running.* Because ballots may be cast for as many candidates as the voter wishes under approval voting, if new candidates enter it is still possible to vote for one or more of them without being forced to withdraw support from old candidates. Plurality voting, on the other hand, is very sensitive to the number of candidates running. As the number of contenders increases, the plurality contest becomes more and more one of who can inch out whom in a crowded field rather than who is the strongest and most acceptable candidate.

Thus, when Jimmy Carter won less than 30 percent of the vote in the New Hampshire Democratic primary in 1976, the significance of his victory could be questioned. This gave the media an opportunity to pass judgment, which they gleefully did. Approval voting, by contrast, by better revealing the overall acceptability of the candidates independent of the field in which they run, more accurately mirrors each candidate's true level of support and gives more meaning to the voter's judgment. A side benefit would be that voters, not the media, would weigh in more heavily in the selection process.

As an example of a recent election in which the overall acceptability of candidates was difficult to ascertain, consider the Democratic primary in the 1977 New York City mayoral election. With no candidate receiving as much as 20 percent of the vote, and six candidates receiving more than 10 percent, a judgment about who the most popular candidate was seems highly dubious. Even the runoff election that pitted Edward Koch (19.8 percent of the plurality vote) against Mario Cuomo (18.6 percent of the plurality vote), said nothing about how the winner, Koch, would have fared in runoffs against the other four candidates who received between 11.0 and 18.0 percent of the plurality vote. Although Koch may have been the candidate more acceptable to the voters than any other candidate in this election, plurality voting, even with a runoff, did not demonstrate this to be the case.

An Example. The following hypothetical example perhaps best dramatizes the different effects of plurality voting and approval voting:

	Plurality Voting	*Approval Voting*
Candidate X	25%	30%
Candidate Y	24%	51%

In this example, which assumes X and Y are the top two candidates in the race and several other candidates split the remaining vote, X just wins under plurality voting. Yet X is approved of by less than one-third of the voters, whereas Y is acceptable to more than one-half of the voters.

Is it fair that X, unacceptable to 70 percent of the electorate, should be considered the "winner" simply because he is the first choice of more voters than any other candidate in a crowded field? He may be liked by the biggest minority of voters (25 percent), but in my opinion the voting system should also register the fact that he is disliked—that is, not approved of—by all but 30 percent of the voters.

Approval voting would show up the fact that Y is acceptable to many more voters than X. Of course, the plurality voting winner and the approval voting winner will often be the same, and then there will be no problem. However, the discrepancy between plurality and approval voting winners seems not so infrequent, even in races with as few as three candidates, to be dismissed as a rare event.

6. *It could increase voter turnout.* By giving voters more flexible options, approval voting could encourage greater voter turnout, although this is difficult to establish until we have some experience with approval voting. It seems likely, however, that some voters do not go to the polls because they cannot make up their minds about who is the single best candidate in a multi-candidate race. By giving such voters the option to vote for two or more candidates if they have no clear favorite, they probably would have more incentive to vote in the first place.

7. *It is superior to preferential voting.* An election reform that has been tried in a few places in the United States (for example, Ann Arbor, Michigan) shares many of the advantages of approval voting. It is called preferential voting and it requires each voter to rank the candidates from best to worst. If no candidate receives a majority of first-place votes, the candidate with the fewest first-place votes is dropped and the second-place votes of his supporters are given to the remaining candidates. The elimination process continues, with lower-place votes of the voters whose preferred candidates are eliminated being transferred to the candidates that survive, until one candidate receives a majority of votes.

Apart from the practical problems of implementing a ranking system, preferential voting has a major drawback: it may eliminate the candidate acceptable to the most voters. In the hypothetical example given in argument 2 above, A would have been eliminated at the outset. Yet, A would have defeated B and C in separate two-way contests, and was, therefore, the strongest candidate and probably would have won with approval voting.

A less serious drawback of preferential voting is that the candidate with the most first-place votes may be displaced after the transfers have been made to determine the majority winner. This may greatly upset that candidate's supporters, particularly if they are a large minority, and lead to questions about the legitimacy of the system. This challenge cannot be mounted against approval voting since approval votes are indistinguishable—whether these votes are first-place, second-place, or whatever is not recorded, so no portion of the winner's total can be judged "inferior."

8. *Practicalities.* It may be thought that, even given the virtues of approval voting, it would make little difference in a real election. This is so because the candidates would encourage voters to vote just for themselves (bullet voting) to keep down the vote totals of their opponents. Yet, even if the candidates made such an appeal, it would probably not be effective, particularly in a crowded race in which voters had difficulty distinguishing their single favorite. As evidence to support this assertion, in an approval voting experiment involving several hundred Pennsylvania voters prior to their 1976 primaries, 72 percent of the voters voted for two or more of the eight candidates listed on their sample ballots.

How can approval voting be implemented? There are a multitude of laws governing the conduct of elections, but consider the statute in New Hampshire for voting in the presidential primaries. To enact approval voting in these elections would require only the substitution of the words in parentheses for the preceding words:

> *Every qualified voter . . . shall have opportunity . . . to vote his prefer-ence* (preferences), *on the ballot of his party, for his choice* (choices) *for one person* (any persons) *to be the candidate* (candidates) *of his political party for president of the United States and one person* (any persons) *to be the candidate* (candidates) *of his political party for vice president of the United States.*

I have been assured by voting machine manufacturers that their equipment could be easily adjusted to allow for approval voting. In jurisdictions which use paper ballots, allowing voters to mark their ballots for more than one candidate will make vote counting somewhat more tedious and time-consuming, but this should not be a major barrier to the adoption of approval voting.

I am completely convinced that approval voting will be the election reform of the 20th century, just as the Australian, or secret, ballot printed by the government with the names of all authorized candidates was the election reform of the 19th century. In effect, the principle of "one man, one vote" in plurality voting becomes the principle of "one candidate, one vote" with approval voting.

Regulation of Political Finance: The States' Experience

Herbert E. Alexander

While the new federal laws governing campaign financing were being conceived and enacted, some noteworthy experimentation in election reform was taking place in many of the states. In the 1970s almost every state changed its election laws in significant ways. These laws imposed on candidates for state offices restrictions similar to those governing congressional and presidential elections. Many states that had adopted campaign laws subsequently had to change them to conform to the 1976 U.S. Supreme Court ruling in *Buckley v. Valeo.* In general, that ruling left intact the public disclosure, contribution limitation and public financing provisions of existing federal (and, by implication, state) election laws. The decision, however, prohibited spending limitations unless they were tied to public financing.

STATE RESTRICTIONS

Disclosure

Forty-nine states have disclosure requirements. Forty-seven of them require both pre- and postelection reporting of contributions and expenditures. Two states, Alabama and Wyoming, require only postelection disclosure. North Dakota is the only state that does not require any disclosure of campaign contributions and expenditures.

Reports The reporting requirements vary by state, but the disclosure laws usually require identification of contributors by name, address, occupation and principal place of business, plus the amount and date of the contribution. The laws also usually require a report of total expenditures and itemization of

From Herbert E. Alexander, *Financing Politics*, 2nd ed. (Washington, D.C.: Congressional Quarterly Press, 1980), pp. 127-129, 133-144. Reprinted with permission of Congressional Quarterly Inc.

certain of them including the amount, date and particulars of each payment. The states differ as to the threshold amount at which reporting requirements take effect. For example, Kansas requires itemization of contributions amounting to $10 or more. Louisiana has a reporting requirement for contributions of $1,000 or more. The states also vary as to when the reports must be filed. Alabama requires one postelection report 30 days after the election. California law calls for filing of two preelection reports, 40 days and 12 days before the election, and one postelection report 65 days after the election. Alaska requires two preelection reports, one month and one week prior to the election, and two postelection reports, one 10 days after the election and the final report on December 31.

Socialist Workers' lawsuits Challenges to disclosure laws have come in the form of a series of suits by the Socialist Workers Party (SWP) supported by the American Civil Liberties Union at the federal level and in several states.[1] Suits were brought in California, New Jersey, Ohio, Texas and the District of Columbia, among others. Where the lawsuits have been successful, the states have provided exceptions for minor-party disclosure insofar as the listing of contributors is concerned. They have based their actions on the Supreme Court's decision in *Buckley v. Valeo*, which stated that case-by-case exemptions for minor parties may be permitted if there is a "reasonable probability that the compelled disclosure of a party's contributors' names will subject them to threats, harassment, or reprisals from either government officials or private parties."[2]

In 1977 a U.S. District Court ordered the FEC to develop a full factual record within six months and make specific findings of fact concerning the "present nature and extent of harassment suffered" by the SWP as a result of the disclosure provisions of the act.[3] The FEC's appeal was dismissed. In 1979 the court approved a consent decree to exempt the Social Workers Party from certain FECA disclosure requirements through the 1984 elections.

Contribution Limits

Contribution limits, sanctioned in the *Buckley* decision, vary by state and by level of candidacy. Approximately 25 states place no limits on donations. Eighteen states have relatively simple restrictions; seven states have rather detailed limitations. Contribution limits for gubernatorial elections range downward from unlimited contributions to as low as $800 per individual in New Jersey's publicly funded general election campaigns for the governorship. Most statewide individual contribution limits range from $1,000 to $3,000 per election or per calendar year. In New York they are based on a specified number of cents per registered voter. Cash contributions usually are prohibited or restricted to $100 or under.

Some states limit contributions for each calendar year, others for each election year and still others for each two-year period. Some limits apply overall to all state campaigns, others only to contributions by individuals, some others to contributions to candidates and still others to contributions by or to political committees or party committees.

Four states—Florida, Kansas, North Carolina and Wyoming—seek to strengthen the political parties by permitting unlimited contributions to and by party committees while restricting contributions by individuals and other political committees. In addition, Maine permits political party committees to distribute slate cards listing three or more candidates and exempts their costs from the contribution limits.

One innovative approach is that used in Connecticut, New York and Minnesota, where stratified contribution ceilings are imposed, depending upon specific races. Some states allow appropriate officials to recommend adjustments in restrictions, or charge a dependent minor's contribution against the parent's limit. Still other approaches provide for exemption of volunteer services, property use and travel expenses of $500 and under. Others permit unlimited individual contributions to political committees, even though these committees may be restricted in the amount they can contribute to a candidate.

Restrictions on business and labor Numerous states prohibit direct corporate contributions, but fewer ban direct labor contributions. Twenty-four states restrict contributions by corporations. Some states restrict campaign contributions by government contractors. West Virginia, for example, prohibits state contractors from contributing to political candidates, committees or parties during the contract negotiation period. Oregon bars contributions from most public businesses such as banks, utilities and common carriers, as well as companies that can condemn or take land. Other states exclude heavily regulated industries, such as public utilities, banks and insurance companies.

Seven states—Delaware, Florida, Indiana, Maine, Maryland, Mississippi, and New York—and the District of Columbia permit corporations to contribute but set limits on the amounts they can give. Even though federal law treats corporations and unions alike by prohibiting contributions from either, only 10 states restrict labor union contributions to campaigns. The 10 states are Arizona, Connecticut, New Hampshire, North Carolina, North Dakota, Pennsylvania, South Dakota, Texas, Wisconsin and Wyoming.[4]

But most states, including those that prohibit direct corporate contributions, now permit corporations and unions to form political action committees that can seek voluntary contributions from employees, stockholders and members. In recent years, business, industry, and trade association PACs have proliferated at the state level as they have at the federal level.

In the past, corporate and union contributions-in-kind, such as the free provision of office space or furniture, or the lending of a car to a candidate, often were not accounted for. Now, federal law and most state disclosure provisions consider contributions-in-kind and loans as gifts that must be reported with reasonable estimates of value received, and the value must be within contribution limits where they exist.

In several states, corporations and unions were prohibited from contributing to ballot initiative campaigns, a logical extension of the restrictions on such contributions to candidates. But the U.S. Supreme Court in 1978 declared unconstitutional a Massachusetts law prohibiting corporations from spending money to influence the outcomes of tax referenda. This decision in *First National Bank of Boston v. Bellotti* was followed by a U.S. District Court action ruling unconstitutional Florida's state law preventing corporations from spending more than $3,000 on ballot initiatives. One result of these decisions may be greater business involvement in ballot referendum and initiative elections.[5]

Improper influence The extent to which campaign contributions are received with expressed or tacit obligations in terms of policy, jobs or contracts cannot be measured, but it undoubtedly is greater at the state and local levels than at the federal level. In many places, systematic solicitation of those who benefit from the system occurs.

In Indiana, for example, the Two Percent Club, composed of certain government employees who are assessed 2 percent of their salaries, is a formal basis of financing the party in power.[6] There also have been clear cases of extortion or conspiracy to obtain campaign money in return for favors or preferment. In New Jersey, a former Democratic secretary of state was convicted in May 1972 on federal charges of bribery and extortion in seeking $10,000 in political contributions from a company that sought a contract to build a bridge. His successor, a Republican, similarly was indicted and convicted in October of the same year for extorting $10,000 for the state Republican Party in return for attempting to fix the awarding of a state highway construction contract. Clearly, corruption crosses party lines.[7]

Another example of the malignant links that can develop between money and politics is the case of former Vice President Spiro Agnew. Routine investigations of corruption in Baltimore County, where Agnew had been county executive, led to the grand jury indictment of Agnew for alleged bribery, extortion and tax fraud. According to witnesses, Agnew allegedly had pocketed well over $100,000 by using his political office to hand out county and state contracts in exchange for personal payoffs from seven engineering firms and one financial institution. Agnew's resignation from the vice presidency in 1973 was one of the conditions of a plea bargaining agreement, under which he pleaded no contest to a single count of tax evasion.[8]

Criminal funds The amount of political money supplied by criminal elements is a subject on which there are few facts. Part of the problem is the difficulty in distinguishing campaign gifts from other exchanges of money.

More than two decades ago, the Second Interim Report of the Special Senate Committee to Investigate Organized Crime in Interstate Commerce (the so-called Kefauver committee) concluded that one form of "corruption and connivance with organized crime in state and local government" consisted of:

"contributions to the campaign funds of candidates for political office at various levels by organized criminals. . . ." Such criminal influence is bipartisan. According to the Kefauver committee, "not infrequently, contributions are made to both major political parties, gangsters operate on both sides of the street."[9] Little has changed to revise this description.

Unfortunately, the extent of such activity is still unknown. Some scholars have estimated that perhaps 15 percent of the money for state and local campaigns is derived from the underworld.[10] Excluding the federal level where the incidence of such behavior is presumed to be low, this would mean that almost $36 million might have come from criminal elements in 1976. If such money is indeed concentrated in nonfederal campaigns, there is special reason to study legislation at the state and local levels designed to regulate such behavior.

BIPARTISAN ELECTION COMMISSIONS

The states vary in their systems of election administration. Twenty-nine states have bipartisan, independent commissions that oversee elections. In most states, the governor appoints the commission members. In other states, such as Michigan, the secretary of state has that responsibility. In Delaware, Massachusetts and Montana, a single officer is appointed instead of a commission.

The commissions represent an attempt to isolate from political pressures the functions of receiving, auditing, tabulating, publicizing and preserving the reports of political candidates and campaign receipts and expenditures required by law. The commissions usually have replaced partisan election officials, such as secretaries of state, who traditionally were repositories of campaign fund reports but whose partisanship as elected or appointed officials did not make them ideal administrators or enforcers of election law. Some commissions have strong powers including the right to issue subpoenas and to assess penalties, powers that also are available for the administration and enforcement of contribution limits and of public funding in states providing it.

Budget and Legal Problems

Generally, the commissions receive and audit campaign contributions and expenditure reports, compile data, write and implement regulations and give advisory opinions. They also conduct investigations that include auditing records. Because of the amount of paperwork handled and because of understaffing and underfinancing, most commissions must rely on complaints filed and on investigative newspaper reporting to detect violations. For example, the Election Board in North Carolina had in 1978 one director, two full-time clerks and a budget of approximately $70,000. During election years, two part-time clerks are hired. In these circumstances, the director stresses administration and processing rather than monitoring of reports.[11]

While independent bipartisan election commissions theoretically are in-sulated from political pressures, they face many constitutional and enforce-ment problems. The original method of choosing the Federal Election Commis-sion was challenged successfully in *Buckley v. Valeo* on the ground that congressional appointments violated the constitutional separation of powers. Similarly, an Illinois court ruled that the manner of selection of the bipartisan State Board of Elections contravened the state constitutional prohibition against the legislative appointment of officers of the executive branch.[12] Mem-bers of the Illinois board were nominated by the majority and minority leaders of each house of the legislature; each leader nominated two persons, and the governor selected one of the two. But an Alaska court threw out a suit that contended the Democratic and Republican parties derived unwarranted statu-tory protection from a law requiring appointment to the state election board from lists submitted by the two parties.[13]

Enforcement

The line between outright bribery and campaign contributions may often be a thin one, but where there is no accounting whatever of campaign funds or of sources of income it is easy to rationalize that one was meant to be the other. Statutory disclosure brings at least some discipline to transactions involving money and elected public officials, and if laws are enforced, even more discipline will result.

Some 30 states require candidates or public officials to disclose their personal finances, but definitions of ethics and conflict of interest are elusive and laws regulating them can be as difficult to enforce as are campaign laws. In some states, such as California, the same commission enforces both areas. Gray areas between compliance and noncompliance sometimes result in antagonisms on the part of state legislators who may work to undercut the administration of such laws. As a result, the responsible offices often exist under severe budget restrictions.

Since the state election commissions have only civil prosecutorial power, they must refer apparent criminal violations to appropriate enforcement officers—normally an attorney general or district attorney, who is a partisan official with discretion on whether to pursue the referrals. While these officials may be less equipped than the commissions to deal with election violations, there is no alternative to referring criminal violations to them.

STATE PUBLIC FUNDING

Seventeen states provide for public financing of state election campaigns (Table 1). The states' approaches to collecting and distributing the money vary widely. Funds are collected by either an income tax checkoff or an income tax surcharge procedure. The latter permits a taxpayer to add a dollar or two onto

Table 1
Public finance of state elections

Year first bill on public financing was passed	States	Years in which public monies have been allocated to parties/candidates
1973	Iowa	1974-78
1973	Maine*	1974-78
1973	Rhode Island	1974-78
1974	Minnesota	1976-78
1975	Montana*	1976
1974	Maryland*	— —
1974	New Jersey	1977
1973	Utah	1975-78
1975	Idaho	1976-78
1975	Massachusetts*	1978
1975	North Carolina	1977-78
1976	Kentucky	1977-78
1976	Michigan	1978
1977	Oregon	1978
1977	Wisconsin	1978
1978	Hawaii	— —
1978	Oklahoma	— —

* States with tax surcharges; all others have tax checkoffs.

Source: Ruth S. Jones, "State Public Financing and the State Parties," in Michael J. Malbin, ed., *Parties, Interest Groups, and Campaign Finance Laws* (Washington, D.C.: American Enterprise Institute, 1980). Reprinted by permission.

one's tax liability, while the former lets the taxpayer earmark for a special political fund a dollar or two that he or she would have to pay anyway. Funds are distributed either to parties or to candidates, or to a combination of both.

Tax Checkoff

Thirteen states use an income tax checkoff provision similar to that of the federal government. Taxpayer participation in using the income tax checkoff varies by state. Although the checkoff system does not increase tax liability or decrease the amount of the tax refund, participation is relatively low; it ranges from 38 percent in New Jersey to 8.8 percent in North Carolina. The average participation rate is 22 percent, somewhat below the rate for participation in the federal system.

Tax Surcharge

Four states—Maine, Maryland, Massachusetts and Montana—have an income tax surcharge provision. The surcharge in Maine adds to the tax liability a $1 contribution to the party designated; alternatively, one dollar of the tax refund may be stipulated for a specific political party.

In Massachusetts, the $1 contribution goes into a general fund for statewide candidates to be distributed on a matching basis. In Maryland, a $2 contribution may be designated to a general campaign fund that also is distributed on a matching basis. Montana, in 1979, switched from a checkoff to a surcharge system and other states also are considering changes.

The surcharge participation rate is considerably lower than that of the checkoff system. For the tax year 1977, in Maine, only 5 percent of the taxpayers participated; in Maryland, 3.2 percent; in Massachusetts, 4.1 percent. In Maryland, the payout to candidates had been planned for 1978 but was postponed until 1982 because the available funds were inadequate.

Distribution of Funds: To Political Parties

Eleven states distribute public funds to political parties.[14] In five states, the money is allocated to the parties and to a general campaign fund designated for candidates. In two states, Idaho and Rhode Island, the money raised is distributed to political parties without restrictions as to how the money can be used other than to prohibit primary election use. In five others, the money goes to parties but with restrictions: In Minnesota, the money must be distributed by parties to selected categories of candidates according to formula; in North Carolina, the money goes from the parties to specified general election candidates only; in Oregon, the money cannot be used to reduce a postelection campaign deficit and half the money received by the party must go to the county central committees; in Iowa, the money cannot go to federal candidates if they receive federal public subsidy; in Utah, the money must be proportionately divided between state and county central committees.

In the nine states where the taxpayer may designate the recipient political party, the Democrats have received far more funds than the Republicans (Table 2). Utah is the only state where the Republican Party has been designated more often than the Democratic Party. In Rhode Island and North Carolina, the ratio is approximately 3-to-1 in favor of the Democrats; in Oregon, it is almost 2-to-1. The Democratic edge has led some observers to be concerned that the system could lead to a "strong-get-stronger, weak-get-weaker" situation. Since the difficulties of forming a new party are great, such a situation could lead to one party dominating a state, with a fractionalized multiparty minority. In Rhode Island, Minnesota and Idaho, suits against the checkoffs claimed that the distributions were discriminatory and unconstitutional. In Idaho, the suit was dismissed; in Minnesota, the court upheld the constitution-

Table 2
Distribution of state checkoff funds to political parties, 1978

	Taxpayer* participation rate	Democrats	Republicans	Other
Idaho	18.4%	$ 12,992	$ 10,701	$ 411†
Iowa	15.2	121,528	94,418	
Kentucky	16.7	180,127	64,738	
Maine (surcharge)	.5	2,132	1,260	
Minnesota	19.8	187,812	132,913	12,013‡
North Carolina	8.8	146,847	50,501	**
Oregon	25.7	167,031	89,444	12,426††
Rhode Island	23.1	82,393‡‡	30,706‡‡	
Utah	25.6	53,958	55,827	7,820

* The states differ in the base used to determine the percentage of taxpayer participation—Iowa, Kentucky, Maine, Minnesota, North Carolina and Rhode Island use percentage of total number of individual taxpayers, whereas Idaho, Oregon and Utah figures are based on the total number of tax returns.

† Idaho's general campaign fund had $38,183.

‡ Minnesota also allocates money to a general campaign fund designated for candidates. In 1977 the general campaign fund had $118,774.

** North Carolina's general campaign fund had $62,341.

†† In Oregon, only the Republican and Democratic parties were eligible to receive funds.

‡‡ Rhode Island's general campaign fund had $82,576, which was disbursed among the political parties. The party checkoff designations were $22,973 for the Democrats and $7,550 for the Republicans.

ality of the checkoff law but required some changes that were made. In Rhode Island, the court determined that the party could not use checkoff funds in favor of an endorsed primary candidate, but refused the requested injunction.[15]

How a party may spend public funds varies from state to state. For example, in Minnesota, though taxpayers can check off a party designation if they wish, the distribution requirements are such that the money goes directly to candidates—whether from the party designations or the general fund—with no flexibility provided the party and no funds available for general party use. Thirty percent of the money must be used in the five statewide campaigns, with a fixed percentage designated for each of the five races. The remaining funds are apportioned to the candidates for the state legislature. Within these quotas, the funds are divided equally among candidates. All the candidates of one party for the legislature share equally in funds allocated to their respective offices from the party account. Some candidates have rejected public funds.

Iowa, by contrast, allows a great deal of flexibility in the way the parties distribute the funds. Other than requiring that candidates at the same level receive the same amount of money—for example, all six congressional candidates of one party must get the identical amount—the Iowa law allows the parties to allocate the money as they wish so long as it is spent for legitimate campaign purposes. Particularly among the Democrats, the money has been used in some instances for strengthening the party effort; in others, the money has aided candidates.

Several states have both a party fund and a general campaign fund whereby the money goes to the former for distribution to parties and to the latter for distribution to candidates. An Oklahoma law provides that the checkoff money be divided equally between parties and candidates. Of the party fund, 10 percent goes to each party while the remainder is distributed according to the number of registered voters per party. The parties may not use the money for primaries or conventions. The other half of the checkoff fund is allocated to statewide candidates in the general election. Twenty percent goes to gubernatorial candidates, 15 percent apiece to candidates for lieutenant governor and attorney general, 10 percent to candidates for state treasurer, and the remainder is divided among the candidates for other offices.

This new source of political money becomes more and more necessary as the recipients begin to depend on it. Ruth S. Jones, in one of the first studies in the effects of state public financing on parties, found that in several states where parties used subsidies to hire staff and pay rent "public funds have apparently had a great impact. . . . [S]taff is viewed by most party leaders as the key to expanding the influence and status of the party."[16]

Noting that the concept was still too novel for a complete assessment, Jones concluded that 1) states are definitely influenced by state public financing policies and that 2) the methods of raising, allocating and overseeing public financing determine the impact of these policies on state parties. Those states that distribute public funds to political parties tend to strengthen the party, while those states that disburse public money to candidates tend to weaken the party. Ironically, the states with strong party systems tend to give public funds to candidates, whereas the weak-party states tend to channel public money to the parties.[17]

The implications of public financing for political parties are discussed below.

Distribution of Funds: To Candidates

Seven states—Hawaii, Maryland, Massachusetts, Michigan, New Jersey, Oklahoma and Wisconsin—distribute money from the public fund directly to candidates. The states that offer public support of state campaigns usually do so on a matching incentive basis. Michigan and New Jersey provide for public financing of the gubernatorial race. Michigan finances both primary and general election gubernatorial campaigns, allocating up to two-thirds of the $1 million spending limit. New Jersey was one of the first states to provide public financing of campaigns without spending limits. It has a matching program under which a gubernatorial candidate in the primary and general election after reaching a threshold of $50,000 in private contributions not exceeding $800 each, can be eligible for matching funds of two dollars for each dollar raised in contributions up to $600.

In 1978 the New Jersey Election Law Enforcement Commission recommended that spending limits, which had been in effect in the 1977 election, be repealed so long as there are provisions for limits on contributions, on candidates' use of personal funds, on loans and on amounts of public funding for candidates. In 1979 Oklahoma adopted a public financing system with no spending limits. In contrast, Hawaii recently enacted a program whereby income tax deductions are recognized only if the candidate receiving the contribution agrees to accept overall expenditure limits.

IMPLICATIONS OF PUBLIC FUNDING

Although public subsidies in campaigns provoke many arguments, scant attention has been paid to the implications that the various state plans have for the political system in general and the two-party system in particular. Questions of fairness, cost, administration and enforcement need to be asked, assumptions challenged and an understanding developed of the conditions that ought to be met if subsidies are to be provided. Public financing is not a panacea, and it will bring fundamental changes in the political structure and electoral processes.

Criteria

The main questions raised about public funding are who should receive the subsidy and how and when it should be made. The goal of government subsidization is to help serious candidates. A subsidy system should be flexible enough to permit those in power to be challenged. However, it should not support candidates who are merely seeking free publicity, and it should not attract so many candidates that the electoral process is degraded. Accordingly, the most difficult policy problems in working out fair subsidies are definitional: How does one define major and minor parties and distinguish between serious and frivolous candidates without doing violence to equality of opportunity or to "equal protection" under the federal or state constitutions? Any standard must be arbitrary, and certain screening devices must be used, based upon past votes, numbers of petitions, numbers of smaller contributions to achieve qualifying levels or other means.

While it is desirable to increase competition in the electoral arena, there are certain related considerations. One is whether the provisions of government funding can induce two-party competition in predominantly one-party areas by means of providing funding to candidates of the minority party; competition may be extremely hard to stimulate. Another is whether public funding of the political parties will serve to strengthen them and, if so, whether that is desirable. Still another is whether government domination of the electoral process will follow government funding.

As the states establish systems of public financing, the cost of electing large numbers of elected officials—a hallmark of this country's political system—will become obvious. In the United States, more than 500,000 public officials are elected over a four-year cycle. Long ballots require candidates to spend money in the mere quest for visibility, and the long ballot and frequent elections combined bring both voter fatigue and low turnout. In New Jersey, there are statewide elections at least every six months because the gubernatorial and state legislative campaigns are held in odd-numbered years. New Jersey, however, elects only one statewide public official—the governor—and then lets him appoint the rest. As financial pressures mount, other states may want to give increasing consideration to reducing the number of elective offices, thus diminishing the amounts of money (whether public or private) needed to sustain the electoral system.

Impact on Parties

Public funding of political campaigns, when the money is given directly to candidates, could accelerate the trend toward candidate independence and further diminish the role of the two major parties. With government funding available and made doubly attractive by limits on private contributions, the candidate's need to rely on party identification is greatly lessened. Supported even partially with government funds, the candidate is less beholden to his party. While traditionally the parties have not provided much money to candidates, they have eased fund raising by opening access to party workers for volunteer help and to contributors for money. Thus as their obligations to the party are reduced, candidates may become even more independent.

At the least, one can speculate that subsidies to candidates without reference to parties will lead to more independence in legislatures and an erosion of party loyalty. A legislator who ignored the demands of the leadership would not be fearful of being frozen out of a reelection bid or denied adequate funds because government would provide at least partial funding. To avoid splintering legislatures and maintain party strength, if policy makers decide that strengthening political parties is desirable, candidate funding—at least in the general election period—could be channeled through the parties.[18]

STATE TAX INCENTIVES

To the extent that campaigns are funded with public funds, the role of large contributors and special interests is reduced. Where there is less emphasis on private money, there is theoretically less chance for corruption or favoritism. But it is also desirable to encourage people to contribute money to politics in small sums, so the federal government and 15 states provide some form of indirect public support. Of the 41 states that impose an income tax, 10 offer a tax deduction for political donations, usually a deduction from gross income for contributions up to $100. Five states, Alaska, Idaho, Minnesota, Oregon and Vermont, plus the District of Columbia offer tax credits, most of them for one half the amount of contributions up to a maximum credit of $10. The tax credit provides greater incentive to contribute because it visibly reduces the amount of taxes paid, while the deduction simply reduces the amount of income subject to taxation.

Other forms of direct or indirect government assistance can be suggested. Rather than provide money, governments can supply services that relieve parties and candidates of the need for certain expenditures. For example, some state governments provide campaign help through the assumption of greater responsibilities for registration of voters, distribution of voter information pamphlets and election day activities. Moreover, public funding can help meet the transition costs between election day and inauguration day.[19]

Among the most important of such services would be government-sponsored universal voter registration. This would vastly reduce the cost to political parties and candidates of performing an essentially public function and would also reduce dependence on special interests for their registration activities. Such assistance would, furthermore, be likely to increase voting participation in a nation having complex registration requirements and a highly mobile population.

TESTING NEW CONCEPTS

Some states have been more experimental than the federal government in dealing with public funding, and the results of their pioneering may affect development of federal electoral regulation policy in the future. Until recent years it has been mostly the other way around, with the evolution of federal reforms influencing the adoption of similar changes in the states.

Eleven states distribute public funds to political parties and, like the federal government, seven states distribute the money directly to candidates. In the nine states where taxpayers can specify which party they want to help, the Democrats have received far more money than the Republicans. But preliminary studies indicate that, Democrat or Republican, the parties are strengthened where public funds are channeled through them—a development that some electoral reformers feel is needed to restore some of the vitality that parties have lost as an intended or unintended result of the vast changes in the American political system. . . .

NOTES

1. *Socialist Workers Party v. Jenings*, Civ. No. 74-1328 (D.D.C.).
2. *Buckley v. Valeo*, 424 U.S. at 68.
3. *FEC Record*, March 1977, p. 6.
4. Wisconsin permits contributions from unions incorporated prior to January 1, 1978.
5. See Karen J. Fling, "The States as Laboratories of Reform," in *Political Finance*, Herbert E. Alexander, ed. (Beverly Hills: Sage Publications Inc., 1979).
6. Robert J. McNeill, *Democratic Campaign Financing in Indiana, 1964* (Bloomington, Ind., and Princeton, N.J.: Institute of Public Administration at Indiana University and Citizens' Research Foundation, 1966), pp. 15-19, 35-40.
7. For a discussion of these New Jersey and other state cases, see George Amick, *The American Way of Graft* (Princeton, N.J.: The Center for Analysis of Public Issues, 1976).
8. See *United States v. Spiro T. Agnew*, Crim. A. No. 73-0535, U.S. District Court, District of Maryland, October 10, 1973.
9. *Second Interim Report of the Special Senate Committee to Investigate Organized Crime in Interstate Commerce*, 82nd Cong., 1st session, Report No. 141, p. 1.
10. According to Alexander Heard, this estimate "embraces funds given in small towns and rural areas by individuals operating on the borders of the law who want a sympathetic sheriff and prosecutor, but who are not linked to crime syndicates. The estimate applies chiefly to persons engaged in illegal gambling and racketeering. It does not extend, for example, to otherwise reputable businessmen who hope for understanding treatment from building inspectors and tax assessors." Alexander Heard, *The Costs of Democracy* (Chapel Hill, N.C.: University of North Carolina Press, 1960), p. 164, fn 73; also pp. 154-168; also see Harold Lasswell and Arnold A. Rogow, *Power, Corruption and Rectitude* (Englewood Cliffs, N.J.: Prentice-Hall, 1963) pp. 79-80; and Donald R. Cressey, *Theft of the Nation: The Structure and Operations of Organized Crime in America* (New York: Harper & Row, 1969) p. 253.
11. Martin Donsky, "Undisclosed Disclosures? A Passive Approach to Campaign Finance Reporting," *NC Insight* Vol. 1, No. 4 (Fall, 1978) North Carolina Center for Public Policy Research Inc., Raleigh, N.C., pp. 12-13.
12. *Walker v. State Board of Elections*, Illinois Circuit Court, 7th Judicial Circuit, No. 364-75 (1975).
13. *Abramczyk v. State of Alaska*, Superior Court, 3rd Judicial Circuit, No. 72-6426 (1975).
14. Some authorities consider Minnesota and Montana to be "candidate" states since the designated parties have no control over the allocation of funds to the candidates. Another state, Oklahoma, will distribute money to both parties and candidates.
15. See unpublished paper by James R. Klonoski and Ann Aiken, "The Constitutional Law of Political Parties and the Emergent Dollar Checkoff," University of Oregon School of Law.
16. Ruth S. Jones, "State Public Financing and the State Parties," prepared for the Conference on Parties, Interest Groups and Campaign Finance Laws, September 4-5, 1979, in *Parties, Interest Groups, and Campaign Finance Laws*, Michael J.

Malbin, ed. (Washington, D.C.: American Enterprise Institute for Public Policy Research, 1979), p. 296.

17. Jones, *State Public Financing*, p. 303.

18. There is extensive literature on party responsibility. Among the more recent books and articles see, for example: Austin Ranney, *Curing the Mischief of Faction: Party Reform in America* (Berkeley: University of California Press, 1975); and Herbert E. Alexander, "The Impact of Election Reform Legislation on the Political Party System," an unpublished paper prepared for the 1975 annual meeting of the American Political Science Association, San Francisco, California, September 5, 1975. For earlier literature, see Herbert E. Alexander, *Responsibility in Party Finance* (Princeton, N.J.: Citizens' Research Foundation, 1963).

19. For a complete discussion of proposals, see Herbert E. Alexander, *Regulation of Political Finance* (Berkeley and Princeton: Institute of Governmental Studies, University of California, and Citizen's Research Foundation, 1966), pp. 16-36.

Discussion Questions

1. Discuss the pros and cons of implementing a national referendum. How has the initiative been used in your state?

2. Does approval voting stand a ghost of a chance of being implemented? What factors seem to be necessary in order for such political innovations to be adopted? What is your reaction to Brams' contention that "I am completely convinced that approval voting will be the election reform of the 20th century . . ."?

3. Try to collect some data on how much money was spent in 1980 by candidates in your local area. Would you recommend the use of public financing of state elections?

CHAPTER FOUR

STATE LEGISLATURES

There has been a strong movement for reform of state legislatures in the past twenty years. As a result, they have been changed and modernized in a great variety of ways. Most legislatures now meet in annual sessions. Salaries have been increased. In a few states, such as Massachusetts, legislatures have reduced their membership. All legislatures have been reapportioned at least twice. Legislators have been given more staff assistance. The number of committees has been reduced and lawmaking procedures have become more flexible. As governors have gained power and state bureaucracies have been enlarged, legislators have sought ways to improve their executive oversight. In short, legislative bodies have become more professionalized.

When each of these reforms was proposed, it was argued that legislative performance would be improved after the change was made. However, in many cases the verdict is still out regarding how closely performance has lived up to promise.

In the early 1960s reformers believed that better apportioned state legislatures would lead to changes in the nature of state policy. They speculated that the change would be in the direction of more liberal education and welfare programs, tax reform, and additional financial assistance to urban areas. They also felt that there would be a greater turnover in membership and the election of more Democrats. Now, twenty years later, political scientists find it difficult to measure the impact of reapportionment. Many other variables, such as the level of economic development, the degree of party competition, legislative professionalism, and the leadership of governors, may also influence the direction and amount of state spending. Moreover, national political events, such as Lyndon Johnson's landslide win in 1964, may affect the political fortunes of those running for state legislative posts. In addition, the federal government has assumed a greater share of funding in several areas.

While reform has had an impact on the top party leaders (Speaker and majority and minority leaders in the House and president pro tem and majority and minority leaders in the Senate) in state legislatures, their basic tasks remain the same. Moreover, the qualities of a good leader—competence, openness, stamina, adaptability, tolerance, patience, firmness, and fairness—remain unchanged. As Alan Rosenthal notes, "The most effective leader, then, is one the members *want to follow* because of their personal regard, and not one that members *have to follow* because of favors, patronage, or special persuasion."

In the first article in this chapter, Cho and Frederickson caution us that the effects of reapportionment have been more limited than reformers anticipated. This does not mean, however, that reapportionment has not caused change in the directions originally predicted. Indeed, these political scientists note that state aid has become less rural biased, higher expenditures have been made for public education and public health, and proportionately less money has been spent on highways.

In the second article Alan Rosenthal reviews the major tasks performed by the top leaders in state legislatures.

The Effects of Reapportionment: Subtle, Selective, Limited

Yong Hyo Cho and H. George Frederickson

State legislative apportionment can be understood at two levels. The first level is normative and philosophical, having to do with alternative definitions of what constitutes representative democracy. Advocates of population equity in apportionment insisted that democracy was diminished when not all citizens were equally represented, and their position carried the day in *Baker* v. *Carr*. The second level is empirical and begins with the question, does population equity enhance the potential for democracy?

Douglas W. Rae, in a convincing essay on "Reapportionment and Political Democracy" (Nelson Polsby, editor, *Reapportionment in the 1970's*, Berkeley, University of California Press, 1971), defines equalitarian democracy very strictly in mathematical modelling terms and analyzes state election data to determine if reapportionment has increased "representativeness" and therefore furthered equalitarian democracy. He concludes that:

> *First, reapportionment made a modest absolute contribution to the democratization of state legislative elections in most cases. Second, however modest the absolute change, it was a very substantial part of the change which might have been achieved within the context of plurality elections. And, third, it follows that the "lion's share" of the feasible democratization under reapportionment per se is behind us, not in front of us. More broadly—and the frequency lines give this a quantitative interpretation—reapportionment seems more than a legal triviality, but less than a democratizing revolution.*

> *What all of this means is that reapportionment has narrowed the set of coincident coalition structures in which the few frustrate or dominate the*

From Yong Hyo Cho and H. George Frederickson, "The Effects of Reapportionment: Subtle, Selective, Limited," *National Civic Review* 63 (July 1974): 357-362. Reprinted with permission of the National Municipal League.

many. There are fewer possible cases, and those cases have smaller numerical disparities, which lead to less arbitrary minority rule after reapportionment than before. It is now less likely that a minority party will win a legislative majority and less likely that in an interelection dispute responsive legislators will form majorities contrary to the numerical division of the electorate. Reapportionment in the 1960s narrowed the prospect of minority rule in the present sense and left only a small margin for democratization by further reapportionment in the 1970s.

If Rae's analyses are correct, and they are compelling, legislative reapportionment has done in elections, at least to some extent, what the reformers said it would do, that is, make state legislatures more representative of the majority.

If elections are more democratic as Rae shows, are the fiscal and nonfiscal policy decisions of state legislatures more democratic? In a longitudinal 50-state study of the impact of reapportionment on fiscal and non-fiscal policy (Cho and Frederickson, *Measuring the Effects of Reapportionment in the American States*, to be issued by the National Municipal League), it was concluded, by using an elaborate series of multiple linear regression equations, that reapportionment is having a generally democratizing impact on state policy.

If it can be agreed that the increased representation for cities and suburbs in state legislatures resulting from reapportionment constitutes significantly higher "quality" or equity of representation, then the findings indicate that there are selected instances in which reapportionment has resulted in policy decisions more generally favorable to the majority. Following are some examples of the capacity of reapportionment to account for policy variation, when controlling for other possible determinants.

Reapportionment brought about a change in state fiscal systems in a significant way. First, greater equity contributed to a higher level of direct expenditures generally, while it is associated with a lower level of rural-biased state aid to local governments. What this change implies is that reapportionment in a more than marginal way enhanced centralization of state fiscal management. It made it more difficult for rural areas to tax at a very low level yet support rural government services funded by state aid which was discriminatory toward cities. It has also resulted in slow growth of state aid spending and in a more equitable distribution of those funds between metropolitan and nonmetropolitan areas.

Second, improvement in apportionment equity resulted in a higher level of state spending for generally urban-related functions such as public education and public health and a lower level for traditionally rural-favored functions such as highways. The growth rate of spending for education and health was also faster in those states where apportionment equity was more improved by reapportionment, whereas the growth rate of spending for highways is slower in better apportioned states.

The reapportionment effect is also evident in some nonfiscal policy decisions of state legislatures, such as firearms control and voting rights legislation.

So, in selected policy areas, and over time, reapportionment is having at least some of the effects that the reformers predicted it would. And if it is agreed that one man, one vote is a necessary precondition to a strict definition of democracy, it can be said that reapportionment is causing a tilt in that direction.

REAPPORTIONMENT AS A TEMPORAL PHENOMENON

The Supreme Court's insistence on numeric equity in the constituencies of state legislators took some time to implement; but it was very quick as political changes go. The question then becomes, "How quickly will the effects of these changes be evident?" Different independent variables were used to approach this question from several angles. To determine if the effects of reapportionment are delayed and, if so, for how long, the first variable was a time-lapse measure indicating the number of years that have passed since it was done. The second was a session-lapse index showing the number of reapportioned legislative sessions. An incumbency index attempted to measure the level of turnover among state legislators. This was used following the logic that under court-ordered reapportionment incumbency would be reduced and non-surviving legislators would be replaced by persons more generally representative of the majority. From previous studies of state election and districting politics we are generally aware that survival instincts among state legislators are very strong, and that in the processes of reapportionment key incumbents would be protected and would likely retain positions of power. Therefore, the effectiveness of reapportionment would be delayed.

The temporal and incumbency measures provide some strong explanations for legislative decision making in selected instances and for selected policy areas. In a nationwide sense, then, it can be argued that the effects of reapportionment were delayed, but that, generally speaking, as a state gets further from the year or session of the initial reapportionment, the effects of that act become more apparent. Here are some salient examples: Those states whose legislatures were reapportioned earlier spent more for general welfare and urban-related functions such as public welfare, public health and hospitals, and less for highways, state aid to local governments in general and to local schools in particular. Similarly, total direct expenditures, direct expenditures for education in general and for higher education in particular increased more rapidly while the growth rate in state aid spending was slower. Of the non-fiscal policies studied, legislative responsiveness is positively influenced by the temporal dimension of reapportionment only in firearms control policies.

The Incumbency Success Ratio was significant in only a few instances — abortion policy in the non-fiscal analysis, and fiscal redistributive policy, and direct spending for education and welfare. In each case the findings seem to suggest a kind of counter-intuitive result, that is, higher levels of incumbency success are associated with greater legislative responsiveness on abortion policy and greater direct spending for education and welfare. It may be that surviving incumbents tended to be "like" their newly elected colleagues, that is, that so few rural incumbents survived that they had little influence on policy. When incumbency did influence policy making it was in the direction of being more majoritarian or responsive, perhaps an indication that urban or suburban incumbents survived and gathered greater strength because of the defeat of their rural counterparts, and then responded to urban/suburban needs. Still, the capacity of the Incumbency Success Ratio to make significant predictions of policy strength and direction is limited and selective.

LINKAGES BETWEEN FISCAL POLICY AND
LEGISLATIVE RESPONSIVENESS

Because the approach to the analysis of the impact of reapportionment has been from two angles—legislative fiscal decision making and legislative responsiveness—it seems important to explore the possible relationships between the two. The differences between fiscal policy and legislative responsiveness must be emphasized before any attempt is made to link them.

In the first place, state fiscal decision making is incremental, based on taxing and other revenue policies that change slowly, and on spending patterns that primarily pay the salaries of state employees or give aid to local governments to help them pay their employees. Budgeting is a conservative process, usually based on a system of using last year's appropriations to predict next year's needs. Budgeting is also highly political, involving attempts by administrative agencies to increase their funds, by governors to find new revenues, and by legislatures determined not to raise taxes. Major shifts in spending are rare, tending to occur at times of crisis or at points of extreme public demand. If reapportionment were to influence spending behavior it would be appropriate to conclude that *Baker* v. *Carr* did induce a kind of crisis or a "system-altering variable" into the matrix of state fiscal policy making. Our findings seem to indicate that reapportionment has had a selective impact which is, like the process of budgeting, incremental, becoming more apparent with the passing of time.

In the second place, the issues studied in non-fiscal legislative policy making usually have few fiscal implications. They are expressions of the interrelationships between public opinion on controversial issues and the stances of state legislatures on those issues. It was hypothesized that if reapportionment increased the general representativeness of legislative bodies those bodies should have an increased capacity for responding to the majority will. The issues analyzed are often highly charged politically. Few public issues are as controversial as abortion, divorce, civil rights, voting rights, firearms control and public employee labor rights. Still, with the exception of public employee labor rights, state legislatures can take either harsh or lenient stances on any of these issues without having to draw heavily on their budgets. As in the case of fiscal policy, the influence of reapportionment on state legislative responsiveness was found to be present and statistically significant, but selective and limited.

What, then, are the possible linkages between the influences of reapportionment on fiscal policy making and legislative responsiveness? Here are some examples: The linkage is not self-evident, but can be delineated. Legislative responsiveness was significantly influenced by reapportionment in politically and socially critical policy issues such as firearms control and civil rights, but not in morally controversial issues such as divorce and abortion legislation. Those spending policies with strong political and social ramifications—state aid to local governments, education, public health and hospitals, and highways—are also significantly influenced by reapportionment. There is little impact on public welfare expenditures, although the issue is socially and politically controversial. The reason for this lies primarily in the fact that expenditure decisions for public welfare are mainly made by the U. S. Congress rather than state legislatures.

Broadly viewed, legislative decision making reveals some discernible sensitivity to reapportionment in both fiscal and non-fiscal policy issues when they clearly manifest intense political and social ramifications.

THE URBAN-RURAL AND CITY-SUBURBAN
DIMENSIONS OF REAPPORTIONMENT

The most arduous point of the reapportionment reformers' argument was that rural-dominated legislatures discriminated against urban areas in spending policies, taxing policies and state regulations on local government generally. The seats gained by urban areas as a result of reapportionment were expected to correct urban-discriminatory state policies. Although urban areas in general were expected to gain a substantial increase in representation, the suburban areas rather than the central cities were perhaps the greatest winners.

The findings indicate that the reformers' argument of urban discrimination was essentially correct in that aid to local governments and direct spending for selected functions were measurably more favorable to nonmetropolitan areas prior to reapportionment. This disparity in state spending policies was generally reduced following the reapportionment, though it still persists. The analysis shows some evidence that reapportionment contributed significantly to the lessening of urban discrimination in state spending policies. Metropolitan-nonmetropolitan disparity was significantly reduced by reapportionment in total state aid and welfare spending, but not in aid to local schools.

As a part of this research project, Robert Firestine studied the impact of reapportionment on state aid to 34 central-city counties and 67 suburban counties in 38 selected metropolitan areas. His findings also corroborate the reformers' argument that urban areas will gain from reapportionment in policy consequences. Both central-city counties and suburban counties received a larger amount of state aid when the reapportioned legislatures were more equitable to the largest counties in the state. Similarly, the level of state aid received by both central-city and suburban county areas increased more rapidly from 1962 to 1968 when the reapportioned legislatures were more equitable and thus more favorable to the most populated counties.

Thus, the evidence resulting from the "first-round analysis" of the reapportionment effect indicates that the cities and suburbs not only have already gained from reapportionment but stand to gain more in the future.

SOME ADDITIONAL OUTCOMES

The court was primarily concerned with the correctness of the vote criteria by which legislators are chosen, and was persuaded that the constitution's "equal protection of the law" clause meant that one vote must be equal to each other vote. While fair and, as contended earlier, advancing the democratization of our representative form of government, the court's decisions may have produced some consequences that either modify or make palatable to incumbent legislators the one-man, one-vote rule.

The two most obvious consequences of reapportionment, aside from the sweeping equity it produced, appear to be an increase in that most basic of districting strategies, the gerrymander, and an increase in the use of multi-member districts. Although the data used here are not designed to indicate the extent to which these two processes are at work, nor the extent to which reapportionment may have caused them, assessments from single state studies seem to indicate that both are on the increase and that both were stimulated by reapportionment.

Perhaps more interesting is the extent to which other political phenomena were influenced by reapportionment. In this analysis many of the variables were used which measure these political factors, such as party competition, gubernatorial strength, administrative professionalism and the like. But, these variables were used to hold constant for these phenomena to ascertain correctly the direct relationship between legislative reapportionment and policy outcomes. The fiscal analysis demonstrated that the political control variables accounted for much more of the variance in fiscal policy outcomes than had been anticipated, seeming to challenge the general view that economic and social forces are the fundamental influences on policy. The political and administrative control variables in the non-fiscal or legislative responsiveness analysis also show unanticipated explanatory power.

Reapportionment occurred in the midst of all of many forces such as urban unrest, rapidly growing government, and the like. An attempt was made to control for as much of this as possible, and if anything too many possible control variables were provided for in the step-wise regression analysis. Still, the study of a phenomenon as basic and complex as legislative apportionment can never be completely stripped of its context. For example, because state spending was growing very rapidly both before and after reapportionment, the variables used in this analysis may have captured some of the explanation of that growth when, in fact, the reapportionment varibles may have been manifestations of other forces in the general context of state spending growth. Also, there is the importance of federal aid to state spending behavior, particularly in those policy areas in which state matching funds are required, such as highway construction. This analysis did not control for federal aid for a variety of reasons, and it is possible that such aid was a factor influencing state highway spending.

Although the era of reapportionment was a basic event in the evolution of American government, the processes of apportionment are constantly at work. This study has focused on the event and its consequences because of its singular importance. As a result of reapportionment, essential equity in both chambers of state legislatures will hold for the foreseeable future. Therefore, state legislative apportionment, in the eyes of the analyst, changes from a variable to a constant. So the job ahead is to continue to assess the results of the change and to focus on some of the unanticipated consequences. It may take many more years and much more analysis to understand fully the extent to which reapportionment altered the manner in which we govern.

Legislative Leadership

Alan Rosenthal

WHAT THEY DO

Top leaders, including the speaker and majority and minority leaders in the house and the president or president pro tem and majority and minority leaders in the senate, bear great responsibility and exert more than nominal influence. Given the magnitude of their jobs, some leaders choose to delegate tasks to their subordinates. But this is not easy. As one leader put it: "The only problem is in having other people you can trust to do these things." Or as a former top staff aide to the New York senate Republicans explained: "The key is to delegate the right amount of power to the right people. . . ."[1] Leaders can delegate power, but they still have to maintain overall control. Generally top leaders delegate authority most effectively where they have the power to appoint their subordinates, and thus can choose individuals whom they trust and upon whom they can rely. In comparatively few states—Connecticut, Florida, Massachusetts, New Hampshire, New York, and West Virginia—do the speaker and president (or president pro tem) appoint the majority and assistant leaders and does the minority leader appoint his lieutenants. In most states, the party caucus selects not only the top leader but others as well. This means that the candidate who lost out to the speaker may be elected majority leader and that different party factions and philosophies may be represented throughout the leadership ranks. The result can be internal friction and even sharp conflict among leaders and factions. In Pennsylvania the speaker and the majority leader were rivals, with the former in control of appointments and calendar, but the latter in control of the house budget. In Illinois it was not unusual to find the speaker and majority leader engaged in a feud which frequently became bitter.

When a leadership "team" is based on trust, responsibilities can be shared. One speaker, who saw eye to eye with his majority leader on most issues, described how responsibility could be divided:

I wanted to spend my time getting the legislature running well, so I concentrated on getting all the staff organized and on getting as much as I could out of the staff agencies. In turn, I let Frank take care of the issues and all the bills. We talked about scheduling and so on, but I mainly left all the coordination of work on getting bills introduced, through committees and to the floor to Frank.[2]

Although Florida's top legislative leaders traditionally have not delegated much authority, the speaker during the 1979 to 1980 session had his own leadership team. The majority leader, a close friend, served as the speaker's chief of staff, taking on some of the tough administrative tasks (such as assigning office space and parking and dismissing a number of the directors of committee staffs) and also assuming responsibility for steering several of the speaker's major programs through the legislature.

Organizing for Work

"Get control of the committee system and you'll be able to manage the entire legislature" is the advice a veteran leader offered at a session for newly elected leaders from the 50 states.[3] It is sound advice, for standing committees are the principal work units in the legislature. Top leaders ordinarily can shape the committee systems in several ways.

First, they help determine the number of committees that will exist, and the overall jurisdictions they will have. The rules of the senate and house list the committees by name and may also briefly specify their jurisdictions. Rules are adopted at each new legislative session, and usually the leaders maintain control of the process. They can establish a new committee, in order to highlight an issue or to create an additional chairmanship for some deserving member. They can consolidate two committees into one or divide one into two. It depends on the issues they want to address and the people they want to satisfy. The process is a fluid one. Second, they help determine the number of legislators on each committee and the ratio of majority to minority members. Here, too, the procedures may be specified in the rules, but the rules are susceptible to change, if the leaders so desire.

Third, and most important, top leaders largely control the appointment of chairmen and members of the standing committees. Senate leaders are less likely to exercise total control, since in a number of states they must work through committees on committees that are formally charged with appointments. This is the case in Arkansas, Georgia, Illinois, Kansas, Kentucky, Michigan, Montana, Nebraska, New Mexico, North Dakota, Ohio, Oklahoma, and Vermont. In Virginia the full senate elects all committee members. In the others the president, president pro tem, or majority leader selects the majority members and often chooses the minority members as well, normally on the recommendation of the minority party. The power of appointment tends to be more centralized in state houses than in state senates, with the speaker having control in nearly four-fifths of the states. In the others, the minority leader has responsibility for minority appointments or a committee on committees may appoint members while the speaker names the chairman. The chairman and members in Kentucky are chosen by a committee on committees and the chairman and members are selected by the party caucus in Hawaii and Wyoming.

Whatever the formal arrangements, leaders usually consult with the minority on minority appointments to committees. Some leaders feel that minority leaders should have full control over their own appointments, so they can take the pressure from their own members and shoulder the blame. Others seek minority recommendations; and in most cases accept them, although, as one speaker explained, "it is a good idea to turn a few down as a demonstration that the speaker has the power and his cooperation cannot be taken for granted." Sometimes, however, the majority will not accept the minority's recommendations for committees. One speaker, for instance, feared that the minority leader would retaliate against minority members who had supported the majority on critical votes if he had the power to assign his members to committees. Moreover, in the event of a majority split into factions, the minority might hold the balance of power on major committees, if it could determine which of its own members would be appointed. There are risks in rejecting minority nominations. New Mexico's Democratic speaker angered Republicans by not accepting some of the committee assignment suggestions of the minority leader. He excluded the minority leader and minority whip from the legislative council, an interim leadership committee on which the minority leaders normally had sat. When Republicans could not obtain a commitment from the speaker to change house rules to allow the minority party to control its own assignments to committees, they joined with dissident Democrats to elect a new speaker.[4]

Chairmanships, and vice chairmanships, are even more important than member assignments. In some states, such as Arkansas and Virginia, seniority is the determining factor in allocating chairmanships. In many other states, and more in senates than in houses, seniority is important, but leaders still have considerable discretion. They can use assignments to punish enemies on the one hand or to build support on the other. A speaker in a New England state, for instance, felt that former enemies could be converted into friends. He took all his caucus opponents and made them vice chairmen. A speaker from a midwestern state felt that legislators who stayed busy were happy legislators. He gave every house Democrat a chairmanship or vice chairmanship. Leaders also use their discretion to maintain control of key committees. What matters most, as far as assignments to important committees are concerned, is a member's responsiveness to the leadership.

Once members have their committee assignments or their chairmanships, the leader's power is diminished. Of course, leaders can always switch a member's position at the next legislative session. Or in exceptional cases they can remove a chairman right in the middle of the legislative session. A western senate leader did this, and in retrospect remarked, "I haven't had too much trouble with chairmen since that time."

Processing Legislation

Leaders have the job of moving bills through the multiple stages of the legislative process—initially referring a bill to committee, scheduling a committee measure for floor action, managing deliberation and decision in the chamber, negotiating the measure through the other chamber and perhaps to conference, and getting it signed by the governor.

At the outset, the presiding officer has responsibility in nearly all the states for referring bill introductions to standing committees.[5] Leaders are somewhat limited by the jurisdictional boundaries of the committees, but they exercise discretion when they want to do so. Usually, if they choose, they can send a sponsor's bill to a committee where the chairmen and members will treat it with favor, or they can send it to a committee where it will receive a cool reception. They may decide on "dual" or "consecutive" referral, so that a proposal has to be considered and reported out by two committees rather than by only one.

Leaders may also manage committee operations, developing a schedule for meetings and encouraging the chairmen to meet regularly. At times management goes further. One speaker divided up the standing committees into four groups, each with one or two major committees and a few minor ones. The majority and assistant majority leaders and the whip and the assistant whip were each assigned one group. During the session they met almost daily with the chairmen, kept on top of what was happening, and made sure that bills important to the party (and to the governor) got out of committee. In another state the leader required that prior to the session chairmen listed important issues their committees would address. The caucus then discussed them, the lists were made public, and the committees and the party were on record.[6] Where deadlines for committees exist, leaders ensure that bills are reported out on time. Where there are no deadlines, they can still prod the committees along.

Although it might not appear so, the scheduling of bills for floor action after they emerge from committee is as critical as any other leadership power. In a few states bills go directly to the calendar and in some they go to the calendar by way of a rules committee. Even where a rules committee decides, however, leaders still can exercise influence—having appointed the membership and making known their views on each bill that comes up. Years ago in the Wisconsin house, once a bill was reported out by a committee, it went on the calendar immediately and was debated in the order reported. If the speaker wanted to affect scheduling, he would have had to persuade chairmen to sit on bills, thereby delaying committee action and consideration on the floor. Then the system changed, with the party caucus each morning determining the day's order of business. The result was that once a week a member of the majority leader's staff prepared a draft calendar for the coming week, and after it was reviewed by the leadership, it went to the rules committee which had final approval.[7]

In most places, the scheduling power resides with the top leadership of the majority party. In New Jersey, one leader commented that "posting the bills is the major power of the speaker." The speaker ordinarily follows the wishes of the committee chairman and he customarily pays mindful attention to the "front office" (the governor and the governor's immediate aides). He will try to include one or two "showcase" bills at each daily session. To a large extent, the leader has to respond to what other people want; and, as a former speaker commented, "You don't have much of a choice after a while." But on the small things, speakers can be extremely powerful. They can help the members get their bills on the board, which almost always means they will go through; and, conversely, they can ignore their wishes and not schedule their bills for floor action. They can hold a member's bill, until the member casts a favorable vote on the budget or on another measure important to leadership. The scheduling power of leadership is probably as great in New York as anywhere else. The speaker here has almost exclusive control over whether and when a bill will come before the assembly. Bills can get lost or can be held up for minor technical amendments. If, by chance, a bill does find its way to the calendar and the speaker decides it should not be brought up for a vote, he may "star" the bill, which results in its being withheld from consideration until the star is removed.[8]

The speaker and the president or president pro tem also affect the processing of legislation in their capacity as the presiding officers of the house and senate. Most of their formal duties, in fact, relate to their roles as presiding officers. In Illinois, to take one illustration, the speaker must do the following: preside at all sessions of the house (but may call upon other members to perform temporarily the duties of the chair); open the session by calling the members to order; preserve decorum; decide all points of order, subject to appeal; decide, without debate, all questions relating to the priority of business; announce the business before the house in the order in which it is to be acted upon; recognize members entitled to the floor; state and put to a vote all questions and announce the results; guide and direct the proceedings subject to the will of the members; lay any bill or resolution before the house acting as a committee of the whole; and have general charge and supervision of the house chamber, galleries, and hallways and passages, and clear them when necessary.[9]

Presiding over the senate or house is a complicated matter. The presiding officer has to keep the session moving along. Some do it casually, but others insist on rigid adherence to the daily calendar, keeping members at their desks—refusing even to recess for supper—until the scheduled business has been done. The presiding officer must take charge and manage debate, recognizing members who want to speak on an issue and determining the order in which they speak. A former presiding officer of the Minnesota house reflected that, "By recognizing whom I want, I can see to it that debate flows and all views are presented."[10]

The presiding officer above all must stay in control, or at least, according to the speaker of Wisconsin's house, "must maintain the appearance of being in control," no matter how great the turmoil on the floor. The elevated dias allows him to see what is going on in the chamber, who is talking to whom, and what the majority leader and whips are about. He must anticipate what is likely to occur, and not allow himself to be surprised by a sudden motion or vote. "When you get in a jam," Oregon's president of the senate advised, "it never hurts to take a recess," thereby getting time to think things through and work them out. If the leader has a thorough knowledge of rules and precedents, he has a distinct advantage as far as maintaining control is concerned. He can be fair, and yet interpret the rules broadly, bend them some, and choose those best suited to his own purposes. The skillful leader is usually a master of the rules, like Republican Fred Anderson, the senate president in Colorado, who was presented by the Democratic minority with a blank rules book titled, "Rules by Anderson."

Negotiating Agreements

The leadership of the majority party will attempt to move major bills, resolve disagreements within the party, and pass legislation with as little conflict as possible. The minority leadership may oppose consistently, in the hope of creating issues to help overcome the majority in the next legislative elections, or it may bargain in order to have the majority's bills modified and to get some of its own legislation enacted. At the very least, the majority leadership can keep most bills that are contrary to party policy from getting out of committee or to the floor.

The initiative for legislation resides with the leaders of the majority party. They can either adopt an aggressive role, by setting an agenda for the legislative party, or a more passive one, by permitting the committees to determine what is important and then lending their support. Needless to say, few leaders can be placed squarely in one category or the other. But on substantive issues some lead more aggressively and others tend to the tasks of building consensus. The majority Republicans in the New York senate illustrate a case of strong issue leadership. The majority leader, Warren Anderson, had a staff of counsels, one of whom was assigned to each standing committee. In conjunction with his program staff, these counsels worked under Anderson's direction in developing a party program. Then the counsels ensured that committee chairmen and their staffs followed along. Florida's speakers of the house traditionally have announced their own programs and charged their committee chairmen with developing legislation to accomplish their general objectives. On some issues, too, leaders are inclined to play a prominent role. On revenue policy, the shots are likely to be called by legislative leaders. In the field of education also, leaders in over half of the states play a significant role along with chairmen of education, appropriations, finance, and ways and means committees. Here, their major involvement concerns matters of budget and finance.[11]

Aggressive policy leadership is probably the exception rather than the rule. On most issues leaders act primarily as mediators and facilitators for proposals advanced by their party colleagues. Kevin Harrington, former president of the senate in Massachusetts, is an example. He saw his leadership role as that of trying to build consensus within the ranks of senate Democrats. Generally he would keep things moving smoothly and fairly in caucus, stating the issues, the alternatives, and even his own preferences, and then "letting the chips fall as they may." If the caucus was sharply split, then Harrington would play a decisive part in moving or blocking a major bill. His ability to step in and take charge earned him the sometimes laudatory, sometimes sarcastic nickname "King Kevin" among legislators, lobbyists, and members of the press. But the critical point about Harrington's leadership on issues was that he intervened only when the Democrats were divided and the welfare of the legislative party was in peril.

Mediation is also the modus operandi in Montana. Leaders here try to keep ahead of controversy—looking for issues that threaten to divide the party and trying to work them out in advance. One majority leader used to keep in touch with the several ideological strains within his party by checking with an advisory group of colleagues. This way he could engineer compromises before an issue had crystallized and participants could no longer afford to compromise. At the same time the leader sought out those issues that would bring members together; then he purposely advanced them as party issues so that the caucus could rally round them.[12]

On issues of import to the majority party (or to the governor), leaders will exert all the power at their command to hold members together and pass legislation on the floor. In some states party discipline is relatively strong. New York is one of them. Joseph Carlino, a former Republican speaker of the assembly, commented:

> *Never once in the 15 years I've been here have we failed to get a Republican majority for a "must" piece of legislation, we Republicans have a tradition of discipline.*[13]

The power of the leaders in New York is considerable. Indeed, if the speaker does not like the outcome of a vote on the floor, he can instruct the assembly clerk "to check his records more carefully before announcing the vote." He will then send his lieutenants to the floor to persuade party members to change their vote or have absent members brought into the chamber in order to get the result he wants.[14] In most places, however, party discipline is lacking. Even in a state like New Jersey, in which party organizations are comparatively strong, most members are too independent to take instruction. A former Democratic speaker, thinking of the old days when a county leader telephoned to Trenton calling members off the floor to get the word, commented: "When you're speaker, you wish they would all go to the phone and find out what to do."

The party caucus (or "conference" as it is sometimes called) is a principal mechanism for a leader's negotiations with party members. Only about 15 percent of the states hold daily party caucuses, at least in one house, but about 50 percent hold weekly caucuses. The rest hold few caucuses, meet on call, or hardly meet at all once the session is underway.[15] Caucuses vary from state to state, from chamber to chamber, and from party to party. In Connecticut caucuses are still integral parts of the legislative process. Although they are held in both chambers, caucuses are more important in the senate than in the house. One member, in fact, asserted that the caucus is the "heart and soul of the senate's operations." Each senate caucus in Connecticut meets and discusses the daily calendar of legislation, with each member having some voice in what is decided.[16] The caucus is also significant in New York. In fact, the entire working of the assembly revolves around the majority caucus. The speaker needs 76 votes to pass a bill on the floor, and therefore makes it his business to gauge how his caucus feels. "On Monday I want to know who is unhappy with a bill, before I bring it up on the floor." If enough members are unhappy so that a majority is jeopardized, the speaker must know. By contrast, the caucus is not as critical in a state like Montana. Here caucuses are not scheduled regularly, but are called by leaders, depending upon whether an issue needs attention. In a Montana caucus a decision can be made on whether or not to make a legislative proposal a party issue. If it is decided to make a proposal a matter of party concern, members are asked if they would be able to vote for it. Individuals can go against the caucus, since there is no rule to bind them; most, however, try to go along with the party, especially if conscience and constituency permit.[17]

The caucus is a means of communication for leaders. In the words of one leader, "It is here that we try to provide all the information a member will need to understand the major bills coming before the legislature." Not only is the caucus a way to educate members, it is also a means for leaders to become sensitive to members' needs and views. A senate majority leader from a midwestern state suggested that it is more important for a leader to listen than to speak at a caucus. It was necessary, he advised, to conduct the caucus according to what he termed the "theory of the dance." To obtain any leadership objective, certain steps have to be gone through, even though it may be frustrating. A leader may want to move quickly to a conclusion, knowing where things will wind up; but he cannot do so, he must patiently bring his caucus along with him.

Today, even more than previously, leaders must be understanding and tolerant of dissent. Several expressed their overall approach to consensus building as follows:[18]

I guess the most important thing to realize is that everyone's view is legitimate.

[A Republican leader from a Democratic district] I could never vote 100% with my party, but I never did anything that would hurt my party. . . . Now I try to be understanding toward my fellow legislators when they *can't go along. By being understanding, I keep a united party when it's really important.*

. . . almost every member thinks that he is more important than almost everyone else and wants things on his *own terms. With all of the big egos around here, I'm sometimes amazed that we're able to get along and accomplish anything.*

Above all, leaders appreciate that legislators represent their own unique districts and that their districts and their reelections come first. On those few occasions when district interests are at stake or public opinion in the district really expresses a mandate, leaders will be extremely tolerant of dissent. Even authoritarian leaders of disciplined legislative parties make allowances for the district. The speaker of the assembly in New York, responding to Governor Carey's tax package in 1977, realized that a "yea" vote would hurt upstate Democrats facing reelection in Republican areas, but would not matter to New York City Democrats. So the speaker did what leaders usually do—he gathered the 76 votes necessary for passage from members with the safest seats, thereby letting the endangered assemblymen from upstate "off the hook."[19]

Although negotiating agreements within their own legislative party is their basic task, leaders must also deal with their opposites in the other party. The relationship between the majority and the minority parties depends in large part on political tradition, on whether one party is always in control or power alternates periodically, and on whose man (or woman) is in the governor's mansion at a particular time. Where party control shifts periodically, relationships are apt to be good. Members in the majority realize that one day they may very well be in the minority, and therefore they treat the minority fairly so that they will be treated the same way when the tables are turned. The relationship also depends on the relative size of the two groupings. If the majority has enough votes to carry all the procedural motions, the minority may be ignored; but if the numbers are close, collaboration may be required in order to get the business of the chamber transacted.[20]

The majority-minority relationship also depends on the individuals involved, and whether leaders respect one another and can cooperate. The majority expects the minority to oppose. And the minority expects to lose most of the time it opposes. But pragmatic majority and minority leaders recognize it to be in their interest to work together to get their business done. "He'll [the minority leader] try to cut my legs off on the floor," was the way one speaker put it, "but I still expect to be able to deal with him as a colleague." Although there are instances where the opposition is dogmatic and relationships are personally tense, much more often than not leaders do work together. It helps the majority leader particularly to have strong opposite numbers with whom to deal. The speaker of the Florida house recalled that it was up to him whether to make the minority leader strong or weak. "In Florida we want to make him strong," he said, "it's easier that way." In more evenly balanced states, too, everyone gains if the minority leader can "keep his boys in line" and not let them run off in all directions.[21]

Leaders not only must deal with their opposite numbers in the same chamber, but they must reach agreements with leaders in the other chamber as well. Here, too, it is generally in their interest to negotiate with opposites who can deliver. After Warren Anderson, the majority leader in the New York senate, lost control of his troops for a period of time on a major issue, the reaction by the majority Democrats in the assembly was sharp. A top aide to the speaker stated publicly: "We've got to be able to negotiate with a leader, knowing his people are behind him. We're not going to be able to negotiate with 30 different senators."[22] The new assembly speaker, however, acknowledged that Anderson usually did have command. On assuming office, he announced, "He doesn't know it yet, but we're going to have a very close and warm relationship"—not necessarily on substantive issues, but on the problems of the two houses.[23]

In places where state and local parties are strong, leaders must also negotiate with them. It is not unusual to find a senate or a house leader in frequent contact with a state or county party chairman. In former days John Bailey, who headed the Democratic party in Connecticut, would actually attend Democratic caucuses in the senate. Nowadays state party control of the Connecticut legislature is much weaker. Yet, legislative and state party leaderships are integrated. Recently integration has been achieved in part because the same individual served simultaneously as legislative leader on the one hand and Democratic state chairman on the other. He saw no conflict between the two jobs and, in fact, viewed them practically as one:

> The State Capitol [he wrote] is the focal point for political action during the legislative session. . . . My predecessor, John M. Bailey, spent most of his time as chairman at the State Capitol during the winter and spring months when the legislature was in session. Thus, I have a head start. . . . I am in constant contact with the Democratic members of the General Assembly as well as the elected officials of the state. The governor's office, for instance, is right down the hall from mine.[24]

A legislative leader must negotiate with the governor on behalf of his house and with his house on behalf of the governor. In some places this is as important as any other aspect of the process. New York is one such place, where the study of legislative politics is "considered to be primarily the story of personal negotiations between the governor and the legislative leadership."[25] Where the governor is especially powerful, leaders see themselves primarily as his or her lieutenants (when the governor is of their own party). Where the legislature is stronger, leaders tend more to be spokesmen for the legislative party. Whatever the relationships, leaders will bargain with the governor for whatever they can get in return. Some are very effective at it. Former speaker William Ryan of Michigan was patient and would spend as much time as necessary negotiating with the governor. One colleague described how he had seen him wear down Governor George Romney in negotiations on a tax bill: "He stole everything but the buttons off the Governor's shirt. . . ."[26]

Dispensing Benefits

Appointive leadership positions and committee chairmanships are the most visible benefits that legislative leaders can bestow on rank-and-file members. But they are by no means the only ones. The "goodies," as benefits are called in many places, range from help with bills and appropriations for the district to patronage appointments and the day-to-day necessities of life in the legislature.

According to one expert on political personality, a large part of what party leadership does is manipulate members' expectations, convincing them that it has control over the distribution of political rewards and punishments, and that it will distribute them in such a way as to maximize support for the party.[27] But for many legislative leaders, conferring (or withholding) benefits is here and now, not in the future.

What they can do to get a bill passed may be as important as anything else for an individual member. Leaders may co-sponsor a rank-and-file bill, thereby giving it greater visibility and obtaining for the member attention in the press. They can assign the bill to an easy committee, bring it up on a good day, and get it through the other house. In case of some hitch, they can persuade the governor to sign it. Also important are what leaders can do to get an item in the state budget for programs or big construction projects in a particular district or how they can shape the drafting of a state aid formula so that one district comes out ahead of others.

There is also political patronage, which varies in abundance from one state to another. In places like Pennsylvania, New Jersey, New York, and Illinois, legislative leaders have considerable patronage power at their disposal. Such patronage ranges from jobs in state agencies to appointments to judgeships and statewide boards and commissions to contracts for favored firms. All of this can go to the friends and constituents of certain members and not to those of others.

Not to be dismissed is what leaders can do to make the daily life of individual legislators somewhat more comfortable. Salaries are not subject to manipulation. But assistant leaders and committee chairmen in some states are paid additional compensation; thus the leaders responsible for such appointments can confer very material benefits here. Additional perquisites range from the somewhat more to the somewhat less, and leaders decide whether the member gets the former or the latter. There is travel to interstate conferences, extra professional or secretarial staff assistance, and additional allotments of stationery.

In some places, such as Florida, leaders have a measure of discretion in assigning seats on the floor of the senate or house. They can make life unpleasant by banishing "uncooperative" members to far corners in the rear of the chamber or seating someone next to a particularly obnoxious rival. A past speaker of the Florida house utilized assignments so well that he became known as "a master of the subtleties of seating when it came to his adversaries."[28] Practically everywhere leaders allocate office space. They may choose to use relatively automatic criteria in their allocations so as to escape the pressure from members and not create ill will. Or they may use offices to reward the faithful with choicer suites, larger rooms, or better locations. Finally, there is the assignment of parking space, frequently as troublesome and as vigorously contested a business as anything else in the legislature. In certain states it is possible to determine one's status by one's automobile's location. Leaders, chairmen, and the closest associates of the speaker in the Florida house park either in the new capitol building garage or near the door of the garage in the house office building. Others park further away, and some park one level down.

What the leaders give, they can also take away. Extra staff, comfortable offices, and convenient parking are occasionally removed if the member gets too far out of line. What happenend to a freshman Democrat in the Pennsylvania house, who defied his leaders by voting repeatedly against the budget in the summer of 1978, may or may not be a mystery. As it was reported in the press, the freshman found workmen in his office on the top floor of the capitol when he arrived one day. "I asked them what they were doing, and they said they were taking my typewriter. I laughed—until they picked it up and left." Several days later the telephone went dead as the legislator was making a call. He suspected that the source of his equipment problems was the house majority leader. But the latter denied it all. "I don't know anything about it," he said. "I doubt that it happened." But after an appeal to the speaker, telephone service was restored.[29]

Leaders can also affect a member's reelection prospects. Some raise and distribute money to their party's candidates. Jesse Unruh, speaker of the California assembly in the 1960s, played a major role in raising campaign funds for Democratic candidates for the assembly. Democratic legislators became dependent on Unruh. Lobbyists did not like it, and as one veteran of the Sacramento scene said: "Most members of the Third House would prefer to give directly to candidates so they know where the money is coming from. When you give to one of Jesse's dinners, the money comes from him." That is exactly what Unruh had in mind.[30] California leaders since Unruh have been primary collectors of campaign funds for members of the legislative party. After almost being ousted from office, Leo McCarthy decided to concentrate on raising campaign money for assembly candidates—whose votes he needed to be reelected speaker in 1981. "We're planning to try to raise $2 million and we think we can do it," McCarthy announced.[31] This California innovation is spreading to other states. Modest amounts have been collected and distributed by Democratic leadership in Connecticut, Kansas, and Michigan. Somewhat more has been contributed by both legislative parties of the senate and house to candidates in Pennsylvania and Washington.[32] In New York state, the funding process works through four campaign committees in the legislature—one for each party in each house. They support incumbents, obscure the sources of funds from candidates, and provide further power for the leadership that has much to say about who gets how much.[33]

Relatively infrequent, but very important to a member's reelection prospects, is reapportionment which occurs after each census. When the legislature does the redistricting, leaders are able to dispense rewards or punishments here. They can help reapportion a member almost out of existence by putting him in a district favoring the other party or putting him in a district with another incumbent. Or they can help ensure that the lines on the map are drawn so that the district is safe for him. It is not surprising in many places that cooperation and loyalty by the rank and file increase as the decennial reapportionment draws closer.

Handling the Press

One of the most difficult and frustrating jobs for legislative leaders is representing their political institution to the capitol press. The relationship between journalists and politicians was never blissful, but it is especially strained today in this era of antipolitical feeling and investigative reporting. A veteran of the New York senate, in anticipation of his retirement from the legislature, commented on the changes that had taken place in Albany. "The days of the reprinted press release and confidential drink at the DeWitt bar are over," he wrote. "In its place has come an adversary journalism which is sarcastic at best and vicious at worst."[34]

The capitol press corps is a challenge for leaders. Novice reporters are unfamiliar with the legislature, ambitious ones want to move up, hungry ones have to move out, and older ones are stuck at the state house and may become cynical. Legislative leaders have begun to despair. They cannot win over the press, no matter how hard they try. As far as they are concerned, the typical press response to a grueling legislative session is: "Besides adjourning, the legislature didn't do anything else that was positive this year."

On getting together to compare experiences at regional and national conferences, leaders waste no time before matching war stories about the unfairness of the press. One leader expresses a fear that when there is no hard news, reporters with time on their hands and blank paper to fill "will surely do the devil's work." Another admonishes, "Don't screw up on a slow news day."

And another recalls that at one time the press would only listen to reliable legislators, but now they listen to the "nutcakes" as well. Because of the competition for colorful news, "if one reporter doesn't print what the nutcakes say, then another one will."

Legislative leaders do their best to persuade the press to be more understanding. There is a story—perhaps apocryphal—of one southern leader who at a national conference moaned to several colleagues about the unfair treatment he was receiving from a newspaper in his district. A few years later, the legislator ran into the same colleagues at another national meeting, and they asked him how the newspaper had been treating him lately. He told them that its treatment had improved markedly. They were printing his press releases, and going out of their way to cover his activities, and even praising him editorially. His colleagues wondered what had happened, and asked, "What did you do to change the paper's attitude?" His reply was, "I bought the paper." Few newspapers are for sale and few legislators, even leaders, can buy out the press. Some try to persuade the press by other means. In several states legislative leaders meet regularly with newspaper editors, and find that their relationships with reporters improve as a result. On occasion, legislative leaders persuade their colleagues to get tough. The house in one state enacted a bill that would have caused newspapers to raise the wages of delivery boys who had to deliver thick advertising inserts in Sunday papers. The bill lost by a narrow margin in the senate, but the lesson was not ignored by the newspaper press. Its attitude toward the legislature became friendlier.

Not too much can be expected as far as the relationship between the press and the legislature is concerned, and most leaders realize this. A speaker of the house of a New England state summed up: "I tried it all ways—but ultimately you get a kick in the teeth." Therefore the only sensible approach is to

> *Acknowledge the press as adversaries—then you won't feel badly when they treat you badly. . . . It's a no-win proposition. The best you can do is get a standoff.*

A standoff is a reasonable outcome. For it is in the very nature of the legislative and press beasts, of their needs, and of their interactions that the legislature will provide a target for criticism rather than an object of respect.

Maintaining the Institution

The maintenance tasks of legislative leaders are essentially twofold. First, there are the day-to-day problems with which leaders must cope; and second, there are the longer-term problems confronting the legislature as an institution.

It is not possible here to enumerate the multiplicity of the nitty-gritty demands on leadership, but the reflections of one majority leader, after a few weeks in office, give some idea of the range:

> *. . . just the other day one member came in and asked me to help him*
> *out. It seems he and another legislator were arguing over whose secretary*
> *should type a bill they were co-sponsoring. Each thought his secretary*
> *could do a better job. I never thought I'd have to spend time on these*
> *things. And then yesterday, someone else came in to get me to talk to his*
> *wife about the problems she was having with him being here all week.*
> *Marriage counselor, father confessor, arbitrator . . . all "rolled into one."*
> *I'm glad I like people or I'd never put up with listening to all these types*
> *of problems people bring me.*[35]

Leaders must soothe their members by having an open-door policy and
holding "confession" sessions or by other means. They have to supervise
administrative staff of the chamber — the clerk and the sergeant-at-arms and
their employees. They have to supervise the other staff agencies, which perform
research, bill drafting, fiscal review, audit, and legislative reference services.
That means taking time to pay attention to what staff is doing and how well it
is doing it. As one leader commented, "Having the right staff helps, but having
a staff that knows that I care and am concerned about what kind of job they
are doing is as important.[36] It is up to leaders to allocate resources, schedule
meetings, plan on the use of facilities, and budget for the operations of the
legislature.

Beyond the immediate necessities, leaders concern themselves not only
with the momentary health of the institution, but with its future health as well.
They are the ones who devote themselves to improving and strengthening the
legislature — making procedures more efficient, expanding facilities, developing
professional staff and information, improving the legislative image, and en-
hancing the ethics, reducing the conflicts of interests, and increasing the
participation of individual members. What distinguishes the best among legislative leaders is that their major contribution has been to the legislative
institution itself.

NOTES

1. National Conference of State Legislatures, *Managing the Legislative Process: A Manual for New Legislative Leaders*, dated 1978 (hereafter referred to as NCSL, *Legislative Leaders' Manual*). Quotations reproduced by permission.
2. Ibid.
3. Ibid.
4. Paul L. Hain, "New Mexico: A Cross-Party Coalition," in *Comparative State Politics Newsletter*, 1 (October 1979), p. 17.
5. In a few places, such as Ohio, the responsibility for assigning bills is with a special reference committee.
6. NCSL, *Legislative Leaders' Manual*.
7. Carol Steinbach and Fran Valluzzo, "Matters of Time: How Legislatures Schedule It, Conserve It, Use It," *State Legislatures* (July/August 1978), p. 25.

8. Peter A. A. Berle, *Does the Citizen Stand a Chance?* (Woodbury, N.Y.: Barron's Educational Series, 1974), pp. 20-21.

9. Samuel K. Gove et al., *The Illinois Legislature: Structure and Process* (Urbana: University of Illinois Press, 1976), pp. 140-141.

10. NCSL, *Legislative Leaders' Manual*.

11. These are the preliminary results of a study of State Legislative Education Leadership being conducted by Susan Fuhrman and the author under a grant from the National Institute of Education and the Ford Foundation.

12. Lawrence Pettit et al., *Legislative Process in Montana* (Helena, Montana, July 1974), p. 20.

13. Quoted in Leigh Stelzer and James A. Riedel, *Capitol Goods: The New York State Legislature at Work* (Graduate School of Public Affairs, State University of New York at Albany, December 1974), p. 29.

14. Berle, *Does the Citizen Stand a Chance?*, p. 22.

15. National Conference of State Legislatures memorandum, dated March 1978.

16. Wayne R. Swanson, *Lawmaking in Connecticut* (New London, Conn.: 1978), p. 44.

17. Pettit et al., *Legislative Process in Montana*, pp. 21-22.

18. NCSL, *Legislative Leaders' Manual*.

19. *The New York Times*, January 16, 1977.

20. NCSL, *Legislative Leaders' Manual*.

21. Ibid.

22. *The New York Times*, April 3, 1978.

23. *The New York Times*, January 4, 1979.

24. William A. O'Neill, "The Art of Compromise and Coordination," in Clyde D. McKee, Jr., ed. *Perspectives of a State Legislature* (Trinity College, Hartford, Conn., 1978), p. 79.

25. Robert H. Connery and Gerald Benjamin, *Rockefeller of New York* (Ithaca, N.Y.: Cornell University Press, 1979), p. 79.

26. Gerald H. Stollman, *Michigan: State Legislators and Their Work* (Washington, D.C.: University Press of America, 1978), p. 75.

27. James David Barber, "Leadership Strategies for Legislative Party Cohesion," *Journal of Politics*, 28 (May 1966), p. 353.

28. *The Tallahassee Democrat*, November 20, 1978.

29. *The Philadelphia Inquirer*, September 13, 1978.

30. Lou Cannon, *Ronnie and Jessie: A Political Odyssey* (Garden City, N.Y.: Doubleday, 1969), pp. 191-192.

31. *The New York Times*, February 3, 1980.

32. *Comparative State Politics Newsletter*, 1 (January 1980), pp. 19-20.

33. *The New York Times*, May 14, 1979.

34. Jack E. Bronston, "The Legislature in Change and Crisis," *Empire* (October-November 1978), p. 41.

35. NCSL, *Legislative Leaders' Manual*.

36. Ibid.

Discussion Questions

1. Contact some members of your state legislature. What are their opinions regarding the impact of legislative reform in the 1960s and 1970s?

2. Try to discover the ways in which the legislative leaders in your state achieved their positions. What are their backgrounds and how did they win party support?

3. Review the process by which your state legislature will be reapportioned after the 1980 census. Have Democrats or Republicans gained legislative seats in your state since reapportionment in the mid-1960s?

4. Are Cho and Frederickson unduly cautious in their evaluation of the effects of reapportionment?

CHAPTER FIVE

GOVERNORS, MAYORS, AND BUREAUCRATS

One of the most important responsibilities that must be met by both governors and mayors is management of their respective bureaucracies—the collections of civil servants who make up the various departments, agencies, and bureaus of state and local governments. One reason for this is the financial significance of such bureaucracies. Their salaries and assorted fringe benefits account for substantial proportions of all state and local budgets. A further reason is their unique importance to the ability of state and local governments to deliver promised services to their citizens. After all, it is bureaucrats, not elected politicians, who fight fires, operate public schools, monitor pollution levels, and provide all the other services that we have come to expect from our state and local governments.

However, effective management of such bureaucracies is not easy. They are often enormous in size, and their formal structure may be so fragmented as to make it difficult for the governor or mayor to know which units have actual responsibility for the delivery of specific services. Such important agencies as a police department or school system may not be directly accountable to the governor or mayor but to a board or commission whose members are not subject to direct control by the chief executive. Bureaucracies have enormous expertise in their specialized fields, an expertise that few politicians can match and that allows them to counter many an executive order with the apparently unanswerable argument that "it won't work." Many have ties to interest groups, legislative committees, and even federal bureaucracies, and these ties can be used to stop executive attempts at control.

Each governor and mayor brings his or her own approach to this task of bureaucratic management, an approach that is a product of such variables as the individual's personality, the importance he or she attaches to this particular task, the unique characteristics of the bureaucratic system that is to be managed, and the political resources available to the governor or mayor. In the first article in this chapter, Martha Wagner Weinberg examines the management

135

style of one governor, Francis Sargent of Massachusetts. The article contains a good analysis of the variables that led Sargent to adopt his particular style, the resources he brought to the task, and the reasons why he treated some agencies differently than others.

Like the federal government, state and local governments have generally established "merit" systems as a basis for managing the personnel who make up their bureaucracies. Such systems emphasize objectively determined merit in the employment and promotion of individuals, and also a precise system of rules and procedures for the determination of relative merit. Theoretically, a merit system should make it easier for governors and mayors to effectively manage bureaucracies by insuring that they are composed of people who are well qualified to carry out their assigned tasks. However, these systems may sometimes become an actual impediment to effective management. In the second article in this chapter, E. S. Savas and Sigmund Ginsburg examine New York City's merit (or civil service) system, and demonstrate graphically just how such a system can in fact evolve into something that makes the governor's or mayor's management responsibilities even more difficult to carry out than they would be otherwise.

Gubernatorial Style in Managing the State

Martha Wagner Weinberg

In the common parlance of politics, the descriptions of chief executives as "managers" and as "leaders of large organizations" often are used interchangeably. In fact they imply quite different things. All governors have to perform certain management functions, but they perform these functions according to their own preferences and styles. Just as it is important to identify what the management functions are that they perform, it is also necessary to understand the dimensions along which they vary in carrying them out and the kinds of choices they make that determine their individual styles of leadership.

Leadership in any large organization is a highly personalized commodity. Implicit in any definition of leadership is some notion of uniqueness of style or attributes that distinguish and identify both the leader and those who are led. Every governor develops his own leadership style. This style does not depend as much on the formal powers that he has or on the number of orders that he gives as it does on how he chooses to spend his time, what resources he uses, and whose advice and pleas for support he heeds.

Understanding the kinds of variation in gubernatorial leadership style is essential to drawing conclusions about the overall effectiveness of a chief executive's management and about how he compares with other chief executives. How he chooses to use his resources in managing agencies and how many of these resources he chooses to devote to management may be a legitimate criterion for judging his performance. In addition, a governor's leadership style may be important in defining the nature of his relationship with agencies. The mesh or clash between his style and the particular style of the agency with which he is dealing may be as important as the substance of policies he espouses in determining his success or failure at controlling the agency's behavior.

This chapter will look at how Sargent's own leadership style and the choices he made affected his management of state government. Sargent's relationship to the agencies was often directly influenced by the obligations he had as governor, by how management issues got on his agenda, and by how he used the resources available to him. By looking at these questions it is possible to understand not only some of the determinants of Sargent's own particular style of management but also some of the dimensions along which all chief executives may vary in their personal leadership styles.

HOW DO THE OTHER ROLES THAT A GOVERNOR HAS TO PLAY AFFECT HIS JOB AS MANAGER?

A governor, even if he wants to, cannot manage all the time. The extent to which he is able to spend time and energy managing his agencies is dependent on the other functions he has to perform and on their importance to him. Perhaps the most significant thing that can be said about Francis Sargent in this respect is that he did not especially enjoy the detailed work of agency management and therefore did not accord it a favored position among his duties. His job as "manager of the bureaucracy" and the demands it imposed on him for his time, attention, and resources had to be balanced against other demands. His own preference to stay clear of the particulars of agency management was reinforced by the fact that his ability to appear a credible manager was heavily dependent on his success at building resources and power in performing his other functions. This was especially true of his ability to remain a successful political figure because his legitimacy as an elected executive depended on his maintaining, or appearing to maintain, electoral support. It is therefore worthwhile to look briefly at the other roles Sargent had to perform and at the importance and attention he accorded them.

An analysis of Sargent's calendar indicates that he spent well over half of his time performing what generally might be labeled the "ceremonial" functions of the governor.[1] These include proclamation signings, swearing-in of public officials, and, especially, large numbers of public appearances. Appearances at ceremonial occasions are intimately tied to any ongoing campaigning a governor does and are often his best way of staying in the public eye. In Sargent's case, the jobs of ceremonial head of government and of campaigner were especially tightly linked and took large amounts of his time. There were two primary reasons for this. First, he was an ebullient and skilled campaigner who enjoyed public appearances. Unlike many governors who neither relish the role of ceremonial head of the government nor perform it with polish, Sargent thrived on it. In addition, to a large extent the Sargent political organization revolved around him personally. Although he is a Republican, Sargent's relationship with the state Republican party was strained to the point of involving Sargent in public disputes with the Massachusetts party leadership. The Republican state committee regarded him with suspicion because of his liberal policies, his appointment of many Democrats to positions in his administration, his refusal to back unilaterally all party candidates, and his lukewarm response to the candidacy of Richard Nixon and Spiro Agnew. Sargent, in turn, did not rely heavily on the state Republican party organization but instead built "Governor Sargent Committees" in each county in the state. Although several times he attempted to purge the Republican State Committee of his opponents, he relied on his own organization to attract the Independents and Democrats whom he needed to survive in Massachusetts, where a large majority of registered voters are Democrats and Independents. His organization was personally based, so public appearances were extremely important to his money-raising and general campaign efforts. Responding to these combined duties as ceremonial head of state, candidate, and head of his own electoral organization, not only was more pleasant personally for him than spending time managing the agencies but also kept him out of his office and used up one of his most valuable resources, his own time.

Sargent's role as spokesman to other branches and levels of government did not greatly interest him or his staff, and consequently they devoted little time to it. Although any governor must deal with the legislature, for several reasons Sargent did not mobilize an especially effective or lively effort to do this. First, during the six years Sargent was governor the General Court of Massachusetts was overwhelmingly Democratic, and partisan resistance to Sargent programs and initiatives was steady. In addition even the Republican minority had no strong loyalty to Sargent as party leader and often balked at his initiatives. His chances of being able to work closely with such a legislature and at the same time appear to be a forceful executive were low. Instead, Sargent's strategy was often to avoid the costs of dealing with the General Court and to portray himself and his policies as the "victims" of a partisan and parochial legislature.

In addition to the fact that the setting for dealing with the legislature was not favorable to Sargent, he did not devote an enormous amount of time to it because his staff was neither especially interested in it nor especially talented at dealing with it. His legislative liaison was a pleasant and mild ex-legislator who had limited interest in or taste for lobbying and arm-twisting bills through the legislature. Sargent's staff kept no records of favors they had done for particular legislators and they made few attempts to change votes or to lobby on any issues exept those that seemed within their grasp.

The governor's unwillingness to deal with the legislature can also be explained by the fact that neither the governor nor his staff members showed any particular fondness or respect for the legislature as an institution. Sargent had not served as a legislator. Two of his staff members (Kramer and Morrow) were former representatives, but when members of the governor's staff dealt with the legislature, they characteristically did so with a good deal of arrogance and in a manner that indicated they felt they were dealing from a superior position.[2] This combination of overwhelming partisan opposition and lack of staff interest and skill at dealing with the legislature meant that Sargent did not devote much time or energy to it. The importance of legislative support or opposition to agency budgets and policies also affected Sargent's ability to influence the outcomes of individual agencies' interactions and dealings with the legislature. This was true both in his enforcing his own policy preferences and in his preventing agency personnel from dealing directly with the legislature and paying little attention to him.

Sargent also took only a limited number of initiatives in dealing and cooperating with the state's other constitutional officers. Perhaps the main reason for this was that during the six years he was in office the other constitutional officers were Democrats. The job of attorney general has always been one potential stepping stone to the governor's office in Massachusetts. Sargent chose to ignore the attorney general as much as possible rather than to attempt to bargain or to joust with him over issues of concern to both of them. Attorney General Robert Quinn was not nearly so aloof from Sargent. He ran for governor in the Democratic primary in 1974, emphasizing in his campaign his investigations of the legality of many actions of Sargent's agencies.

Sargent did not devote much of his own time to dealing with other government jurisdictions, and he did not organize his staff so that the job fell naturally to any one of them. He had a representative in Washington who attempted to keep track of the Massachusetts congressional delegation and to serve as a liaison to large federal agencies, but his ties to the Nixon administration were neither strong nor close. As the Republican governor of the only state in the union in which Richard Nixon did not receive a majority of the popular vote cast in the 1972 election, he was not in a good bargaining position with the Nixon administration. He exacerbated his isolation from the national administration by being a spokesman for the liberal wings of the New England and national Republican governor's organizations, particularly on such issues as welfare, corrections, and the environment. In addition, he did not hold a prominent place in the hierarchy of the national Republican party. This meant that the little time he spent dealing with the federal government was as an advocate for a specific cause or as a supplicant, begging for funds.

The consequences of this for his management of the agencies were twofold. First, he had no easy or special access to federal monies to supplement state appropriations. Second, many of the agencies that built up special relationships with their federal counterparts did it without his help and therefore had access to funding and expertise that allowed them independence from him.

Sargent had no formal ongoing relationship or channel of communications with the cities and towns of Massachusetts, including Boston. Robert Wood argued in 1949 that the City of Boston and its problems are so influential for any governor of Massachusetts that "the organization of the executive branch is best discussed in terms of aids or deterrents to the governor's representation of the Boston interest."[3] The major movement of population to suburbs outside the Boston city limits made this not as true during the Sargent administration as it had been in 1949. But because of the overlap of government services as well as the location of the electorate in the state, cities in general and Boston in particular were important to Sargent. Despite this fact, however, neither the governor nor any staff person attempted to keep track of Boston's activities on a day-to-day basis or to work on a series of joint programs or policy plans. Kevin White, the mayor of Boston, had been Sargent's opponent in the 1970 gubernatorial campaign. Sargent kept himself informed of White's activities to the extent that they made him a potential rival and cooperated with him on issues on which both men could gain. However, neither in Sargent's own office nor in his administrative agencies was there a formalized liaison to the City of Boston. Kramer left his job as urban affairs advisor to become chief of the policy staff, and his old job was never filled. The major crises involving the City of Boston and other municipalities were handled on an issue-by-issue basis through informal channels of negotiation.

Sargent, like most other chief executives, devoted enormous amounts of time and personal resources to the duties of a governor that traditionally would not be regarded as "management." Most of his attention had to be directed to one primary objective: ensuring his political survival. Even when he "managed," he often did so because handling a crisis involving the agencies was important to his political future. Much of his ability to manage the agencies depended on his success at being able to perform these other roles credibly and to build up his resources with other institutions of government and with the electorate. These resources useful in managing the agencies could have been built up in a variety of different places with different results. Sargent's choice of investing his time primarily in his electoral organization, in campaigning, and in public appearances was the result both of his need to preserve his political constituency and of his own personal style.

For Sargent, the job of performing the managerial functions commonly associated with running a large organization often had to be forgone in favor of more pressing matters. If they were done at all, they had to be carried out by staff members or administrators in line agencies acting in behalf of the governor. The irony of this kind of management is that precisely because a political executive draws his legitimacy from being the single person elected to fill the job of governor, his managerial authority is difficult to delegate. Though Sargent supported his chief staff personnel in their policy decisions, there were many management issues on which he was legally and formally the final authority. Even if disputes were resolved or policies handled by virtue of his having delegated them to a staff member, he was often viewed as a weak executive by his agency personnel precisely because it was known that he had not made the final decision himself.

HOW DOES A MANAGEMENT ISSUE GET ON THE GOVERNOR'S AGENDA?

One important dimension along which governors differ is the importance they accord obligations other than management and the capital or leverage their performance of these obligations gives them in the political and administrative system. Equally important in understanding how chief executives manage and how they differ from each other is the question of how issues involving agencies get on their agendas in the first place. There is great variation among executives on this point. The way an issue gets on the governor's agenda and the extent to which a governor can control it may vary because of the differences in states. For example, one might speculate that a governor of a heavily populated, highly industrial state like Massachusetts or New York might have to spend more time dealing with issues put on his agenda by well-organized constituencies than the governor of a state like Wyoming or Idaho, where the population is less dense and where crises are likely to occur less frequently. In addition, how issues get on a chief executive's agenda may vary because of the style and interests of the person who holds the office. For example, in this respect Francis Sargent was extremely different from Richard Ogilvie of Illinois. Though both Sargent and Ogilvie were Republican governors of large industrial states, their agendas often consisted of very different kinds of issues. Ogilvie was fascinated by the question of how well the bureaucracy was working. He spent a great deal of time trying to measure the efficiency and effectiveness of agencies and working to improve the performance of large organizations he felt were not doing well. Sargent, on the other hand, when given a choice rarely put this kind of issue on the top of his agenda and, in fact, actively avoided working on questions of this kind as much as possible. Differences of this kind may indicate a good deal both about a particular governor's personal commitment and style and about the reasons for the autonomy or control with which individual agencies operate.

There are three distinctly different ways in which an issue can get on a chief executive's agenda. The first involves issues put on the agenda by the governor himself. A governor may take a firm stand on an issue or set of issues that he wants implemented, changed, or handled in the agencies because of his own personal commitment to them. The hallmark of the group of governors who might be labeled "activists" is the large number of these kinds of issues they publicly place on their agencies. This may involve overseeing a single set of issues during a limited period of time or it may involve a governor's "adoption" of a policy area or agency that becomes his pet project throughout his administration. In either case, he becomes closely identified with the management of this particular issue or agency because he has chosen it, because he has taken a strong stand on which his position is known from the outset, and because his own credibility is tied up with how it fares.

The second way a management issue may get onto the governor's agenda is if the public or some large group of the electorate puts it there. This kind of issue is similar in many ways to the first kind. Though the chief executive may not have been deeply involved with a particular department or agency, he must take a strong stand on the issue immediately because the electorate as a whole or some important segment of it may *see* him as responsible.[4] As on the first kind of issue, he becomes personally involved at the outset and his ability, real or perceived, to deal with the agencies involved and to convince or coerce them to respond to him becomes crucial. These are often "crisis" situations, such as a prison revolt or discovery of major fraud or errors in a welfare department. In instances of this sort, where his own credibility is at stake, his role as manager of the agencies may take on overwhelming importance and may force him to become intimately involved with the agencies. Even if one single issue is not important enough to determine his electoral future, the cumulative "box score" of how many issues with which he was closely identified he won or lost may become extremely important.

The third distinct kind of management issue that may get on the governor's agenda is different from the first two because of its visibility, its implications, and the demands that are made on the governor. These issues could be labeled "technocratic" or "bureaucratic" issues and are characterized by the fact that they first surface within the administrative agencies or because of a highly technical problem with which the agencies deal.[5] They may be the result of a clash between agencies over jurisdiction, method of operation, or allocation of scarce resources. They may involve highly technical issues that because of their complexity or because of the expertise required to understand them have little potential for arousing immediate public concern or public pressure. At least in its initial stage, this kind of issue may work its way up the administrative hierarchy to be dealt with by agency heads, commissioners, or division directors. Though the issue may become publicly visible, the individuals held responsible by those following the situation are likely to be administrators identified with one particular agency or substantive area of the bureaucracy. For example, a commissioner of public health may be perceived as the immediately responsible official in a controversy over whether a hospital should be allowed to expand. The first contact the governor's office has with such an issue is through a staff person. If the issue cannot be resolved, it may work its way up to the governor for a decision. Unlike issues on which he is personally involved, however, in this situation his major role is as mediator, not as advocate. His job is to be above the fray, to listen to arguments made by both staff and line personnel, and to hand down a decision. Although he may eventually end up with credit for such a policy or program, he does not involve himself initially either by visibly taking a strong stand or by going to war with or exerting strong pressure on the agency or agencies involved. In this situation, unlike those in which the governor is involved from the beginning, the advocates tend to be agency or staff personnel and it is their credibility, not the governor's, that is tied up with resolving or winning the issue.[6]

Technocratic issues are not immediately public, but a chief executive may sustain "losses" on them that may affect his ability to manage. He may become known for taking no initiatives at all on technical issues or for having an incompetent group of people working for him. Or he may "lose" because by deciding in favor of one advocate or another he may destroy the morale, effectiveness, or goodwill of a staff person or agency head who in day-to-day activities is supposed to speak for him. It is also possible to find out a good deal about the nature of the long-term strength and responsiveness of the relationship between the governor and any particular set of agencies by looking at whether the governor attempts to manage and maintain an interest in an agency only at a time when his personal credibility is at stake or whether he takes a more active interest in the day-to-day workings and activities of the agency.

Though it is possible to find individual examples of all three kinds of issues' getting onto Sargent's agenda, it is clear that his own style and personal preferences dictated that most of the time he spent on management issues involved those he dealt with because he perceived a public demand that he manage or avert a crisis. When Sargent took office, he had no strong personal commitments to particular agency policies. His natural inclination was toward being a mediator rather than an activist, and this personal preference caused him to wait for technocratic issues to surface on their own rather than to rummage around the bureaucracy searching them out. Because his own and his staff's temperamental preferences were to deal with crisis issues, often resulting in the "crisis of the day" receiving enormous amounts of attention, most of Sargent's management effort was directed toward dealing with a few highly visible issues. The kinds of bureaucratic issues that had little potential for ballooning to crisis proportions often went unnoticed. Whether there was any initiative taken on them at all depended heavily on the strength and imagination of the staff person assigned responsibility for that functional area, of the cabinet secretary, or of agency personnel.

Policy areas in which the Sargent administration became known for taking initiatives included health regulation, environmental policy, provision of children's services, right to privacy legislation, transportation policy, "deinstitutionalization," welfare management, and correctional reform. Sargent took firm stands on environmental management, correctional reform, and deinstitutionalization after specific possibilities for policy in these areas were presented to him by his staff. He associated himself closely with bold policies in these areas and had to take an ongoing interest in the agencies that dealt with them. When he had to fire his radical and highly controversial commissioner of corrections, John Boone, public response focused on the governor personally and on his ability to handle the situation. The issue became a crisis as well as a question of personal commitment for the governor and caused him to become intimately involved with the Department of Corrections.

The governor's initiatives in welfare made him equally visible and vulnerable. Like his concern over correctional issues, Sargent's interest in managing the welfare issue was the result not of a strong set of beliefs about welfare management but of the chronic sense of public dismay about the Department of Public Welfare. Sargent asked that the state assume control of the welfare system and made major administrative changes in department operations because of the system's high cost and because of the public's anger over the issue. He as governor was seen as responsible for the welfare issue, so he *had* to take initiative and *had* to familiarize himself with the department and with the most controversial of its policies.

Sargent's moratorium on highway building was not as clear cut a response to crisis, but it was a response to crisis just the same. His announcement of the highway moratorium was precipitated both by public outcry and by his having been persuaded by Kramer and a series of allies from a variety of anti-highway constituencies that the issue had reached crisis proportions.[7]

On all of these issues involving an immediate and highly visible position taken by the governor, control of the agencies involved became an important issue for the governor and his staff. These agencies were often closely scrutinized and constantly had broad (and sometimes strict) parameters of action laid down for them by someone close to the governor, if not by the governor himself. Their performance was closely watched, and commissioners or high-ranking agency personnel were removed from office or resigned at a far greater rate than those of other agencies.[8]

Some of the policy positions for which Sargent was known did *not* involve immediate action on his part initially but instead surfaced first at lower levels of the government. These included protection of the public from large-scale data gathering by government and limitation of access to data-gathering facilities, creation of an Office for Children to extend the state's network of children's services, and initiation of a strong health regulatory mechanism. These issues differed markedly from the crisis issues both in the governor's treatment of them and in the consequences of that treatment for the state's agencies. They involved problems that normally would have been considered "technicalities" of running a bureaucracy and as such might have escaped public notice indefinitely. They usually surfaced because of the particular preferences, interests, and talents of someone in an agency or a junior "functional specialist" on the governor's staff or a combination of both. For example, the emphasis on children's services (particularly on foster care and adoption) came from Elton Klebanoff, a lawyer who by adopting a child had become involved with the state's array of children's service agencies. Andrew Klein, who initiated the effort to block massive accumulation of data on individuals by the state and federal governments, had picked the issue as a nonthreatening one with which to deal with the agencies for which he had been designated the governor's liaison and in order to focus his job beyond the amorphous assignment of being a special assistant for welfare, law enforcement, and public safety.

The staff member from the governor's office worked closely with agency personnel on each of these issues, providing support for and receiving support from the agency involved. Both Klebanoff and Stephen Weiner, the staff person most responsible for initiating the state's health regulatory legislation, made an effort to spend much time in the agencies assigned to them and based their opinions of what should be done more on the views of the personnel working in the agencies than on the guidance of the senior staff in the governor's office. The circumstances under which Weiner secured cooperation within the Executive Office of Human Services and the Department of Public Health were among the most fortuitous of any experienced by any functional specialist on the governor's staff. He knew the agencies and personnel involved in health regulation well and enjoyed the goodwill and confidence of the agency staffs. He began to work for the state at the same time that the secretariat's leading expert on health did, and he helped recruit and hire the commissioner of public health. He showed himself to be willing to work on the details of health regulatory policy and functioned at times as if he were a staff member of the agency. Finally, he enjoyed the confidence of both Kramer and the governor and was known in the governor's office as a person who asked for attention only when it was absolutely necessary.

The crisis orientation of Sargent's style was not without its costs, particularly as it affected the relationship between the governor and his agencies. There was intense competition among staff members and between staff members and agency personnel to provide a solution in a crisis. Because Sargent liked to hear all sides of an issue and then decide it, there tended to be losers and winners. Agency heads and agency personnel resented getting attention from the governor's office only in times of crisis, when they were often at their most disorganized. This style also promoted competition for the governor's time between the staff and the secretariats and agencies. The staff was concerned with and liked "managing crisis," even if the issue involved was simply the "crisis of the day." The agency and secretariat personnel, on the other hand, did not tend to see the major issues that concerned them as potential electoral crises for the governor but, rather, as issues that affected their working conditions and the capacity of the agencies to deal with policy. Finally, although there were some unspectacular policy initiatives on which agency personnel worked closely with members of the governor's staff, there was a certain randomness about these. They were highly dependent on whether anyone on the governor's staff was assigned to their agency and on the personality, talent, and personal preferences of the governor's staff member who was assigned.

WHAT MANAGEMENT RESOURCES DOES A GOVERNOR HAVE?

Having looked at variations in executive agendas, it is important to ask, once an item gets on a governor's agenda, what influences how it is managed and the success or failure of an executive's intervention? A governor's ability to manage a particular incident or to control an agency over a sustained period of time depends, more than on anything else, on the resources he is able to mobilize. Resources vary in kind and in importance. A resource is any identifiable set of goods, services, or skills that help someone reach a desired end. Political resources may be useful in only one situation or may be used continuously over a period of time. Political resources are often highly personalized—a resource for one political executive may not necessarily be a resource for another. For purposes of analysis, political resources important in management may be divided into three categories: personal resources, situational resources, and enabling resources.

Personal Resources

Personal resources include personal traits such as intelligence, humor, verbal facility, and personal political skill. They are the resources most difficult to generalize about because they are highly dependent on the individual manager's particular personality. Richard Neustadt has argued that the most important power a chief executive has is "the power to persuade," describing the chief executive's main task as "to induce them [those agencies with which he is dealing] to believe that what he wants of them is what their own appraisal of their own responsibilities requires them to do in their interest, not his."[9] One could argue that it is in exercising this "power to persuade" that personal resources are especially important, though difficult to identify or catalog from one situation to the next.

Sargent's personal appeal was considerable. Though he was not overwhelmingly articulate, even his detractors conceded that Sargent's charm and humor were among his strongest political assets. He was especially effective at using the media both in campaigns and during crises in his administration because of his ability to project a likeable, easy-going quality. For example, in his debates in 1970 with his Democratic rival for governor, Kevin White, the general consensus of the press was that though White had made his arguments more sharply and more articulately, Sargent had "won" the debates by appearing to be the nicer, more easy-going, less "political" of the two. The fact that he was not an "arm-twister" had both negative and positive implications for his ability to manage. He did not like "horsetrading" and bargaining with political favors, which meant that he did not exercise as much leverage with the legislature, other jurisdictions, his party, and even his own agencies as he might have. On the other hand, he was not negatively perceived as a "politician" who would sell his soul for a vote by either the other branches of the government or by the electorate in general.

Situational Resources

"Situational resources" are those highly diverse sources of help in managing particular situations that vary according to the particular combination of circumstances of an agency and the issues with which it deals. They are not constant in their value. For example, having a close and well-informed relationship with the chairman of the Committee on Ways and Means may be an extremely valuable resource for a governor when he wants to prevent cuts in the state's welfare budget, but it may not necessarily be a resource to him in attempting to pass a measure to change the process of judicial selection. Of all the kinds of resources a governor uses, situational resources are the most variable in their applicability and importance within any single administration. There are four especially salient kinds of situational resources: knowledge of the jurisdiction and of the political climate, technical expertise, clear authority, and the ability to define the management task or objective clearly. In dealing with one agency or situation he is trying to control, a governor may have to rely on his ability to manipulate and master only one of these resources; but in dealing with another situation, he may need to summon several or all of them.

Knowledge of the jurisdiction and of the political climate One resource that is important to any public manager, especially to a governor, is a detailed knowledge of the particular political environment in which he operates. For a governor whose jurisdiction is broad, this may involve detailed knowledge of the personalities and particular quirks of the other governmental institutions with which he has to deal. It also involves having enough experience to be able to identify key actors in any given political situation and to understand the composition and size of the pool of those politically talented or active in a given area. This kind of knowledge may be particularly important in making management decisions on issues with a long or controversial history or in selecting personnel for new jobs or to fill vacancies.

Sargent, like most governors, had spent most of his life in his native state, Massachusetts. Unlike many other governors, however, his career in Massachusetts government had been confined to jobs in the state bureaucracy in natural resources and public works and did not include service in the legislature, in any other constitutional offices, or in local government. He was familiar with the workings of two state agencies but not with the agencies of administrative oversight like the Executive Office of Administration and Finance. Although as governor he had to deal with a variety of governmental institutions, his only "apprenticeship" had been in an administrative agency. The result of this was that his knowledge of the important actors and of relevant information about the political process was largely confined to the general political climate of Massachusetts and did not include in-depth familiarity with or fondness for such institutions as the legislature or the lower levels of the bureaucracy.

Technical expertise Another crucial resource in any managerial situation may be technical expertise. Understanding a particular situation fully may require knowledge of one technical area. This may be especially crucial to a public manager at a level below that of the governor because the governor's responsibility is so broad that he could not possibly be an expert in all substantive areas falling under his jurisdiction. Even for a governor, however, technical expertise or access to someone possessing that expertise who is also loyal to him, may be a crucial management resource. The resource of technical expertise may also involve knowledge of how highly complex general government functions such as personnel systems or resource allocation mechanisms work. It may include an understanding of certain techniques for operations research, capital budgeting, or accounting. On questions that are so highly technical that how the question is put and what choices are outlined may determine the answer, trusted technical expertise may be a crucial management resource.

Sargent was an architect by training and, except in the fields of natural resources and engineering, he had had no formal academic or management training in any of the highly technical fields for which he was responsible. Because he took great pains to recruit competent professionals for high-level government jobs, his access to trusted technical expertise in such areas as transportation, housing, and welfare was good. His own grasp of the details of these particular areas or of the general complexities of administrative management such as budgeting or financial transactions was limited. His style of management was not to be a "details man." This meant that his access to the resources of technical expertise was not based on his own understanding of many issues, that it was highly dependent on the ability of his own appointees in those areas, and that it was extremely variable from one functional area to another.

Clear authority A third kind of situational resource is presence of clear authority. This authority may stem from the formal legal authority granted by the constitution or by law. It may also be informal and may be the result of a chief executive's ability to convince everyone that he is and should be in control of a situation or an agency. For an elected public manager such as the governor, this authority may come from an electoral victory widely interpreted as a "sweeping mandate." It may also come from the appearance of general support within agencies. In any case, the resource consists of being able to assume control of a situation in a context in which everyone involved believes that the governor has the legitimate right to do so.

The Massachusetts governor's formal authority is broad compared with that of governors in many other states.[10] The governor has a four-year term, can submit his own budget to the legislature, and can hire and fire his cabinet and most commissioners at will. Although Sargent submitted a budget to the legislature each year, he did not have the staff, the expertise, or the personal inclination to develop his budgetary power to be a significant resource and to use it as a mechanism to maintain day-to-day control over his agencies. He was less reluctant to use the power to hire and fire and to make it clear that he had the authority to do this.

Sargent was less adept at establishing his authority where there was no formal grant of power than he was at exercising his constitutional authority. Although he occasionally made policy by use of administrative fiat, he seldom used his budgetary power as a carrot or a stick in asserting his authority over the agencies. Similarly, he made little effort to use his legal staff to interpret agency statutes or regulations to give him leverage with the agencies. Finally, although he did often appeal directly to the electorate for support, very seldom did he use the argument that his decision should be final because of his popular mandate to govern.

Ability to define the management task clearly A fourth situational resource that may be the most crucial in determining how well an executive is able to manage a problem is his ability to define the job to be accomplished in such a way that it is capable of being reduced to a clear, simple, straightforward task. Whether this resource is present or absent may depend on the governor's ability to reduce a highly complex management situation to be a single task or to define the task in such a way that this becomes possible. It may also depend on the nature of the task itself, which may be so complex that it cannot be simplified without being distorted out of proportion.

Because it varies so much from situation to situation and from agency to agency, it is difficult to generalize about Sargent's use of this resource during his administration. To define the task of the Division of Employment Security ("to mail out unemployment checks") is less difficult than to define the task of the Department of Public Welfare. However, it is true that Sargent's temperament and style did not lead him to want to set fixed goals, especially arbitrary ones, for agencies. He did not deal frequently enough or closely enough with the agencies so that he could constantly measure or evaluate their performance according to any definition of their tasks. This meant that he did not make the effort to state or to simplify the complex goals of most agencies and then to take credit or blame for their performances or failures based on those goals. This was especially true of those agencies whose tasks were difficult to define. Sargent was more likely to ignore those agencies than to insist that they meet any goals set by him.

Enabling Resources

A third set of resources on which any governor draws might be called "enabling resources." These resources are much less likely to vary within any executive's term of office than situational resources and often allow a governor to develop his situational resources. Perhaps the most important of these enabling resources is staff assistance.[11] Also included among these resources are funding for the governor's office, time, and easy access to information. Although these resources are not always separable from situational resources, what distinguishes them from other kinds of resources is that they are not as valuable in and of themselves as they are for *enabling* a governor to build up other kinds of resources. For example, a large and well-funded staff may not by virtue of its existence be valuable to a chief executive but may only become important when it is used to build up other resources. Like all political resources, enabling resources have no inherent value, and their importance depends on whether and how they are used.

Sargent was aided in developing some of the resources necessary to control the agencies by several factors. Compared with many other governors, he had a large, well-financed staff.[12] Perhaps the greatest single determinant of how he was or was not able to utilize resources to manage was the way he designed his staff, which in turn often determined the other resources to which he had the best access. Sargent recognized his own penchant for being a mediator and built into his staff a variety of political views. By ensuring representation of a variety of views along the political spectrum, he made it possible for agencies with extremely diverse interests and for groups outside the government to find allies on his staff. He had some functional policy specialists on his staff who were willing to work as closely with the agencies with which they dealt as with their peers in the governor's office and who knew a great deal about the resources and information necessary to make the agencies behave as they wished. In addition, Sargent received a special bonus by being able to appoint all ten of the first cabinet secretaries to take office. The secretaries were to be "deputy-governors," appointed by the governor to manage clusters of agencies in particular functional areas. By deciding what individuals he was going to appoint, he was able to shape the expectations of both the agencies and the public of what the job of secretary should be and at the same time command personal loyalty from the individuals who took the jobs because they were *his* appointees.

Although the way he constructed his staff and the style with which it operated provided him with access to one set of resources, it also had its costs. The fact that he and his staff opted to concentrate most of their scarce resource of time on maintaining and polishing the governor's electoral image and on managing crises, coupled with the size of the job of running state agencies with a budget of more than $2.5 billion, meant that his attempts at dealing with complicated day-to-day issues were uneven. Particularly because he himself did not devote personal attention to agency matters, his "control" of the administration often depended on the agility with which his staff was able to perform in the difficult "minister-without-portfolio" role. They often had to speak "for the governor" in situations about which the governor, and often the staff member, knew nothing. This difficult role was especially complicated in the Sargent administration for two reasons. First, the incentives for any staff member to want to devote his time to dealing with the big issues, the "crises," were powerful because those issues were high on Sargent's own agenda. But the greater the competition to propose the solution to a crisis, and the more extremely and visibly a staff member stated his own position, the less likely he was to be seen as "speaking for the governor" by the agencies, especially if his solutions "lost" frequently. Second, not only did Sargent create a large number of situations for ministers-without-portfolio, but he also filled these positions, particularly those of "functional specialists," with young inexperienced generalists. An agency that wished to be intractable could mask what it was doing with technicalities and complexities totally unfamiliar to the staff person with responsibility. Also, because few of the members of the governor's staff aspired to holding down their positions after the governor was gone, the agency personnel could count on simply outliving the generalists.

The secretaries and commissioners were appointed by the governor, but because of the Sargent style of operating they were often pitted in deadly competition with the governor's own staff. The staff, busy with dealing with the issue of the day, had little time to focus on any but the most spectacular problems arising in the agencies. The secretaries and commissioners, on the other hand, were hired as full-time administrators and generally concerned themselves with issues different from those with which the staff dealt. Though to a certain extent this meant that responsibility was divided and delegated, it led to bloody battles and extreme competition between the staff and the agencies when each had to compete for the governor's time and attention or when the issue on which the governor had to focus lay in the agencies themselves. Often this competition, coupled with the governor's own reluctance to deal with the legislature, led some agency personnel to negotiate directly with members of the legislature, end-running the governor.

The style and quality of gubernatorial leadership of public agencies varies from governor to governor along several dimensions including the personal temperament of the chief executive, the kind of management he is called on to do, and the resources he can mobilize. But even within one administration, gubernatorial leadership and control can vary greatly from one agency to another. A governor's control and an agency's responsiveness depend not only on conscious decisions on the part of the governor but also on the nature of individual agencies. Different kinds of agencies demand different kinds of management. It is useful briefly to differentiate among kinds of agencies according to the kinds of circumstances in which a governor may deal with them.

The typology of these agencies corresponds roughly to that used to describe how particular issues get on a governor's agenda. Certain agencies require constant scrutiny because the public perceives the issues with which they deal to be on the governor's agenda. Other agencies require constant scrutiny because the governor has dictated that the issues with which they deal be given priority. A third kind of agency receives a governor's attention only when it is responsible for a crisis issue. Finally, some agencies handle matters that seldom if ever get on the governor's agenda.

Those Agencies Requiring Constant Scrutiny

The agencies that demand constant scrutiny may vary from one state to another and from one governor to another, depending on the governor's priorities and his own personal style. These agencies are of two kinds. The first kind is one in which a crisis would be so spectacular or in which the cost of a malfunction would be so high that the governor under no circumstances could affort not to attempt to anticipate it. In Massachusetts, for example, despite the limitations under which he operated in dealing with the bureaucracy, Sargent had to be familiar with the Department of Public Welfare and the Department of Corrections.

The second kind of agency a chief executive must constantly watch differs subtly but significantly from the first kind. It is an agency that must be monitored because it involves such heavy commitment of state money or personnel or such well-organized interests that a problem can cause an outcry or a response from some important constituency or constituencies and, potentially, from the public as a whole. The response to an error or a crisis may not be as clearly immediate as that to the volatile first category, but it may be equally important, either because of the implications for the long-run service provided or because of the importance of the constituencies involved. In Massachusetts one might cite the Department of Public Works or the Department of Public Health as examples of this second sort of agency. It is also important to point out that for these agencies in Massachusetts the more imminent the threat of crisis, the more likely it is that they will get the kind of attention that the agencies threatening constant spectacular crisis receive.

Those Agencies That Receive Constant Scrutiny Because of the Personal Preferences of the Governor

Some agencies receive attention not because of their size or importance or because they bristle with political bombshells but because the governor has some other interest in them. They may represent a substantive policy area in which he is interested or they may offer a particular resource on which he can capitalize, such as patronage jobs.

Francis Sargent came into office with no strong interest in how any one substantive area or agency of government ran. He was more interested in dealing with agencies on the basis of the seriousness of issues raised within their boundaries than in consistently following any agency or group of agencies that dealt with a substantive policy area of personal interest to him. Perhaps the closest he came to this sort of personal interest was his emphasis on the de-institutionalization of persons in state facilities. However, he was not a governor like Paul Dever, a Massachusetts chief executive who during his term adopted mental health as his pet issue and chose to keep close track of the Department of Mental Health.

Those Agencies That Receive Gubernatorial Attention Because of a Single Crisis

Every governor has a series of agencies that he generally ignores but that may suddenly become very important because of an unanticipated crisis. For example, in Massachusetts, until the time of the controversy over whether or not to develop the large section of downtown Boston known as Park Plaza, the governor and his staff had no idea who worked in the Department of Community Affairs or what went on there. As a consequence, during the crisis they had to act quickly on the basis of very little previous knowledge of how the agency worked or who in the agency could handle some of the decisions that had to be made. The fact that an agency is the source of a crisis does not necessarily ensure that it can be "crisis-managed," especially if neither the governor nor his staff has invested any resources in it before.

Those Agencies the Governor Leaves Alone

Finally, there is always a series of agencies that a governor makes no effort to control and that he deals with in a limited way or ignores. These agencies fall into two categories: those he leaves alone because of some calculated consideration on his part and those he leaves alone because of the nature of the agencies themselves.

There are several reasons a governor may make a deliberate choice to ignore an agency. First, he may not attempt to exert control over an agency because it performs as he would like. He does not have to use his scarce resources to persuade its personnel to behave as he would like or to make policies he wants because the agency personnel share the chief executive's goals for the agency. During the Sargent administration, the Massachusetts Housing Finance Agency was an example of this kind of agency.

A governor also may not intervene because he realizes that he does not have the resources or the authority to control an agency and may therefore be unwilling to go to battle with it and lose. Even in what may normally be regarded as a crisis, he may hold back from dealing with the issue (as Sargent did, for example, on issues involving higher education in Massachusetts) because he may not be certain of appearing to "win." Or a governor may not deal with an agency because he wants it to be known publicly that he is not fully responsible or in control of that agency. For example, Sargent often made it known that he did not go to battle with the Massachusetts Port Authority because he had no legal control over it.

Finally, a governor may not deal with an agency at all purely because of the nature of the agency. The governor or his staff may see it as having no potential for crisis. For example, in Massachusetts, most governors have assumed that the Massachusetts Department of Agriculture is an agency of this type. An agency may also be left alone because of the highly technical nature of its work. Or it may be ignored because it serves easily identifiable, single, specialized goals. In Massachusetts during the Sargent administration the job of the Division of Employment Security was to send out checks for unemployment compensation, a procedure that varied little from one month to the next.

This chapter has looked at gubernatorial leadership and style and at the characteristics of and limitation on it that affect how the governor manages his agencies and holds them accountable. It has also examined the variation in the kinds of response a governor may make to these agencies and has attempted to explain some general reasons for this variation.

NOTES

1. In order to find out how Sargent spent his time, I looked at his daily schedules, divided into fifteen-minute intervals, from 1970 until 1974. This analysis was obviously a rough one because often the calendar was changed at the last minute to meet a crisis and the issues considered at appointments with individuals or "staff time" often were not detailed. Still, over the period of four years, such an analysis of the calendar made it possible to arrive at a gross approximation of how the governor spent his time.

2. For documentation of two specific instances of this, see my papers on "Reorganization of Government: the Massachusetts Case" and "Correctional Reform in Massachusetts."

3. Robert Wood, "The Metropolitan Governor — Three Inquiries into the Substance of State Executive Management." Ph.D. dissertation, Harvard University, 1949, p. 112.

4. Though the leadership styles of political leaders to a certain extent are the result of conscious choices by political executives, it is clear that the issues with which they deal and the style with which they deal with them is often heavily influenced by the publics that are important to them. Leadership style is not only the result of the executive's personal traits but also of his perceptions of public expectations. As Murry Edelman points out in *The Symbolic Uses of Politics* (Urbana, Ill.: The University of Illinois Press, 1964) on p. 188: "Through taking the roles of publics whose support they need, public officials achieve and maintain their positions of leadership. The official who correctly gauges the response of publics to his acts, speeches and gestures makes those behaviors significant symbols, evoking common meanings for his audience and for himself and so shaping his further actions as to reassure his public and in this sense "represents" them."

5. The term "technocratic politics" is Samuel H. Beer's, and much of the discussion that follows is based on a helpful conversation with him. The distinction between a "public" issue and a "technocratic" one is not always clear cut. The number of paragovernmental groups in society makes it difficult to enforce this definition strictly. For example, technical advisors who work for government but who advise citizen groups may use their technical skills to clarify a public issue. However, the distinction is useful in trying to determine whether an issue reaches the governor's desk because of immediate public pressure or because it first surfaced within a technical elite and was "translated" into public business.

6. This is one of the points at which the distinction between a governor and his staff becomes obvious. In such a situation, when a staff person is operating as a "minister-without-portfolio" and/or as an advocate, he cannot sustain a large number of losses and still be closely identified as speaking for the governor.

7. For fine documentation of the whole highway moratorium incident, see Alan Lupo, Frank Colcord, and Edmund P. Fowler's *Rites of Way: The Politics of Transportation in Boston and the U.S. City* (Boston: Little, Brown and Co., 1971).

8. For example, the commissioner of public works, Edward Ribbs was fired in the middle of the highway crisis. Robert Ott was replaced by Steven Minter as commis-

sioner of public welfare immediately before the initiation of the flat grant system in the Department of Public Welfare. John Fitzpatrick was replaced by John Boone as commissioner of corrections after the first major uprising at the Massachusetts Correctional Institution at Walpole. Boone was subsequently removed when the prisons continued to flare up.

9. Richard Neustadt, *Presidential Power* (New York: Signet, 1960), p. 53. Although it is difficult to generalize about personal resources, most students of executive management of large organizations, both public and private, stress their importance. See, for example, James Sterling Young's *The Washington Community 1800-1828* (New York: Columbia University Press, 1966), p. 157ff and Kenneth Andrews' *The Concept of Corporate Strategy* (Homewood, Ill.: Dow Jones-Irwin, 1971), p. 227ff.

10. For a comparative analysis of the limitations on gubernatorial power see Douglas Fox, *The Politics of City and State Bureaucracy* (Pacific Palisades, Calif.: Goodyear Publishing, 1974), p. 26ff. It is important to note, however, that Thomas Dye has concluded that "there is little evidence that a governor's formal powers significantly affect policy outcomes in the fifty states." See Thomas Dye, "Executive Power and Public Policy in the United States" in Richard Leach and Timothy O'Rourke, eds., *Dimensions of State and Urban Policymaking* (New York: Macmillan, 1975), p. 128.

11. For an excellent analysis of how several presidents arrayed and used their staffs and of the consequences for public policy, see Richard T. Johnson's "Management Styles of Three U.S. Presidents." One of the points Johnson makes well is that there is no single "best" way to design a political staff, that each style has its costs and benefits.

12. Of all the governors or ex-governors attending the 1974 John F. Kennedy Institute of Politics seminar on "The Governor's Office"—including Hoff of Vermont, Peterson of New Hampshire, Holton of Virginia, Ogilvie of Illinois, and Evans of Washington—only Ogilvie had had a staff of comparable size.

The Civil Service: A Meritless System?

E. S. Savas and Sigmund G. Ginsburg

The nation's basic civil service law was written in 1883, following the assasination of President Garfield by a disgruntled job seeker. The goal at the time was both noble and urgent: to assure that the merit principle, rather than the patronage principle, would be used for the selection and promotion of federal employees. Subsequently, in reaction to the excesses of the spoils system which had prevailed for the preceding half-century, a civil service reform movement swept the land, spreading through states, counties, cities, and school systems during the next few decades. Today, the so-called merit system—the name given to the elaborate web of civil service laws, rules, and regulations which embrace the merit principle—covers more than 95 per cent of all permanent federal (civilian) employees, all state and county employees paid by federal funds, most state employees, many county employees (particularly in the Northeastern states), most employees in more than three fourths of America's cities, and almost all full-time policemen and firemen.

However, vast changes in government and society have taken place in the last 50 years, and the rules and regulations appropriate for 1883 have now become rigid and regressive. After 90 years, the stage is set for a new era of civil service reform. Recent court decisions have ruled out several civil service examinations which had no demonstrable relation to the job to be performed; scholars and political leaders recognize the many shortcomings of today's civil service systems; and now the general public is stirring as well. The citizen sees that government—and tax collection—is a growth industry. (If we extrapolate the current rate of growth of the governmental work force, by the year 2049 every worker in America will be a government employee!) He sees that job security (tenure) exists for his "servants" but not for him. State and local

Reprinted with the authors' permission from *The Public Interest*, No. 32 (Summer 1973), pp. 72-85.
© 1973 by National Affairs, Inc.

governments spend as much as the federal government (excluding defense), and the citizen can see *their* work at close hand in his daily life. And what he sees is *not* a merit system—certainly not in the common usage of the word "merit." The low productivity of public employees and the malfunctioning of governmental bureaucracies are becoming apparent to an increasing number of frustrated and indignant taxpayers. The problem shows up all over the country in the form of uncivil servants going through pre-programmed motions while awaiting their pensions. Too often the result is mindless bureaucracies that appear to function for the convenience of their staffs rather than the public whom they are supposed to serve. It is the system itself, however, rather than the hapless politician who heads it or the minions toiling within it that is basically at fault.

COUNTERPRODUCTIVE POLICIES

Imagine a large, multi-divisional organization with an annual budget of 10 billion dollars. Imagine further that the organization has the following personnel policies and practices:

- Most entry positions are filled on the basis of written examinations scored to two or three decimal places.

- There is no scientifically supportable evidence that these examinations are related to subsequent on-the-job performance.

- Once a ranked list of examination scores is established, management must choose one of the top three names on the list regardless of special qualifications, knowledge, experience, aptitude, or training or other applicants on the list.

- After an employee has spent six months on the job, he is virtually guaranteed the job for life, unless his supervisor files a special report urging that the employee be discharged or at least that the granting of tenure be deferred; it is very unusual for a supervisor to take such action.

- An employee, after acquiring such tenure, can be fired only on grounds of dishonesty or incompetence of a truly gross nature, and cannot be shifted to a less demanding assignment.

- An employee is "milked" of his ability and dedication, while given little significant opportunity for advanced training, personal development, career counseling, mid-career job change, or an enriched job that fully engages his evolving interests; no manager cares about this situation.

- Promotions are generally limited to employees who occupy the next lower position within the same division; qualified employees in other divisions of the organization are discriminated against, as are applicants from outside the organization.

- Promotions are made primarily through written examinations, with no credit given for good performance.

- Salary increases are virtually automatic and, with rare exception, are completely unrelated to the employee's work performance.

- Supervisors belong to unions, sometimes to the same unions as the employees they supervise.

- All personnel practices are regulated by a three-man commission, whose powerful chairman is the Director of Personnel. Managers and supervisors must defer to his judgment on all personnel matters except those involving top-level executives.

- The employee unions have enough political power to influence the decision concerning whether or not the chief executive is permitted to stay on; furthermore, they also influence the appointment of top-level managers.

One does not have to be a management expert to be appalled at this array of counterproductive policies or to predict that the hypothetical organization employing such policies would be laughably ineffective.

Unfortunately, neither the policies nor the organization is hypothetical. The foregoing is an accurate description of the venerable civil service system under which New York City is forced to operate. In summary, the system prohibits good management, frustrates able employees, inhibits productivity, lacks the confidence of the city's taxpayers, and fails to respond to the needs of the citizens. While this bleak picture may not yet be fully representative of all civil service systems in the country, neither is it uncommon. Furthermore, considering that New York often serves as a leading indicator of societal problems, this pattern, if it has not already been reproduced elsewhere, may be soon — unless a groundswell of popular opinion leads to a new wave of reform.

More than half of New York's 9.4-billion-dollar budget is spent on the salaries and fringe benefits of its employees. In the last decade, personnel costs have risen by roughly 150 per cent, while the number of employees has increased by about 75 per cent — to 400,000. (Genghis Khan conquered Asia with an army less than half this size; however, he used certain managerial techniques of reward and punishment which are mercifully denied to today's more circumscribed and more humane chief executive.) Of this number, about a quarter of a million (!) constitute the "competitive class" of civil service — that is, employees who are hired and promoted on the basis of competitive examinations. This is the aspect of the civil service system dealt with here.

In order to understand fully the shortcomings of the current system in New York, it is useful to look in turn at each of its major elements: the jobs themselves, recruitment practices, examinations, selection procedures, promotions, and motivational rewards.

JOBS, RECRUITMENT, AND EXAMINATIONS

Jobs

Very narrow, specialized jobs have gradually emerged, in part because this makes it much easier to produce an examination specific enough to give an appearance of relevance and fairness. Credentialism runs rampant, and pre-requisites are sometimes introduced with no discernable value except bureau-cratic convenience in the subsequent selection process. As a result, artificial and nonsensical divisions have proliferated, and New York City now has Methods Analysts, Management Analysts, and Quantitative Analysts, as well as Office Appliance Operators, Photostat Operators, Audio-Visual Aid Tech-nicians, Doorstop Maintainers, and Foremen of Thermostat Repairers. When the human cogs in the General Motors assembly line at Lordstown stopped working, it was a clear and obvious revolt against the dehumanizing nature of their activity. Could it be that the human cogs in the municipal machinery stopped functioning long ago, for the same reason, and we are just now indirectly noticing their sullen revolt?

Recruitment

The recruiting process for civil service is similarly arbitrary. The law requires only that advertisements of openings appear in certain specified, obscure places and in formidable terminology: the formal descriptions, in "bureaucrat-ese," of the narrow kinds of specialties mentioned above. The Personnel Department seldom goes far beyond this minimal legal requirement. This means that current employees (and their families) have an advantage over outsiders because they know where to look and how to decode the message. This fact, coupled with job qualifications of questionable value, serves to limit access into the service by other potential applicants.

In fact, this traditional process has been so ineffective that out of exaspera-tion a competing recruiting organization was set up within the Mayor's office, not for dispensing patronage, but for recruiting the kind of professional and technical personnel without which modern government cannot really function. The most capable managers in the entire organization devote much of their effort and ingenuity to subverting and bypassing the regulations in order to hire such recruits from outside the system.

Examinations

About 400 civil service examinations are conducted each year in New York City, at great effort and expense, and about half of them consist primarily of written tests. *Yet not a single case could be found where the validity of a written test—with respect to predicting performance on the job—was ever proven.* That this problem transcends New York's borders is indicated by the following statement by the U.S. District Court in Massachusetts in regard to an examination for police officer:

> *The categories of questions sound as though they had been drawn from "Alice in Wonderland." On their face the questions seem no better suited to testing ability to perform a policeman's job than would be crossword puzzles.*

Heavy reliance on written examinations at least has the advantage of being "safe." No bureaucrat need be saddled with the difficult task of using his judgment somewhere in the selection process. Exclusive reliance on an "objective" test score creates a situation where no one can be accused of favoritism or overt bias, even though a test may demonstrate inherent discrimination against certain cultural minorities.

At present, candidates who pass an examination are ranked on an eligible list based on their adjusted final average, *carried to as many as three decimal places.* (Adjusted final average is derived from the candidate's scores on the individual tests which comprise an examination: written, practical, technical, oral, etc., plus veteran's preference credit, where applicable.) A manager must appoint one of the top three scorers. Now, no one seriously contends that a person who scores 92.463 on an examination of dubious validity is likely to perform better on the job than someone who scores 92.462, or even 91.462. This scientifically unsupportable custom is just another defense against accusations of bias and should be abandoned. Test scores should be rounded off, thereby creating more ties and giving managers more choice and flexibility in selecting their subordinates from among those candidates with the same score. The potential impact of this change, recently endorsed in New York City by Mayor Lindsay, can be indicated by noting that on the 1968 examination for Fire Lieutenant, 25 men scored between 86 and 87, and 203 scored between 81 and 82.

Another vexing problem with the existing system was described by one frustrated manager:

> *The City's unimaginative recruitment mechanism, combined with generally unappetizing work surroundings, makes it virtually impossible to recruit stenographers at the entry level. Accordingly, we keep filling entry-level stenographer positions with candidates who make it through a relatively undemanding stenography test which has been watered down to qualify those with minimal skills. No attempt is ever made to differentiate between candidates on the basis of intelligence, work attitudes, motivation, reading comprehension. Thus, we start with an entry group whose competence has not really been tested—and may well be minimal —and proceed to lock ourselves in by demanding that all candidates for higher level positions be selected from this pool, even though the pool may be drained of some of its best talent over time.*

An example of the straitjacket created by this rigid procedure can be found in the agency that needed a mechanical engineer for maintenance of heating, ventilating, and air-conditioning equipment. The experience of the six highest-ranking candidates on the "Mechanical Engineer List" was inappropriate, consisting of machine design, drafting, and the like; the seventh-ranked engineer, however, was ideally suited for the job. Nevertheless, the agency was constrained by civil service rules to hire one of the top three. Only by finally persuading four of the top six to waive their legal claims to the job, thereby elevating Number Seven to Number Three, was the agency able to hire the man with the needed experience. If any one of the four who reluctantly withdrew had joined the other two of the top six in refusing to do so, the agency would have faced the choice of hiring either no one or someone with an inappropriate background, even though a suitable candidate was available only a few meaningless points further down the list.

SELECTION PROCEDURES: AN INVERSE MERIT SYSTEM

The most surprising finding is that the current legally mandated selection procedure, ostensibly designed to hire the most meritorious applicants into city service, appears to be a failure according to that very criterion: *It discriminates against those applicants who are most qualified according to its own standards.* Candidates with low passing grades are actually *more* likely to be hired than those with high passing grades! Furthermore, this perverse result seems to hold true for all skill levels.

This finding emerged from a careful study of three representative (written) examinations, which span a broad gamut of entry-level skills: Railroad Porter, a position which requires minimal education; Clerk, a position which requires some educational attainment; and Professional Trainee, a job which requires a college degree. Each examination showed the same general pattern — roughly speaking, the *lower* the percentile ranking, the *greater* the number of hires drawn from that percentile group! Conversely, the *higher* the percentile, the *fewer* the number of people hired from it.

Corroborating evidence was found by analyzing a 10 per cent sample of those 1970 and 1971 examinations which resulted in actual hiring: In almost half of the examinations analyzed (14 of 30), none of the four highest scorers was appointed; in a third of the examinations no one was appointed from the top 10 per cent; and in two of the 30 examinations, no one was appointed from the upper half of the eligible candidates.

These anomalous and unexpected results are presumably due to the long delay between the closing date for applications and the date of the first appointment. Delays are produced by a combination of administrative procedures and applicant-initiated protests, appeals, and law suits. The sample of examinations revealed that in 1970, the median delay was *seven months* and the maximum (of the sample) was *15 months*. If we assume that the "best" people score highest, then it seems reasonable to assume that many will find jobs elsewhere and that as time goes on a decreasing number of them will still be available when "their number is called." Analysis of the data showed that the greater the delay, the deeper into the lists one had to dig to find people still willing to accept appointment. When the delay was "only" three months, the openings were filled from the top 15 per cent of the list, but when the delay was six months, hires were drawn from the top 37 per cent, and when the delay was 15 months (for the Clerk examination), it was necessary to dip all the way down to 63 per cent in order to fill the vacancies.

One could argue that this finding is true but irrelevant, and that the 6,000th person on the Clerk list, for example, is really not significantly worse than the fifth, both of whom were hired. But if this assertion is accepted, then one is essentially admitting that the entire examination process is virtually useless.

In summary, as far as drawing new recruits into public employment via examination is concerned, the evidence strongly suggests that *New York City's civil service system functions as an inverse merit system* (something the public at large has cynically assumed for years). Although additional verification is needed before this finding can be generalized, at the moment the burden of proof must fall on those who would maintain that New York's civil service really is a merit system in this respect. Indeed, to anyone familiar with both public and private personnel systems, it is quite obvious that large corporations today are much closer to a true merit system than are our governments.

PROMOTION AND MOTIVATION

With regard to promotions, the civil service can be described more accurately as a seniority system than as a merit system. The rules discourage "lateral entry" into upper-level positions by outsiders. This means that one usually starts at the bottom and works his way up, which sounds fine: All organizations find it beneficial as a general practice to promote from within, and their current employees have a natural and desirable advantage over outsiders. In New York's civil service, however, this practice is carried to an extreme and becomes an exclusionary device that limits competition. One frustrated high-level city official offered a striking example of the problem:

> In an occupational area like computer operations, applying the usual rigid procedures denies us the option of hiring experienced computer programmers, systems analysts, and data processing managers. It would force us to appoint only computer programming trainees and to wait for these to be trained and developed by years of experience. This is patently absurd.

The current promotion procedure is as follows: Vacancies in positions above the lowest level in an agency are generally filled by promotion on the basis of competitive examination from among persons holding tenured positions in the next lower grade *in the same agency.* If the Civil Service Commission concludes that there are not enough people available at the lower grade to fill all the vacancies via promotion examination, it may decide to conduct an open-competitive examination as well. An open-competitive examination is open to individuals in other city agencies, to individuals in other grades within the same agency, and to complete "outsiders."

But this openness is illusory. Assuming that the "outsider" has somehow ferreted out the fact that an open-competitive examination is being conducted, he is still at a significant disadvantage compared to the "insiders" who take the promotion examination. Any "insider" who passes the promotion examination will be offered the vacant position before it is offered to anyone who passes the open-competitive examination. Even if one accepted the validity of the examinations, one can seriously question whether it is always better for the public to promote an "insider" who scores 70 than to hire an "outsider" who scores 99.

A study was made of 10 pairs of written open-competitive and promotion examinations given for such positions as engineer, accountant, stenographer, planner, and so on. For each position the promotion and the open-competitive examinations were almost identical. Though the results are not conclusive, they are suggestive, to say the least: The lowest-ranked "insider" was selected over the highest-ranked "outsider" despite the fact that the latter scored higher than the former in all cases but one; "insiders" who averaged 14 points below "outsiders" were nevertheless chosen before the latter. One can legitimately ask how the public interest is served by this policy.

Damning though such findings may be, the worst feature of the promotion system is that an employee's chance of promotion bears no relation to his performance on the job. It is the promotion examination that counts and not performance, motivation, or special qualifications. Distressing examples of the unfairness that this system produces are legion. For instance, a man responsible for the successful completion of an important health program failed to pass the promotion test for Senior Public Health Sanitarian. To all who were familiar with his excellent work, this result was positive proof that the examination was completely invalid. At the top of the list on that examination was someone who has never been able to supervise people and has been mediocre on the job. The demonstrated inability of such tests to predict supervisory competence remains one of the major weaknesses of the examination system.

Given the nature of the promotion procedures, there are relatively few ways in which an agency head, manager, or supervisor can motivate, reward, or penalize his workers. Yearly salary increases are authorized under union contracts, while cost-of-living and comparability adjustments occur automatically for non-union employees. In principle, an outstanding employee can receive a special salary increase, but in fact the vast majority of employees are never really evaluated for such increases, as few agencies and few positions come under this policy. How long will a highly motivated and competent individual be willing to put forth extra effort when he receives no real reward compared with others who do much less? A sensible individual would conclude that instead of spending extra energy and effort on doing his job well, his time would be better spent studying for promotion examinations, or simply relaxing. Also demoralizing for supervisors is the knowledge that it is almost impossible to penalize or discharge the barely competent or even incompetent permanent employee. The administrative procedures involved, the time lags, the large amount of managerial effort needed "to make a case," all force the manager to live with the problem rather than to solve it.

COLLECTIVE BARGAINING VS. CIVIL SERVICE

The single most compelling reason for major reform of public personnel systems—even aside from the mounting evidence of their meritlessness—is the fact that a new system, collective bargaining, has grown up atop the old system, civil service. The enormous growth in membership, power, and militancy of unions of civil servants has resulted in increased protection, wages, and benefits for New York City employees—and in decreased productivity. The ultimate monopoly of power held by municipal unions raises fundamental and disquieting questions about public employee unionism that are not yet resolved.

It is an inescapable fact, however, that union power has produced a second personnel system overlapping and at times conflicting with and negating the civil service system. Job classifications and duties, recruitment, promotion paths, eligibility for advancement, and grievances all fall within the purview of the civil service system, yet all are in fact negotiated, albeit informally, with the municipal unions. Initial selection of employees had remained the one area under the exclusive regulatory authority of the Civil Service Commission, but this, too, is now becoming subject to joint policy determination with the unions.

A strong argument can therefore be made for acknowledging reality and abolishing the civil service system, relying instead on the collective bargaining system. In effect, this has already been done in one area, the municipal hospitals, which have been taken over by the independent Health and Hospitals Corporation. Its employees are no longer civil servants but continue to be represented by a union, and there has been no discernible harm to them or to the body politic. At the very least, a "Blue Ribbon Commission" should be appointed to consider long-term, fundamental reform of New York's civil service system, with particular focus on the overlap between collective bargaining and civil service.

WHAT SHOULD BE DONE?

In trying to prevent itself from doing the wrong things—nepotism, patronage, prejudice, favoritism, corruption—the civil service system has been warped and distorted to the point where it can do hardly anything at all. In an attempt to protect against past abuses, the "merit system" has been perverted and transformed into a closed and meritless seniority system. A true merit system must be constructed anew, one that provides the opportunity for any qualified citizen to gain access non-politically, to be recognized and rewarded for satisfactory performance, and even to be replaced for unsatisfactory service. The improvements that are needed are obvious:

• The principal determinant of promotions should be a performance appraisal and potential assessment system, based upon performance standards and established with union cooperation. Such a system should include an employee's right to review and appeal the appraisal report.

• An individual's salary increase should be a function of his performance. Salary Review Boards with union representation should be established in each agency to set annual guidelines for allocating salary increases in the agency out of a lump-sum annual budget for raises; for example, "standard" performers might get a five per cent raise, "superior" performers a larger one.

• Examinations should be for broad categories of related positions, with "selective certification" used to appoint specialists from within the pool of qualified candidates.

• Written examinations should be employed only where their validity can be demonstrated. Oral examinations should be used more extensively for both selection and promotion. (We are not referring to the kind of "oral examination" now sometimes given—namely, a stilted interview in which competent interviewers are asked to camouflage their reasonable but subjective impressions of the interviewees by asking the exact same questions in the same sequence and giving numerical ratings to the responses. These "oral examinations" are then graded by employees who conscientiously average the interview scores.)

• In selecting new employees, the emphasis should be on evaluation of qualifications, experience, assessment by prior employers, and an oral or practical examination.

• The custom of scoring examinations to several decimal places should be abandoned. Round off the test scores; this will create more ties and give the appointing authority more freedom to use his judgment.

• Positions should be evaluated regularly to weed out rampant credentialism.

• More upper-level positions should be filled at the discretion of management. A good model can be found in the New York Police Department, where the highest rank attainable by examination is captain, and the Commissioner has the authority to assign captains to higher ranks as long as he is satisfied with their performance.

• The system should stop discriminating against "outsiders." Open-competitive and promotion examination lists for a given title should be merged into a single ranked list; alternatively, "outstanding" outsiders should be selected before "good" insiders, and so on. Experience in New York City government should be one of the criteria used in evaluating individuals.

• A flexible system of probationary periods should be instituted, with the duration of the period bearing some logical relationship to the job. The granting of tenure should require a positive act, as it does in universities.

• To improve the performance and motivation of employees, training opportunities should be greatly increased. Job counseling and career planning should be introduced, and tuition-refund plans, evening courses, and released-time programs should all be utilized. Job responsibilities should be enlarged ("enriched") commensurate with employee acceptance. The constricted domain of the unfortunate doorstop maintainer might be expanded to include hinges and doorknobs, and in time even simple locks. So far Victor Gotbaum, the municipality's farsighted union leader, has done more for job training and enrichment than anyone on the management side.

The recommendations presented above would tend to make New York City's system more similar to the federal civil service. The federal system 1) makes far greater use of selective certification; 2) more readily accepts outside applicants for middle and upper positions, and evaluates them on the basis of their education and upper positions, and evaluates them on the basis of their education and experience rather than by written examination; 3) bases promotions on performance rather than examination; 4) has a much shorter average time span for promotions; 5) identifies talented individuals early, at the time of the entrance examination; 6) encourages movement between government agencies; 7) is more concerned about training and identification of persons with higher potential; and 8) has a one-year probationary period for new appointees, with positive action by supervisors necessary for retention.

People who have served in both consider the federal system vastly superior to the one under which the city operates. However, some of the recommendations we have made would also apply to the federal government: 1) the need for evaluating duties and responsibilities of positions regularly to insure against demanding greater or different qualifications than the job requires, 2) strengthening the performance evaluation and potential assessment system; 3) doing away with automatic raises and tying them more closely to performance; and 4) making it easier to reward good performers and to demote or remove incompetent performers.

RACIAL AND ETHNIC PROBLEMS

The managerial virtues of such proposed changes are clear, but would they create an even worse problem of racial and ethnic patronage? In New York today, the civil service system is undergoing strain in part because of the widespread belief that to be successful in certain jobs one must possess traits that the system was designed to ignore: culture, class, neighborhood, and other such euphemisms for race and ethnicity. Hence the color-blind hiring practices which successfully staffed city agencies a half-century ago are not well suited for staffing the new municipal agencies that deal with problem families, drug addicts, and unemployed youths. Nor do they adequately provide the recruits needed by a police department whose job has changed significantly and now requires considerable community cooperation for effective crime control. Cultural rapport is vital for success in both the new agencies and old ones facing new challenges.

Ingenious job descriptions (with the adjective "community" frequently in the titles), public employment programs aimed at reducing unemployment in particular neighborhoods, and carefully targeted recruitment campaigns are being used to get around the color-blind system, but such policies have hardly gone unnoticed. Those groups that are already well represented within the civil service decry the "decline in standards," and attack such hiring programs in the courts and at the bargaining table. They may recognize the irrationality of the system, but they fear that civil service reform and greater managerial flexibility will be used to advance newcomers at their expense.

Those major groups that are not yet proportionally represented, black and Spanish-speaking New Yorkers, recognize the irrationality of the system; they are successfully challenging discriminatory examinations which exclude them, and thereby introducing greater flexibility into the system. At the same time, though, they fear that a reformed civil service will allow supervisors the flexibility to discriminate against them.

We conclude that the civil service system is already enmeshed in all the strains of racial and ethnic politics in the grand New York tradition, and that a reformed system would be embroiled in similar, but hardly worse, fashion. This endemic condition, therefore, offers no grounds for abandoning the civil service changes advocated here, changes that are likely in time to provide improved delivery of public services to all citizens and neighborhoods.

THE PROSPECTS FOR REFORM

How can civil service reform be brought about? At first glance, the picture is not very promising. Elected chief executives are understandably wary of the issue, on two counts. First, an attempt at reform might easily lead to demoralization of the work force, with employee resentment leading to a further drastic decline in government performance, to the chagrin of its head. Second, elected officials fear the voting power of the growing army of civil servants. In New York City, the conventional wisdom runs as follows: There are some 400,000 employees. Each one votes himself and influences several relatives and friends. Hence municipal employees represent a voting block of more than a million votes, more than enough to ensure victory or defeat. Therefore, the logic goes, don't do anything that might antagonize the work force—and be sure to treat it especially well in election years.

It is not at all clear, however, that this simplistic arithmetic really applies: At least one seventh of the work force lives out of town and is therefore ineligible to vote in New York's municipal elections; voter registration, turnout, and bloc voting may be no greater for civil servants than for other groups; many of those influenced by government employees are themselves in public service and should not be counted twice; and other friends who are not on the public payroll might resent the "good deal" that they attribute to the tenured civil servant, and hence would approve of reform.

Furthermore, candid discussions with many public employees reveal support for civil service reform; able and devoted civil servants—and there are many thousands of them—resent it when they see incompetent co-workers receive equal pay and pass promotion examinations, and they are tired of being vilified by the public for the lethargy of such colleagues. They would respond favorably to sensible improvements, for the overwhelming majority want to be effective in their work and to have pride in their organization. Therefore, the irreconcilable opposition to civil service reform probably numbers far, far less than one million, and political leaders should be able to deal with such opposition by mobilizing the many latent forces for reform.

But for too long there has been a mutually convenient conspiracy of silence among civil service employees, their unions, and public officials about the quantity and quality of work performed, the productivity of government agencies, and the level of service delivered to the public. Employees received security, generous fringe benefits and pensions, and constantly improving salaries. (The top civil service salary is now close to $40,000.) The unions acquired members and political power. The public officials' reward was the possibility of reelection or reappointment. However, that era is drawing to a close as taxpayers demand better performance and as alert political leaders sense the popular mood.

The time now seems right for a long-overdue reform of the civil service. The intent of reform should be to adapt the civil service system to changing times and changing needs in order to bring about more efficient and more effective government. Several of the steps recommended by us were accepted in New York and are being implemented. Although the procedures will generally vary from state to state, many of the changes needed in the nation's civil service system can be effected by the direct and indirect authority of the chief executives. Other changes may require enlightened rule-making by appointed civil service commissions. Still others will require action by state legislatures.

Inevitably, there will be opposition to any changes, and the dread spectre of the 19th-century spoils system is already being exhumed and summoned to the battlements. Certainly, safeguards will be needed. But the surest safeguard of all is the fact that current political realities have greatly reduced the threat of the spoils system. Today, an elected official can best secure his own reelection by creating and maintaining an efficient and effective organization to deliver governmental services to the public. He cannot do this without a competent work force. Trite though it may sound, the best protection against abuses is an enlightened citizenry, demanding performance and accountability of its government, and aided by a vigilant free press. These conditions exist today in New York, and in other places as well.

The argument for reform is overwhelming. The potential future imperfections of a revitalized personnel system are small and distant compared to the actual weaknesses, large and immediate, of today's illusory merit system. Undoubtedly, the prescription should be applied selectively. Some states and cities are still suffering under a corrupt spoils system and can benefit from the kinds of changes introduced long ago by the *first* wave of civil service reform. By far the most common affliction, however, is the rigor mortis of over-developed and regressive civil service systems. If these are reformed, no doubt the time will come again, in another 50 or 100 years, when the disadvantages of the system advocated here will outweigh its advantages. At such time, new reforms—reforms that meet the needs of those new conditions—will again be in order, for no system devised by man works well forever.

Discussion Questions

1. How would you characterize Francis Sargent's relationship to the state legislature, to other state agencies, and to the federal government? How did this relationship affect his ability to manage the bureaucracy of Massachusetts? Can you identify similar patterns in the case of your own governor or mayor?

2. Weinberg identifies several different ways in which management issues can get on the governor's agenda. Can you identify any management issues that are of concern to your governor or mayor? How might they have gotten on his or her agenda?

3. How would you compare the management resources possessed by your governor or mayor with those possessed by Sargent?

4. Savas and Ginsburg argue that where public employees have unionized and help determine personnel policy through collective bargaining, it might be wise to simply abolish the civil service system and rely entirely on collective bargaining. Do you agree? How would you feel about the utilization of private firms for such municipal services as garbage collection and fire protection? Would this be a viable alternative to the use of unionized public employees?

5. Do you feel that a reformed civil service system of the type Savas and Ginsburg advocate would be compatible with society's need for a public work force that reflects its racial makeup? What problems might arise?

6. Could a mayor with Francis Sargent's attitude toward bureaucratic management reform a civil service system such as Savas and Ginsburg discovered in New York City?

CHAPTER SIX

COURTS AND CRIMINAL JUSTICE

The American criminal justice system—including the courts, the police, and corrections agencies—has been subjected to long-standing criticism. Attack has come from both liberals and conservatives. As crime rates increase, there is growing pressure from conservatives for a "get tough" policy. They believe that police should make more arrests, judges should not "coddle" criminal defendants, and a large percentage of those convicted should be sent to jail. Liberals, on the other hand, contend that the system is unnecessarily harsh and that greater care should be taken to protect individual rights.

The indictment of our court system includes the following charges. Few cases come to trial because of the prevalence of plea bargaining. When trials do occur, it often is only after considerable delay. Many "minor" offenders are handled on an assembly line that gives only passing attention to the charges against them. Incompetent lawyers and bail bondsmen prey on their unsuspecting clients. Minority persons and the poor do not have the same opportunities to see justice served as do white, upper-class landlords, merchants, and creditors. Poor court organization often results in jurisdictional confusion and an unequal distribution of resources. Professional management is not utilized in most trial courts.

The police, of course, are always fair game for critics who charge that they are poorly trained, insensitive to minorities, corrupt, and undisciplined. For their part, police often have a paranoid reaction to the world. Norval Morris and Gordon Hawkins describe police as follows in *The Honest Politician's Guide to Crime Control:* "They huddle together, an anxious ingroup, battling the forces of wickedness, political corruption, citizen irresponsibility, and declining morals, particularly the immorality of youth. Their extra-corps contacts are cautious in the extreme. They are, they believe, insufficiently esteemed, inadequately rewarded, but gallantly carrying the burdens of society for a parsimonious and misguided citizenry."

In fact, American police *are* poorly paid, inadequately trained, and often hostile toward blacks and Hispanics. Police have made relatively little use of modern technology to combat crime. Petty corruption often exists because of their low level of professionalization.

American prisons are perhaps the most strongly criticized part of our criminal justice system. It is argued that they neither rehabilitate criminals nor act to deter crime. Many prisons are old and overcrowded. Destructive riots occur at a distressingly regular rate. In February 1980, prisoners gained control of the New Mexico State Penitentiary in Santa Fe. They took 11 guards hostage, burned cell blocks, and did 25 million dollars worth of damage. While no guards were killed, 33 inmates were brutally murdered by their fellow inmates. Another 100 inmates were injured. This was the worst prison riot in American history.

In the first article in this chapter, James Eisenstein and Herbert Jacob discuss the roles played by various actors in the courtroom workgroup and their relationships to each other. While judges are the formal leaders in most courtrooms, the authors suggest that the attorneys for the prosecution and defense possess the greatest influence on the operation of courts. Eisenstein and Jacob contend that all parties in the workgroup wish to avoid conflict; thus they have established a variety of techniques to control uncertainty. Because the same people interact on a regular basis, strong patterns of mutual dependence emerge in the courtroom.

In the second article James Q. Wilson identifies three basic styles of police organization. The "watchman" style is found in the traditional police department, where officers are locally recruited, given minimal training, and paid poorly. They exercise a great deal of discretion in law enforcement and are willing to ignore minor violations so long as general order is maintained. The "legalistic" style of enforcement often exists in cities that have recently had scandals in their police departments. Officers in "legalistic" departments energetically make arrests for minor violations and enforce all laws equally against all classes of people. Police in "moralistic" departments are well-trained, well-paid, and courteous. Such departments often are found in affluent suburbs where residents demand a high standard of police performance.

The Courtroom Workgroup

James Eisenstein and Herbert Jacob

Courtroom workgroups have characteristics commonly found among other organized workgroups.[1]

1. They exhibit authority relationships.

2. They display influence relationships, which modify the authority relationships.

3. They are held together by common goals.

4. They have specialized roles.

5. They use a variety of work techniques.

6. They engage in a variety of tasks.

7. They have different degrees of stability and familiarity.

These traits establish a complex network of ongoing relationships that determines who in the courtroom does what, how, and to whom.

COURTROOM AUTHORITY PATTERNS

The judge is the formal leader of most courtrooms.[2] In a sense, the courtroom belongs to him; he enjoys considerable formal powers to force others to conform to his desires. Most decisions the courtroom produces, including those made by others that affect the disposal of cases, usually require formal judicial approval. The judge must ratify the defendant's decision to enter a guilty plea, the prosecutor's decision to dismiss some or all charges, and an agreement on sentence. Finally, by participating in a number of decisions affecting case outcomes, judges gain influence over other courtroom organization members. Judges make preliminary decisions on bail, on motions and hearings. They rule on specific objections during courtroom proceedings and thus influence whether a compromise is reached—and if so, its content—as well as the verdict when no bargain is consummated.

Judges are universally considered the linchpins of courtroom workgroups. They are the formal leaders of the court and have the formal responsibility for making decisions that affect the flow of cases. They set dates for motions, hearings, trials, and other proceedings. The courtroom's work load is affected by their willingness to grant or deny extensions of deadlines, the time they take to render decisions on motions and in hearings, the procedures they use to empanel juries, the degree to which they cut short attorneys' examination of witnesses, and the amount of time they are willing to work. Judges also govern courtroom conduct. They are responsible for the actual behavior of attorneys, witnesses, spectators, and defendants; for example, they regulate voice level and physical movement, and decide when conversations will be allowed.

Attorneys represent interested parties to a conflict, but the judge is the neutral arbiter; even in criminal trials, he is not supposed to favor the state, even though he is a public official like the prosecutor. He represents the ideals of justice; he sits above the others, wears a robe, and requires all others to show visible respect for him by addressing him as "your honor" and by rising when he enters and leaves the courtroom. No one may openly criticize him in the courtroom; he may charge those who do with contempt of court (not contempt of the judge) and fine or imprison them on the spot. Moreover, this formal authority is often reinforced by the age and experience of the judge. He is often older and more experienced in the law than the attorneys who practice before him.

The judge, however, has less authority than many superiors in workgroups. He does not hire or fire others who work in the courtroom. Almost all of them are assigned by independent authorities—we call them sponsoring organizations—such as the state's attorney, the public defender, the clerk of courts, the sheriff (who assigns the bailiffs in many courtrooms), and the marketplace, which brings private attorneys representing individual clients to the courtroom. Each of these sponsoring agencies imposes its own requirements on the participants it sends to the courtroom workgroup. Consequently, the judge's authority is quite limited.

Judges also have few budgetary controls over the courtroom. Unlike most workgroups, courtroom workgroups typically do not have their own budget. Each participant brings his own resources to the workgroup and uses them himself or shares them with others. Neither judges nor anyone else in the courtroom workgroup can decide to install a new public address system or to hire several additional clerks; judges cannot reward hardworking prosecutors or bailiffs with a salary raise, nor can they directly withhold salary increments from malingerers. Lacking personnel and budgetary powers, judges have less authority than many workgroup supervisors.

Even on legal matters the judge's authority is not absolute. He renders decisions, of course, and they have the force of law. But they are subject to reversal by other judges. Attorneys sometimes seek to influence their content by citing statutes and appellate decisions. In addition, a judge generally can rule only when someone else raises the issue and requests a decision. Thus, his legal decisions are molded by the activities of others.

COURTROOM INFLUENCE PATTERNS

The influence of other participants in the workgroup limits the formal authority of the judge. Their influence stems from formal authority that the law also provides them, and from superior information or control over access to the courtroom.

The law gives the state's attorney the right to determine whom to prosecute and what charges to press. In addition, the prosecutor routinely has more information about a case than anyone else in the courtroom. He possesses the police report, records of previous arrests and convictions, witness reports, laboratory tests, and the physical evidence if there is any. The prosecutor, more than anyone else, knows what the strength of a case is and when it is ready for disposition. Thus in many courtrooms, the prosecutor controls the scheduling of cases and the dispositional pattern. The judge—although possessing greater formal authority—responds to the prosecutor's actions. No experienced prosecutor will routinely overlook the judge's sentiments about how the courtroom is to be run, but many run it instead of the judge. Even where the judge maintains more control, he must take into account the prosecutor's opinion of what should be done.

Defense counsel also possess considerable influence in the work of the courtroom. They are charged with representing their client in a number of crucial proceedings. The defense attorney has a duty to insist that evidence seized illegally be thrown out of court and may ask for a hearing to accomplish that end. He can demand a hearing to determine the legality of an arrest or confession. A conscientious and skilled defense counsel may make the work of a prosecutor much more difficult and may require detailed rulings on the law from the judge.

The defendant is notably absent from most interactions of courtroom workgroups, assuming the role of a very interested spectator with a front row seat.[3] But he possesses several rights—the right to a jury trial being the most important—which cannot be waived without his formal direct participation in a ceremony. Before a defendant can waive his right to a jury trial or enter a plea of guilty, he must be questioned directly by the judge and answer in his own voice, not his attorney's. But defense attorneys may convince defendants to waive these rights and may school them in the proper responses to the judge's questions. If defense counsel is unwilling or unable to influence and control clients most of the time, the smooth operation of the workgroup is jeopardized.

Under some circumstances, clerks also possess some influence in the courtroom workgroup. In busy courtrooms where dockets are not arranged by a central computer, the clerk often determines which case will be heard next. The order in which cases are heard is important for busy lawyers who want to avoid fruitless hours of waiting for their case to be called for a two-minute ritual. Where the sequence of cases has an effect on the outcome (because one case is affected by the outcome of the case just before), the clerk's decision may also lead to more or less severe results for the defendant.

Finally, police have significant influence on the operation of criminal courts. In many cities they determine who will be sent to court by the arrests they make; at the least, they share that determination with the prosecutor. They also are the most frequent witnesses in criminal court. Their appearance or absence, their demeanor, the care with which they preserve evidence—all have a considerable effect on the work of the courtroom. Prosecutors, especially, depend on the police, but defense counsel and judges also have a considerable stake in how the police act in the courtroom.

The precise pattern of influence in courtroom workgroups varies with the degree to which each of the participants possesses these resources and how he uses them. When everything else is equal, an aggressive defense attorney will exert more influence than a reticent one. A diligent prosecutor exerts more influence than one who forgets details of the cases he is handling. An assertive judge retains more of his authority than one who sees his role solely as responding to the initiatives of others in the courtroom. Some courtrooms appear to be governed almost entirely by their judges, although that appearance almost always is an exaggeration. Other courtrooms are ruled by the prosecutor; a few are dominated by defense counsel. Many are governed by a collective decision-making process encompassing judge, prosecutor, defense attorneys, clerks, and police.

SHARED GOALS OF COURTROOM WORKGROUPS

Courtroom workgroups have a job to do. Like most people pressed for time, their members do not often pause to philosophize about their ultimate purpose or goals. It is difficult enough just to keep going. Although they may not realize it, all courtroom workgroups share values and goals.[4] These shared perspectives undermine the apparent conflicts generated by the formal roles of workgroup members—the prosecutor's push toward conviction, the defense attorneys' quest for acquittals, and judges' inclination toward neutrality.

Four goals present in courtroom workgroups are summarized in Table 1. They are produced by the interaction of two dimensions: the function performed (expressive or instrumental) and the origins of the goals (external or internal to the group).[5] Expressive goals serve symbolic functions and infuse meaning into activity. Instrumental goals serve material functions and help get things done. Externally oriented goals are imposed by the workgroup's environment. Internal goals are produced by the need of the members to share perspectives that sustain the organization itself.

External goals reflect pressures on the workgroup from outside the immediate bounds of the courtroom and from the sponsoring organizations that send the major participants to the courtroom. The police, the media, governmental agencies, including the legislature and appellate courts, and ultimately the general public, all expect results from the courtroom workgroup. These "outside" groups impose both instrumental and expressive goals on courtroom organization. The most important instrumental goal is that cases should be handled expeditiously. Many people believe that expeditious disposition will deter crime. In addition, quick convictions or acquittals tie up fewer resources of the police. They also fulfill requirements imposed by appellate courts for a speedy trial and might reduce appellate business. They produce a steady flow of news to the media and assure the public that the courts are doing their job. Disposing of cases without attracting undue attention or criticism from outsiders is also intepreted by many as doing justice.

All members of the courtroom workgroup are interested in disposing cases, although the reason for this interest varies. Judges and prosecutors want high disposition rates in order to transmit an aura of efficiency and accomplishment. Prosecutors also prefer speedy dispositions because as cases age, memories dim and witnesses scatter, weakening the evidence and lowering the chances of conviction.

Retained attorneys face a more complicated set of incentives. Most attorneys who specialize in criminal cases depend on a high turnover of clients who can afford only modest fees. Without high volume and the investment of a modest amount of time in each case, many a private defense counsel would go broke. Yet private counsel must maintain a reputation for vigorous defense in order to attract new clients. Public defender organizations charged with representing all indigent defendants prefer quick disposition because their manpower barely suffices to handle their case load. But they also seek to establish a reputation for effective representation of defendants.

Table 1
Goals of courtroom workgroups

| Function of goal | Origins of goal | |
	External	Internal
Expressive	Doing justice	Maintaining group cohesion
Instrumental	Disposing of case load	Reducing uncertainty

The expressive goal imposed by the external environment is to do justice. All the principal participants are attorneys, and are bound to that goal by their professional training. For that matter, nearly everyone in American society values doing justice. The specific content of the term, however, is ambiguous. For some, justice is done when criminals are caught and severely punished regardless of procedures. For others, adherence to the principles of due process and equal treatment produces justice. The ambiguity and disagreement contained in the notion of justice in society are mirrored in the varying perspectives of workgroup members. For the defense, doing justice may mean either obtaining an acquittal or a mild sentence for its clients, or forcing the prosecution to prove its case beyond a reasonable doubt. The prosecution often sees doing justice in terms of its conviction rates, because it is convinced that most defendants are in fact guilty. Judges generally see this goal as requiring impartial behavior, although their definition of impartiality often favors either the defense or the prosecution. Thus surface agreement within the courtroom organization on the goal of "doing justice" often engenders behavioral conflict.

Internally oriented goals facilitate the functioning of the courtroom workgroup. The expressive form of these goals is maintaining group cohesion.[6] Pervasive conflict is not only unpleasant; it also makes work more difficult. Cohesion produces a sense of belonging and identification that satisfies human needs. It is maintained in several ways. Courtroom workgroups shun outsiders because of their potential threat to group cohesion. The workgroup possesses a variety of adaptive techniques to minimize the effect of abrasive participants. For instance, the occasional defense attorney who violates routine cooperative norms may be punished by having to wait until the end of the day to argue his motion; he may be given less time than he wishes for a lunch break in the middle of a trial; he may be kept beyond usual court hours for bench conferences. Likewise, unusually adversarial defense or prosecuting attorneys are likely to smoothe over their formal conflicts with informal cordiality. Tigers at the bench, they become tame kittens in chambers and in the hallways, exchanging pleasantries and exuding sociability.

The instrumental expression of internal goals is reducing or controlling uncertainty.[7] The strong incentives to reduce uncertainty force courtroom members to work together, despite their different orientations toward doing justice. More than anything else, trials produce uncertainty. They require substantial investments of time and effort without any guarantee of the result. The difficulty of estimating how long they will last makes everyone's schedule very uncertain. Even bench trials require some preparation of witnesses and throw the other participants at the mercy of these witnesses, whose behavior on the witness stand is unpredictable. What witnesses say and how they say it may make the difference between conviction and acquittal. Jury trials are even worse, because attorneys must deal with the jurors as well as the witnesses. In ordinary cases very little is known about the jurors, and jury decisions are proverbially unpredictable. Even after presenting a "dead-bang" case to a jury, prosecutors suffer nervous hours while the jury deliberates. The judge is also committed to avoiding uncertainty. Most judges like to have some control over their dockets; they like to see where actions are heading and what further activity is required of them.

The desire to reduce uncertainty leads to the development of several norms designed to make behavior predictable. One is "stick by your word and never mislead deliberately." Attorneys who violate this norm find they are punished. Another is "no surprises." It is often illegal to call surprise witnesses or to introduce evidence that the opposing counsel is unaware of; it is almost always regarded as a dirty trick.

The instrumental goals we have identified are generally mutually supportive. Caseload disposition and reduction of uncertainty go hand in hand; the former is often articulated (partly because it is directed at the external environment), whereas the latter is more often an unspoken commitment by courtroom members. Expressive goals, however, are not as frequently mutually supportive. The quest for justice often threatens courtroom cohesion, and the desire to maintain a cohesive workgroup may seem to jeopardize the quest for justice. The general political culture more explicitly legitimates the externally oriented goals. There is much public discussion of the need for justice and for the clearing of dockets in criminal courts. Organizational maintenance goals are almost furtive by contrast. They are rarely articulated in public by members of the courtroom organization; they can best be deduced from private statements and courtroom behavior. Although they are not illegitimate, they have not yet been publicly legitimated.

Courtroom workgroups vary in their adherence to these goals. For instance, some workgroups value cohesion less than others because they find conflict less threatening to their survival. But in general we believe that the variation is not great. Nevertheless, it is important to identify these goals, because common adherence to them keeps the groups together.

WORKGROUP SPECIALIZATION

Although courtroom participants have common goals, they play radically different roles. The participants rigidly adhere to the specified role differentiation. The judge maintains an air of impartiality; he responds to requests for rulings on the law and makes decisions when called on by others. He may intervene in the scheduling of cases or in questioning witnesses, but he may not take sides. The prosecutor, on the other hand, represents only the state and never the defense. Defense counsel only defend and never prosecute. There is no alternation of roles in the criminal courtroom.

However, the three leading members of the courtroom workgroup — the judge, prosecutor, and defense attorney — are all lawyers and possess the professional qualifications to do each other's work. Although role orientations are distinct and specialized, the work these three principals do is very similar.

All of them manipulate information in order to reach decisions on the cases before them. They ask questions of witnesses—in private interviews or on the witness stand. They search out relevant aspects of code and case law and seek to apply them to their cases. All three are familiar with the techniques employed in adversarial proceedings; they are equally familiar with negotiations.

Little disagreement exists in the courtroom about this division of tasks and roles. It creates a situation in which everyone quickly fits into his accustomed place and in which the principals readily understand each other's work. Even novices readily fit into the work routine of a courtroom.

The other members of the courtroom workgroup engage in quite different tasks. The clerk keeps records. Although judges and lawyers may keep their own, the clerk's record is the official one. He records decisions, the dates when they occurred, and the motions and appearances that are filed with him. Together with the stenographic record of the proceedings, the clerk's file is the official record of the case and is used by everyone in the courtroom to determine what has happened in the past and what still needs to be done to complete disposition of the case. In addition, the court reporter—often a private contractor—makes a stenographic record of public proceedings. Those records, however, are not transcribed unless the defense or the state asks and pays for the transcription. Finally, bailiffs work in the courtroom to maintain decorum and guard prisoners who appear as defendants or witnesses.

Each of these members of the courtroom workgroup knows his task, role, and physical location in the courtroom. He knows it before he enters the courtroom. Little formal training or socialization occurs in the workgroup. If a participant needs additional skills, he learns them informally.

THE WORK TECHNIQUES OF COURTROOM ORGANIZATIONS

Organizations are more than stable groups of people who share goals and divide tasks in a purposive manner. Organizations also employ a technology, which in turn helps shape them.[8] The technology consists of procedures to manipulate resources into desired outputs. For courtrooms, resources consist principally of information and the authority to make decisions that bind others. The outputs are dispositions. The courtroom organization's task is to transform information and authority into dispositions by applying its work techniques.

Courtroom workgroups require an externally validated, comprehensive, readily available, and generally accepted set of techniques, because the participants are sometimes unfamiliar with one another. This unfamiliarity means that they have not developed common patterns of interaction. When strangers meet and interact, they fall back on commonly accepted formulas to guide their behavior. The procedures embodied in statute and case law relating to the conduct of trials and the hearing of motions provide such formulas. These techniques are not only justified because they employ norms and values relating to equal justice and due process; the very nature of courtroom workgroups also requires that some work techniques be codified and generally accepted.

Courtrooms use three sets of techniques: (1) unilateral decisions, (2) adversarial proceedings, and (3) negotiations. Each of them requires highly specialized knowledge and involves courtroom members in intense interactions.

Any attorney member of the courtroom workgroup may make unilateral decisions that eventually turn into dispositions. The defense counsel may file a motion; the prosecutor may file a dismissal; the judge or clerk may call up one case rather than another in his docket. In each instance, the participant uses his information and authority to impose a condition on other members of the courtroom team. The extensive interdependence of workgroup members, however, restricts their ability to impose unilateral decisions on the group. Consequently, unilateral decisions play a rather minor role in the courtroom's work.

Adversarial proceedings play a much more prominent role. They may be invoked by any of the three attorney members. Some of them are preparatory proceedings, such as preliminary examinations or hearings on motions; others are full-scale trials before a judge or jury. Adversarial proceedings are highly stylized interactions for revealing and sharing information that can become the basis for a disposition. During adversarial proceedings, information must be elicited in the approved manner, through oral arguments on legal points or questioning of witnesses. Neither prosecution nor defense ordinarily knows the full story a witness may tell, but the side presenting the witness generally knows more about what he might reveal than the opposing party. The judge knows almost nothing. Each side attempts to elicit the information most favorable to its cause while blocking the presentation of damaging information. This activity requires a high degree of skill in questioning and a thorough knowledge of the technical rules of evidence which guides courtroom hearings. Participants whose skills are inadequate not only jeopardize their case, but also hinder the output rate of the courtroom. It is common to see a judge take over questioning from inept prosecutors or defense counsel, or to cut them off when he thinks that sufficient evidence has been presented to reach a disposition. Similarly, counsel often advise judges about the legal basis for a decision.

Hearings require considerable coordination by the prosecutor or defense counsel rather than the judge. Witnesses must be assembled and prepared; each side must have an overview of its argument so that witnesses can be called in the most convincing sequence. Witnesses who might make an unfavorable impression or who appear fragile are often held in reserve and used only if absolutely necessary. If the hearings involve legal as well as evidentiary matters, the attorneys must read up on the law and have appropriate appellate citations at their fingertips. All of this preparation involves coordinating many people outside the ordinary ambit of the courtroom workgroup. Consequently, coordinative skills are almost as valuable as debating skills in adversarial proceedings.

Negotiation is the most commonly used technique in criminal courtrooms.[9] Plea bargaining—although most widely publicized—is only one use of negotiation. Continuances and the date of hearings are often bargained; the exchange of information is also commonly negotiated. Negotiation involves persuasion and the search for common ground. The common ground is generally based on agreement about the courtroom's goals; most members of the courtroom implicitly agree on the need to dispose cases and to reduce uncertainty. They also recognize the value of accommodating those on whom they are partially dependent. Each party to the negotiation attempts to convince the other that his solution is acceptable; in the course of negotiations, both parties are likely to move from their original positions toward a mutually acceptable outcome.

Information and the ability to make unilateral decisions that affect others significantly are the principal resources in negotiations. Courtroom participants utilize two types of information. One type is information about legal matters: the character of admissable evidence, the authorized sentence for a particular offense, the meaning of "lesser included offense," and similar matters. Most attorneys who specialize in criminal cases routinely possess this legal information. They also need to know the future details of the case. Normally the prosecution possesses more information about the incident, on the basis of police reports and sometimes as a result of preliminary interviews with witnesses. Often there are disputes about what "really" happened, with the defense attorney attempting to put a less serious interpretation on the events than the prosecutor. At the same time, the character of the defendant is also in question. The defense attorney often claims to know more about that; he will tell of his client's family background, his employment record, his standing in the community, in addition to any disadvantages he has had to overcome. The prosecutor usually possesses only the defendant's police record. Negotiations proceed through a careful manipulation of this information. Even when both prosecutor and defense make "full disclosure," they often interpret the information at their disposal rather than simply laying it out on the table.

Information about the way in which other courtrooms handle similar incidents is also important in negotiations. What happens in other courts of the city or state is communicated principally through these negotiations. If other courtrooms readily grant continuances, that constitutes a useful argument that a continuance ought to be granted in the case under discussion. If, in an adjoining courtroom, aggravated assault seems to carry a normal sentence of two to four years, defense counsel will try hard to achieve at least as low a sentence. Because prosecutors usually work in a single courtroom, whereas private defense counsel circulate throughout several courtrooms in the city, some defense attorneys possess more of this kind of information.

Negotiations also invoke claims on workgroup cohesion. None that we witnessed did so overtly, but many were impregnated with hints that the continuing need to work together required reasonableness in negotiation. Participants joked about it; at the end of a negotiation, they often stood around and chatted about other matters as if to imply that they were still friendly partners of the same workgroup. Only when negotiations broke down did either prosecutor or defense counsel occasionally stalk out without the usual social amenities.

Clearly the techniques of presentation, the manipulation of information, and the invocation of common workgroup values are quite different in negotiations than in adversarial hearings. Not only are the negotiations much less formal, but they also depend less on the rules of evidence and other legalistic formulas that pervade so much of the adversarial performance. In negotiations much more depends on the long-run relationships between bargaining members of the workgroup. Trust, empathy, mutual understanding are important in negotiations, but matter little in adversarial proceedings. In bargaining, information is narrated; formal testimony from witnesses is the principal mode in adversarial proceedings.

Implicit threats to make unilateral decisions underlie the uses of information in all negotiations. The ability to take such actions gives weight to the efforts to control the exchange of information. Judges can render decisions that affect the outcome of specific cases and the work life of attorneys in general. The prosecutor can proceed to trial on the original charges if the defendant does not plead guilty to them. And the defense attorney can insist on a full jury trial regardless of what anyone else does, unless a complete dismissal is forthcoming. Without the existence of these threats, negotiations based on the exchange of information would carry little weight. Indeed, much of the manipulation of information is directed toward demonstrating what would happen if the case went to trial.

COURTROOM TASKS

Courtrooms everywhere must complete similar tasks. These tasks flow from their fundamental responsibility in one way or another to dispose of every defendant charged. That responsibility requires maintaining physical control over defendants who may be prone to flee or to express their anger in violent outbursts. Much record-keeping is also required. A case file must be kept, containing information about all major actions taken. Then cases must be scheduled and the participants for each case assembled at the same time. All major proceedings must be recorded by a court reporter in case verbatim transcripts are required at a later stage. Finally, the law requires a variety of actions at different stages of criminal cases. Defendants must be arraigned and informed of the charges against them. Bond or release conditions must be set.

In order to proceed against the defendant, a court must determine whether there is "probable cause," or a grand jury must return an indictment against him. "Discovery"—the exchange of information between prosecution and defense—must take place.

These tasks may be handled in many different ways. In some places, a single courtroom workgroup performs all of them, processing a criminal case from beginning to end. More commonly, courtroom workgroups specialize in subsets of these tasks. For instance, arraignments, bond setting, and preliminary hearings are often handled by one set of workgroups, whereas final dispositions are the domain of another workgroup. In some places, specialized workgroups process all motions; in others, all negotiations take place in a single setting. Specialized workgroups obviously operate differently than generalized ones. The more specialized the tasks of the workgroup, the more it can routinize procedures and the more familiar its members will be with the tasks they perform. On the other hand, specialized workgroups often do not see the final outcome of the case, and their decisions may hinder rather than help the work of other courtroom workgroups that later process the same case.

WORKGROUP FAMILIARITY

Courtroom workgroupings almost always contain some persons who are quite familiar with one another and some who are more like strangers. The familiarity among major participants is an important characteristic of workgroups, because it has a significant effect on the manner in which they work. The more workgroup members are familiar with one another, the better they can negotiate; the more familiar, the less they need to rely on formalities and the more they can utilize informal arrangements. The more familiar courtroom members are with each other, the more likely it is that they will agree about courtroom values and goals and the less they will conflict with one another.

Workgroup familiarity depends on two factors. The first is the stability of the workgroups themselves.[10] The second is the size of the pool from which workgroup members are drawn; the smaller the number of judges, prosecutors, defense attorneys, clerks, and others working in the courthouse, the more familiar courtroom members will be with each other.

Generally, the most stable assignment is that of the judge. Except during vacation or illness, a single judge ordinarily sits for a year or more in a single courtroom. However, in courtrooms hearing misdemeanors, assignments may last for as little as a month; in other courtrooms, where the judges are elected or appointed to the criminal court itself, the assignment may extend over many years. The stabilizing effect of long assignments of judges is well illustrated by what happens when one is temporarily replaced by another judge. Work routines become substantially altered. Everyone suffers from more uncertainty about what to do and how to do it, because an important stranger is in their midst. Where possible, the remaining members postpone significant proceedings until the judge returns. If action cannot be delayed, proceedings switch into an adversarial mode, because the unknown qualities of the substitute judge can best be neutralized in a jury trial.

The assignment of prosecutors and defense attorneys is much more variable. These differences have profound consequences.

The less change there is in workgroup personnel, the more interaction will occur. Frequent interactions produce familiarity with each other's intentions and probable behavior. In stable courtroom workgroups, the principal actors know each other's preferences; they have been able to develop standing accommodations with each other. They work together enough to share organizational maintenance goals; they learn to understand the pressures that each must bear from his sponsoring organization. Thus, prosecutors and defense attorneys learn what information the judge wants in routine cases; they know the sentence he will likely mete out. They know how to present a case in order to provoke the harshest response or the mildest reaction from the judge. They know what plea offers were made in the past, and can evaluate the present case in the light of that common past. The uncertainty in negotiating with each other is considerably reduced by their familiarity with one another. In addition, frequent interactions provide innumerable informal opportunities for negotiation. Prosecutor and defense counsel may talk about a case not only when it is on the docket but during the many other occasions at which they encounter each other. They can test possible compromises informally, without putting the case on the judge's desk for formal decision. By contrast, in fluid workgroups, information about each of the participants is much more sparse; members of the courtroom workgroup deal with each other more as strangers than as friends; formal roles govern them more completely. In fluid workgroups, members work in a much less certain context. They are less likely to know the judge's preferences or each other's. They do not have a great storehouse of common experiences by which to evaluate the present case. They have not had an opportunity to develop a set of shared accommodations or an understanding of each participant's work pressures.

Finally, low interaction means that no one heavily depends on the actions of any other individual to accomplish his work. Where the same individuals interact continually, however, strong patterns of mutual dependence and accompanying abilities to influence one another emerge. In addition, if interaction is high, circulation of defense counsel and prosecutors from one courtroom to another will be low. A lower circulation, in turn, facilitates the development of distinctive styles of behavior within the rather isolated courtrooms located in the same building.

Even in unstable workgroups members may be quite familiar with each other, if the pool of active participants in the courthouse is fairly small. Where there are only a handful of judges, a half-dozen prosecutors, and a dozen defense attorneys, familiarity develops as if the workgroups were the same every day. But the familiarity found in smaller cities and in rural areas can be approximated in large cities if a small group of specialized attorneys monopolizes the work.

SUMMARY OF WORKGROUP CHARACTERISTICS

All courtroom workgroups confront the same basic task—to dispose of defendants' cases. All have the same composition—a judge, prosecutor, and defense attorney, who are familiar with each other's roles but who specialize in their own tasks. They share expressive and instrumental goals generated from within the workgroup and from the external environment. Workgroups utilize three work techniques—adversarial proceedings, negotiations, and unilateral decisions. These characteristics are found regardless of city. But workgroups also differ in several significant respects. Nowhere do judges completely dominate influence patterns within the workgroup, but the precise distribution of influence does vary. When the membership of workgroups is stable, patterns of mutual dependence develop, resulting in a more even distribution of influence. Stability also produces familiarity, but familiarity can exist even when workgroup composition is fluid, if the total number of people who form workgroups is fairly small and unchanging. When members are familiar with one another, negotiations are facilitated. When they are not, adversary proceedings are more likely.

Courtroom workgroups are like many other organizations. They are labor-intensive, are staffed by professionals, and provide services rather than products. Courtroom workgroups have an authority structure that is modified by influence relationships, but they are not hierarchies. The judge does not rule or govern; at most, he manages, and often he is managed by others.

Although workgroups dispose of many cases during a day, they are not assembly lines. Even routine decisions involve discretion. Setting bond, for instance, does not involve putting the same nuts and bolts into a piece of sheet metal (as on a typical assembly line); rather, it requires fitting a variety of factual assertions into a limited number of possible bail-bond decisions. The information required for such decisions may be communicated rapidly, and decisions may follow one another in quick succession. But it is no assembly line. On an assembly line, one worker simply relies on all the others doing their jobs; an assembly line requires few verbal or social interactions. Workgroup members must interact with one another to reach a decision.

NOTES

1. Our understanding of organizations is based primarily on the work of Herbert A. Simon, *Administrative Behavior*, 2d ed. (New York: Macmillan, 1957); Peter M. Blau and W. Richard Scott, *Formal Organizations: A Comparative Approach* (San Francisco: Chandler, 1962); Amitai Etzioni, *A Comparative Analysis of Complex Organizations* (New York: Free Press, 1961); Charles Perrow, *Organizational Analysis: A Sociological View* (London: Tavistock, 1970); and James D. Thompson, *Organizations in Action* (New York: McGraw-Hill, 1967). As will be evident to the reader familiar with organizational studies, we have been eclectic in our construction of the framework presented in the following pages.

To our knowledge, no organizational analyst has studied courts. However, several students of courts have used fragments of organizational analysis for their presentation. The most influential of these are Abraham S. Blumberg's *Criminal Justice* (Chicago: Quadrangle Books, 1967) and Herbert L. Packer's *The Limits of the Criminal Sanction* (Stanford, Calif.: Stanford University Press, 1968). Neither Blumberg nor Packer, however, lays bare the elements of an operative organizational model for courts. A more recent, but also only partial, attempt to explicate an organizational model for courts is Malcolm Feeley, "Two Models of the Criminal Justice System: An Organizational Perspective," *Law and Society Review* 7 (1973): 407-426; Feeley focuses on court systems rather than courtrooms, and again presents only a very partial model. The organizational context of the work of criminal courts is also emphasized by Lief Carter, although he focuses on the prosecutor's office rather than the courtroom in his analysis; see Lief H. Carter, *The Limits of Order* (Lexington, Mass.: Lexington Books, 1974). Exchange relationships in an organizational context are emphasized by George F. Cole, *Politics and the Administration of Justice* (Beverly Hills, Calif.: Sage Publications, 1973), esp. pp. 200-203.

2. The judge's formal role is the focus of much legal literature. It is epitomized by Bernard Botein, *The Trial Judge* (New York: Simon and Schuster, 1952).

3. Note the analysis of criminal proceedings from the defendant's perspective by Jonathan Casper, *American Criminal Justice* (Englewood Cliffs, N.J.: Prentice-Hall, 1972).

4. We are conceptualizing goals as incentive mechanisms and the goal structure as multifaceted. They help orient the calculus of decision-makers and serve to bind organization members together. An insightful discussion of the problems associated with operationalizing goals and placing them in a theoretic scheme is Petro Georgiou, "The Goal Paradigm and Notes toward a Counter Paradigm," *Administrative Science Quarterly* 18 (1973): 291-310. Despite Georgiou's arguments, we find the concept of goals and incentive structures essential to the organizational paradigm.

5. This discussion reflects what Mohr calls transitive and reflexive goals. Lawrence B. Mohr, "The Concept of Organizational Goal," *American Political Science Review* 67 (1973): 470-481, esp. 475-476.

6. For partial evidence in support of the following see "Lawyers with Convictions," in Abraham S. Blumberg, *The Scales of Justice* (Chicago: Aldine, 1970), pp. 51-67; George F. Cole, *The American System of Criminal Justice* (North Scituate, Mass.: Duxbury Press, 1975), pp. 238-241 and 271-272; Carter, *The Limits of Order*, pp. 75-105; Jerome Skolnick, "Social Control in the Adversary System," *Journal of Conflict Resolution* 11 (1967): 51 ff; Lynn M. Mather, "The Outsiders in the Courtroom: An Alternative Role for the Defense," in Herbert Jacob (ed.), *The Potential for Reform of Criminal Justice* (Beverly Hills, Calif.: Sage Publications, 1974), pp. 268-273.

Note, however, that cohesion is not the only goal of actors and that it sometimes conflicts with others.

7. Cf. Carter, *The Limits of Order*, pp. 19-21.

8. See especially Thompson, *Organizations in Action*.

9. We have drawn from descriptions of courtroom negotiations by Blumberg, *Criminal Justice*; Casper, *American Criminal Justice*; Carter, *The Limits of Order*; Mather,

"The Outsiders in the Courtroom"; and Albert W. Alschuler, "The Prosecutor's Role in Plea Bargaining," *University of Chicago Law Review* 36 (1968): 50-112.

10. Stability or cohesiveness is taken for granted by many organizational analysts. For instance, the much-cited article by D. S. Pugh, D. J. Hickson, C. R. Hinings, and C. Turner, "Dimensions of Organizational Structure," *Administrative Science Quarterly* (June 1968): 65-106 does not count stability as one of the dimensions of organizational structure.

Styles of Police Systems

James Q. Wilson

THE WATCHMAN STYLE

In some communities, the police in dealing with situations that do not involve "serious" crime act as if order maintenance rather than law enforcement were their principal function. What is the defining characteristic of the patrolman's role thus becomes the style or strategy of the department as a whole because it is reinforced by the attitudes and policies of the police administrator. I shall call this the "watchman" style, employing here for analytical purposes a term that was once—in the early nineteenth century—descriptive generally of the mission of the American municipal police.[1]

In every city, of course, all patrolmen display a watchman style, that is, a concern for the order maintenance aspect of their function, some of the time, but in a few places this style becomes the operating code of the department. To the extent the administrator can influence the discretion of his men, he does so by allowing them to ignore many common minor violations, especially traffic and juvenile offenses, to tolerate, though gradually less so, a certain amount of vice and gambling, to use the law more as a means of maintaining order than of regulating conduct, and to judge the requirements of order differently depending on the character of the group in which the infraction occurs. Juveniles are "expected" to misbehave, and thus infractions among this group—unless they are serious or committed by a "wise guy"—are best ignored or treated informally. Negroes are thought to want, and to deserve, less law enforcement because to the police their conduct suggests a low level of public and private morality, an unwillingness to cooperate with the police or offer information, and widespread criminality. Serious crimes, of course, should be dealt with seriously; further, when Negroes offend whites, who, in the eyes of the police, have a different standard of public order, then an arrest must be made. Motorists, unless a departmental administrator wants to "make a record" by giving a few men the job of writing tickets, will often be left alone if their driving does not endanger or annoy others and if they do not resist or insult police authority. Vice and gambling are crimes only because the law says they are; they become problems only when the currently accepted standards of public order are violated (how accurately the political process measures those standards is another question). Private disputes—assaults among friends or family—are treated informally or ignored, unless the circumstances (a serious infraction, a violent person, a flouting of police authority) require an arrest. And disputes that are a normal business risk, such as getting a bad check, should be handled by civil procedures if possible. With exceptions to be noted, the watchman style is displayed in Albany, Amsterdam, and Newburgh.

The police are watchman-like not simply in emphasizing order over law enforcement but also in judging the seriousness of infractions less by what the law says about them than by their immediate and personal consequences, which will differ in importance depending on the standards of the relevant group—teenagers, Negroes, prostitutes, motorists, families, and so forth. In all cases, circumstances of person and condition are taken seriously into account—community notables are excused because they have influence and, perhaps, because their conduct is self-regulating; Negroes are either ignored or arrested, depending on the seriousness of the matter, because they have no influence and their conduct, except within broad limits, is not thought to be self-regulating. But no matter what his race, if a man's actions are "private" (gambling, for instance, or driving while intoxicated) or if they involve only another person with whom he has a dispute (an assault or a petty larceny), then, unless the offense is a "serious" one, the police tend to overlook the violation, to handle it informally (by a reprimand, for example), or to allow the two aggrieved parties to resolve it between themselves as if it were a private matter (a store-keeper getting restitution from a shoplifter or an assault victim bringing a civil action). If, on the other hand, the public peace has been breached—creating a disturbance in a restaurant, bothering passers-by on a sidewalk, insulting an officer, causing a crowd to collect, endangering others, or publicly offending current standards of propriety, then the officer is expected to restore order. If order cannot be restored or respect for authority elicited in any other way, an arrest is appropriate.

This "privatization" of the law defining misdemeanors and offenses and the emphasis on keeping order in public places is squarely within the nineteenth-century tradition of American law enforcement. As Lane notes in his history of the Boston police, the present-day force grew out of men appointed as part-time watchmen to keep the streets clear of obstructions, human and material, and to supervise a number of ordinances pertaining to health, lighting, and animals running loose. Vagabondage, raucous behavior, public lewdness, and street fights were the "criminal" matters handled by the watchmen and later by the police. *Real* crime—theft, robbery, murder, a private assault—was not in their province at all; detecting the perpetrators was essentially a private matter. If the victim could learn the identity of the thief or assailant, he applied for a warrant, which was then served, for a fee, by a constable. Later, detectives added to the force aided in the apprehension of criminals, but still on a fee-for-service basis; they were paid with a share of the recovered loot. The object of the process was not so much punishment as restitution.[2] Prostitution flourished, as did illegal drinking establishments; when they became too noxious—that is to say, when their toleration became impolitic—a "descent" (in modern terms, a raid) was carried out, never to eliminate the nuisance but to contain it.[3] As late as 1863, a Boston alderman, the aristocratic Thomas Coffin Amory, objected to proposals that the police play a more aggressive role in enforcing laws, especially those against drinking, and proclaimed: "It is the duty of the police officer to serve . . . warrants, when directed to him. It is nowhere made his duty to initiate prosecutions."[4] A few years later, Alderman Jonas Fitch rejected complaints against detective procedures and argued instead for a return to purely private enterprise.[5] When a visitor to Albany or Newburgh remarks that the city appears to be still in the nineteenth century, he is making a more significant observation than he may realize.

Cities where the police follow a watchman style will not thereby have identical standards of public order and morality. The quality of law enforcement depends not simply on how the police make judgments, but also on the socioeconomic composition of the community, the law enforcement standards set, implicitly or explicitly, by the political systems, and the special interests and concerns of the police chief. A city like Amsterdam with almost no Negroes and few derelict drunks obviously cannot ignore petty Negro crime or chronic alcoholics. Whether or not a city is "wide open" with respect to vice and gambling depends as much on what the political leadership will allow as on what the police are willing to ignore. And although the police in all three cities tend to make very few misdemeanor or juvenile arrests and issue very few traffic tickets, there are exceptions—the Albany police arrest drunks in large numbers, the Newburgh police issue many more speeding tickets.

The police style in these cities is watchman-like because, with certain exceptions dictated by the chief's policies or the city's expectations, the patrolman is allowed—and even encouraged—to follow the path of least resistance in carrying out his daily, routine assignments. His desire "to keep his nose clean" is reinforced by the department's desire "not to rock the boat." The police handle the problem of an adversary relationship with the public by withdrawing from as many such relationships as possible. As in all cities, these departments are highly sensitive to complaints from the public, though they differ in their handling of them. There is no formal complaint procedure nor any internal review or inspection system; instead, the chief handles such matters personally. Depending on the kind of political system of which he is a part, he may defend the department vocally, or hush the matter up quietly, or, if an influential person or segment of opinion has been offended, "throw the man to the wolves" by suspending or discharging him. (There were cases of officers dismissed in all three cities.) The chief tries to avoid such difficulties, however, by tightly restricting the discretionary authority of his patrolmen ("don't stick your neck out" unless you can make a "good pinch") and by having them refer all doubtful matters to the sergeants, the lieutenant, or even the chief himself.

In none of the three cities did even the critics of the police allege that serious crime was overlooked, nor did anyone deny that police tolerance of vice and gambling had declined somewhat over the years. All three communities were once a good deal gaudier and there is still a lot of life left in Albany and Newburgh. But all have become, at least publicly, more decorous, and this was accomplished without any significant change in the police—it was simply understood that the politicians and the community and church leaders wanted things a bit quieter, a process aided in Albany by the fact that the governor tore down the wooliest part of the city. (As in all land clearance programs, a large proportion of small businessmen, illegitimate as well as legitimate, never survive the relocation process.)

To a watchman-like department, the penal law is a device empowering the police to maintain order and protect others when a serious infraction has occurred; the exact charge brought against the person is not so important—or rather, it is important mostly in terms of the extent to which that particular section of the law facilitates the uncomplicated exercise of police power and increases the probability of the court sustaining the action. The charges of public intoxication and disorderly conduct are useful, and thus frequently used, in this regard—they are general, they are difficult to dispute, they carry relatively light penalties and thus are not likely to be resisted, and they are not technically, in New York, "crimes" that might hurt a man's record.

In these cities, the patrolman is expected to ignore the "little stuff" but to "be tough" where it is important. For example, the police have essentially a "familial" rather than law enforcement view of juvenile offenders. Their policy is to ignore most infractions ("kids will be kids") and to act in local parentis with respect to those that cannot be ignored: administer a swift kick or a verbal rebuke, have the boy do some chores ("Tom Sawyer justice"), or turn him over to his parents for discipline. An Albany probation officer who handles many young people told an interviewer that "sometimes a cop has to do things that aren't strictly legal, like taking a kid into the back room . . . The parents should do it, but don't."

The Amsterdam police recall fondly the days when such elaborate procedures were not necessary. The officer who caught the window smasher or bicycle thief meted out curbstone justice that would instill, if not the fear of God, then at least the fear of cops. "You used to be able to take care of the whole thing yourself," one officer told an interviewer, "but if you hit a kid today, you would really get clobbered." Whatever was once the case, it is clear that the police still rely largely on informal means for controlling juveniles—lecturing them on the street corner, taking them home to their parents, or telling them to "break it up" or "move along." Such informal methods have even been institutionalized in what one department calls "Saturday morning probation." Juveniles who commit more serious, or more frequent, offenses are told to come to police headquarters every Saturday morning for a few weeks or months to report on their behavior. The parents are informed and told the alternative could be an arrest. The chief conceded to an interviewer that "It's probably not kosher," but the family court judge is aware of the system and cooperates. If the offense is not, in the eyes of the police, a "real" crime at all—as, for example, drinking under age—nothing is done. If it is a "real" crime—such as auto theft or a burglary—then an arrest is made.

Informal settlements are also the rule with minor adult offenses. In Amsterdam, for example, in cases where disorder occurs or is likely, the police commonly tell the aggrieved party to "see the judge" and the abusive party to "go home" or, if he has no home, to "get out of town." All nontraffic incidents recorded by the Amsterdam police during June 1967 were examined; there were twenty-nine. About half—fourteen—involved a fight, dispute, disturbance, or drunkenness. In three cases the persons were arrested; they were charged with resisting or abusing the police.

There appear to be two exceptions to the watchman style in these three cities. First, the Newburgh police issue many more traffic tickets than Albany or Amsterdam. Second, the Albany department arrests many more drunks than not only other watchman-like departments but more than almost any kind of department. Traffic, however, is that police function most easily brought under the control of the administrator . . . his interest in ticketing, and almost nothing else, determines how many shall be issued. And in Newburgh, it was not even the chief, but his deputy who, together with the city manager, put on the pressure for ticketing. But that pressure was limited to the men assigned to traffic and never became a department-wide policy.

The high drunk arrest rate in Albany has a somewhat different explanation. There appear to be simply more drunks—especially derelicts—on the streets: Albany is a major transportation center for people moving up and down the Hudson River, east and west between Boston and Buffalo, Cleveland, and Chicago, and to and from the summer resorts in northern New York State. In the past, the city was a place where people went looking for a good time. When the famous "Gut" was flourishing, a large number of arrests for intoxication were required to maintain some semblance of order and, more important, keep the carousers from leaving the area to annoy the "decent people" elsewhere in the city. What the detectives condoned the patrol force had to cope with. Though much of the Gut is gone, the city still attracts derelicts from all over the state. Thus, part of the high arrest rate can be explained by the fact that there are not simply more drunks, there are more *homeless* drunks in Albany than in most other cities. The tendency of a watchman-style police force to go easy on local drunks cannot, obviously, operate if the drunks are not locals — not only will out-of-towners not be bound by local norms, they may become a burden on local charity. Albany, accordingly, makes proportionally seven times as many arrests for vagrancy as does Oakland. As a high law enforcement official in Albany told an interviewer:

> We're pretty tough on vagrants here. We give them summary justice and send them to jail. There, the police rough 'em up a bit and then we send them out of town. These people could work if they wanted to. There's plenty of jobs here, what with all the construction going on . . . The only reason these men don't work is that they don't want to work.

There may be other explanations as well, but they must remain conjectural.[6] What is clear is that in Albany there is not, as in Oakland, a concern for the law enforcement implications of drunkenness — its relation to strong-man robberies, for example. Drunkenness in Albany is a matter of public order; it so happens that for various reasons, drunks are more likely in that city (than in, say Newburgh) to be seen by the police as a threat to order.

In a watchman system, little emphasis is placed on a "correct" appearance or manner. Since the task of the police is to be ready for a serious crime or to restore order, neatness or courtesy are not especially important, though by the same token one does not wish to do anything that will needlessly antagonize the "respectable" element in the city, for that could cause "trouble." A watchman-like department is as interested in avoiding trouble as in minding its own business.

It would be a mistake to assume that a watchman-like department is necessarily a corrupt one, though there may be a little corruption in all such departments and a great deal in a few. The predisposition to avoid involvement — to control (not eliminate) public disorder rather than to enforce the law — depends not on corrupt motives, but on the inclinations of the men recruited into police work and the norms of the organization to which they belong. In a small town, the police may tolerate illicit businesses because no one with any influence wishes to have it otherwise; if tolerance rests on community indifference rather than police forbearance, then the police have nothing to sell and, except for small gifts, nothing to gain. Of course, if such enterprises operate on a scale larger than what public opinion would tolerate, then the police can sell their ability to "keep things quiet." In a larger city, with an organized political opposition and formal institutions (newspapers, churches, civic groups) that might wish to act as keepers of the community's conscience, tolerance is more valuable because more precarious. It may, therefore, be sold, though not necessarily by the police. A strong political party may sell "licenses" to run illegal businesses and simply order the police to respect the licenses; if there is no strong party to which they are beholden, the police may sell the licenses themselves. The Amsterdam police, for example, are not bribed to be tolerant of gambling; rather, they believe that the community expects them (and pays them) to behave as mere night watchmen, and they do. . . .

THE LEGALISTIC STYLE

In some departments, the police administrator uses such control as he has over the patrolmen's behavior to induce them to handle commonplace situations as if they were matters of law enforcement rather than order maintenance. He realizes, of course, that the officer cannot always act as if his duty were merely to compare observed behavior with a legal standard and make an arrest if that standard has been violated—the law itself, especially that governing misdemeanor arrests, does not always permit the application of its sanctions. But whenever he acts on his own initiative or to the extent he can influence the outcome of disorderly situations in which he acts on the initiative of the citizen, the patrolman is expected to take a law enforcement view of his role. Such a police style will be called "legalistic," and it can be found in varying degrees in Oakland and Highland Park and to a growing extent in Syracuse.

A legalistic department will issue traffic tickets at a high rate, detain and arrest a high proportion of juvenile offenders, act vigorously against illicit enterprises, and make a large number of misdemeanor arrests even when, as with petty larceny, the public order has not been breached. The police will act, on the whole, as if there were a single standard of community conduct—that which the law prescribes—rather than different standards for juveniles, Negroes, drunks, and the like. Indeed, because such persons are more likely than certain others to commit crimes, the law will fall heavily on them and be experienced as "harassment."

The Oakland and Highland Park police departments began functioning this way in about the mid-1950's; Oakland continues to do so, and Highland Park has modified its policies only slightly since the appointment of a new chief in 1965. Syracuse began moving in this direction in 1963, with the arrival of a "reform" police chief and deputy chief; it is too early to tell how far it will proceed. For now, it has only some of the earmarks of a legalistic department —and these primarily in the field of traffic enforcement.

The concept "legalistic" does not necessarily imply that the police regard all laws as equally important or that they love the law for its own sake. In all the cities here discussed, officers distinguish between major and minor crimes, feel that private disputes are usually less important than public disorders, and are willing to overlook some offenses and accept some excuses. Indeed, because the "normal" tendency of police officers . . . is to under-enforce the law, a legalistic police style is necessarily the result of rather strenuous administrative efforts to get patrolmen to do what they might not otherwise do; as such, it is never completely successful. Though there may be a few zealots in a watchman-like department, they will be few indeed and will probably concentrate their efforts more on making "good pinches," which in any department are rewarded, than on "pushing paper" (that is, writing tickets or citing juveniles). In a legalistic department, there is likely to be a sizable number of patrolmen with comparatively little zeal—typically older officers, or officers "left over" from a previous and different administration, or officers of any age who do not regard the benefits (in terms of promotions, official recognition, or good duty assignments) of zealousness as worth the costs in effort and possibly adverse citizen relations.

The legalistic style does mean that, on the whole, the department will produce many arrests and citations, especially with respect to those matters in which the police and not the public invoke the law; even when the police are called by the public to intervene, they are likely to intervene formally, by making an arrest or urging the signing of a complaint, rather than informally, as through conciliation or by delaying an arrest in hopes that the situation will take care of itself.

Though in many cases they are required by law to rely on citizen arrests, the police in following the legalistic style do not try to privatize the handling of disputes and minor offenses. Citizen arrests are facilitated, prosecution of shoplifters is encouraged, juveniles are handled formally, and drunks are arrested "for their own protection." Prostitutes are arrested (but drug-store pornography, because the law affords fewer grounds for an arrest, is pretty much left alone). Even in Highland Park, though a small town, drunks and juveniles have been handled more formally since the mid-1950's and bad-check passers are often prosecuted even when the merchant is willing to drop charges. As the chief told an interviewer, "Once we get that check, we'll sign a complaint and we'll prosecute. We've got the check with their name on it and the date, and it's marked 'insufficient funds,' so we've got all the evidence we need. A lot of the stores would just as soon not prosecute, I suppose, but . . . we're not a collection agency." At the same time, as Highland Park is a small and affluent town, the police are hardly eager to intervene in domestic disputes —to be precise, wife beatings—which, unlike the barroom brawls of the big city, are rich in opportunities for an officer to get himself in trouble. The police once handled such dilemmas occasionally by calling the local magistrate (until recently, an elected magistrate handled all local cases) and asking him to try informally to reach a settlement and, of course, to take responsibility. This is no longer the case; now, the victim would be asked to sign a complaint ticket.

Though the legalistic department will issue a large number of traffic tickets, not every department with a high ticketing rate can be called legalistic. Because he has an unambiguous performance measure, the police administrator can obtain almost any level of ticketing he wishes without necessarily altering the way the police conceive their function, as when ticketing is delegated to a specialized traffic enforcement unit. A legalistic department will typically go beyond this, however, and put all patrolmen, not just traffic specialists, under some pressure to "produce." To the extent this policy is followed, some change in the patrolman's conception of his function ensues. Sometimes, however, the opposite occurs. In Highland Park, the chief responsible for the heavy emphasis on traffic enforcement was replaced, in 1965, by a chief who shifted the department's strategy without greatly affecting its ticket productivity and without abandoning its general law enforcement orientation. He did this by substituting specialization for quotas—easing somewhat the pressure to produce on the force as a whole and giving the task to one or two officers who would do little else.[7]

A better test for the existence of the legalistic style can be found in those situations where the administrator's control of his subordinate's conduct is less certain and where therefore greater and more systematic efforts must be made to achieve the desired behavior. The handling of juvenile offenders is just such a case. In Oakland and Highland Park, and perhaps to a growing extent in Syracuse, the police take a law enforcement rather than familial view of their responsibilities in delinquency cases. Perhaps "institutional" view would be more correct, because the police in none of these cities feel their task is simply to make an arrest whenever possible. Indeed, the officers are keenly aware of the importance of the family and spend considerable time talking to parents, but the relationship between officer and juvenile or officer and parent is formal and institutional—the officer seeks to involve specialized, professional services (probation officers, judges, child guidance clinics) rather than to apply his own form of discipline or to resort to appeals to clergymen or others presumed to wield "moral" influence. Of course, to take advantage of the professional services the community provides, the juvenile must be brought into these institutions—and that, typically, requires an arrest. . . .

THE SERVICE STYLE

In some communities, the police take seriously all requests for either law enforcement or order maintenance (unlike police with a watchman style) but are less likely to respond by making an arrest or otherwise imposing formal sanctions (unlike police with a legalistic style). The police intervene frequently but not formally. This style is often found in homogeneous, middle-class communities in which there is a high level of apparent agreement among citizens on the need for and definition of public order but in which there is no administrative demand for a legalistic style. In these places, the police see their chief responsibility as protecting a common definition of public order against the minor and occasional threats posed by unruly teenagers and "outsiders" (tramps, derelicts, visiting college boys). Though there will be family quarrels, they will be few in number, private in nature, and constrained by general understandings requiring seemly conduct. The middle-class character of such communities makes the suppression of illegal enterprises both easy (they are more visible) and necessary (public opinion will not tolerate them) and reduces the rate of serious crime committed by residents; thus, the police will be freer to concentrate on managing traffic, regulating juveniles, and providing services.

Such a police policy will be called the "service" style, and it can be found especially in Brighton and Nassau County. In such communities, which are not deeply divided along class or racial lines, the police can act as if their task were to estimate the "market" for police services and to produce a "product" that meets the demand. For patrolmen especially, the pace of police work is more leisurely (there are fewer radio messages per tour of duty than in a community with a substantial lower class)[8] and the community is normally peaceful, thus apparent threats to order are more easily detected. Furthermore, the citizenry expects its police officers to display the same qualities as its department store salesman, local merchants, and public officials—courtesy, a neat appearance, and a deferential manner. Serious matters—burglaries, robberies, assaults— are of course taken seriously and thus "suspicious" persons are carefully watched or questioned. But with regard to minor infractions of the law, arrests are avoided when possible (the rates at which traffic tickets are issued and juveniles referred to Family Court will be much lower than in legalistic departments) but there will be frequent use of informal, nonarrest sanctions (warnings issued to motorists, juveniles taken to headquarters or visited in their homes for lectures). . . .

NOTES

1. A social scientist reading this and the next two sections will understand that any typology is an abstraction from reality that is employed, not to describe a particular phenomenon, but to communicate its essential or "ideal" form—in this case, the "flavor" or "style" of the organization. The lay reader should bear this in mind and guard against assuming that because two or three police departments are grouped together they are identical in all respects. They are not. Furthermore, a typology can only suggest, it cannot prove, that a particular operating style is associated with certain organizational characteristics. Finally, merely because it was found convenient in this study to group these departments together into three styles, no one should assume that these are the only police styles or that every police department in the country displays one or the other of them. I assume if enough departments were studied that one would probably learn of other styles in addition to these and that one would certainly learn that many, if not most, departments display a combination of two or more styles.
2. Roger Lane, *Policing the City: Boston, 1822-1885* (Cambridge, Mass.: Harvard University Press, 1967), pp. 7, 56, 57, 150. See also Seldon D. Bacon, "The Early Development of American Municipal Police," unpublished PhD. dissertation, Yale University (1939), p. 784. Professor Herbert Jacob suggests another way in which the law may become privatized. In his study of bankruptcy and wage garnishment proceedings in four Wisconsin cities, he found that in some, such as Green Bay, there is relatively little inclination to invoke the legal processes to handle debts, while in others, such as Madison, there is a strong inclination. Green Bay prefers to settle such matters privately, Madison to settle them formally and publicly. Herbert

Jacob, "Wage Garnishment and Bankruptcy Proceedings in Four Cities," in James Q. Wilson, ed., *City Politics and Public Policy* (New York: John Wiley & Sons, 1968).

3. Lane, *Policing the City*, pp. 115-116.

4. Quoted in *ibid.*, p. 130.

5. Quoted in *ibid.*, p. 154.

6. A former Albany police officer to whom this manuscript was shown offered in a letter to me an additional explanation for the high drunk arrest rate: "Many times a person will go to a police station to make a complaint. This could be anything from an auto accident, an argument, or of being rolled. The policeman on the desk will inform the person that he will look into the matter and then ask the person if they have been drinking. No matter how many or few beers he may have had, he will be booked for public intox."

7. When the specialized enforcement strategy replaced the quota system, the morale of the Highland Park patrolmen improved. But the new methods did not substantially reduce the chance that a motorist would be ticketed. In 1965, though the new chief was in office for about nine months, the number of moving vioation tickets issued was about the same as the average for the preceding three years when the former chief, and thus the quota system, prevailed.

8. During the first week of June 1965, the Brighton police sent 124 nonadministrative radio messages to patrol cars and the Newburgh police sent 173; the towns are approximately equal in population, but the median income in Brighton is twice that in Newburgh. Furthermore, a substantially higher fraction of the Newburgh calls (8.9 per cent) were for "crimes in progress" than of the Brighton calls (3.2 per cent).

Discussion Questions

1. In what ways does Eisenstein and Jacob's description of the courtroom workgroup differ from the more commonly accepted view of courts? How did the article affect your previous opinions about judges and lawyers?

2. How would you describe the style of your local police? Do you believe that there is a trend toward more service style police departments? What types of people are most likely to pursue careers in law enforcement?

3. How accurate a picture do you believe most Americans have of life in prison? If our correctional system is irrational, uneconomic, and ineffective, how can it be improved?

CHAPTER SEVEN

FINANCING STATE AND LOCAL GOVERNMENTS

The subject of finance is often viewed by students of state and local govern-ment as one of secondary interest, and on occasion this viewpoint seems to be shared by textbook writers who treat it briefly in one of their later chapters. This is unfortunate, for finance is one of the most basic subjects to come before state and local governments in any given year. There are many reasons for this. One obvious reason is that the adequacy of state and local revenues is an important determinant in the ability of those governments to meet the needs of their citizens. Federal aid is a big help, but for the most part state and local governments must finance their activities out of their own revenue sources.

Further, the tax structures utilized by state and local governments deter-mine the relative shares of the cost of government to be borne by different income groups within the jurisdiction being served. Some forms, notably the progressive income tax, put a heavier burden on the wealthy than on other income groups, while regressive forms, such as the sales tax, put a heavier burden on middle- and lower-income people. Public perception of the "fairness" of a state or local tax system helps determine public willingness to support that government, but it is not always easy for the public to understand the real impact that different kinds of taxes may have on different income groups. Thus sales taxes are sometimes perceived as fairer than progressive income taxes because everyone pays the same tax rate. In fact, however, they take a greater percentage of their income from middle- and lower-class people than they do from the wealthy.

Finally, the extent to which a state or local government allows itself to rely on federal grants as a revenue source will help determine the extent to which it is subject to federal influence. As was suggested by the ACIR study reprinted in Chapter 1, accepting federal money means accepting at least some federal direction. Not only must those funds be spent for purposes for which the federal government has given its approval, but they often must be "matched" in varying proportions by state or local funds. The recipient government must also abide by a variety of other "strings," such as the avoidance of racial or sex discrimination and the implementation of an affirmative action program.

In recent years the cost of government has gone up dramatically, and inevitably so have taxes. One result has been the so-called taxpayers' revolt, a determination on the part of many Americans to make use of devices such as the citizen initiative to limit state and local taxes. In the first article in this chapter, Frank Levy examines Proposition 13, a California initiative that severely limited property taxes in that state and that marked the beginning of the taxpayers' revolt. He argues that the circumstances surrounding Proposition 13 were unique to California and that its passage had the effect of shifting power from local governments to the state government.

The world of government finance sometimes appears to be one best reached through the looking glass, a world where the politicians responsible for imposing taxes and creating budgets do their best to convince both themselves and the voters that they have done something different from what they have actually done. Thus as this is written Congress is congratulating itself for creating a "balanced" budget, while the concurrence of outside experts is that a large deficit will quickly be created by the various costs associated with the current recession. In the second article Arnold Meltsner argues that city officials in Oakland, California, engage in a variety of such deceptions. Perhaps most notably, they seem willing to deceive themselves about the fairness of the tax system they utilize, assuring themselves that it is fair when this is patently not the case.

On Understanding
Proposition 13

Frank Levy

Any subject worth studying spawns at least two schools of thought. So it is with the current taxpayers' revolt. There is, first, a "macro" school of analysis, which views events of the last 14 months as a series of similar responses to a few root causes. The causes are rapid inflation, rising taxes, and the growing size and arrogance of government. The responses include California's Proposition 13, subsequent ballot initiatives in other states, and calls to limit Federal expenditures through a constitutional amendment. This broad view, congenial to the requirements of television news, has little use for the details that distinguish one state's tax-reform initiative from another's. As one young economist put it: "Those who would look [for explanations] to the circumstances of individual states are wasting their time."

For persons of the opposite view, the circumstances of individual states provide interesting and important variations. Some ballot initiatives proposed cutting current expenditures. Others proposed limiting future expenditure growth. Some focused on property taxes. Others applied to taxes in general. Some took place where budgets were in surplus. Others took place in states that were broke. And some initiatives won while others lost. Adherents of this form of analysis—the "micro" school of thought—argue that examining these variations will yield a more precise understanding of voter concerns—concerns that in fact may have differed from one state to the next.

What follows is a micro-school examination of Proposition 13. Because, in Eugene Bardach's phrase, the good is in the particulars, it is appropriate to begin with a summary of the initiative itself. Proposition 13, passed in June 1978, contained three major points:

Reprinted with the author's permission from *The Public Interest*, No. 56 (Summer 1979), pp. 66-89. © 1979 by National Affairs, Inc. Frank Levy is Senior Research Associate at The Urban Institute. Funding for the study was provided by a grant from the Department of Housing and Urban Development.

1. For purposes of taxation, a property's full value would be set at its estimated market value in 1975 or its price at the time of its last sale, whichever occurred later. As long as a property was retained by the same owner, its full value could increase by no more than 2 percent per year. At time of sale, the full value could be increased to the actual sale price.

2. The combined property taxes of a city, a county, a school district, etc., would be limited to 1 percent of a property's full value. (In 1977, total property taxes on a typical California home averaged about 2.6 percent of market value.) The only exception to this limit was made for property taxes needed to retire bond issues that were outstanding as of June 1978.

3. Any general state increase would require a two-thirds vote in the legislature rather than the majority-vote requirement then in effect. Similarly, local governments could not increase property taxes above the 1-percent limit but could increase other local taxes, subject to a two-thirds majority in a referendum.

In at least one important respect Proposition 13 differed from most of the initiatives that were proposed in other states later in the year. At the time of its passage, voters were uncertain about the size of California's budget surplus and so Proposition 13 was perceived by them and by the national press as a potentially substantial expenditure cut. By contrast, in most other states electorates voted not on possible cuts in public spending, but on tax shifts or limits to future expenditure growth. Of the 17 states with one or more fiscal initiatives on the November ballot, only four voted on actual expenditure cuts. In two states (Michigan and Oregon), the cuts were defeated. In one state (Idaho), the cut passed. And in the fourth state (Nevada), the cut passed but it was a "free vote": Voters knew they would have to approve the initiative again in 1980 before it would take effect.

A limit on future expenditure growth promises controlled, if unpleasant, adjustments. A cut in current expenditures suggests something much more unsettling, something voters will not lightly embrace. The willingness of California voters to approve such a cut (by a two-to-one margin) suggests they were more angry than most. And so it is particularly useful to understand their motivations.

A natural line of inquiry is offered by recent California history. From 1968 through 1976, Californians saw numerous attempts to reduce property taxes and/or government expenditures by initiative. Many never qualified for the ballot. Those that did all failed. By examining these efforts we can ascertain those factors that changed between previous failures and Proposition 13's success.

THE DAWN OF PROPERTY-TAX REFORM

The story of the recent taxpayers' revolt in California begins in the summer of 1965, when the *San Francisco Chronicle* began a series of stories on the bribery of property-tax assessors across the state. The *Chronicle* reported that elected assessors had received "campaign contributions" to "review and adjust" assessments on business properties. A similar series of articles was soon published in the *San Francisco Examiner*.

Several state legislators had been longtime proponents of property-tax reform. Reform, as they defined it, meant a uniform statewide ratio of a property's assessed value to its market value, with sufficient reassessment to keep the ratio current. Until the scandal, however, the legislature as a whole was unenthusiastic. In the spring of 1965, it had once again shunted aside a reform bill.

But once the scandal gained publicity, the legislature's attitude changed dramatically. By the middle of 1967, a strong reform bill had been signed into law. Assembly Bill 80, or the Petris-Knox bill, gave county assessors three years to reassess all property at 25 percent of market value and required frequent reassessments to keep the ratio intact.

Property-tax reform achieved great popularity because the newspaper stories had focused on abatements purchased by businessmen. From these stories, most voters drew the conclusion that business was not paying its fair share of the tax bill. The conclusion was not well founded: Businessmen often received tax breaks in preference to other businessmen, but in many jurisdictions, business properties as a whole were paying a disproportionately *high* percentage of the tax bill. Ironically, it was in San Francisco County that the discrepancy was greatest. As Diane Paul documented in *The Politics of the Property Tax*, single-family housing in San Francisco was assessed at about 9 percent of market value while commercial buildings were assessed at about 35 percent. Across the bay, in Alameda County, single-family housing was assessed at an average 22 percent while commercial property was assessed at 28 percent.

It followed that the adjustment to a uniform 25-percent assessment ratio often brought about a rapid increase in homeowner assessments. In theory, increased assessments need not mean increased tax bills: Local governments can reduce tax rates to compensate. But in California such compensation was rare. Local governments were required by the state constitution to tax all property at the same rate. As assessments on single-family housing were rising, assessments on commercial property were falling. As a result, the total tax base often changed relatively little. Local governments wishing to maintain property-tax revenues could not cut tax rates, even though single-family housing was assuming a greater proportionate share of the tax load. By the 1970's, in California and elsewhere, a similar shifting of the tax burden would become a major stimulus to the taxpayers' revolt.

Largely as a response to the increase in homeowners' tax bills, the "Watson Initiative" appeared on the ballot of November 1968 as Proposition 9. The initiative was developed and sponsored by Phillip Watson, County Assessor of Los Angeles. It involved a constitutional amendment that would have required property-tax revenues to be divided into two classes: Revenues going to "people-related services" (primarily education and welfare); and revenues going to "property-related services" (all uses except people-related services, for example, public safety and general government). Under the initiative, property-tax revenues for people-related services were to decline annually by 20 percent of their 1969-1970 levels until they were eliminated in 1973. Property-tax revenues for property-related services would be limited to 1 percent of a property's current market value.

The Watson Initiative was not so much concerned with reducing public spending as with changing the way it was financed. Both Watson and his opponents assumed that the state would fund those local-government functions that the initiative eliminated. But because Proposition 9 was unclear as to how this funding would occur, it provided the opportunity for opponents to paint a fearsome picture of the income- and sales-tax increases the initiative would require. In the end, voters were faced with a choice between an evil they knew and one they didn't.

The state legislature responded by passing a more moderate tax-relief alternative. By 1968, both legislators and then-Governor Reagan knew that assessment reform had produced unanticipated consequences. They also realized that were the Watson Initiative to pass, they would be in the unenviable position of having to raise state taxes sharply or implicitly approve sharp cuts in public schools and welfare payments. To help avoid this situation, the legislature passed California's first homeowner's property-tax exemption. Under the exemption, the first $750 of assessed value of an owner-occupied home would be exempt from property taxation. The revenues lost by local government under the exemption would be replaced by the state. In a county like Alameda where there had been relatively large assessment adjustments, the exemption would have cut the typical homeowner's Petris-Knox tax increase in half. In a county like Los Angeles with smaller assessment adjustments, the exemption would have offset the typical tax increase entirely.

To be sure, the legislature did not act with great dispatch. The homeowner's exemption, like the Watson Initiative, would require voter approval of a constitutional amendment. But by the time the legislature finished action, the November ballots had already been printed. The homeowner's exemption had to be placed on a supplemental ballot with a special explanation sent to all voters. Nevertheless, the need for the amendment gave the legislature and Governor the opportunity to confront the Watson Initiative directly. The initiative was portrayed as having large and uncertain impacts on state taxes, while the exemption was said to embody "responsible tax relief."

But voter attitudes were also influenced by the economic context of the times. With one or two exceptions—San Diego County and the now-famous Marin County—housing market values were growing at moderate rates of 5 to 6 percent per year. Rapid assessment increases were not occurring in many counties, and where they did occur they could be attributed to one-time-only Petris-Knox adjustments, rather than to long-term trends. At the same time, according to the monthly *California Poll*, Californians felt optimistic about the economy in general. The absence of rapid, long-run assessment growth and the relatively favorable economic outlook together played a large part in determining the election outcomes. The homeowner's exemption passed with 54 percent of the vote. The Watson Initiative lost by better than two-to-one.

The Watson Initiative campaign was a prototype of the way the property-tax debate would go for nine more years. Property taxes were distasteful, but as long as they did not become outrageous people would remain cautious—too cautious to approve large cuts in public spending. And so long as spending cuts were regarded as unacceptable, proposals for property-tax relief would continue to raise the specter of large increases in sales and income taxes—a trade most voters were unwilling to make.

At the same time, it was unlikely that the property-tax issue would go away. The Petris-Knox bill ensured that property assessments would retain a 25-percent relationship to market value. By the early 1970's, most counties were on three-year, and some on two-year, reassessment cycles. The system had little political discretion to mitigate the effects of housing inflation on homeowner assessments.

In June 1970, Californians had the chance to vote on another tax-shift measure, Proposition 8. Whereas the Watson Initiative was clearly designed to cut property taxes, Proposition 8's motivations were more cloudy. Proposition 8 called for an expansion of the homeowner's exemption and a substantial increase in the state share of welfare and education costs. At the same time, Proposition 8 *did not* require local governments to translate the savings for localities into reduced property taxes. This lack of an explicit statement on tax reduction together with the nature of the proposition's sponsorship—for example, the California Teacher's Association—brought the immediate fire of taxpayers' associations and the League of Women Voters. Proposition 8 lost with 28 percent of the vote.

There was also an attempt in 1970 to place a more standard tax-limitation initiative on the ballot. The amendment's sponsor was Howard Jarvis, a lobbyist for a Los Angeles association of apartment-house owners. The attempt failed for lack of signatures.

In 1972, Phillip Watson qualified a second initiative for the November ballot. Proposition 14, like Watson's earlier Proposition 9, limited local property taxes and shifted most educational and welfare expenditures to the state. But Proposition 14 and Proposition 9 differed in two respects. First, Proposition 14 sought to anticipate the criticism that it would shift great costs to the state without creating corresponding sources of revenue. It specified a set of increases in the state sales tax, liquor tax, cigarette tax, and the tax on corporate income, which Watson claimed would be enough to pay for the increased state costs. Second, Proposition 14 began to deal with expenditure limitations rather than just tax shifts. It specified a new state-local educational finance arrangement in which every district would receive total revenues of $825 per child, about $100 per child below the then-current statewide average expenditure. The uniform educational-expenditure formula was intended to deal with the then-recent California Supreme Court decision in *Serrano v. Priest*, the decision which required California to revise its school finance formula to disassociate a school's available resources from its property-tax base.

By 1972, California was recovering from the national recession but its economic outlook was still uncertain. Thus economic conditions were more favorable to Proposition 14 than the optimistic 1968 outlook had been to Proposition 9. More important, assessments for single-family homes were beginning to increase at 7 to 8 percent per year as the result of housing-market inflation—not simply one-time government-mandated adjustments. Nonetheless, Proposition 14 failed badly with only one-third of the vote.

The wisdom of hindsight suggests the proposition's failure was due in large part to its own specificity. Its proposed increases in alcohol and tobacco taxes enraged the alcohol and tobacco industries, which became the chief financiers of the anti-14 campaign. Similarly, the explicit proposal to reduce and make uniform expenditures for education unnerved many persons who felt that education was still worthy of strong support and that educational-spending decisions were best left at the local level. Moreover, Proposition 14's specificity did not keep Watson's critics (including Governor Reagan) from charging that his calculations were wrong and that the proposition would leave the state with a large revenue gap which could be made up only by substantial increases in income and sales taxes.

As in 1968, the state legislature moved to draft a moderate alternative, once again somewhat belatedly. The resulting legislation, known as Senate Bill 90, was not completed until after Proposition 14's November defeat. Nonetheless, Senate Bill 90 spoke directly to many of Proposition 14's concerns and demonstrated that the legislature was aware of the homeowner's plight. The bill contained an expansion of the homeowner's exemption to $1,750 (from $750), a modest income-tax credit for renters, limits on city and county tax rates, and limits on school-district expenditure levels. Its costs—estimated at $1.1 billion in its first year—would be funded by an increase in the state sales tax.

SOME RECENT HISTORY

In 1973, California confronted another tax-reform measure, Governor Reagan's Proposition 1. Unlike previous initiatives, Proposition 1 was not concerned with shifting taxes but with limiting the size of the public sector. It elaborated on the local tax limits in Senate Bill 90 and increased the majority required for state tax bills to two-thirds. The proposition also required that total state expenditures could increase no faster than the increase in state income. Governor Reagan's authorship gave Proposition 1 some credibility, but the proposition was written in complex language that aroused substantial suspicion. Opponents argued that any limit on state spending would force necessary services back onto local government and the property tax. This argument combined with group interests—for example, those of state employees —and Proposition 1 lost with 44 percent of the vote.

Sometime after 1973, California entered into a period of rapid and accelerating housing inflation. Federal Home Loan Bank Board data indicate that between 1973 and 1977, housing prices in the Los Angeles and San Francisco metropolitan areas were increasing at an average rate of 14 to 15 percent per year, a rate significantly higher than that in most other areas of the country.

The reasons for the particular intensity of housing inflation in California are not entirely clear. Leo Grebler and Frank B. Mittelbach, of the Graduate School of Management at UCLA, suggest in their recent book, *The Inflation of House Prices*, a number of factors that intensified California's excess demand, including rapidly rising incomes and immigration. John J. Kirlin and Jeffrey I. Chapman of the University of Southern California point to the extensive use of bank financing via trust deeds rather than mortgages, the more common instrument in most states. They note that a trust deed makes it relatively easy for a bank to reacquire a property in default, without encumbrances and without litigation. From the banks' perspective, the trust deed made housing that much more liquid an asset. Correspondingly, banks were encouraged to accommodate the housing inflation through 30-year mortgages and other devices.

In a world of "unreformed" property taxes, tax assessors might have reacted to the housing inflation by exercising discretion or increasing assessments at a slow pace. But California's property-tax system, as reformed by Petris-Knox, kept assessed values and market values in a fixed ratio. These reassessments raised the possibility that a family would find itself financially distressed by housing costs well above what they expected when they had purchased their home.

Consider a family in Los Angeles that made $18,000 in 1973. At that time a typical home was financed at a 7 3/4-percent rate of interest for 25 years. Institutions required a 20-percent down payment and used a 25-percent rule of thumb: The sum of the monthly housing payment and property-tax payment should be less than 25 percent of gross monthly income. The combined Los Angeles tax rates for city, county, and the Los Angeles Unified School District stood at about $12.25 per $100 of assessed valuation (and the first $1,750 of assessed valuation was tax exempt under Senate Bill 90). Taking all these factors into account, a bank would have judged the family capable of purchasing a $47,500 home. The annual property-tax bill would have been slightly over $1,000 per year. By 1976, typical reassessments would have increased the family's annual property-tax bill by $730. By 1977, their tax bill would have risen by an additional $400 per year, a nominal tax increase of over 100 percent in four years!

In addition, public concern was aggravated by several factors. In practice, the rate of housing inflation was accelerating, not constant—so homeowners could well believe things were "getting out of control." Moreover, even the most efficient counties fully reassessed properties only every two years, and thus individual assessments did not rise smoothly over time. Rather, each year one-third to one-half of all homeowners would receive an assessment increase of 25 to 40 percent, and their protests would remind other homeowners, who in the previous year or two had received a similar increase, that they could expect another whopping boost in the not-too-distant future.

In 1976, there were two attempts to place property-tax initiatives on the ballot. One was sponsored by Phillip Watson. The other was sponsored by Paul Gann, a retired Sacramento realtor. Surprisingly, neither initiative got the necessary number of signatures.

There is more to the story but events to this point should give comfort to those who argue that there is nothing new under the sun. Proposition 13 was not a spontaneous phenomenon, but was rather the latest inning in a biennial event, a restitching of numerous earlier initiatives. A limitation on state expenditures, passed in seven states last fall, was almost passed in California six years ago.

And what of Jarvis and Gann? They were both good campaigners but not the great initiators portrayed in the media. By 1976, both men had tried standard tax initiatives and, unlike Watson and Reagan, they had failed to stir a ripple. History will record that in 1978 Jarvis and Gann hit a home run. But good history will also record that circumstances served them a fat pitch.

WHERE WERE THE LOCAL GOVERNMENTS?

The Los Angeles homeowner's tax calculation cited above implicitly assumes that increased assessments led to increased tax bills or, put another way, that local jurisdictions did not lower their tax rates to compensate for higher home-owner assessments. Over the 1973-77 period this was the case, by and large. Estimates prepared by the California Office of the Legislative Analyst suggest that the average combined tax rate faced by a California homeowner declined about 5 percent from FY 1974 to FY 1978, or about 1.2 percent per year, but this was not nearly enough to offset the assessment increases. Why was local governments' response so weak?

The commonplace view holds that tax rates did not fall because local governments were greedy, taking in all they could while they could. A second view holds that, for a variety of reasons, local revenues increased more slowly than assessed values on housing would suggest, and that as a result local governments were left with an undeserved reputation. There is, as in most cases, some evidence on each side—but the second view seems the more accurate.

The case for local-government greed is weakened at the outset because none of the available data sources shows an excessive growth in local expenditures. Figures from the Office of the State Controller show aggregate local expenditure grew at about 9 percent per year in per capita terms. This was about 2 percent per year above the growth in the Consumer Price Index, but well below the 15 percent annual growth rates in the assessed values of single-family homes.

Similar data come from the Federal *Census of Government*, and show that between 1973 and 1977, local-government employment per capita grew at about 1 percent per year while average earnings grew at 7 percent per year. The earnings growth rate was higher than that of most private-sector wages, but it did not keep pace with inflation. Here too, the data suggest that local-government payrolls were increasing but their growth was far more moderate than the growth of housing assessments.

Some persons have charged that local-government greed was expressed not in increased payrolls, but rather in the establishment of large, unrestricted surpluses. There are, however, no hard data to support this proposition and at least some soft data to support the opposite view. To be sure, the State Controller's data, the Census's employment data, and existing data on local surpluses are all open to question. But together, they suggest that during the period of rapid assessment increases, local governments were not exploding but were growing slightly faster than the rate of inflation. In particular, the growth rate of local expenditures—less than 10 percent per year—was significantly below the growth rate of assessments of single-family homes.

It is this last fact which opens the door to a more charitable view of local governments, a view justified by several institutional factors.[1] One such factor was the composition of the property-tax rolls. In 1973, about 33 percent of the value of the rolls represented owner-occupied, single-family housing. Another 5 to 7 percent was single-family housing occupied by renters. The remainder was commercial property. Commercial-property assessments are typically based on discounted income, and during the early and middle 1970's—the era of stagflation—business incomes were not doing well. Accordingly, commercial assessments were growing relatively slowly.

For example, the counties sampled by the State Board of Equalization in 1973 and 1976 had an average annual-growth rate of 12.8 percent for single-family homes but only 7.6 percent (per parcel) for all other properties.[2] Similarly, estimates by the Office of the Legislative Analyst indicate that between FY 1977 and FY 1978 the value of all owner-occupied single-family homes increased by 20 percent while the value of all other property on the rolls increased by 10.5 percent. *The difference in these growth rates was important because, as noted earlier, a local jurisdiction had to tax all properties at the same rate. If a local government wanted to reduce sharply the tax rate faced by homeowners, the rate reduction would apply to commercial properties as well, thereby risking a substantial revenue loss.* In practice, tax rates fell only slowly. As a result, property taxes on single-family homes exploded while total property-tax collections grew only slightly faster than general inflation. The apparent paradox can be resolved by seeing that in the mid-1970's, as in the original Petris-Knox adjustments, single-family homes were assuming a greater share of all property-tax revenues.

This shifting of the property-tax burden was reinforced by a number of specific circumstances. For cities, property-tax collections were a relatively small portion of all revenues—about 25 percent. No matter how fast they grew, they were insufficient to finance any spending spree. In addition, many cities had one eye on the financial troubles of New York and so were in no mood to cut property taxes sharply or do anything else which might undermine their financial positions.

School districts—which in California are autonomous governmental units—had a problem of a different sort. Through 1977, California distributed much of its aid to education through an equalization formula. Calculated on the basis of a predetermined, "appropriate" level of expenditure per child, the formula was designed to concentrate state aid on districts with low tax bases. However, the formula presupposed static economic conditions. In a dynamic situation, in which assessed values are rising everywhere, every district will *appear* to be richer and so all districts will lose state aid. Thus, increases in a school district's property-tax base were offset by declines in state aid—leaving the school district in a poor position to reduce tax rates.

In the face of the growing burden on homeowners and local governments, the fiscal limits passed in 1972 by the legislature in Senate Bill 90 were generally ineffective. The limits on cities and counties referred to permissible tax *rates*. The tax bills on owner-occupied housing were growing not from increased tax rates, but from increased assessments. Actually, tax rates were marginally declining even as tax bills rapidly grew. Similarly, the expenditure limits on local education generally kept increases in educational expenditures at about the rate of inflation, but the design of the state-aid formula shifted the burden of educational funding onto the local tax base and, thereby, onto the single-family home.

CALIFORNIA TAXES: HOW HIGH WERE THEY?

To this point, we have focused on rapidly increasing property taxes for single-family homes. But rational voters should respond to the level of taxes as well as the rate of increase. Moreover, the macro school of analysis would argue that voters are rebelling against all taxes rather than the property tax in isolation. It would thus be useful to know whether California's taxes, as perceived by the voters, were out of line with taxes in the rest of the nation.

Unfortunately, most existing studies are not really suited to this purpose. Several authors have examined state-by-state ratios of aggregate taxes to personal income. But this ratio lumps together taxes that voters perceive directly with taxes that are perceived indirectly if at all, such as the portion of property taxes paid by business.

It is possible to construct a crude estimate of a state's "perceived property taxes" by taking total property-tax collections multiplied by the proportion of all assessed valuation in the state comprised of residential property. Such a statistic, of course, has problems of its own. In particular, it assumes that residential and other property are taxed at equivalent rates, even though the two property types may be concentrated in different jurisdictions. It also does not correct for homeowner exemptions, "circuit breakers," and other existing property-tax relief. Nonetheless, the statistic provides a rough estimate of what voters are facing. Table 1 contains the 1976 ratio of each state's perceived property taxes to its total personal income. The table also contains a second ratio—the sum of perceived property taxes, state and local personal-income taxes, and state ,and local sales taxes, all divided by personal income. This can be used as a rough index of states' "total perceived taxes."

The data show on both measures that California ranked quite high. Nationally, perceived property taxes are, on average, 2.2 percent of a state's total personal income. California's perceived property taxes were 3.9 percent of personal income, a ratio higher than all but five other states. Total perceived taxes average 6.3 percent of a state's income. California's ratio was 9.2 percent, a figure tied with Wisconsin and topped only by Hawaii and New York. Thus the assumption of some that the rapid increase in property taxes caused Californians to react to what were, in fact, relatively low tax bills is simply incorrect.

WHERE WAS THE STATE GOVERNMENT?

How local governments should have responded to the tax calamity is a debatable question. That the state government "dropped the ball" is not. In the middle months of 1977, before most voters had heard of either Howard Jarvis or Paul Gann, the state had the opportunity to pass a moderate program of tax relief. Several tax-relief bills were before the legislature, and at least some funding sources were available. But in September 1977, the legislature adjourned in disarray, unable to come to an agreement. The result was almost the mirror image of 1968 and 1972: In those years Governor Reagan and the legislature had acted relatively late, but they produced moderate alternatives to ballot initiatives. In 1977, Governor Brown and the legislature tried to act early and their failure was a major cause of Proposition 13's subsequent success.

The state's failure to act had two major causes: disagreement over the design of a property-tax bill, and uncertainty over the amount of relief the state could afford. This uncertainty arose from confusion over the size of the state's budget surplus—a subject which even now remains a source of great confusion.

By any measure, the recent growth of the state surplus was extraordinary. In January 1977 estimates of the surplus were in the range of $940 million, or about 7.5 percent of state revenues. By June of 1978 people were discussing surplus estimates in the range of $6.1 billion. The increase of $5.2 billion had three primary sources:

Table 1
State-by-state computations of perceived property taxes and perceived total taxes as a percentage of personal income, 1975-76

State	Perceived property taxes/total personal income	Perceived total taxes/total personal income	State	Perceived property taxes/total personal income	Perceived total taxes/total personal income
Alabama	0.7%	4.9%	Nebraska	1.8%	4.8%
Alaska	4.0	8.9	Nevada	1.9	4.7
Arizona	2.0	6.6	New Hampshire	4.4	4.5
Arkansas	0.9	4.9	New Jersey	4.7	6.5
California	3.9	9.2	New Mexico	0.8	6.3
Colorado	2.4	7.6	New York	3.2	9.6
Connecticut	3.8	6.4	North Carolina	1.3	5.6
Delaware	1.2	4.9	North Dakota	1.0	5.9
D.C.	1.6	6.8	Ohio	1.7	4.2
Florida	2.1	4.8	Oklahoma	1.1	4.5
Georgia	1.7	6.0	Oregon	2.8	6.3
Hawaii	1.6	10.2	Pennsylvania	2.0	5.4
Idaho	1.4	5.8	Rhode Island	3.6	7.2
Illinois	2.1	6.4	South Carolina	1.0	5.6
Indiana	2.1	6.4	South Dakota	1.8	4.8
Iowa	1.6	5.8	Tennessee	1.1	4.8
Kansas	1.8	5.4	Texas	1.5	4.0
Kentucky	1.1	5.2	Utah	1.7	7.7
Louisiana	0.9	5.4	Vermont	3.8	7.3
Maine	4.1	8.1	Virginia	1.9	5.8
Maryland	2.2	6.4	Washington	1.9	6.7
Massachusetts	5.1	9.1	West Virginia	1.1	7.2
Michigan	3.2	7.0	Wisconsin	3.3	9.2
Minnesota	2.4	7.9	Wyoming	1.1	4.8
Mississippi	1.1	6.7			
Missouri	1.7	5.4	Average for all states and the District of Columbia	2.2	6.3
Montana	2.2	4.6			

Sources: Various publications of the Bureau of the Census, U.S. Department of Commerce.

1. *Planned current surpluses ($2.19 billion).* When the FY 1978 budget was first presented in January 1977, it had a $540 million estimated current surplus.[3] When the FY 1979 budget was first presented in January 1978, it had an estimated current surplus of $1.65 billion.

2. *Revenue underestimates ($1.56 billion).* Between January 1977 and May 1978, revenue estimates for FY 1977, FY 1978, and FY 1979 increased by $1.93 billion. This was partially offset by expenditure underestimates of $370 million.

3. *Expenditure cuts ($1.35 billion).* In June of 1978, after Proposition 13 had passed, FY 1979 expenditures were reduced by $1.35 billion. These changes were direct and indirect results of Proposition 13 itself.

The first two factors—the factors prior to Proposition 13—resulted from the combination of a relatively progressive state income tax, a sustained economic recovery (coupled with inflation), and Governor Brown's desire to shield the developing surplus from what he saw as pressure for unnecessary spending.

Governor Brown took office in January 1975. In the two preceding years, a severe national recession had seriously damaged California's economy. Nonetheless, Governor Reagan had left Brown with an FY 1975 accumulated surplus (as of June 30, 1975) of $380 million, about 5 percent of state revenues.

More important, Reagan left Brown an elastic tax system. When Brown took office about 30 percent of the state's general fund came from a personal-income tax, while almost 40 percent came from its sales tax. Both taxes were responsive to economic activity. The income tax, in particular, was highly progressive. (It had bracket rates for a single earner running from 1 percent to 11 percent with the top bracket being reached at $15,500 of adjusted gross income.) Its "elasticity" during the middle 1970's was such that a 1-percent rise in state income would increase state income-tax revenues by 1.6 percent. In the inflationary environment of the 1970's, taxable income was typically rising at 10 percent per year. An assemblyman involved in passing the income tax said, "When we [Governor Reagan and the legislature] passed it, we knew we were taking care of taxes for a long time to come." It was, as the assemblyman noted, a money-making machine.

A review of the FY 1977 budget illustrates how efficient this money-making machine actually was. When the budget was first proposed in January 1976, it was assumed that the FY 1976 budget would close with an accumulated surplus of $301 million and FY 1977 revenues would be $10.4 billion. When these figures were combined with anticipated expenditures, they produced an FY 1977 accumulated surplus estimated to be $350 million. By January 1978, final FY 1977 estimates were complete: They showed that FY 1976 had an actual accumulated surplus of $904 million (rather than $301 million) and FY 1977 revenues were actually $11.4 billion (rather than $10.4 billion), leading to a FY 1977 accumulated surplus of $1.8 billion!

After the fact, these revenue underestimates by the Department of Finance came under attack from legislators and the public alike. From first to final estimates, FY 1976 revenues were underestimated by $500 million, and FY 1977 revenues underestimated by $1.0 billion. And despite these earlier lessons, FY 1978 revenue estimates needed to be increased $1.1 billion only six months into the fiscal year.

In part the miscalculations were due to an unexpectedly vigorous economic recovery—the extent of which was something the Department of Finance, like any good budgeting organization, was likely to underestimate. It is always easier to distribute an unexpected surplus than to make up for an unexpected deficit. But there is also strong anecdotal evidence to suggest that Governor Brown himself encouraged the Department of Finance to avoid any changes — such as revisions of revenue-estimating procedures—which would bring the surplus into focus. The less that was known about the size of the surplus, the more the Governor could preserve his freedom of action: to spend the surplus on some special project, to cut taxes in a bid for re-election, to avoid having to increase taxes during a second term, or whatever.

By the spring of 1977, when the legislature first began to debate property-tax relief, they were looking at an accumulated surplus of $2.4 billion. However, the accumulated surplus was only one part of the problem. A politically feasible property-tax relief program would have to be ongoing; future budgets would have to generate necessary funds even after the accumulated surplus had diminished. Put another way, few legislators wanted to cut property taxes in 1977 only to have to raise other taxes or cut aid to localities in 1979 or 1980.

It was on this point that the legislature received conservative advice not only from the Department of Finance, but also from its own staff. In May 1977, the State Senate received testimony from John L. Vickerman, a ranking official in the Office of the Legislative Analyst, who warned that even a moderate package then under consideration—one costing about $600 million in its first year—might necessitate a tax increase at some time in the next two or three years. Vickerman's warning was based on specific considerations—such as, that the state would soon have to increase school aid markedly to comply with the *Serrano* decision—but it was also based on revenue estimates more conservative than those issued by the Department of Finance. Moreover, the long-run surplus estimates of both the Department of Finance and the Office of the Legislative Analyst were based on assumptions of "business as usual," assumptions which Proposition 13 would eventually overturn. For example, the Department of Finance's five-year budget projections issued in the fall of 1977 and the winter of 1978 assumed that expenditures for existing state programs would increase at slightly over 10 percent per year, while expenditures would increase by an additional 2 percent per year due to new legislative programs. To have altered these assumptions radically—to have assumed that in a given year there would be a pay and hiring freeze, or to assume that the government would sharply curtail new programs—would not have been reasonable in the absence of a radical shift in the political environment. In fact such a shift was coming, but the legislature had not yet sensed it.

THE COLLAPSE OF THE TAX-RELIEF BILL

The legislature's problem was further complicated by splits over the design of a property-tax bill. When debate began, there were two camps: those who wanted a moderate-to-large bill requiring some new taxes, and those who wanted a smaller bill financed by the surplus alone. By April 1977 the legislature had three property-tax bills under consideration. Two were larger bills: an Assembly bill costing $775 million in the first year and a Senate bill costing $925 million in the first year. Both required new taxes. The third was more moderate, a Senate bill costing $605 million in the first year which was to be financed by the surplus alone. All three bills focused property-tax relief on low- and middle-income families, a departure from past practices.

By May 1977, the extent of the legislature's disagreement was clear as the Senate passed *both* its larger and smaller bills and sent them to the Assembly. The Assembly, in turn, passed its $775 million bill. By June all three bills had gone to a conference committee.

At the end of the summer, the conference committee reported out a bill costing $4.7 billion over five years. Its tax relief was tied to a household's income and the bill itself was to be financed largely from the accumulating state surplus. While the bill was supposed to be a compromise, the problems of the spring remained. The legislature came under a stream of attacks suggesting they were inviting future tax increases. Moreover, Senate Republicans began to object strenuously to the absence of tax relief for higher-income households. Such disagreements were important because in the California legislature, any appropriations bill must pass each house by a two-thirds vote of the members. It was because of this requirement that tax relief ultimately failed. The Assembly passed the conference-committee bill 56 to 22, but the Senate—the more conservative chamber—defeated it 16 to 23. With time running out, the conference committee brought forth a revised bill. This time the Assembly postponed action until they knew the outcome in the Senate. The Senate voted in favor of the bill but only by 21 to 15, less than the two-thirds majority required. (One Democrat joined all 14 Republicans in opposition.) The legislature adjourned with no bill.

It is natural to contrast the legislature's failure to act in 1977 with its tardy but effective action in 1968 and 1972. Both 1968 and 1972 had been statewide-election years. 1977 was not an election year and presumably this gave all parties the illusion of time for maneuver.[4] Equally important was that, by the fall, Republicans—and particularly Senate Republicans—appear to have adopted a rejectionist stance, condemning proposals similar to those they had supported in the spring. Some have suggested their newfound opposition was part of a general electoral strategy. Republicans were entering 1978 in an unexposed position. Of the 80 Assembly seats, Republicans held only 23. Of the 20 Senate contests (the California State Senate has four-year-terms, with half the seats elected every two years), only three involved Republican seats and all three incumbents would retire before the primary. And the only Republican statewide officeholder, the Attorney General, was running for governor. In this situation, Republicans could risk an obstructionist strategy designed to make the Democrats look bad, for if people reacted by attacking all incumbents, Republicans had little to lose.

Normally, a Democratic governor would try to counter such obstruction by a campaign of opposition-bashing. But Governor Brown also had an eye on 1978. Since his election, his administration had developed a strong anti-business image by elevating environmental concerns far above economic growth. As the election approached, the Governor was attempting to adopt a more pro-business stance. Such a move made good political sense since defections from the Democratic center—especially by big labor—were far more likely than defections from the Democratic left. But courting business interests effectively ruled out a virulent anti-Republican campaign. The Republicans could proceed unscathed.

The rest of the story is well known. Shortly after the legislative session collapsed, Howard Jarvis and Paul Gann began circulating petitions for an initiative to limit property taxes. Their initiative was more concerned with tax cuts than tax shifts. Like the Watson initiatives, they specified a large cut in local property taxes, but unlike the Watson efforts they did *not* allocate the cut to specific services (with the implication that these services would be funded by the state.) And like Reagan's Proposition 1, they sought to control the ability of the state to compensate for reduced local revenues by increasing the majority required for all new state tax legislation to two-thirds. Finally, in a departure from past initiatives, Jarvis and Gann sought to limit the future growth of local revenues by separating assessed values from market values as long as the property was retained by the same owner. The initiative was estimated to cut property taxes by $7 billion in FY 1979. Proposition 13 qualified for the ballot within one month.

In January 1978 the legislature reconvened and attempted to construct what was now an alternative proposal. By this time, the size of the state surplus was becoming clearer, but the legislature continued to disagree over the appropriate distribution of benefits. Ultimately, they passed a compromise package, costing $1.6 billion for FY 1979. But it labored under substantial handicaps. The legislature's squabbling in January and in the previous fall gave the bill a reluctant, second-best quality, as something that would not have been undertaken at all but for Proposition 13. Moreover, the compromise contained provisions for separate tax rates on residential and commercial property and this, in turn, required a constitutional amendment, listed as Proposition 8 on the June ballot. This could have provided a good opportunity to confront Proposition 13 directly, but as the legislature's bill was written, Proposition 8 spoke only of taxing residential and commercial property separately. It said nothing about tax relief *per se*. Consequently, at least some voters perceived Proposition 8 as only a vague promise of tax relief in the future and did not realize it was, in fact, the final piece required to implement a bill that had already been signed by the Governor.

Despite these handicaps, Proposition 8 had some chance of passage (and Proposition 13 of defeat) until May 1978, when Los Angeles County received its FY 1979 assessments. The data showed the total value of the property-tax rolls had increased by 17.5 percent — a remarkable figure considering that only one-third of the properties had been reassessed. Assessment increases on single-family homes of 50 to 100 percent were not uncommon and these results were broadcast widely across the state. While other counties had not yet released their assessments, the numbers from Los Angeles made the election a foregone conclusion. Proposition 13 won with 65 percent of the vote.

WHAT HAPPENS NEXT?

This detailed history of California tax-reform initiatives gives us a more precise picture of voter concerns: It appears that California voters were primarily concerned with high and rapidly increasing property taxes. Homeowners were caught in a system of taxation and aid formulas that shifted an increasing portion of the tax bill onto single-family homes. Local-government officials were relatively powerless to solve the problem. The Governor and the legislature showed no great enthusiasm for solving the problem. And so voters took the matter into their own hands.

This interpretation of the event is surely a modest one. Shortly after the election, members of the previously mentioned macro school — most notably, Howard Jarvis — described the vote as an attack against inflation, large and arrogant government, and taxes of all kinds. This interpretation was soon adopted by the media, but existing evidence suggests it is hyperbolic.

Ascertaining voters' true attitudes is a chancy business but a variety of data is available from tabulations of the monthly *California Poll*. With respect to inflation, the most relevant data come from a question posed in January 1978 asking respondents to compare their current economic status with their economic status in January 1977. Forty-one percent said they were doing better in 1978 than in 1977, a far more optimistic outlook than in other recent years. With respect to taxes, the relevant data come from a *California Poll* taken in the middle of 1977. One question asked respondents to identify those taxes which they felt were too high. Multiple answers were permitted. Sixty percent of the sample (including 70 percent of homeowners) felt that property taxes were too high, about double the national response to similar questions. By contrast, the Federal income tax, the state income tax, and other taxes were mentioned no more than 15 percent of the time, about one-half the typical national response.

Data on voter attitudes toward government come from a *California Poll* taken in the week before the Proposition 13 vote. Included in the poll was a series of questions concerning the appropriate level of spending on services such as mental health, court administration, street and highway maintenance, and building repair. In each case the respondent was asked whether the amount of taxpayer money going to the service should be increased, left alone, or cut back. The poll results have been extensively analyzed by Jack Citrin, from the University of California at Berkeley, who found that only four of the fifteen services examined received a response which was close to or actually negative. Two of the criticized services were welfare and public housing. The other two were "City and County Administration" and "Environmental Protection Regulation." These last two, as Citrin notes, were loaded issues: Discussing "administrators" without reference to what they administer and discussing anything with the word "regulation" in the title both invite a negative response.

Citrin's analysis also shows that support for Proposition 13 was not confined to voters who wanted significant budget cuts. Citrin defined a voter as "generally satisfied" with government services if he or she wanted spending cuts in no more than three of the fifteen services listed. Yet he found that even these "generally satisfied" voters favored Proposition 13 by 52 to 48 percent.

To be sure, a variety of other sentiments existed. But the data, taken as a whole, suggest that Proposition 13 was a referendum on property taxes: Property taxes had to brought under control and if that necessitated cuts in government spending, it would be an unfortunate but necessary by-product. Had homeowner property taxes not been increasing so quickly, Californians might well have preferred more moderate alternatives. In particular, they might have led other states in approving a limit to future spending growth, something they almost did five years earlier.

If Californians are satisfied with the current size of the public sector, they are fortunate, because evidence indicates the public sector will remain at roughly its current size for some time to come. To see why this is so, it is necessary to re-examine the state's financial position.

By May 1978 the available surplus for FY 1979 had reached a reported figure of $3.3 billion. But this figure was in a sense artificially small, since it assumed expenditure of $1.6 billion for the legislature's compromise tax-relief bill. When Proposition 8 was defeated, the $1.6 billion was returned to the state surplus.

The simultaneous passage of Proposition 13 further increased the surplus by cutting $700 million from anticipated FY 1979 expenditures. By lowering local property-tax bills, Proposition 13 lowered state property-tax relief via the homeowner's exemption. Finally, Governor Brown, a Proposition 13 opponent, quickly shifted positions and made last-minute budget cuts totaling $600 million, including a pay freeze, a hiring freeze, a freeze on benefit levels in the welfare program, and deletion of a program to make the state of California part owner of a communications satellite. Together, these changes increased the available surplus for FY 1979 from $3.3 billion to $6.2 billion, all apparently in three weeks time.

Before June was out, the Governor and legislature began to dispose of the surplus in several ways. They passed a one-year emergency assistance bill for local governments at a total cost of $4.2 billion. They passed a large round of one-year tax cuts together with a smaller, permanent, partial indexation of the state income-tax system. Under the indexation, certain personal exemptions were adjusted annually for changes in the price level. But tax-rate-bracket limits were adjusted only for the portion of inflation in excess of 3 percent, leaving the income-tax system relatively elastic.

The result of these changes was a modest decrease in public expenditures.— something short of Armageddon. The Governor's state budget cuts represented a reduction of about 7 percent in expenditures on existing programs. Local governments lost $7.2 billion of property-tax revenues under Proposition 13, but the infusion of the $4.2 billion emergency state aid compensated somewhat, leaving them with a shortfall of $2.9 billion—a 10-percent reduction in their total revenues received from all sources.

At the time these measures were announced, various observers—encouraged by members of the state administration—shifted their concern from Armageddon today to Armageddon tomorrow. While the state could get through FY 1979, they said, it could not continue such emergency local aid through FY 1980. But such a view does not square with the numbers. The Department of Finance's own revenue estimates, combined with the Governor's determination to hold down state costs, suggest the state can bail out localities for the foreseeable future. In fact, Governor Brown has made the continuation of such aid part of his FY 1980 budget and there is no reason to expect radical readjustments any time soon.

In essence then, California, like other states, has approved a limit to the growth of its public sector. But it is a limit with a difference, for it involves a substantial shift of power from localities to the state. For many years, California liberals had an agenda of reform for state and local fiscal relations. Initially it included the state assuming county welfare and health costs. Later it was expanded to include the larger, restructured state role in education described in *Serrano*. The agenda was developed not out of specific concern with property taxes but because liberals perceived they had greater power in the state legislature than in hundreds of local governmental units. The passage of Proposition 13 has caused almost the entire liberal agenda to be *de facto* adopted. The state now pays for most county welfare and health costs, and state support of public schools has increased from about 40 percent of all expenditures prior to Proposition 13 to 67 percent today.

Passing a liberal agenda is not, however, equivalent to achieving a liberal result. Though funds at the state level are sufficiently tight to preclude substantial funding increases in existing programs, the revised fiscal structure has made counties, school districts, and to a lesser extent cities, far more dependent on Sacramento for their year-to-year financing than had previously been the case. In the future, as local preferences change and diverge from one another this centralization of power will become increasingly confining.

LESSONS FOR THE REST OF US

It is natural to conclude by asking what California can teach the rest of the country. At this point micro-school members are usually at a disadvantage. The story just presented is, after all, a history of only one case. Its numerous idosyncracies make generalizations difficult.

Nonetheless it appears that Proposition 13 has been generalized and, in most cases, quite accurately. Few other states had California's precise circumstances: explosive property-tax growth for single-family homes, a potentially large state surplus, and a state government that would not deal with the problem. Nor did many states pass initiatives as drastic as Proposition 13. To the contrary, the rest of the country seemed quite capable of accepting California's general message without developing false conclusions from the details. For example, Massachusetts voted to retain the possibility of different assessment ratios on different kinds of property precisely to avoid the kinds of problems California had.

If there was an exception to this happy process, it was Governor Brown's embrace of the Federal balanced-budget amendment, a particularly illogical conversion. California, like almost every other state, requires a balanced budget in its own constitution. The requirement did nothing to stop a dramatic growth in state revenues and the development of a surplus equal to one-third of state expenditures.

It can be argued that the Federal government would never allow such a surplus to develop, but a second, more serious gap in logic remains. The origin of California's recent dilemma was its rigid, highly reformed property-tax system. The performance of this system in the 1970's re-emphasized what every working politician should know: In government one should not rely too heavily on rules to replace political discretion. Had California's assessors retained some of their pre-1965 authority to set assessments, they could have mediated at least some of the housing inflation. Homeowners would have been less battered. Local governments would have retained most of their powers. To conclude from the California experience that the Federal budget should also be purged of political discretion is to read between the lines what isn't there.

NOTES

1. I am particularly indebted to David Doerr, Chief Consultant on the staff of the California Assembly's Revenue and Taxation Committee, for an explanation of these points.

2. The 1973-76 cycle includes Alameda, Los Angeles, Fresno, and San Joaquin counties, among others, and accounts for about one-half of the assessed valuation in the state. In interpreting these calculations, note that assessed value per commercial property is a number highly subject to sampling variability.

3. The state's fiscal year begins on July 1. A current surplus refers to an excess of revenues over expenditures within the budget of a given year. An accumulated surplus refers to total uncommitted funds on hand at a particular time. Thus, for example, the funds available for allocation over FY 1979 would be the sum of the accumulated surplus the last day of FY 1978, June 30, 1978, plus the current surplus in FY 1979.

   For simplicity, we will use the term "surplus" to refer to the unrestricted portion of the surplus, exclusive of funds in restricted accounts. We will also exclude from consideration the unrestricted funds in the Federal revenue-sharing account which remained relatively constant over the period.

4. I am thankful to Dean Tibbs for a discussion of these events.

Let's Pretend

Arnold J. Meltsner

One of the frustrating but fascinating aspects of studying revenue is that appearances are deceptive. Fiscal reality is such that actors cannot always do what they claim to do; norms are established and have to be ignored; and words do not mean what they usually mean. Local revenue is a world of pretense and make-believe behavior.

LET'S PRETEND THAT REIMBURSEMENTS ARE NOT REVENUE

. . . [R]evenue [is] any financial resource that flows into the city over which the city has some expenditure control. The city receives money called reimbursements, which it excludes from the budget and does not consider to be revenue. In one year about $800,000 was reimbursed [to Oakland, California] for services provided for outside agencies, such as the state of California, Alameda County, the Rapid Transit District, the Redevelopment Agency, the Port of Oakland, and even for private utilities and individuals.

Does a reimbursement for a service constitute payment of a service charge, or is it, in accounting parlance, a nonrevenue receipt? The distinction between service charges and reimbursements is murky. Formally, a reimbursement applies to city activity that is beyond the usual scope of city functions. This bit of speciousness means essentially that it is possible to define when a specific service is within the scope of city functions. Many of these reimbursed services have *standard* rates and procedures indicating that for all practical purposes there is no difference between a service charge and a reimbursement. And if there is no difference in the clients, or the service, or the methods of charging, then there is not much reason to maintain the distinction.

From Arnold J. Meltsner, *The Politics of City Revenue* (Berkeley and Los Angeles: University of California Press, 1971). Reprinted by permission of the University of California Press.

The distinction between service charges and reimbursements may at times be only a matter of the auditor-controller's interpretation. Once a revenue is put in one pocket or another, a precedent is established. To take a minor example, Oakland conducts elections for the Board of Education, the Peralta Junior College District, and the Port of Oakland as a service to these agencies and to avoid duplicating elections. Oakland computes the total cost of running the election and then receives reimbursements on the basis of the number of offices reserved on the ballot. For instance, in the nominating municipal election held in April 1965, Peralta Junior College accounted for three of the sixteen offices on the ballot. Therefore, Peralta paid the city three-sixteenths of the total cost of that election.

LET'S PRETEND THAT TAXES ARE NOT TAXES

One of the great arts of the tax game is to design revenue sources so that people will not know that they are paying taxes. Taxes should not be seen nor felt, only paid. There is a contrary school of thought, which I believe to be in the minority, that claims that taxes should be visible and that the taxpayer should know he is paying. However, the revenue behavior of Oakland officials is consistent with the hide-the-tax rule. Furthermore, the state helps in this endeavor by establishing fines and setting procedures for some in lieu taxes.

The municipal courts of Alameda County are a source of revenue to the city of Oakland. Court revenue is collected when bail is forfeited, and for fines relating to vehicle code violations and to misdemeanor arrests for nonvehicle-code violations. The yield from this revenue source has steadily increased over the years. In 1962/63 it was $1.5 million and by 1966/67 it was $2.1 million. Of the $2.1 million total, approximately half a million dollars came from fines and forfeitures for nonvehicle-code violations, while the rest came from vehicle-code violations. The nonvehicle-code court fines become part of the city's general fund, while the vehicle code fines, by state law, are deposited into a special earmarked fund called the Traffic Safety Fund.

The city has no discretion over what these fines will be or what revenue it will receive. The maximum and minimum penalties are set by various state legal codes, and the Alameda municipal court judges determine the fine and bail schedules within these state limits. The only possible area of discretion is related to who actually does the arresting. For example, if an Oakland police officer writes the citation for a vehicle-code violation, then the resulting fine money is split with 22 percent going to the county and 78 percent going to the city. On the other hand, if the individual is cited or arrested by state officers within the city, the city only gets 50 percent of the money and the rest goes into a special county road improvement fund.

The normal procedures for the property tax do not apply to certain kinds of property. The taxes paid on these kinds of property are usually called in lieu taxes because they are paid instead of the locally assessed property tax. For example, motor vehicle license fees provide the city with in lieu taxes amounting to $2.4 million without the pain of collection or taxpayer resistance. Because apportionment and collection procedures are complicated, most Oakland citizens probably do not realize that their motor vehicle license fee includes a 2 percent in lieu tax, based on the market value of the vehicle, part of which goes to the city. Apportionment for the motor vehicle licence fee is based on county population within the state. Each county keeps 50 percent of the money it receives and the rest is redistributed to its cities on the basis of their populations. Oakland's per capita amount for 1967/68 was $6.80.

Besides being palatable another feature of in lieu taxes is that "in lieu" often does not mean "instead." The term is misleading, because the city does not receive as much revenue as it would if the property were subject to the usual real property procedures. Consider the in lieu tax on private aircraft. This tax is levied locally by the county assessor at a rate of 1.5 percent of market value, and the collected taxes are distributed evenly between the city, the county, and the school district. If aircraft were treated as real property, the property would be assessed as a percent of market value and then a tax rate for each jurisdiction would be applied. The in lieu procedure, applied to 365 private aircraft (worth about $8 million), yielded the city approximately $35,000. The city would have received about twice this amount if the real property procedures could have been used.

LET'S PRETEND THAT EARMARKED FUNDS ARE NOT EARMARKED

A primary characteristic of an earmarked fund is that the money is set aside for a special use. The primary reaction to such funds by city officials is to broaden the use of the money. By using particular funds for general purposes, officials are able to reduce the impact on their general fund and keep their property tax rate stable. The California Penal Code, for example, specifies items which can be expended out of the "fine" revenue that is in the Traffic Safety Fund. Officials then attempt to cover general fund traffic safety expenditures, such as traffic control devices, with money from this special fund.

The city also establishes its own earmarked funds, usually as a means to justify a new tax. A few years ago it adopted a service charge to be collected from users of the sanitary sewer system and to be used for the replacement of sanitary sewers. Gradually, officials have extended the use of the Sewer Service Charge Fund to cover not just replacement but maintenance, billing, and collection costs and other city overhead expenditures. . . .

For all practical purposes, the Transient Occupancy Tax Fund is no longer an earmarked fund. Both the special use of the money and the special interests that were involved have disappeared. When the transient occupancy tax was instituted in 1965, it imposed a 4 percent charge on hotel and motel accomodations rented for periods of less than thirty days. The League of California Cities had urged its adoption in order to avoid state preemption of the tax. The tactic was that if the state levied a similar tax after many cities had adopted it, the cities would then have to be given part of the revenue.

On the home front, Oakland officials got support for the tax by stressing the special purpose for the funds and by including their opponents, the hotel and motel owners, in the decision process. The tax was passed and justified because of the specific requirement to encourage tourism and convention promotion for the city and not as a general revenue device. Since it was a tax which directly affected hotel and motel interests, a special Transient Occupancy Tax Committee was established to make recommendations for the allocation of these funds. The original membership of this Committee included two members from the Eastbay Hotel Association, two from the Motel Association, two from the Chamber of Commerce, two from the City Council, and one from the city manager's office. In theory, this committee was to make recommendations on how the money should be spent and these recommendations would then be endorsed by the City Council.

Historically this fund, like other earmarked funds, was operated to broaden the original use of the money and to provide some offset or alleviation to the general fund. As the fund was administered, there was an emphasis on using the money to cover costs that were being paid out of the general fund. One time, officials attempted to use the fund for entertainment and advertising activities and became involved in a set of legal entanglements. The city auditor claimed that a charter restriction on entertainment and advertising appropriations applied to the Transient Occupancy Tax Fund. The charter was then amended by the voters, which freed the fund from the restriction. Officials continue to broaden the use of the money, so that practically any general fund expense for tourism, visitors, entertainment, and advertising is paid out of the Transient Occupancy Tax Fund. In the 1968/69 budget, all expenses for community improvement activities, such as support of the Chamber of Commerce, the Oakland Symphony, and Columbus Day, Fourth of July, and special celebrations were transferred from the general fund to the Transient Occupancy Tax Fund.

The Transient Occupancy Tax Committee has also disappeared. Originally, the city gave the hotel and motel people representation on the committee to gain their concurrence for the tax. Now, allocation decisions and rate increases are made by city officials with some advice from the Chamber of Commerce; but no direct consultation with hotel or motel operators takes place.

The state gasoline taxes are another example of the operation of earmarked funds. Although the average citizen may worry about control of city government by the state, control is not an adequate word to describe the bizarre set of arrangements that result from the establishment of such funds. It is not a simple matter to say to a city, "You will spend this money in only this way." Problems of definition and legality are widespread when earmarking takes place. The League of California Cities, for example, does more than lobby for funds from the state legislature; it also provides an important educational service by informing cities as to what and how they can spend existing state donations.[1]

A great deal of activity in past years has been devoted to trying to "beat the system" legally. The art of city administration of earmarked funds lies in avoidance of the constraints imposed by the authorities who originally established the fund. The idea is to spend the money on what you want to spend it on without losing any in the process. This objective requires a small army of clerks to shift funds from one pocket to another.

Californians pay a tax of seven cents per gallon of gasoline of which the state keeps four cents for highway construction; the rest is sent to the cities and counties. Part of this revenue which the city receives is usually termed the "old gas tax." This tax has a more formal legal description, but I will use the City Hall name. In 1966/67 the old gas tax brought in $1.7 million. State law provides that at least 40 percent of the city's old gas tax receipts must be used for construction of the "Select System of Streets." These streets are determined by the City Council and approved by the state. What this means in practice is that the *major* city streets which serve as arteries for traffic coming from outside city limits, as well as for local traffic, are included in the list of select streets. The other 60 percent of old gas tax funds may be used for maintenance or, with the approval of the state Department of Public Works, for construction purposes. What constitutes maintenance, construction, or a select street is subject to negotiation and is defined by administrative fiat and practice.

Another source of revenue is the "new gas tax" established in 1963 that allows 1.04 cents per gallon to be apportioned directly to cities and counties for street construction purposes. In fiscal year 1966/67 new gas tax funds amounted to $1.5 million. When the new gas tax fund was established, it required the city to match the grant with its own money. This requirement was eliminated in 1967. Elimination of matching requirements for the new gas tax alleviates an administrative headache and saves the cities from having to find additional revenue. Until then Oakland officials worried that the city would be unable to find enough money to match on a dollar-to-dollar basis.

The city's final source of gas tax revenue is known as the Alameda County Street Aid Fund. Since 1955 the mayors of Alameda County cities have had an agreement with the Alameda County Board of Supervisors to share a portion of the county's gas tax funds for city street construction. Funds are to be used for streets that have more than local importance. The agreement between the mayors and the county has been renewed every five years and is based on the recognition that, although the cities may receive more gas tax funds in absolute figures, it is the cities which suffer the greatest deficiencies in the Select Street System. It is also recognized that the cities have used a greater percentage of their own local sources of financing for street-related expenditures than have the counties. Revenue from this source was around $800,000 for fiscal year 1966/67. This type of agreement is typical for urban counties, like Alameda

County, where the total city street mileage accounts for 78 percent of the total county streets and highways.

The fact that the county gives away some of its revenue is an indication that the state allocation of gas tax revenue is not satisfactory. In addition, there are inequities in present apportionment procedures, which are based on population. Current distribution rates for Oakland are over $3.00 per capita. The apportionment procedure tends to favor the city with a rapidly expanding population. In Oakland's case, that of an old city with a set of deteriorated streets and a stable population, the apportionment procedures are to the city's disadvantage. The money is not being placed where the need is. Thus, resorting to higher-level government allocations of funds does not necessarily result in a rational distribution.

The administration of gas tax funds is complicated, and the central administrative headache is to find matching funds. Not just any city expenditure on streets qualified for matching. The state wants the city to spend nongas-tax revenue on the Select System of Streets and for only certain street improvements; for example, expenditure for sidewalks did not qualify for matching. In the past the city would use expenditures from its Traffic Safety Fund for its matching requirements because this fund is derived from nongas-tax revenues. However, one year a significant part of the Traffic Safety Fund was scheduled to be used for construction projects which would not qualify as matching expenditures.

Oakland's superintendent of streets had a way out of the dilemma which would allow the city to construct what it wanted and still not lose any state funds. His ingenious suggestion was to get Alameda County Board of Supervisors to agree to a confusing accounting substitution of funds. First, the county would be asked to approve the use of Alameda County Street Aid Funds to help finance some freeway construction. Second, the county would agree to the city transferring funds from the city's Traffic Safety Fund to finance the same freeway construction. Thus the Alameda County Street Aid Funds, which were made available by the transfer, could be used for the originally scheduled noneligible construction projects. The net result of these machinations would be that the county would get some select system street work accomplished which it wanted, and at the same time the city would be able to show that it had the necessary matching expenditures. By the marvels of accounting the city could meet all state qualifications for matching. The eligible construction projects would be aligned with the eligible funds.

LET'S PRETEND THAT GRANTS ARE NOT REAL MONEY

I have been discussing recurring revenues which have a fairly stable impact on the city. The area of grants is an important one, but it is unpredictable, involving one-time projects without sufficient continuity for the city to rely on this revenue source.

Cities are not expected to rely on grants to pay for their usual functions. Grant systems are established to take care of extras; grant programs are deliberately designed to prevent recipient cities from relieving their own tax burdens. Unfortunately, cities like Oakland need fiscal aid for the traditional functions of local government as well as money to deal with pressing social and economic problems. Oakland officials search elsewhere to relieve their revenue constraint.

Currently $95 million of federal funds comes into Oakland, and only a relatively small part of these funds is included within the budget for usual functions.[2] To get some perspective on the impact of federal and other agency funds, one only has to consider that the entire budget for Oakland for 1968/69 was $56.7 million. As an example of funds excluded from the budget, it was estimated that a little over $8 million for fiscal 1967/68 would be coming to the city for urban renewal. Such funds are under the jurisdiction of Oakland's Redevelopment Agency, which is a separate agency created by the City Council to administer the federal urban renewal programs within the city.

Some grants, such as the Urban Planning Grant from the U.S. Department of Housing and Urban Development, under Section 701 of the Housing Act of 1954, do go directly to city officials and are in the city budget. This act provided around $600,000 to the city in 1966/67. It is expected that the total planning grant will be approximately $1.5 million. The planning grant is designed to support an extensive city-wide planning study which will attempt to develop a comprehensive plan to deal with all the physical and social problems of the city. The grant is, however, for a one-time planning project. From a variety of local, state, and federal agencies there is a miscellaneous set of grants amounting to about $400,000 per year which supports city activities. This amount includes repayments on the Hall of Justice by the county, state grants for training police officers, and federal funds for civil defense and a library demonstration project. Within the total for grants, the details vary from year to year as to what the money is being spent for and who is actually the contributor. Only about 1 to 2 percent of the annual budget is conceivably supported by federal funds.

LET'S PRETEND THAT TAXES ARE JUST

Equity is an elusive goal which local taxation will never reach. At the local level fiscal cynicism supplants fiscal justice. The question is seldom who should pay but rather who will pay. Local officials emphasize yields and leave the problem of income distribution to the federal government.

The property tax is inequitable because not everybody pays. Certainly it is legitimate to have welfare exemptions, but sometimes reductions in the tax base can be excessive. During past years property has been excluded from assessment due to exemptions, welfare considerations, and illegal or under-assessment practices. Oakland budget officials estimate that over $300,000 will be due to the city because of past underassessment. In Oakland and throughout California, exemptions from property tax such as those for veterans, churches, homes for the aged, hospitals, schools, and cemeteries resulted in about a 5 percent reduction in assessed value. Oakland's exemptions reduce its assessed valuation by $35 million. In other words, the city "loses" over a million dollars of tax revenue annually because of exemptions. If, for example, the 17,000 veterans in Oakland had to give up the exemption on their $14 million worth of property, the city would gain over $400,000 and its tax rate could be reduced by about six cents.

Reduction in assessment is also due to the fact that some public property, particularly that controlled by the Port of Oakland, is leased to owners and is appraised only for the occupant's possessory interest in the property. By leasing a person can pay less taxes. The appraisal of possessory interest is made by an estimation based on use and not on the value of the property itself. The port uses such leases for warehouses and office buildings to attract business. These possessory interests had been assessed at 14 percent of value, but with the new assessment procedures of 1967/68 the ratio was to be increased to 25 percent. However, there still remains the difference between the value of use under a possessory interest basis and the actual appraisal of the property as if it were owned rather than leased. Officials would like to have a study of possessory interest practices of the port because the city believes that revenue could be increased if the port would sell property rather than lease it. Unfortunately, one government's benefit is another government's cost.

The property tax is inequitable because old people have different burdens. Old people who live in their own homes must pay property tax, but those who live in homes for the aged do not share a similar burden. Not only are the aged treated unequally because of the exemption for old age homes, but rich old people can escape property taxes by living in "luxury" old age homes. Oakland has eleven old age homes, and several new homes are currently under construction. Some of these, like Lake Park (California-Nevada Methodist Homes), satisfy a California legislative committee criterion for a home that "could be strongly suspected of opulence."[3]

A regressive tax is one where the burden of the tax decreases as one's ability to pay increases. The property tax is inequitable because it is regressive. A recent study for the state concluded, "the relative burden of the property tax on income tends to drop substantially as income increases."[4] For the second important source of Oakland's revenue, the sales tax, the evidence indicates that, with different measures of ability to pay, the California sales tax is roughly proportional. However, . . . some leaders consider the sales tax to be regressive while businessmen and other leaders, to some extent, deny this. Because of major exemptions of food and prescription drugs, one analyst says, "this regressivity may be more apparent than real in the case of California's type of sales tax."[5] So the property tax remains the necessary evil of local finance, perhaps mitigated by the benefits received. One student describes the property tax: "This tax is shown to have many faults. It cannot be defended on the grounds of the ability-to-pay principle, and its use can only partially be justified on the basis of benefits received by the tax payers. Its regressivity is acknowledged; its incidence is often uncertain; its failure to contribute to economic stability is recognized; and its administration results in frequent and serious injustices."[6]

NOTES

1. See League of California Cities, *Limited Expenditure Funds of Cities*, March 1963.
2. Oakland, *Digest of Current Federal Programs in the City of Oakland*, prepared by Jeffrey L. Pressman with the assistance of the Redevelopment Agency of the City of Oakland, October 1968.
3. California, Legislature, Assembly, Interim Committee on Revenue and Taxation, *Problems of Property Tax Administration in California*, vol. 4, no. 20, Final Report, Part 1, December 1966, pp. 63-65.
4. California, Legislature, Senate, Fact Finding Committee on Revenue and Taxation, *Property Taxes and Other Local Revenue Sources*, Part 9, March 1965, p. 77.
5. California, Legislature, Assembly, Interim Committee on Revenue and Taxation, *The Sales Tax*, prepared by Harold M. Somers, December 1964, p. 31. For another study that indicates proportionality in the sales tax, see State of California, Legislature, Senate, Fact Finding Committee on Revenue and Taxation, *General Fund Consumption Taxes*, Part 2, January 1965, pp. 11-14.
6. California, Legislature, *Property Taxes and Other Local Revenue Sources*, p. 33, citing C. Ward Macy, "The Property Tax in the Fiscal System," in *Proceedings of the 51st Annual Conference*, National Tax Association (Columbus: National Tax Association, 1958), p. 74.

Discussion Questions

1. Levy argues that the enthusiasm with which California voters supported Proposition 13 should not be taken as an indicator of general public dissatisfaction with taxes of all kinds. Do you perceive this as an accurate reading of the public's current mood?

2. Levy argues that we should not conclude from California's experience that the federal budget "should also be purged of political discretion" through the passage of a constitutional amendment requiring the federal government to balance its budget. Do you agree?

3. In general terms, how would you describe the impact of the federal and state governments on Oakland's system of taxes and revenues?

4. Given the opportunity to do so, what approach would you take to restructuring Oakland's system of taxes and revenues? Outside of city officials themselves, which other public officials would have to cooperate?

5. Can you see a connection between Levy's assessment of the underlying causes for Proposition 13 and Meltsner's assessment of Oakland's tax system and the attitudes of its public officials?

CHAPTER EIGHT

METROPOLITAN POLITICS AND PROBLEMS

For most of its history, the United States has been a decidely rural country, but today most Americans live in urban areas, or what the U.S. Bureau of the Census likes to refer to as Standard Metropolitan Statistical Areas (SMSAs). According to the bureau, an SMSA consists of a "county or group of contiguous counties which contains at least one city of 50,000 inhabitants or more, or 'twin cities' with a combined population of at least 50,000." This rather innocuous term and its definition fail to convey any real sense of the tremendous ethnic, political, and economic diversity that characterizes urban America. Our major cities and their suburbs contain many of the richest and poorest of Americans. They hold multiple ethnic and racial communities whose inhabitants continue, in varying degrees, to see themselves as somehow different from the rest of American society. They are inhabited by numerous supporters of our two major political parties, but also contain numerous third parties and pressure groups representing every conceivable political ideology.

The term *SMSA* also fails to convey a sense of the wide array of challenges facing those responsible for the governance of these areas. All the various racial, political, and economic differences that exist among SMSA inhabitants serve as actual or potential bases for group hostility. The level of hostility between urban blacks, who tend to be poor, supportive of the Democratic party, and confined to central city ghettoes, and suburban whites is likely to be particularly high. The most important challenge facing metropolitan governments today is to keep such hostility under control and prevent it from breaking out into open conflict.

Beyond this most basic challenge lie others. Urban regions commonly contain a bewildering variety of municipalities, counties, special districts, and other forms of government. Somehow this fragmented collection of governments, exercising jurisdiction over different segments of the same urban region, or responsible for providing different services to the same communities, must be made to work. It must be made to operate in a fashion that is economical and responsive to the widely varying needs of the people in the region.

⌈ An especially difficult challenge for metropolitan governments is to meet the social-service needs of the urban poor. To do so effectively requires a level and quality of service delivery from welfare agencies, public schools, police departments, and other bureaucracies that is not often provided. In addition, it requires more financial and administrative support from federal and state agencies than is usually forthcoming⌋

Urban pollution is also a difficult challenge. The crowding of people, automobiles, and industry into limited areas causes dangerously high levels of air pollution, water pollution, and noise pollution. If metropolitan America is to be inhabitable, these pollution levels must be reduced. At the same time, the costs of pollution control cannot be allowed to grow to the point that they threaten urban economies and employment levels. ⌉

During the 1960s, stories about crime, pollution, and unrest in America's central cities became depressingly commonplace. Liberals especially began to speak of the "urban crisis," a term they used to refer to the apparent deterioration and impending doom of the largest and oldest of American cities. In the first article in this chapter, T. D. Allman examines the underlying reality of the whole notion of an urban crisis and the ability of the federal government to influence the future of the cities through deliberate policy decisions. He concludes that the real problems of metropolitan America are very different from what they are perceived to be, and that the ability of the federal government to have a positive effect on the future of the cities through its deliberate policy decisions is very limited indeed.

In the second article Thomas Andrzejewski and Denise Stinson examine the public housing program in Cleveland. The purpose of this program is to provide decent housing for those who cannot provide it for themselves. It is supposed to do this by bringing together the superior economic resources of the federal government and the superior insight of local administrators into local needs and conditions. However, the public housing program in Cleveland has generally failed to meet this goal.

In the third article G. Christian Hill looks at the current status of the decades-old fight against metropolitan air pollution. He suggests that, for a variety of reasons, the fight is going badly and may very well be lost. The implications for the quality of life in metropolitan America, especially for those who cannot escape to less crowded, less polluted places, are harsh indeed.

The Urban Crisis Leaves Town

T. D. Allman

Whatever happened to the urban crisis?

Last year, the cities of the Northeast and Midwest seemed less in the midst of municipal difficulties than in the path of the Four Horsemen of the Apocalypse. The Bronx was in flames and Buffalo was buried in snow. The "underclass," perhaps the most subtle epithet ever directed against nonwhite Americans in need of a job, was looting Brooklyn, and taking over Washington east of Rock Creek Park. In Hartford the civic center had fallen down. All the statistics and all the media images testified to the same melancholy truth: Jobs were still disappearing from cities, and so were taxpayers. While the welfare class dismantled the temples of urban America stone by stone, selfish people in the suburbs refused to share their wealth, and smug people in the southern climates lounged beside their swimming pools. The federal system was robbing the poor to give to the rich; America's cities were writhing in poverty, arson, and decay. At stake, as a group of big-city mayors pointed out, was not just "the survival of our cities" but the "survival of the American way of life as we have known it." "While every American city is not tottering on the brink of disaster," they said, "all are moving toward it."

The press, politicians, and urbanologists all agreed on one thing. With cities and their people, as a Presidential policy group put it, in distress, the only hope left was for a national urban policy, the kind of "massive effort to achieve the revitalization of our cities" that Jimmy Carter had promised in the 1976 election. So through the summer of 1977 and the cold and bitter winter that led into 1978, the northern cities waited, as the idiom current at that time put it, to be "saved." Finally the President spoke.

"I am convinced that it is in our national interest," Jimmy Carter announced last March, "to save our cities. The deterioration of urban life in the United States is one of the most complex and deeply rooted problems we face. The federal government has the clear duty to lead the effort to reverse that deterioration. I intend to provide the leadership." He then announced a series of programs "designed to marshal the immense resources of America in a long-term commitment to pursue that goal." Had not our cities become disintegrating warrens of poverty and despair? The President promised a labor-intensive public-works program to put the chronically unemployed back to work rebuilding decaying business districts. Had not private corporate capital callously abandoned its social obligations in the very cities that had generated its enormous profits? The Carter national urban policy promised a National Development Bank to provide venture capital for inner-city economic revival. Had not the suburbs, like shortsighted parasites, selfishly shirked their metropolitan responsibilities, refusing to share revenues and closing their borders to the urban unemployed? The White House would create federal incentives to make the states part of the urban solution. Had not Southern Shift, and Washington's own irrational proclivity for pouring federal money into Atlanta and Phoenix at the expense of Cleveland and Baltimore sentenced the northern cities to fiscal doom? Under Jimmy Carter, the Treasury would provide direct federal budgetary assistance to help impoverished inner-city governments stand on their own two feet again.

"Let there be no doubt," the President concluded, "that today marks a turning point."

THE HORSEMEN PASS BY

These days, to look at what has happened to cities since the President made his pledge is to look in the face of a paradox. Big-city politicians, bureaucrats in Washington, urbanologists around the country agree on two things that, at first glance, seem contradictory. The first is that Jimmy Carter's urban programs are inadequate—and abysmally inadequate—either to save cities, or to confront the urban crisis that so recently was considered this nation's most troublesome domestic problem. The second thing on which they agree is that the catastrophe has not taken place. In spite of the dire consequences predicted for the nation if Washington did not come to the rescue, 1978 was not the year the sky fell on St. Louis, the skyscrapers were abandoned on Wall Street, or Detroit burned to the ground. It was the year the northern cities confounded the prophets of inner-city doom. Once dismissed as anachronisms of the pre-suburban past, cities like Boston and Baltimore proved themselves to be vital human centers with futures far more promising than either their detractors or their beleaguered proponents imagined possible.

In the months following his announcement of the national urban policy, Jimmy Carter's grandiose promise to rebuild the South Bronx "brick by brick and block by block" never went beyond tokenism. But the World Trade Center, once dismissed as a white elephant, achieved a 90 percent occupancy rate, and the Citicorp Tower, the eighth highest skyscraper in the world, opened in midtown Manhattan. The Administration's commitment to revive decaying inner-city neighborhoods never was translated from the drawing boards to the tenements of Bushwick and Dorchester. But from Boerum Hill in Brooklyn to Capitol Hill in Washington the fastest growing social problem was not the departure of the white middle class; it was the displacement of the poor and nonwhite, as affluent, taxpaying professionals bid up the prices on brownstone houses and cooperative apartments in what once were dismissed as unsightly slums. Urban specialists now refer to this process as inner-city "gentrification."

Today the National Development Bank, like the incentives for state aid, remains no more than a proposal on a piece of paper, marked over by Congress, and seemingly forgotten in the White House. But without waiting for Washington to show them how, small businessmen competed avidly for rental space in downtown Boston's Quincy Market and a major utility expanded its operations in Newark. The Urban Land Institute estimates that 70 percent of all sizable American cities today are experiencing a significant revival in what once were called "deteriorated" areas. According to a study for the Pacific News Service City Project by Thomas Brom, corporate investment is flooding American cities, and the influx of American capital into downtown areas is being matched by funds coming from Europe, the Mideast, Japan, as well as from other areas that were once supposed to offer investment opportunities far better than devastated Detroit or run-down old New York. While automobile money flowed into Renaissance Center in downtown Detroit, Olympia and York Developers of Toronto began sinking $350 million into a real estate package of seven office buildings in New York. Money Market Directories estimates that over the next few years America's 300 largest corporate funds will invest more than $6 billion in real estate, and for many foreigners, American cities seem to be the most alluring investment opportunity. Nowhere else can Europeans invest money and have some assurance that it will still remain their property ten years later.

But wasn't New York destined to become a ghost town unless President Carter provided money and jobs? The President's labor-intensive public-works bill was never passed, yet over the past two years, in spite of the fiscal crisis and the layoffs at City Hall, New York has added more than 100,000 jobs — nearly half the workforce of Atlanta — to its payrolls. Today the unemployment rate in Cleveland, erstwhile ruin beside Lake Erie, is 6.8 percent. In Atlanta, workshop of the New South, it is 7 percent. Miami has more of its workers unemployed than Boston. Baltimore, Detroit, and St. Louis all have lower unemployment rates than El Paso. Houston and Dallas are still booming, but Chicago, with its run-down ethnic neighborhoods, has a lower unemployment rate than Los Angeles. (See Table 1).

But aren't America's cities going broke? What happened to the municipal bonds no one would buy? What was the fate of the teachers and policemen whom northern cities couldn't pay unless heroic action was taken in Washington? NEW FISCAL PROBLEM: TOO MUCH MONEY; FEARS OF DEFICIT CRISIS VANISH AS CITIES, STATES FACE PROBLEM OF RISING SUR-

Table 1
Northern cities narrow the unemployment gap (comparison of unemployment rates in select cities for 1976 and 1978)

	1976			1978		
	Employed	Unemployed	Unemployment rate (%)	Employed	Unemployed	Unemployment rate (%)
Northern cities						
St. Louis	210,629	19,582	8.6	226,972	10,144	6.6
New York	2,730,000	344,000	11.2	2,838,270	279,999	8.8
Cleveland	287,744	32,892	10.3	297,731	21,818	6.8
Baltimore	379,815	40,133	9.6	385,781	26,799	6.5
Boston	272,246	34,074	11.1	299,368	23,979	7.4
Detroit	600,183	74,085	11.1	631,805	62,009	8.9
Southern cities						
Denver	222,429	16,873	7.1	240,774	15,960	6.2
Los Angeles	1,221,611	134,526	9.9	1,273,114	114,779	8.3
Dallas	428,876	25,408	5.6	478,094	22,473	4.5
Houston	709,008	36,192	4.9	816,233	40,333	4.7
Phoenix	313,017	33,939	9.8	353,725	19,645	5.3
Atlanta	244,376	31,676	11.5	216,225	16,319	7.0

Source: U.S. Department of Labor, Bureau of Labor Statistics.

PLUSES, read one headline during 1978. The Carter proposal for direct budgetary assistance for cities still has not been enacted either. Yet the prophecies of urban fiscal disaster, serious as the economic condition for many cities remains, have been disproved by an astonishing fact: in calendar 1977 the aggregate state and local government budget surplus reached the remarkable level of $29 billion, the highest in history. Instead of being "black, brown, and broke," cities are attracting affluent people from all over the world, and in some fortunate cases at least, finding themselves with more revenues than they know how to spend. For all the diagnoses of senility, and all the prognoses of imminent death, it is increasingly difficult to deny that the northern cities have turned out to be remarkably durable—holding their own economically and fiscally, in spite of the people and jobs they lost from the end of World War II through the early 1970s, while reasserting their traditional social and cultural preeminence at the very moment it was supposed to be gone forever.

Since the beginning of the year the whole tenor of urban discourse has changed, with visions of inner-city renaissance prevailing over the old prophecies of doom. In August I asked several members of the House and Senate, and a number of urbanologists and staff members in Congress, the Department of Housing and Urban Development, and in the White House—all grappling with urban problems—how they thought America's "dying inner cities" would be faring five or fifteen years hence. Without exception they believed the cities would be much better off than they are now. Where policy makers once were so pessimistic, they now seemed to foresee a future for cities that the so-called Sunbelt and suburbs might envy. "For the next twenty years," Kenneth McLean, staff director of the Senate Committee on Banking, Housing and Urban Affairs, told me, "the good life in America will be urban." "I'm optimistic," added Rep. William Moorhead of Pittsburgh, who is chairman of the similar committee in the House. "There has been a fundamental shift. People are rediscovering, in a massive way, the advantages of city life." Moorhead—who lobbied diligently to win Congressional support for fiscal aid to New York—has never been one to pretend that urban problems don't exist. But he doesn't see cities as needy relics of the Industrial Revolution any more, but rather as pacesetters of the post-industrial age. "We won't get back the old manufacturing jobs," he points out, "but cities will benefit greatly from the explosion in the service sector. Today in Pittsburgh, the biggest single employer isn't U.S. Steel or the government bureaucracy. It's the University of Pittsburgh."

Pittsburgh, of course, cleaned up pollution years ago. It has one of the most homogeneous populations of any big American city—and the incredible wealth of the Mellon family on its side. Surely spokesmen for cities that are less fortunate don't buy all the new talk of urban revival.

"I made a mistake when I propounded the abandonment theory," Rep. Parren Mitchell of Baltimore, the chairman of the Congressional Black Caucus, told me when we sat down to talk in the ornate cloakroom of the House of Representatives. "I did not reckon with the fact that white capital would not let its urban investment go down the drain." Mitchell, who represents a predominantly black district, thinks his city, and others, have turned the corner. The 1980 census, he concedes, will reflect the population losses many older cities suffered in the early 1970s. But he points out that while city populations may decline more, the per capita wealth of those who remain seems bound to increase. Mitchell believes long-term events will show that the last few years were not the nadir of the urban crisis, but the period when the American city turned around. "When I moved deeper into the ghetto a few years ago," the Congressman said "even my black friends said I was crazy. Today the next street over is predominantly white middle class, and on my own block, black professionals are buying up houses and renovating them.

"In fifteen or twenty years," Mitchell concluded, "America's worst national problems won't all be concentrated inside cities as they are now. Cities at the worst will be doing fairly well."

CATCHING UP WITH REALITY

What is going on when a national crisis seems to abate, without the President of the United States having vindicated the great-man theory of history, without Congress having passed a single piece of major national urban legislation? Elinor Bachrach, who, in her work for the Senate Banking Committee, has been intensively involved in urban fiscal problems for years, suggested that it might be a matter of fashion. "Washington is a town of fads," she said. "I can remember when 'environment' was the buzz word. Then we got all excited about the energy crisis. The city craze," she elaborates, "has now been killed off by the Prop 13 fashion." Politicians last year were saying only new programs could bail cities out; this year they are cutting every tax they can find. With so many swings in the Washington tiller, why has the national ship not run aground long ago? "It is fortunate," Ms. Bachrach said, "that beyond the limits of the District of Columbia there exists a real world, with real forces that manage to operate without an Act of Congress."

While that sentiment is little shared on the banks of the Potomac, Roger Vaughan, an economist who has made many studies of urban problems for the Rand Corporation, has a theory even more disconcerting for those who imagine that by debating policy they determine events. As one of the authors of a study on the urban impact of federal policies sponsored by both private funds and the federal government, Vaughan has said, "There always is a gap of at least several years between the problem, and our political perception of it." After years of gathering and analyzing thousands of statistics, Vaughan works on the assumption that if a problem provokes the greatest possible public concern, it already is being solved. He remembers how environmental pollution became the raging public concern at the precise moment when the flight of industry was dissipating city smog; that the energy crisis came to obsess political discourse in the midst of the greatest oil glut in history. "It was the same way with the urban crisis," Vaughan told me. "By the time we became aware of Southern Shift, it already was beginning to ebb. We were too busy suddenly discovering what harm we had done to cities in the 1950s and 1960s to notice that, in the 1970s, events had started to favor cities again." Vaughan does not suggest that there is never anything to worry about, just that Presidents, Congressmen, and journalists tend to run around worrying about the wrong things. He suggests that "we should be worrying about what we're not worrying about."

So while tax surpluses increase, a President tells us about "the distress of the most fiscally strained communities"—and when word of the taxpayers' revolt reaches the capital a few months later, the political elite reacts with astonishment and alarm. Prestigious newspapers print editorials about the crisis of urban disinvestment while the Arabs put up a skyscraper next door. In the halls of Congress, Senators and Representatives make speeches about the advancing blight in our cities while outside their office windows, on Capitol Hill, seedy sandwich shops are being metamorphosed into pretentious French restaurants, and rundown, $15,000 welfare rooming houses are being sub-divided into apartments costing $85,000 apiece. The divergence between policy and reality—most graphically illustrated in the happy divergence between the fate of Jimmy Carter's urban programs and the fate of America's cities—in fact operates on two separate levels. The first concerns the federal government itself, and involves the gap between "news" and what really is happening even when no one notices it; between "debate" and what already has been decided by events even when the crisis managers go home at five; and between "policy" and what the federal government, with its immense weight on affairs, effects even when there is no policy at all. The second level concerns a national and international reality larger than the federal government. It involves the gap between what the government is doing, whether it knows it or not, and those immense social, demographic, economic, and technological forces that exceed the capacity of the federal government to control them.

On the first level—that of the effect of the federal government on events— it is now clear that the concentration in the press, in Congress, and in the White House on specific urban programs frequently has blinded almost everyone to the effects on cities of unprogrammatic federal spending, whatever its inten-tion. This was true in the 1960s when, under the rubric of the War on Poverty, ostensible policy and programs were as pro-city as they ever have been, but the aggregate of federal spending nonetheless was accelerating the outflow of capital, jobs, and people from inner cities at a rate no amount of Great Society programs could reverse. Today it is the continuing tendency to confuse *programs* (that is, what the President, Congress, and the federal bureaucracy say, and sometimes even believe, they are doing) with what the federal government is actually doing, and an almost complaisant lack of attention to *spending* (that is, to what the government is really doing, whether it wants to do it, or even knows it is doing it) that continues to becloud understanding of the impact of the federal government on cities.

Lyndon Johnson said he was trying to help cities; Lyndon Johnson believed he was helping cities, with "urban renewal" programs that destroyed neighborhoods, and with "equal opportunity" programs that gave the jobless and poor incentives to stay in northern cities at the very moment opportunity was shifting to the suburbs and the South. So the conventional wisdom grew up that Lyndon Johnson poured so much money into so many cities to so little effect that he proved "you can't solve problems by throwing money at them." Richard Nixon, in his turn, made it very clear that it was not his policy to throw money at problems. So it became the conventional wisdom that cities got into trouble because of Nixon's stinginess. Later, as city problems got worse, Gerald Ford demonstrated his insensitivity to New York City. Such, even after Watergate, was the implacable faith of Americans in their supreme magistrate that it was widely assumed a metropolis of more than 7 million people might expire before our very eyes, because a President of the United States had indicated it was fine by him if it did. Finally Jimmy Carter promised his national urban policy; again it was believed a fundamental change in direction would occur, because the man in the White House had said so.

The statistics (which, like policy, always lag behind events) are now available. They make short work of all those conventional wisdoms.

It now is clear that, whatever his intentions, Lyndon Johnson's Great Society Programs bore no more relationship to the real problems of America's cities than the Domino Theory did to the security of Connecticut. Far from throwing money at urban problems (and much future grief might have been avoided if he had), President Johnson presided over a federal money machine that as late as 1968 still was constantly sucking wealth out of northern cities, and enfeebling urban industrial economies that already were in trouble. While LBJ paid ghetto dwellers to stay put in Harlem and Roxbury studying obsolete trades, he used New York and Massachusetts tax dollars to build the manned space center in Texas. The Great Society was not misplaced largesse; it helped set up cities for the crisis that broke a few years later. Nixon and Ford, for their part, may not have intended to throw money at problems, but throw money they did, or rather the federal bureaucracy and Congress, sometimes in spite of Presidential vetoes, did. To the extent American cities faced a major crisis during the Nixon-Ford years, the cause lay as much in the federally encouraged outflow of urban assets that had occurred under the Democrats as in the anticity policies of their Republican successors. (Of course, Nixon's partisan use of revenue sharing to help Republican suburbs hurt cities, and above all Republican mismanagement of the economy, resulting in two major recessions in the early 1970s, greatly intensified the problems cities already faced.)

Nonetheless, a truly remarkable influx—not outflow—of federal moneys into cities had occurred by the end of the Nixon-Ford Administration. The transfer of federal wealth to cities that occurred under two Republican Presidents has played the same causal role in helping cities now that the outflow of money under Johnson earlier played in creating the urban crisis of the Nixon-Ford years. Under Jimmy Carter the direction of federal spending in cities has not changed at all, even though the direction of policy ostensibly has. It has only accelerated. What was the merest trickle of federal funds into municipal coffers in Johnson's day had become a flood by the time Ford left office. Today it is a deluge, so that urban analysts who once feared that cities would expire for lack of outside money now fear that cities might become sick with surfeit. As data assembled by the Advisory Commission on Intergovernmental Relations indicate, a fundamental change has occurred in the financing of city budgets over the last twenty years, largely independent of the specific policy of the specific President in the White House. And when these figures are linked with the other indications of urban revival we now have, they would tend to debunk that most hardy perennial of all policy myths: It seems that at least some problems in cities begin to be solved, if you throw enough money at them.

As Table 2 indicates, so far as cities were concerned the transition from Eisenhower, with his fear of deficit spending, to the Administrations of Kennedy and Johnson and all their Keynesian advisers, made little difference at all. Under Lyndon Johnson, direct federal aid amounted to only 1 percent in St. Louis, only 1.7 percent in Newark, and only 2.1 percent in Buffalo of the general revenues those cities raised themselves, from their own local property, sales, and other taxes. These sums were too small even to compensate for the competitive advantage other federal programs—notably FHA mortgages and the Interstate Highway System—then were lavishing on the suburbs and the South and West, let alone to help solve social problems. Meanwhile Phoenix—in the heart of the so-called Sunbelt[1]—was getting 10.6 percent from Lyndon Johnson. By the end of the Nixon-Ford years, direct federal aid to many cities had skyrocketed—to 23.6 percent of the revenues St. Louis raised, 11.4 percent in Newark, and no less than 55.6 in Buffalo. Of course Nixon and Ford—as their liberal critics often pointed out—also rained money down on affluent suburbs and the southern areas when the money was more needed elsewhere. Phoenix by the end of the Nixon-Ford years was getting direct federal aid amounting to 35 percent of its own burgeoning revenues, while direct federal aid to expanding cities like Denver, Los Angeles, and Houston—where the problem wasn't urban decay at all, but uncontrolled growth—had risen from almost nothing to a full fifth of those cities' own revenues.

Under Jimmy Carter, or much more accurately speaking, under the tendency of federal programs, once started, steadily to gain in both mass and velocity, the federal manna falling on cities has become a blizzard. St. Louis, which was getting less than $3 in annual per capita direct federal aid during the War on Poverty, was getting $86 by the time President Ford turned his back on the cities. Today St. Louis receives $223 in direct federal aid for every man, woman, and child within the city limits. It would be astonishing under such circumstances if economic conditions did not improve. Over the past two years, St. Louis has gained more than 16,000 new jobs, and the number of

Table 2
Accelerating federal aid to cities (direct federal aid as a percent of city's general
revenue, selected cities and fiscal years 1957-1978

| City | Fiscal years | | | | Per capita federal aid based on 1975 population | |
	1957	1967	1976	1978 (est.)	1976	1978 (est.)
St. Louis	0.6	1.0	23.6	54.7	$86	$223
Newark	0.2	1.7	11.4	55.2	47	251
Buffalo	1.3	2.1	55.6	69.2	163	218
Cleveland	2.0	8.3	22.8	68.8	65	217
Boston	*	10.0	31.5	28.0	204	203
Baltimore	1.7	3.8	38.9	53.3	167	258
Philadelphia	0.4	8.8	37.7	51.8	129	196
Detroit	1.3	13.1	50.2	69.6	161	248
Atlanta	4.3	2.0	15.1	36.0	52	150
Denver	0.6	1.2	21.2	24.2	98	140
Los Angeles	0.7	0.7	19.3	35.7	54	120
Dallas	0	*	20.0	17.8	51	54
Houston	0.2	3.1	19.4	22.7	44	68
Phoenix	1.1	10.6	35.0	58.3	57	116

* Less than .05 percent.
Source: Advisory Commission on Intergovernmental Relations staff computations based on U.S.
Bureau of the Census data.

unemployed has been cut almost in half—from 19,852 then to 10,144 this year
[1978]. Since 1976, per capita aid to Newark has risen from $47 to $251, and
now amounts to 55.2 percent of all locally raised revenues. In Buffalo, the
current figures, respectively, have risen to 69.2 percent and $218; in Baltimore,
to 53.3 and $258; and in Phoenix, the ever fortunate, to 58.3 and $116. Since
the end of the War on Poverty, some $400 billion has been spent in direct federal
aid for cities and the people who live there. On an annual, virtually self-
renewing basis, without any aditional new programs, some $80 billion in
federal money now goes specifically for urban aid programs, and for social
programs aiding people who live in cities. These figures do not include other
federal spending in cities, for example salaries for federal employees, or the
share of this year's mammoth $117 billion military budget that will be spent in
urban areas in spite of the continuing southern and suburban bias of most
defense spending.

ELUSIVE CRISES

How can such a stupendous, in many instances desirable, transfer of wealth into cities not merely have been ignored so totally in analyses of the urban "crisis," but the policy debate on cities have been premised so universally, and for such a long time, on the completely opposite assumption — the assumption, as Senator Moynihan, for example, never ceases to iterate, that the real reason for urban problems is that the federal government keeps taking much more out of cities than it puts back? A major reason, it needs to be reemphasized, is the perpetual tendency of the press, Congress, even the policy makers themselves to confuse policy with what really is going on. A year ago, inner-city spokesmen were calling for a "Marshall Plan" for cities. When Jimmy Carter finally announced his urban policy, it contained specific new program proposals that would have added $4.4 billion in direct new federal spending for cities. The conventional wisdom at the time was that Carter was "the most fiscally conservative Democratic President since Grover Cleveland," that he had decided to make cities eat crumbs, and give them no cake.

But alarming as the thought to policy makers may be, policy is not where the action is. Sen. William Proxmire of Wisconsin no doubt is right when he points out that to give American cities today what Europe got under the Marshall Plan would be to inflict mass cutbacks in urban spending that not even the lunatic fringe of the Proposition 13 crowd would espouse. The Marshall Plan provided $13 billion over five years — or $2.6 billion a year — to seventeen countries with a population larger than the whole of the United States. Today cities are getting $2.4 billion each year in mass transit funds alone, and $4.5 billion annually from the Environmental Protection Agency. "The federal government spends twenty-three times per year the amount we spent per year under the Marshall Plan," Proxmire points out. "Even when we allow for inflation, we now put about ten times more into our cities each year than we put into Europe under the Marshall Plan."

Proxmire — like others who no longer support the urban catastrophe scenario — is no enemy of cities; he is not trying to invent excuses to stop spending money where it is needed. But he is appalled to see federal funds shoring up affluent neighborhoods while garbage goes uncollected in marginal areas; to watch Community Development grants pouring into the richest census tracts, while poor neighborhoods collapse further into ruin. Proxmire wonders why so little of the federal money goes to Harlem, or to give tax breaks to struggling factories providing jobs in Queens, why the only significant piece of urban legislation Congress passed in 1978 was a $1.6 billion loan guarantee for the big Wall Street banks. "Providing credit for New York City, the credit capital of the world," he suggests, "was like shipping dairy cows to Wisconsin."

Without a doubt much of what Proxmire says is correct; a large portion of this influx of federal money into cities is utterly wasted, so far as solving inner-city social, economic, and fiscal problems is concerned. As much as $20 billion of the $80 billion given to cities each year leaks into the suburbs. An enormous amount of it goes to people and neighborhoods that don't need help at all. Meanwhile much of the money that actually reaches inner cities and people in distress serves to create a permanent dependent population, rather than new jobs; it does absolutely nothing to revive inner-city school systems, or to preserve municipal capital, ranging from bridges to sewers, which is deteriorating at an alarming rate. To the extent that cities suffered in the past from the unprogrammatic impact of federal spending, whatever the policy of the moment happened to be, for the foreseeable future they will benefit to a similar extent from the reverse phenomenon. But the inflow of federal money into cities certainly until now has not had, and may never have, whatever the rhetoric current in Washington, that surgical precision that the advocates of "targeting"—the great new urban policy buzz word—talk about. Instead, the federal funds being spent in cities should be regarded more as an act of nature, like a change in climate, than as an act of conscious policy implementation. And one should be just as wary of the "countercyclical" claims made for federal spending. In both cases the theory is straightforward. When the economy goes down, the conventional doctrine holds, federal spending should go up; this is the theory of countercyclical programs. The theory behind targeting is that, whatever the overall state of the national economy, federal money should be spent on the areas, and people, that need help the most.

These theories are attractive, not merely because we should minimize the human costs of a cyclical economy, or because we should help people who need help even when the economic indicators are going up, whether they live in East Orange or south Texas—these theories are attractive because they foster the illusion that the federal government is more a policy instrument, and less an act of political nature. Alas, our whole experience with trying to use a big government to solve big social problems over the past few decades shows not, as the conservatives pretend, that it can't, but simply, as liberals won't accept, that we really don't have all that much control over whether it does or not. It is one thing to rain down money on the South for twenty years, and then move the rainmaking machine to the cities. But there are several problems with trying to do much else.

The first problem is political. It is far easier to get the 535 members of the House and Senate to approve legislation that helps all their constituents than it is to get them to vote funds that help only a few districts and states, however deserving they may be. In a political system in which it is also much easier to extend old programs than to initiate new ones, "countercyclical" money tends to go on being spent, even when the economy enters a new cycle, just as "targeting" tends to broaden out into pork barrel legislation that helps Riverdale as much as it does the South Bronx. We have seen this tendency operating with particular force during the current session of Congress. The problem is not that the legislators have failed to help people and cities in distress, but that, jumping on the Proposition 13 bandwagon, they have cut taxes for everyone. The

President started out by asking Congress for some labor-intensive public works to help chronic unemployment; he may wind up having to veto legislation that would give every corporate vice-president's son a summer job.

The second problem is far more serious; it might be termed cultural. It quite simply is that, In American society, programs once in effect, whatever their initial intent and specific provisions, invariably help the rich more than the poor, the white more than the black, the educated more than the functionally illiterate, and those who have something more than those who have nothing at all. In the 1960s, Project Head Start was metamorphosed quickly from a program for underprivileged ghetto youth into an amenity for the preschool children of the affluent. CETA jobs help those who already know the ropes in City Hall more than they help the chronically unemployed. Today anti-redlining legislation, currently a great reformist cause, is the most conspicuous example of this tendency. In the long run it probably will hurt the very people it is supposed to help, by encouraging white middle-class families to buy up inner-city houses, and displace the poor blacks and browns who live there now. Even among the disadvantaged this tendency operates: It takes a high level of literacy, considerable industry, and a keen sense of how bureaucracies work to be a successful welfare chiseler. One of society's real victims is unlikely even to know how to get food stamps.

These warps in causality between what we achieve and what we have set out to achieve are not, as those who mistake making policy for manipulating reality like to think, indications that what is needed is just a little more fine tuning. Like the distortion in an amplifier, like the errors of margin in the weapons we used in Indochina, they are inherent parts of the process. And finally, because of the inevitable lag between crises and the political perception of them, to say nothing of the chronic delays in appropriating money and then spending it, one must count in the tendency of the federal government to throw money at the places where problems once were, not at the places where they are now.

Today the perception lag remains, and all the other limitations of what we try to do with policy, too. Does this worry Jimmy Carter? The surprising thing is that this advocate for Zero-Base Budgeting, with his dream of an end to deficit spending, appears far more aware of what really is going on, and far less troubled by it, than those who spend their time picking over his proposals for a National Development Bank. Last March, for example, when the President announced his national urban policy, he divided it into three parts, in descending order of significance. Carter first pointed to "the very substantial increases" he already had made in the volume of federal moneys flowing into cities, and correctly pointed out that "total assistance to state and local governments already had been increased by 25 percent," from $68 billion to $85 billion, even before he announced the policy. The second major element in his urban policy, the President said, was "the reorientation of federal activities to make certain that they support our urban goals." Only third and last did the

President mention the "new initiatives"—the programs that offered so little new money, and that Congress has not enacted anyway—that left so many urban advocates disappointed. Two other sentences from the President's speech are worth quoting. "The Defense Department," he said, "will set up a new program to increase procurement in urban areas." "And the General Services Administration will retain facilities in urban areas and will put new ones there." He later followed these promises up with executive orders.

Thus—as with the New South and the suburbs before—the money seems likely to keep pouring in, whether it goes where it is needed or not, and whether we know it or not. Jimmy Carter in fact has put himself in the business, whether he fully realizes it or not, of taking back with the right hand what Lyndon Johnson once gave—while giving back with the left hand what LBJ took away. The reverse symmetry hardly could be more exact. The War on Poverty was a *policy* that purported to cure America's gravest social ills; but while Johnson was raising millennial expectations, federal *spending* patterns in fact were making inner-city problems worse. Jimmy Carter's policy didn't offer very much, beneath the rhetoric, in new programs; and what he offered has not become law. But the new federal spending patterns that Carter did not originate, but which he is certainly helping to accelerate, are offering cities something all the liberal rhetoric of the Great Society never could: money, which is like manure. Spread enough of it around, no matter how indiscriminately, and something is bound to spring up. If the urban crisis has not turned out to be the gaping wound in our society it once seemed, neither has the balm spread upon it.

The easiest way to dispose of old myths is to create new ones. Cities were believed to be dying only a short time ago, asphyxiating for lack of money. Nothing would be easier now than to suggest that cities are in the midst of an amazing renaissance that has solved all their problems. The truth is that many double-edged forces, cutting into the lives of millions of people in complex ways, are at work in cities, and on the whole country. If there never was an "urban crisis," at least not in the terms assumed by those who make policy and report it, the lesson to be drawn is not that the opposite conventional wisdom is true. It is that we should stop bounding every few years from one inadequate metaphor for the situation we face to another.

The energy crisis; the population crisis; the pollution crisis; the crisis of crime in the streets and the crisis created by the revolution of rising expectations. The crisis of the falling dominoes, and the missile gap crisis. The whole history of policy discourse over the past twenty years often has been no more than a pantomime in which vast amounts of money and officials, technology and newsprint have been marshalled to fight crises that, it eventually was discovered, weren't really crises at all. We have tended to confuse unstoppable evolutions with sudden breaks in the dike. We have assumed that events which threatened our preconceptions were "problems"—and conversely, we have imagined that when the problems turned out to be not what they had seemed to be, we had nothing to worry about at all. We shall hear less and less about the "urban crisis" in the future; new buzz words are already taking its place.

AN ODD RENAISSANCE

For two years, Prof. Franz Schurmann, an expert in international relations at the University of California at Berkeley, has been studying the problems of America's cities. Starting on the outside and working in, concentrating on the worldwide forces affecting Anacostia or the Upper West Side, he has come to the same conclusion that many urbanologists have reached, beginning with tenements and tax receipts—that American cities face a dynamic future, not slow death as relics of an outmoded past. Rather than trying to sort out the "crises" and break them down into "problems" that can be solved, he and other members of his Third Century America Project, working with a grant from the Ford Foundation, have tried to understand the whole: to discover how situations like the declining rate of return on European capital investment or the growth of agribusiness in Mexico relate to the Manhattan condominium market, or the dynamics of the illegal labor market in Chicago.

By forgetting about the crises for a little while, and the "policy implications" of his research, too, Schurmann has discovered that what we face is less an urban crisis, and much more a national transformation. He sees the influx either of poor Third World peoples or of foreign capital into our cities not as problems to be solved, but simply new facts of life we must begin to understand. With Manila and São Paulo looking more and more like Manhattan, he wonders, is it so surprising to see New York and Los Angeles looking more and more like Third World cities? American cities, he points out, are getting richer and poorer at the same time. The problem is not merely that any one conventional wisdom is wrong, but that when put together, so many of them are true: He sees an urban crisis and an urban renaissance going on at the same time. What he considers most important is not that affluent whites are rediscovering the urban life-style at the same time Third World migrants are filling our cities, or that petrodollars are flooding New York while industry continues to leave. What he considers important is the convergence of all these events. Efforts to turn back the clock—whether New Left attempts to save archaic steel mills, Nixon's stab at "Project Independence," or Carter's own efforts to reduce dependency on foreign oil—only create the illusion, he warns, that scattershot policies can be a substitute for taking advantage of fundamental new changes that we cannot reverse. "What the economic realities say," according to Schurmann, "is that our dependence on the world economy is not due to oil. By the middle of this year, oil had slipped to third place on the list of U.S. imports; machinery and transport equipment headed the list, followed by manufactured goods. The U.S., which a century ago became the world's leading industrial nation, is now rapidly becoming primarily a trading nation."

And far from being bypassed by events—whether we consider those events good or bad—cities instead are becoming, as Professor Schurmann puts it, "the nodal points in a great transition not just of American society but of the whole world economy."

After trying to piece all the "crises" together, Schurmann has worked out his own scenario of what is happening to American cities. It falls into three parts, and bears little resemblance either to the old prophecies of urban doom, or to the new talk of a happy urban ending. First, he believes, "downtown centers of U.S. cities will continue to boom, with office buildings like the new Citicorp Tower going up, and areas of gentrified living like [New York's] SoHo continuing to expand." Barring a major change in the world economy, he has concluded that American cities will continue to benefit from the worldwide transition into a new "post-industrial era involving compact high technology, a huge service sector encompassing everyone from millionaire real estate analysts to Spanish-speaking housemaids earning less than the minimum wage, as well as sizable culture and leisure sectors. Cities," he emphasizes, "are central to the new era."

But what will happen, as this metamorphosis goes on, to the people who already are in cities? "Second," he observes, "as downtown and gentrified areas expand, the poor and jobless are being crowded into the outer cities, and beyond." As Schurmann and members of his project see it, the fact that cities will become richer doesn't mean that problems like poverty will go away. Far from it. "The difference," he points out, "the characteristic of this new urban era, is that this time it is the rich who are coming in and pushing the poor out." Our cities will become more and more like the European cities American urbanologists have envied—but in ways they have not anticipated. "The likelihood," Schurmann comments, "is not just that downtown America will become more like the smaller charming European towns—high-finance and high-culture centers with lots of palaces, theaters, and restaurants—but that the revived centers of cities like Boston and Baltimore, like the bombed-out European centers that were rebuilt following World War II, will be ringed by dingy working-class suburbs or, as one now frequently sees in Europe, 'bidonvilles,' tin-can and clapboard shacks housing Europe's migrant workers, the counterparts of our own illegal aliens." As American cities become increasingly internationalized, he has concluded, the American economy will not just more and more resemble foreign ones, but American society will change, too. In the third phase of Schurmann's scenario, "stratification will turn more and more into class, as the lines between different kinds of people no longer are sociological abstractions, but become visible traits" under these new urban circumstances. He foresees many more white affluent city neighborhoods, many more expanding slums in which English is hardly spoken, money being poured into new skyscrapers and elegant restorations, while elsewhere the deterioration has only begun.

If these kinds of changes amount to a solution of an urban crisis, it is an odd sort of renaissance, in which urban problems are not so much solved as switched around within metropolitan regions; in which problems once considered the exclusive bane of northern cities increasingly afflict the suburbs and the South, too, while the inequalities in our society are not diminished by a period of great social ferment and economic transformation, only made more intense. Not even the most optimistic forecasts of inner-city revival see the big-city ghettos disappearing. But are there Sowetos in our future too?

"Slumming of the suburbs is already evident in many American metropolitan regions," Schurmann comments. "It is especially evident in many close-in suburban centers." "The suburban crisis is no longer on the horizon," Roger Vaughan adds. "In the older and inner suburban cities it is already here." Research by the Rand Corporation (see Table 3), conducted for the Economic Development Administration, compares how fast cities were generating new jobs with how fast their suburban counterparts were generating them during the period when perceptions of the urban crisis were most intense, and fears for the economic future of cities were greatest. Covering the years from 1970 to 1975, these data indicate that even back when the alarums about the urban crisis were shrillest, it already was time to disabuse ourselves of another policy myth—the conventional wisdom that downtown business districts were turning into deserts of joblessness, while the suburban shopping mall was the scene of perpetual economic miracle. Instead, all across the country, inner suburban growth rates were slowing down, while the rate at which the cities were generating new jobs was catching up. Though the pattern was the same everywhere, it was particularly instructive in the old manufacturing-belt metropolitan regions, where the flight of jobs to the suburbs was supposed to be most serious.

The data show that during the 1960s, the suburban centers indeed were outperforming the downtown economies at an extraordinary rate. In the Northeast and Midwest, suburban centers like Cherry Hill in suburban Philadelphia and Nassau County in suburban New York were generating new jobs more than four times faster than their respective city centers. In the South and West, this was the period when Orange County began to outperform Los Angeles, and San Jose to overtake San Francisco in job growth. There, suburbs were generating new employment twice as fast as the inner cities.

But by 1975—the very year the fiscal crisis broke and urban economic decline became a major national issue—the situation had changed dramatically. In the South and West, the ratio had reversed itself. Cities were now generating new jobs twice as fast as the nearer suburban centers. And in the Northeast and Midwest, cities were outperforming suburban centers, if one takes into account the fact that while the growth of new jobs in cities continued, their populations were declining—that the new jobs cities were creating had to be shared out among fewer and fewer people.[2]

Table 3
City-suburban gap narrows (in the 1960s, suburban economies were growing faster than cities, but in the 1970s the gap began to close*)

	Old manufacturing belt		Sunbelt		Mountain & West		National average
	Central cities	Suburban centers	Central cities	Suburban centers	Central cities	Suburban centers	
1960-1970							
Employment growth	4.2%	18.0%	28.2%	58.9%	25.1%	53.1%	19.4%
Population growth	5.8%	17.1%	34.6%	72.2%	22.7%	99.7%	13.3%
1970-1975							
Employment growth	4.2%	5.4%	21.7%	18.2%	25.8%	14.9%	7.9%
Population growth	−3.5%	0.4%	13.3%	9.2%	11.0%	10.9%	4.2%

* Analysis compared 388 central and suburban cities of populations exceeding 50,000.
Source: Rand Corporation analysis of Bureau of Labor Statistics data for Economic Development Administration.

All this hardly means that Harlem is becoming the showplace of the American economy, and that Scarsdale soon will have to go on the dole. But it does show that inner-city economies were stronger, even in the depths of the recessions of the early 1970s, than seemed possible. In fact, since 1975, as the employment statistics for cities like St. Louis and Cleveland show, cities have accelerated the rate at which they have generated new jobs. Outlying exurban areas and the newer suburban districts are still growing fast, but what can be said is that factors once actively biased against cities now are increasingly favorable toward them. It seems likely that both the Southern Shift and the great migrations to the suburbs have largely run their course. Many inner cities already have passed through the social trauma associated with deindustrialization; it is now Westchester and North Carolina that must worry about losing jobs—to Taiwan and Korea. The suburbs also face structural limitations on growth that cities do not. Cities expand vertically, suburbs laterally, and there is not much horizontal space left for new growth in many suburban areas, as one discovers when one seeks cheap, large tracts of developable land these days in either Nassau or Los Angeles County. The result is that while cities today are generating new employment opportunities sometimes faster than, or at least as fast as, many suburban areas, the suburbs themselves are falling prey to social problems once confined within city limits. Interstate highways, on which the suburbs heavily depend, have begun to deteriorate, as have stocks of suburban housing, hastily built with FHA mortgages in the 1950s. New York's Suffolk County has one of the fastest growing dependent populations in the country. It would be as simplistic to herald doom for suburbia now as it once was to regard skyscrapers as tombstones. But it hardly seems too early to point out that the controversy over "suburban exclusion"—like the one over redlining—has come too late, and is an example of yet another lag in perception between the social problem and the political debate. There is no doubt now that increasing numbers of the poor and of racial minorities finally are getting their chance to move to suburbia. But barriers preventing the poor, jobless, and nonwhite from getting a house with a picket fence around it are beginning to tumble precisely at the moment when suburban opportunities are beginning to ebb—and the affluent are beginning to discover not just the charms of urban life, but the high cost of suburban mortgages and commuting.

Like most urban "solutions," the changing composition of inner-city populations creates as many problems as it solves; not the least of these is the danger that what political influence black Americans have been able to gain as a result of their long march from the rural South into the slums of urban America now will be eroded as the forces of gentrification gather momentum. Urban policy debate still tends to focus on the immense losses in white middle-class populations that cities suffered from the end of World War II into the middle 1970s. We take far less note of the fact that poor and nonwhite populations are leaving their ghettos today almost as dramatically as ethnic whites deserted the old neighborhoods in the 1950s. According to U.S. Census Bureau data, of the fifty Congressional districts that have lost 5 percent or more of their population since the 1970 census, forty-six of them have a majority of their populations in urban areas—and almost all of these districts have populations that are largely nonwhite or poor or both. Fourteen of fifteen Congressional districts represented by blacks have lost population since 1970, and the nation's only predominantly Puerto Rican district, New York's 21st, has lost nearly a third of its total population in less than eight years. Where are these people going—or being pushed? Many are simply being transferred to other areas within the same city, but black migration to the suburbs is now a significant demographic pattern, and for the first time since the inauguration of the Underground Railroad, more blacks are emigrating to the South than are leaving it. (See Table 4.)

The conclusion is an obvious, and in many ways unflattering, one about the way our society works. So long as suburban land was cheap, and the South booming, we could afford to cede our downtown areas to dependent populations, and abandon their stagnant economies to the "underclass." But now that the scent for an urban revival is in the air, cities increasingly look like those reservations we ceded so solemnly to the Indians—until we noticed they had uranium underneath. While sociologists detect changing cultural attitudes toward city life, it is probably best to seek the reason for what is happening in market forces. The truth—whatever cultural enlightenment may be involved—is that the cost of a suburban split-level has only to soar so high, and the price of an inner-city brownstone to plummet so low, before people in Westchester start finding even certain neighborhoods in The Bronx colorful and cultivated places to live. As with the bombed-out cities of Europe thirty years ago, one of the northern cities' greatest present assets is their past misfortune. For thirty years the cost of inner-city land, real estate, and labor has been declining, and the cost of those commodities in the suburbs rising, in relationship to each other. Whether the arsonists of the South Bronx have created a graveyard of urban civilization, or the biggest bonanza for the smart money developers yet, depends on the eye of the beholder. But even if one does consider Walter Wriston a philanthropist for building Citicorp Tower, or Henry Ford's investment in Renaissance Plaza a selfless gesture of noblesse oblige, it does no harm to keep in mind the comment of one big-time realtor: "Any corporation today that decided to sell in Baltimore and buy in L.A.," he said, "would be acting irrationally in terms of the market. Everything would cost more in California, and they would be putting 3,000 miles between themselves and what is still the richest, biggest market in the world, the Northeast megalopolis."

PROBLEMS MOVE OUT

What will be the long-term effects on cities of the sudden rediscovery that they not only can be pleasant places to live, but profitable places to buy land? Even while working hard to attract private investment, many city officials have

Table 4
Black flight

In the 1950s and 1960s the influx of poor, nonwhite populations created social and fiscal problems for cities. Today the problem is reversed. Nonwhite political gains are threatened by ghetto flight. Every one of the sixteen urban Congressional districts with either black or Puerto Rican majorities has suffered major population losses in the 1970s. The result: Nonwhites may lose political representation after the 1980 census, in spite of urban "revival." (N.B.: Two black members of Congress, Ronald Dellums and Yvonne Brathwaite Burke, both of California, represent districts that do not have a black majority.)

	Majority nonwhite Congressional districts		
District	City	Represen-tative	Per cent population loss, 1970-1976
California 29	Los Angeles	Hawkins (*)	−6
Illinois 1	Chicago	Metcalfe (*)†	−15
Illinois 7	Chicago	Collins (*)	−12
Maryland 7	Baltimore	Mitchell (*)	−9
Michigan 1	Detroit	Conyers (*)	−11
Michigan 13	Detroit	Diggs (*)	−19
Missouri 1	St. Louis	Clay (*)	−20
New Jersey 10	Newark	Rodino	−9
New York 12	Brooklyn	Chisholm (*)	−15
New York 14	Brooklyn	Richmond	−11
New York 19	Manhattan	Rangel (*)	−14
New York 21	Bronx	Garcia	−29
Ohio 21	Cleveland	Stokes (*)	−21
Pennsylvania 2	Philadelphia	Dix (*)	−7
Tennessee 8	Memphis	Ford (*)	−9
Texas 18	Houston	Jordan (*)	−6

(*) Member of Congressional Black Caucus.
† Rep. Ralph H. Metcalfe died in October.
Sources: The Almanac of American Politics 1978; Congressional Quarterly; U.S. Census Bureau.

mixed emotions about the strategy. Officials in Hartford recently mounted a major campaign to persuade an airline to open a headquarters downtown. The effort was a success, but virtually all the new jobs created are held by commuters, not the inner-city unemployed. Officials in Boston point out that the revival of Quincy Market and the surrounding area, impressive as it has been, has saddled the business district with tax-exempt government offices, and that most of the revenues the new restaurants and boutiques bring go into the state treasury. Meanwhile, more than one thousand small-scale loft industries, employing mostly low-wage workers who are now on the unemployment rolls, were destroyed by the redevelopment process.

It is already clear that many problems once considered exclusively "urban" now seem less troublesome for cities not because they are being solved, but simply because they are being pushed beyond the city limits. Meanwhile even more serious city problems are not even being displaced. They are only being masked by current political, economic, and social trends. Inner-city education, for example, is in appalling shape. But we are hearing less and less about the blackboard jungle for two reasons, both of which have nothing to do with the fact that we seem to have lost the knack for teaching people how to read and write. The first reason is that more and more Americans, including nonwhite Americans, are having fewer and fewer children. The second is that the kind of people who can command attention in Congress and in the press now increasingly send their children to private schools, especially when they live in cities. Nineteen-seventy-eight was the year it became fashionable for cultivated people with high incomes to extol the charms of city life, to confess they had found life in the suburbs just a little dowdy. But it was also the year that Congressmen and state legislators fell all over each other in a mad scramble to give tax credits to those who take their children out of public schools. New York, having earlier abolished free tuition at City University in the name of fiscal solvency, this year enacted generous tax credits for parents who send their children to private universities. So while the tax revolt spreads, and there is less and less money for P.S. 10 or the Bronx High School of Science, the academies of the new urban gentry enjoy important new indirect subsidies. This is hardly a prescription for solving inner-city social problems, let alone restoring American cities to their former roles as the Great Integrators of American life. Education in most American cities today is not only separate and unequal, but scandalously so. The real question is not whether the deterioration of most big-city school systems can be stopped, but how to begin constructing new ones. The issue is hardly even raised.

We also should take less comfort than we do from the declining crime rates in cities. They bespeak no particular victory for either law or order, let alone any success in making our courts more just or converting our prisons into institutions of rehabilitation. It is just that violent crime is essentially teenage crime, and with Americans showing less and less of an interest in reproducing themselves, teenagers of all races form a rapidly dwindling proportion of most inner-city populations. We have demography—not any new wisdom in transmitting civility and skills to city youth—to thank if there is less terror in the subways, fewer assaults on city streets. (See Table 5.) Indeed, if the death of the American city has proved to be an illusion, part of the reason is that the death of the American family is becoming a fact. As Dr. Thomas Muller of the Urban Institute points out, families are still fleeing big cities; one must go to much smaller cities in upstate New York and Pennsylvania to find any real renaissance in traditional neighborhood life. Instead the new gentrified neighborhoods are filled with trendy restaurants, not family markets; and big old houses are broken up into one-room studios, for that majority of our adult population that now either divorces or never marries at all. Commuting becomes intolerable, a place in town suddenly becomes attractive, when both spouses work. But it would be quite wrong to suggest that urban areas suddenly are becoming

Table 5
The declining significance of crime*

The larger the city, the faster crime has been declining

Cities by population	Number of cities	Percent change in crime rate 1977-78
more than 1 million	6	−4
250,000-1 million	49	−2
50,000-250,000	371	−1

Crime is decreasing fastest in the Northeast and in the Midwest

Crime index trends by geographic region

Region	Percent change in crime rate 1977-78
Nationwide	−2
Northeast	−6
Midwest	−5
South	−1
West	+2

Number of crimes are decreasing in Northeastern and Midwestern cities, while they are still growing in Southern and Western cities

Increase or decline in numbers of offenses known to police

Northeastern and Midwestern cities	Changes in number of crimes 1977-1978	Southern and Western cities	Changes in number of crimes 1977-1978
New York	−26,505	Los Angeles	+7,025
Chicago	−7,892	Houston	+4,103
Boston	−2,201	Phoenix	+3,050
Baltimore	−929	Atlanta	+2,988
St. Louis	−2,066	Miami	−326
Detroit	−6,527	Dallas	−1,433

* Statistics compare change from 1977 to 1978 during the period January-June.
Source: Federal Bureau of Investigation Uniform Crime Reports, September, 1978.

more congenial to the nurturing of our national future. In many ways it is just the other way around.

Another looming problem for the northern cities and the whole country is the massive deterioration of our public capital stock, which no amount of private restoration or speculation in real estate can reverse. As much as a third of the drinking water piped into New York City is lost through seepage before it reaches the city limits. Arson, abandonment, and other forms of disinvestment continue to extort an enormous public cost even when property values rise. As to the potholed streets and seeping tunnels of the North, the collapsing freeways and disintegrating sewer systems of the suburbs and South will be added sooner than we imagine. Probably the most serious mistake in urban policy always has been the tendency to confuse the fiscal solvency of cities with their physical health. If a city's budget is in the black, it is always assumed, then it is somehow a successful human society; if a city is going bankrupt, it must bespeak some terrible crisis of urban civilization.

The truth is that there tends to be little difference in the black teenage unemployment rate in solvent cities like Houston and fiscally troubled cities like New York. States like Connecticut, New Jersey, and New Hampshire for years escaped financial trauma by keeping taxes low. But this did not turn Newark into the Dallas of the North, or make the little mill towns of New England, with their vanishing industries, better places to look for a job than Manhattan or Boston. It is very instructive, as one looks back at what has happened to cities over the last few years, to note how successfully our political and economic system has dealt with the money problems, while scarcely addressing the human ones at all. For all the scare headlines and Congressional questioning, the bank guarantees for New York came through. Indeed all the members of what President Carter calls his "new urban partnership"—federal officials, state officials, city officials, Congressional officials, corporate officials—did not so much bail out the city as themselves from the financial and economic complications default would have entailed.

But one can hardly say the same things about New York's—or most other cities'—underlying problems. What is the value of a balanced budget if it means a continual deterioration in city services? What is the benefit of a deluge of federal spending if it means a widening, not narrowing, gap in incomes between the very rich and the very poor? What will have been accomplished, even if cities enjoy a real renaissance—if all the problems we formerly kept locked in the ghetto are just sent off to roost someplace else?

There was a fiscal crisis in American cities three years ago, one which was mistaken for an urban crisis that never existed in the terms that were assumed. Today the fiscal surplus in some American cities—the cities with the worst problems are still very short of cash—risks being interpreted in a way that bears no more relationship to the complex problems of city life than the old scare-talk did. What is especially troubling is not that some local governments had so little money three years ago, and that they have so much of it now. It is that the financial response of our system remains so unpredictable and volatile, and so unrelated to the chronic problems we face. For decades cities and their budgets have tended to be both more vulnerable to recession and more responsive in times of recovery than the nation as a whole. While default has been avoided, cities still face the unsolved fiscal problem that they are given the least money when they need it most, and have to carry burdens that other levels of government can shirk as they please, while remaining so vulnerable to the irrationalities of both our cyclical economy and the flow of federal dollars. What will happen if there is another big recession by 1980, and in the interim the taxpayers' revolt means that the federal Treasury is no longer throwing money at problems? The gnawing doubt behind all the rosy urban forecasts now is that the favorable indicators we see reflect only the general, and relatively modest, recovery of the national economy since 1975. It will be interesting to see how all the new theories stand up, which way all the straws of urban revival will blow, when they are exposed to an unfavorable wind.

Oddly enough, one of the first times I heard the urban catastrophe thesis disputed, and a much more positive future for American cities predicted, was at a time when inner-city unemployment rates were still at Depression levels, and the municipal deficits had not yet begun to turn into surplus. I did not hear it from an investment banker or academic or a politician in Washington, but from Mayor Kenneth Gibson of Newark, the city Americans still somehow consider to exist outside the framework of our national possibilities. For years Gibson has had a quite opposite view. He has called Newark "the city of the future"—the place where the hardest problems hit first, but also where the outlines of the future might first become visible. "Watch where Newark is now," Gibson said for years, "and you will see where your own city will be five or fifteen years from now." It always seemed like a prophecy of doom. But more than a year ago, Gibson was saying that the urban crisis had bottomed out, that cities were on the way up again. "Newark is a city with a future," he told me back in those days when that seemed difficult to believe. "The energy crisis has guaranteed the future of the American city."

Even earlier, about the time of the New York City blackout and riots in the summer of 1977, Nicholas Carbone, head of the Hartford city council, was predicting urban recovery too, and appending to his prediction a question. "There is no doubt cities will be saved," Carbone was saying at a time when so many cities seemed doomed. "The real question is who cities will be saved for: the big corporations and the returning middle class, or for the poor, the jobless, the people who always seem to be shortchanged by our society? Are cities collections of skyscrapers, or groups of human beings? Who will cities be saved for?"

Perhaps that was the real question underlying the great urban debate, and today we have the answer. It is visible in the newly gentrified neighborhoods with their marble fireplaces and parquet floors, in the ticky-tacky little suburbs where the blight has already begun; in the soaring new palaces downtown, and in those downtrodden parts of rural south Texas where, for all the talk of Southern Shift, the glitter of Houston has never reached. As always we face a maddening inability to grasp the conditions that plague us, a truly American genius for casting them into brilliant new forms.

NOTES

1. Like most conventional wisdoms, the arbitrary antithesis between "Sunbelt" and "Frostbelt" is a crutch that has crippled understanding of cities and their problems, and should be eschewed. In some of the frostiest of the "Frostbelt" cities—notably St. Paul, Minneapolis, Milwaukee, and Chicago—urban problems have been far less severe than in cities like St. Louis, Baltimore, and Oakland, where the snow falls less often or not at all. The distinction also ignores the problems of growth in cities like Houston and Los Angeles, even though these are often as severe for human beings as the problems of stagnation and decay.

2. Cities probably have performed better in generating new employment than these data indicate, because the official statistics by definition disregard the "subterranean" economies flourishing in most U.S. cities. One whole stratum of urban America—illegal aliens—and the work they do is almost entirely left out because of the way we collate numbers. Another group, U.S. blacks, also is significantly disfranchised from the statistical life of the nation because of the inherent bias in how we count urban population and assess economic activities in cities. Does a houseful of Caribbeans in The Bronx not exist because our census takers do not speak Spanish? Do the profits and losses of a drug dealer have any less effect on a city than those of a corner grocery? Most inner cities have not lost nearly as many people or jobs as official statistics indicate, and as anyone who has ever lived in a ghetto—or experienced poverty—knows, life on the other side of the tracks is an existence not of indolence, but of constant hustle. We should not imagine "they don't want to work" or are not even there, just because their livelihoods and lives fall outside the purview of what is considered legitimate economic and social activity.

Public Housing: The Plight of Cleveland's Forgotten Citizens

Thomas S. Andrzejewski and Denise L. Stinson

Adeline E. Turner thought she was finally getting ahead when she was accepted for a Cuyahoga Metropolitan Housing Authority apartment. But that was five years ago, and the harsh realities of public housing have changed her mind.

After being widowed in 1967, Mrs. Turner, 39, supported her family with Social Security survivor's benefits and a job as an elevator operator in a downtown department store, until she suffered a heart attack. When she was able to leave her E. 103d St. apartment for CMHA's Riverview Estates, she leaped at the chance.

She could get a decent place to live, she thought, on W. 25th St. near conveniences such as the West Side Market, for only $84 a month.

"I had been on the waiting list for quite a while," Mrs. Turner recalled.

Now she regrets the move. Two of her boys, whom she said had never been in trouble before, fell into bad company and have been to Juvenile Court.

And her public landlord, Mrs. Turner discovered, was no better, and perhaps worse than, the old private one.

Mrs. Turner, her family and her fellow tenants at CMHA family estates are victims of a combination of forces working against housing the poor. Those include bumbling by CMHA, indifference by the federal government, neglect by local governments and social agencies, racism and segregation and the cruelty of unruly tenants CMHA does nothing about.

Some CMHA housing—especially some of the newer buildings for the elderly and some duplexes and single homes away from projects—is a showcase and has no more problems than exist in better private housing.

From Thomas S. Andrzejewski and Denise L. Stinson, "Public Housing: The Plight of Cleveland's Forgotten Citizens," *The Plain Dealer, Cleveland*, January 7, 1980. Reprinted by permission from The Plain Dealer, Cleveland.

But the bulk of families living in CMHA estates suffer numerous indignities, ranging from roaches crawling across their buttered breakfast toast to raw sewage from backed-up sewers filling their slippers on bathroom floors.

That is the kind of housing provided by a government supposedly committed to providing modest but livable shelter for the poor.

Most of CMHA's 32,000 residents have incomes less than half the national poverty level, which in 1978 was $6,662 for a family of four.

Almost half of the residents are under 18.

More than 75% of the families with children receive Aid for Dependent Children (ADC), and more than 90% of all elderly and disabled residents are on Social Security or Supplemental Security Income.

All CMHA family estates are in Cleveland, in poor neighborhoods with high unemployment and high juvenile and adult crime.

Most residents realize they are victims of CMHA and the type of housing it provides—which in many cases is unsafe and unsanitary. But, like Mrs. Turner, the victims of public housing have nowhere else to turn.

But Mrs. Turner has not sat back idly wallowing in her plight. She is one of CMHA's activist tenants, as president of the tenants' council for Riverview Estates. But residents have not had much influence on CMHA's operation.

Meanwhile, she is stuck with CMHA.

"If I knew all this would have happened, I would have never moved," she said. "I would have put up with the water dripping in my kitchen and the plaster falling."

The waiting lists for even the worst CMHA projects show that there are places even worse on the private market. The persons who live in the projects have no place else to go.

As Norman Krumholz, former city planning director now with Cleveland State University's college of urban affairs, said:

"There is virtually no other game in town."

PUBLIC HOUSING: A THOUSAND HEADACHES

Although Cuyahoga Metropolitan Housing Authority projects suffer from maintenance and management problems that have been pointed up repeatedly, little has been done to remedy them.

Many criticisms have gone unheeded by the staff, the board and the politicians who appoint the board.

In fact, while CMHA has been the target of critical barrages from tenants, neighborhood groups, the media and others, Director Robert J. Fitzgerald and Board Chairman Msgr. Francis W. Carney have stiffly resisted change and staunchly defended the authority's poor performance.

Some housing experts interviewed by The Plain Dealer said Fitzgerald and Carney are the main problems, but others disagreed. Many, however, said the board and the staff of CMHA cannot escape at least some blame.

Former Cleveland Planning Director Norman Krumholz, now with Cleveland State University, said administrators or board members could be better, more effective or even more caring or concerned. But the state of public housing depends on more than the personalities involved, he said.

Substantive criticisms have been made about how CMHA is managed. Some detailed ones come from the tenants' organization, the Central Advisory Council.

Clara E. Bell, president of CAC, said her group wants to get more active in CMHA budgeting. She said there are basic problems such as the housing authority not being able to predict future costs.

"They present a flat budget," said Mrs. Bell. "The only thing they project is their income."

But the most damning criticisms do not deal with style and do not come from amateurs such as tenants trying to find out why their living conditions have deteriorated so badly.

Instead, they have come from internal management studies and audits by the government. An otherwise routine management review by the Department of Housing and Urban Development (HUD) in 1973 went so far as to call for Fitzgerald's removal.

Carney, Fitzgerald and the CMHA staff often have issued statements decrying the lack of money for public housing. But the latest management review, completed last year, concluded that spending was apparently inefficient.

HUD officials reported they were concerned with "increasing costs of operation, in excess of normal inflation, and the apparent decrease in services to residents and (in) living conditions on the estates."

As one example, federal investigators said CMHA had detailed its $19,302-a-year skilled servicemen to picking up litter for two hours daily. The allegation was corroborated by tenant leaders who have complained about slowness in fixing up vacant apartments. Fitzgerald claimed the practice was done only when servicemen could not get into apartments of late-sleeping tenants.

One flurry of memos dealt with what HUD called CMHA's unusually high legal fees.

While Fitzgerald, Carney and other CMHA officials decry the lack of money, the housing authority was able to find $416,129 to pay legal fees out of its regular operating budget. The money was paid for 1978 and the first three months of 1979, according to a recently completed special audit of CMHA's legal fees.

The bulk of that, $328,710 was paid to the firm of Kelley, McCann & Livingstone, according to HUD documents obtained by The Plain Dealer. Housing officials had questioned the fees, charging that Kelley, McCann & Livingstone's rates for routine work, $70 per hour for senior lawyers, appeared high.

The fees were for representing CMHA in Workers Compensation cases and other lawsuits, miscellaneous agreements, the rent subsidy (Section 8) program and developing new housing. The largest costs were for working on apartments for the elderly in Berea, Cleveland Heights and University Circle.

The government also questioned the manner of payment of the fees, that is, whether the money was drawn properly from certain accounts.

But even though the investigation was begun a year ago, it is still unresolved.

The government has not been the only critic.

In a confidential letter to the CMHA board last year, the accounting firm of Peat, Marwick, Mitchell & Co. said it found weaknesses in internal control that left the housing authority vulnerable to theft and fraud, such as:

- Duplicate payments to suppliers and contractors were possible because of the way in which receiving and inspection reports were being made.

- There was a possibility that supervisors could collect the pay of fired employees without being detected.

- In three years that were studied, the amount of liabilities that were not recorded at year's end was as high as $181,000 and totaled $437,000.

- Estate managers could allow persons to live in vacant suites and either pocket the rent or collect favors without being discovered.

- Inventories were not being taken so hardware and supplies could be easily pilfered.

Fitzgerald said controls have been tightened in accord with the audit's findings.

The Plain Dealer was able to obtain the letter and other reports about CMHA through Freedom of Information Act requests of the government.

A comparison of the 1973 management review and the 1979 one shows many items appearing in both documents, such as:

- More emphasis should be placed on repairing vacant units so they could be occupied and thereby increase rental income.

- Tenants should be screened better.

- CMHA's organization is cumbersome and unwieldly.

Both reports also suggested that there be fewer estate managers.

When CMHA has had the opportunity for reform, it has either rejected changes outright or left conditions alone to eventually be forgotten.

Poor management has aggravated CMHA's inability to raise money. In September, HUD divided $10 million among 29 housing authorities, for good performance in rent collection and occupancy rates. New York, Chicago and Philadelphia each received about $1.5 million.

CMHA got none.

PUBLIC HOUSING: POLITICS OF RACISM

Since the pioneering of public housing in Cuyahoga County, politics and racism have guaranteed its segregation.

In a society that traditionally has shunned its poor and persecuted its minorities, public housing tenants have been consistently separated from the mainstream, branded as undesirables and blamed for the conditions of the projects.

In Cuyahoga County, the segregation of public housing—including segregation of Cuyahoga Metropolitan Housing Authority projects—has been no accident.

Historically, CMHA has had white projects and black projects. And regularly, the invisible walls that separate rich from poor have been erected around all but the worst city and suburban neighborhoods.

In the late 1930's CMHA workers reportedly lowered and raised window shades in vacant suites at the all-white Cedar-Central Estates to feign occupancy when there were black applicants.

In 1949, 99% of the residents in Carver and Outhwaite projects were black, although overall CMHA had 31% black tenants, according to testimony before the Civil Rights Commission in 1966.

In 1966, 81% of the blacks living in CMHA were concentrated in Carver, Outhwaite and Garden Valley.

Even today, 15 projects on the city's East Side are more than 90% black, and eight on the West Side are more than 90% white, according to CMHA's own figures. CMHA makes little attempt to integrate public housing.

One city official said in a recent interview that Irving M. Kriegsfeld was the only public housing director here "who aggressively tried to decentralize and desegregate public housing. But that cost him his job."

Other housing authorities in the country have had at least minor success by offering residents incentives such as moving families up on waiting lists, in hopes of easing the racial stagnation in the projects.

CMHA's poor management of its family estates in the city has further narrowed the slim chances of suburbs accepting any forms of public housing.

Even housing for the elderly, usually thought of as more desirable, does not have much of a chance of being built in the suburbs.

In 1972 U.S. District Judge Frank J. Battisti ordered Cleveland to locate all future public housing west of the Cuyahoga River.

"The most appropriate way of dispersing public housing, especially scattered-site, is to put a very large percentage of it on the West Side of the city and continue to place it there until a substantial portion of the population of the West Side is black, or at least until the tipping point is approached," he said in his ruling.

Juanita T. Williams, vice chairman of the CMHA board and a black, said segregation follows patterns in the community.

"Public housing isn't a separate little entity that isn't a part of the city," she said. "It's part of the composition of Cleveland. The segregation you see is part of the city.

"How do you change it in the rest of the city? The same thing you do there, you do in public housing."

She said public housing should not be concentrated in any one place, but scattered throughout the community.

CMHA director Robert J. Fitzgerald contends that because of HUD restrictions where new public housing can be located—away from flight paths near airports, freeways and railroad tracks—there is not much room on the West Side for more family housing. Therefore, little has been built.

The problem, however, runs deeper than technical limitations.

Fitzgerald's attitude in getting blacks to move into public housing on the West Side or whites on the East Side, promotes continued segregation.

"Young black families do not want to live on the West Side of the river," he said. "The first weekend they do when friends come over is they go to a bar and there's a fight.

"The next day they're in the office wanting to move over to the East Side. White families also don't want to move east of the river."

Fitzgerald maintains that his tenants are segregated from the rest of society because of economics, not race.

Compared to the reactions of communities where CMHA has attempted to place public housing, Fitzgerald sounds like a rabid integrationist.

Most of the fights against public housing have been on the West Side, mainly in Wards 4, 9, and 22. Only in Ward 9 were residents successful—with the aid of former Mayor Ralph J. Perk—in keeping out public housing.

Perk made a campaign pledge in 1971 to cancel building permits for public housing. He fulfilled the promise immediately after taking office and CMHA never was able to build in Ward 9.

PUBLIC HOUSING: WHO WATCHES THE WATCHDOGS?

The federal government, which bankrolls and is supposed to oversee public housing, has in many instances contributed to the poor condition of Cuyahoga Metropolitan Housing Authority estates.

The Department of Housing and Urban Development and its predecessors have mostly neglected the basic agreement between them and public housing authorities. The agreement provides:

"Each project . . . will be developed and administered to promote serviceability, efficiency, economy and stability to achieve the economic and social well-being and advancement of the tenants thereof."

Unlike most contracts, this agreement is not enforced.

In the case of CMHA, the contract is for $13 million in federal money annually, plus additional millions for updating the more than 12,000 apartments CMHA operates. The agency also administers rents subsidies for 3,400 others.

On one hand, the money is not enough. It cannot be stretched to meet the ideals stated in the contract. And on the other, HUD is a toothless watchdog—barking only occasional criticism.

HUD has been lax in watching CMHA closely enough to discover waste, such as duplicate payments. The Plain Dealer found in September that the government may be paying twice for Severance Towers, a $56-million apartment building for the elderly near Severance shopping center in Cleveland Heights.

The situation, apparently still unresolved, is that there exist two Severance Towers on HUD's inventory—one a 190-suite apartment building that opened earlier this year and one a project existing only on paper.

CMHA had switched the Severance proposal from a "turnkey" project (for which a developer builds apartments and then sells it, or turns over the keys, to a public housing authority), to a conventional project and then to a so-called "Section 8," or rent-subsidy development. According to HUD memos obtained by The Plain Dealer, HUD has been paying for both.

Fitzgerald denies anything is awry and claims CMHA has not benefited from any extra money.

HUD refused The Plain Dealer access to the documents under a Freedom of Information Act provision which bars revelation of even the most trivial documents when an investigation is involved. Officials denied the government was trying to cover up a sensitive matter.

Meanwhile, The Plain Dealer obtained the documents through other means.

Most officials agree that Congress has not appropriated enough money to keep public housing livable. The entire public housing appropriation for 1980 was $742 million—an increase of less than 2% from 1979, which was also inadequate. CMHA's share suffers proportionately.

Moreover, when HUD found inefficiency in CMHA's operation, it never issued more than advice paired with gentle reprimands.

"HUD would no more want to do away with the current operation of CMHA because CMHA is fiscally solvent," said Dr. Joseph M. Davis, research director of the Federation for Community Planning. "Their bottom line is, 'Can you keep your doors open?'"

The recourse, said Hayward Sparks, supervisor of HUD's Cleveland office, is to place CMHA into default when management shortcomings are discovered.

"You have 16,000 units and 32,000 people, and what do you do, stop funding them?" asked Sparks.

"You can do a lot of yelling, or go for an injunction, but no court in the country is going to throw 32,000 people on the street."

Rather than providing enough money for CMHA and other large-city housing authorities to operate, the federal government doles out cash according to a formula called the performance funding system—which even HUD admits is unworkable, cheating the larger housing authorities out of money.

The intent was to have housing authorities operate on a spartan but sufficient budget. In reality, the formula failed because of unforeseen inflation and rising utility costs.

The government now says it realizes the formula is flawed. But its study to revamp public housing funding is not due to be completed until 1982.

"Performance funding" is also a contradiction, because it does not encourage certain improvements, such as mixing tenants by income. Segregating them thusly—such as placing mostly welfare clients in certain estates—is acknowledged as one of CMHA's major problems. But the money formula system does not encourage improvement.

A Congressional Research Service survey found this aspect of performance funding "works perversely with regard to tenant income and rents: If rental receipts rise . . . operating subsidies will be correspondingly reduced."

Meanwhile, little is being done to upgrade public housing, compared with acknowledged needs, except for a few grants for specific projects such as security.

For example, housing experts here pointed to the so-called Target Project Program for public housing earlier this decade. Hundreds of housing authorities, including CMHA, participated with various kinds of projects to upgrade estates.

But the program ended in failure. While the government blamed local housing authorities, it had assigned only one official in Washington to monitor its progress.

Some housing experts note the irony of HUD making money available for new developments but not caring for the present public housing.

One study being done for HUD says well over $1 billion is necessary to make livable the worst 20% of the nation's public housing.

While HUD allowed for $545.5 million in fixup money for 1979 (which was almost $100 million more than in 1978), its 1980 budget allows just $409 million. Stephen F. Coyle, former assistant to the secretary of HUD, said most of the country's 1.2 million public housing units are pretty good. The exception is between 200,000 and 600,000 (units).

He also said, "The buck for the poor conditions and problems in public housing just keeps passing. The locals blame the feds, the feds blame the locals and the locals blame the tenants."

But he also told The Plain Dealer during an interview in Washington that while federal response to public housing has improved in the last few years, it has been indecisive and intermittent at best.

Los Angeles's Setback in Smog Battle Raises Doubts on Other Cities

G. Christian Hill

The Los Angeles area is losing its fight against smog.

It achieved some victories in the 1950s and 1960s but hasn't made any progress in several years. In fact, air pollution has significantly worsened over the past 18 months or so, and the siege in early September was the worst in 25 years.

"Despite a multibillion-dollar effort, there has been no net progress in the last six years," the South Coast Air Quality Management District, the air-pollution-control agency for the 6,600-square-mile Los Angeles air basin, conceded in a recent letter to President Carter. The AQMD told the President:

"We are deeply concerned we may be losing the war on air pollution." The lack of progress "tells you that the present strategy isn't working," says Thomas Heinsheimer, vice chairman of the district's board and a physicist with a background in atmospheric research. "There has been a failure in public planning," he says. "Before we pass more costly rules based on existing misconceptions about smog, we should stop and take a long, hard, serious look at the situation."

BEYOND CALIFORNIA

The failure here has implications that extend beyond California. Since Los Angeles has been battling smog longer and harder than most cities and states, its setback raises troubling questions for many other Sun Belt metropolitan areas. Pollution-control officials in Phoenix, Denver and Dallas also report little or no progress in reducing smog levels during the last five years. Under the 1977 Federal Clean Air Act, regions that don't make "reasonable progress" toward meeting a stringent set of standards by 1987 face Washington-imposed restrictions on growth.

As recently as 1975, pollution fighters here predicted that bad sieges of smog would be eliminated by 1980. What went wrong? Regional, state, and federal officials don't all agree on which factors are most responsible, but they cite several reasons.

- The highly touted devices for controlling vehicle-exhaust emissions haven't performed up to expectations. Federal data indicate that the devices deteriorate sooner than expected because of tampering, illegal use of leaded gasoline, and poor engine maintenance or adjustment.

- Weather conditions have been unusually adverse during the past two years.

- The push for controls on industrial pollutants isn't producing the sizable reductions it once did, because most of the easy "technological fixes" have already been made. Thus, some officials suggest, gains from this effort may no longer be able to offset the failures of other attacks on dirty air.

- Continued economic growth and increasing population are generating additional vehicles and industry. That makes it more difficult to achieve net reductions in pollution.

- Decisions by federal and state energy regulators have forced utilities in the air basin to use fuel oil instead of cleaner natural gas or nuclear power.

Interagency conflicts color the analysis of just which factor is most critical. The AQMD, which controls industrial air pollution, puts most of the blame on unexpectedly high vehicle emissions. The state Air Resources Board (ARB), which polices vehicle emissions, blames industrial polluters and adverse weather conditions.

A WORSENING PROBLEM

Everyone agrees that the smog is getting worse. One indicator is the number of days when the air in the basin is rated "very unhealthful" by the federal Environmental Protection Agency. Last year there were 76 such days in Los Angeles County, compared with an average of 62 days in 1972-77, an increase of 23%. In the eastern part of the basin, the number of such days last year totaled 72, compared with an average of 47 days in 1972-77, an increase of 53%. The air is rated "very unhealthful" when it contains at least 0.20 part per million of ozone, a key constituent of smog.

(The number of "hazardous" days, those on which ozone peaks exceed 0.35 part per million, has declined since the 1950s, a trend that gives the AQMD some consolation. There were 11 such days in Los Angeles County this year, compared with 33 in 1969 and 34 in 1959.)

As the ARB suggests, meteorological conditions probably have contributed to the generally worsening smog here. Smog is generated when certain by-products of combustion, mainly unburned hydrocarbons and nitrogen oxides, are trapped under a still blanket of air known as an inversion layer. Plentiful sunlight causes the pollutants to explode in a photochemical reaction that produces ozone and more than 100 other constituents of smog.

The Los Angeles basin, particularly in the summer, is probably the most poorly ventilated site in the world for a major city. Inversion layers normally occur under its sunny skies more than 200 days of the year. In 1978, according to the chief of the AQMD's air-quality division, the inversion layers here were lower and lasted longer than normal, sunny days were considerably more frequent and wind speeds were lower. The result: more smog.

But federal and local meteorologists believe that weather conditions can't account for the bulk of the recent increase. The AQMD takes each day's highest ozone reading in the basin, adds all the high readings for the June-to-September smog season and averages them. In 1978, it says, these maximum readings averaged 14% higher than those for the previous six years. Adjusting for the weather, the agency says, the increase becomes 8.7%—still a "significant increase," in the words of AQMD officials. The weather, these officials conclude, thus wasn't the prime factor.

"We have to focus on the realities," says the agency's Mr. Heinsheimer. "Ozone isn't getting any better, and that isn't because of a quirk in nature."

A chief cause of this worsening pollution, according to the EPA, the AQMD and some independent analysts, is that the auto-emission-control system built around the catalytic converter isn't living up to its billing.

"The only reasonable explanation (for the rise in smog) is that vehicle controls aren't performing as well as they were projected to perform," asserts J. A. Stuart, AQMD executive director. James N. Pitts Jr., director of the state-financed Air Pollution Research Center, suggests that "auto emissions may be one of the major factors in the smog increase during the last two summers."

CARS FLUNK TESTS

State tests begun about eight months ago on late-model cars that change ownership in Southern California clearly indicate that something is amiss: More than 50% of the autos fail to meet the California emission standards. Car owners are part of the problem. The AQMD says that the emission controls on about half the cars that flunk have been tampered with in some way, presumably in an attempt—a needless and futile one, the EPA says—to improve power. Nationwide, EPA studies show, about 19% of emission-control systems have been tampered with, making them less effective.

Drivers also seem to be causing other problems. Federal pollution laws require that unleaded fuel be used in 1975-model and later cars. But EPA investigators who have kept watch on service-station transactions find that about 10% of the drivers of these cars are "poisoning" their pollution-control devices by using leaded gasoline. Motorists either use special funnels or enlarge the size of their tank inlets with crowbars so that their cars can receive leaded gasoline from the large nozzles through which it is pumped.

These drivers use the leaded fuel because it is cheaper and more plentiful and because they feel, rightly or wrongly, that leaded gasoline has more zip. If leaded gasoline is used three or four times, the pollution-control system becomes worthless. Many of these cars are spewing out uncontrolled emissions at up to 10 times the levels expected.

(The ARB and auto makers say that their own surveys show that only 2% to 3% of late-model-car owners are using leaded gasoline.)

The catalytic converter, which traps and scrubs waste gases, also suffers from its sensitivity to poor engine maintenance and adjustment, the EPA says. In a seven-city study, the agency concluded that this factor alone caused the average car of recent make to produce three to five times the emission levels that the converters were capable of achieving.

"The implications are quite significant in terms of additional air pollution," says James J. Sakolosky, an administrator in the EPA's automobile enforcement office. "We have a very severe problem."

Pollution fighters are banking heavily on a mandatory annual vehicle-inspection program to deal with the problems of the emission systems on the basin's seven million cars. Such an inspection program was ordered by the 1977 Clean Air Act for high-vehicle-pollution areas such as Los Angeles; but most states still don't have them in operation, and California's legislature is balking at adopting one for fear of enraging car owners.

The recent upturn in smog here also reflects the slower progress being made as regulators tackle the "hard-core" sources of industrial pollution. The AQMD asserts that industrial pollution was reduced 21% from 1970 to 1978, nearly twice the national average reduction calculated by the EPA. Industrial sources now account for less than 40% of the basin's most important pollutants, the AQMD says.

But "we've reached the point of diminishing returns on controlling stationary sources," Mr. Heinsheimer says. "There's not an awful lot we can still do that is economically justifiable or politically acceptable." George Thomas, the district's supervising engineer, stresses that "it will be quite difficult to offset future pollution increments (from vehicles)" with reductions in industrial-plant emissions.

The state Air Resources Board, however, contends that the district can be tougher than it has been on industrial pollution. "We've had to kick their butts and hold their hands to get them to move" against industrial polluters, an ARB spokesman says in an interview.

PEOPLE AND GASOLINE

The increase in the number of people, factories and vehicles in the basin also helps explain why smog has proved such a persistent foe since 1972, several scientists say. Daily gasoline consumption in Los Angeles County rose to 10.1 million gallons last year from nine million gallons in 1975, despite an increase in the percentage of high-mileage cars.

"Over the past five years, there is no question that emissions from existing sources have been reduced, but that has been offset by the population, which has exploded and continues to explode," says Mr. Pitts of the Air Pollution Research Center. The basin's population next year is expected to be half a million larger than it was in 1975.

Smog's intractability in Los Angeles seems likely to add to the pressure on the federal government to either push on with the politically sensitive task of limiting growth in certain regions or sharply relax its clean-air standards. The limits on growth would come in the form of restrictions on industrial, highway and sewage-treatment construction. Limiting growth would mean significant changes in the way people live here—possibly forcing them out of their cars and suburbs.

Neither bureaucrats nor politicians in this state believe that the public would accept such changes, despite the worsening smog. "The public says air pollution is their No. 1 concern," notes the AQMD's Mr. Stuart. "But based on their willingness to do something about it, I have to believe it's way down the list."

There seems to be a growing consensus that the region can't achieve truly clean air and must seek congressional relief from the federal standards. But the EPA is adamant right now, and its air chief, David Hawkins, predicts, "There won't be any bail-out by Congress."

Discussion Questions

1. In general terms, how does Allman's perception of the "urban crisis" differ from the traditional perception of it?

2. Why do you suppose that, as Allman suggests, it is so difficult for the federal government to maintain an accurate, up-to-date perception of the state of urban America? Should we expect a better performance from state and local governments?

3. Like other investigators, Andrzejewski and Stinson find that racism is a serious problem confronting public housing programs. In particular, suburbanites resist the construction of public housing in their communities. What might be the most appropriate approach to this problem?

4. Should the responsibility for constructing and operating public housing be given entirely to the federal government?

5. Given the current difficulties in achieving federal air pollution standards in American cities, should these standards be relaxed or should federal pressure on state and local officials to achieve them be increased? Should urban growth be restricted?

CHAPTER 9

EDUCATION AND CIVIL LIBERTIES

Education is the largest single expenditure of state governments. Record numbers of students are enrolled in public colleges and universities. Nearly one-third of all Americans are directly involved in education as teachers, staff, or students. Because so many people are touched by our educational system and because expenditures are so high, it is little wonder that it has always been a favorite area for criticism. The situation always appears at its worst at any current point in time.

Still, public dissatisfaction with schools increased markedly in the 1970s. While standardized test scores dropped, grades rose. Vandalism and assaults on teachers grew. Teachers went out on strike. Voters refused to approve new operating levies. Children seemed uninterested in education. Many teachers quickly burned out—some of them quit teaching, while others made only a minimum effort to educate students. As elementary and high school enrollments declined in many large cities, teachers were laid off and buildings were closed.

While the educational system certainly does not suffer from a lack of recommendations for reform by government officials and social scientists, few significant changes have occurred. The most publicized "innovation" of the 1970s was a return to the "basics," with a stress on fundamental competencies and discipline.

Public schools continue to be caught up in civil rights issues. Many schools have spent millions of dollars defending themselves against racial discrimination charges and then millions more to implement busing. In both the North and the South there has been a strong reaction among whites against busing. Many blacks also oppose busing. It has become a major issue due in large part to federal court decisions that have ordered busing as a means to remedy past discrimination.

One of the most influential of all social science studies in recent years was the 1966 Coleman Report. This government-financed study by sociologist

James S. Coleman documented the existence of unequal educational opportunities for black children. It suggested that black children achieve better in schools that are racially integrated. This led to the decision to bus children as the only practical means to avoid all-white and all-black schools in many cities.

The Coleman Report was highly controversial. Many blacks objected to the implication that black educational achievement was related to the presence of white children in the classrooms. Whites objected to busing. In 1975, Coleman released an equally controversial follow-up study. This time he found that court-ordered busing was causing whites to leave cities and flee to suburbs. In this second study Coleman stated that home environment had a greater impact on learning that did school integration. He noted that busing could become counterproductive by increasing segregation in public schools as whites leave central cities. Supporters of busing criticized Coleman, arguing that none of the cities he studied had a court-ordered busing plan during the time of his research (1968-1972). One critic contended that his conclusions were "statistically unfounded, morally tainted, and distorted by the press."

The first article in this chapter, a *Time* magazine cover story, reviews much of the current criticism of American public schools. The article suggests that there is plenty of blame to be shared by teachers, students, administrators, and parents. While the article concludes with some proposals for reform and notes instances where changes have been made, the reader is left with little optimism regarding the improvement of our educational system in the near future.

In the second article, Diane Ravitch closely analyzes the 1975 Coleman Report and the responses to it. She concludes (and her interpretations are themselves a point of controversy) that Coleman's concern about whites leaving cities is valid. That is, there has been significant "white flight" from cities where there has been court-ordered busing. As Ravitch cautions us, however, this is not to say that we should continue to maintain racially segregated schools in order to avoid the loss of whites from cities.

Help! Teacher Can't Teach!

Like some vast jury gradually and reluctantly arriving at a verdict, politicians, educators and especially millions of parents have come to believe that the U.S. public schools are in parlous trouble. Violence keeps making headlines. Test scores keep dropping. Debate rages over whether or not one-fifth or more adult Americans are functionally illiterate. High school graduates go so far as to sue their school systems because they got respectable grades and a diploma but cannot fill in job application forms correctly. Experts confirm that students today get at least 25% more As and Bs than they did 15 years ago, but know less. A Government-funded nationwide survey group, the National Assessment of Educational Progress, reports that in science, writing, social studies and mathematics the achievement of U.S. 17-year-olds has dropped regularly over the past decade.

Rounding up the usual suspects in the learning crisis is easy enough. The decline of the family that once instilled respect for authority and learning. The influence of television on student attention span. The disruption of schools created by busing, and the national policy of keeping more students in school longer, regardless of attitude or aptitude. The conflicting demands upon the public school system, which is now expected not only to teach but to make up for past and present racial and economic injustice.

But increasingly, too, parents have begun to blame the shortcomings of the schools on the lone and very visible figure at the front of the classroom. Teachers for decades have been admired for selfless devotion. More recently, as things went wrong, they were pitied as overworked martyrs to an over-burdened school system. Now bewildered and beleaguered, teachers are being blamed—rightly or wrongly—for much of the trouble in the classroom.

One reason is simply that it is easier for society to find someone to blame than to hold up a mirror and see that U.S. culture itself is largely responsible.

But the new complaints about teachering also arise from a dismaying discovery: quite a few teachers (estimates range up to 20%) simply have not mastered the basic skills in reading, writing and arithmetic that they are supposed to teach.

Of course, among the 2.2 million teachers in the nation's public schools are hundreds of thousands of skilled and dedicated people who, despite immense problems, manage to produce the miraculous blend of care and discipline, energy, learning and imagination that good teaching requires. Many newcomers to the field are still attracted by the dream of helping children rather than for reasons of security or salary. The estimated average salary of elementary school teachers is $15,661, and of high school teachers is $16,387, for nine months' work. The average yearly pay of a plumber is about $19,700; for a government clerk it's approximately $15,500. The best-educated and most selfless teachers are highly critical and deeply concerned about the decline in teaching standards and educational procedures. Their frustration is perhaps the strongest warning signal of all.

Horror stories about teaching abound. In Oregon a kindergarten teacher who had been given As and Bs at Portland State University was recently found to be functionally illiterate. How could this be? Says Acting Dean of the School of Education Harold Jorgensen: "It was a whole series of people not looking closely at her."

In Chicago a third-grade teacher wrote on the blackboard: "Put the following words in alfabetical order." During the weeklong teacher strike last winter, many Chicago parents were appalled by what they saw on television news of schools and teachers. Recalls one mother: "I froze when I heard a teacher tell a TV reporter, 'I teaches English.' "

In the Milwaukee suburb of Wales, Wis., school board members were outraged when teachers sent them written curriculum proposals riddled with bad grammar and spelling. Teachers had written *dabate* for *debate, documant* for *document. Would* was *woud,* and *separate* was *seperate.* Angry parents waved samples of their children's work that contained uncorrected whoppers, marked with such teacher comments as "outstanding" and "excellent."

A Gallup poll has found that teacher laziness and lack of interest are the most frequent accusations of half the nation's parents, who complain that students get "less schoolwork" now than 20 years ago. Whether the parent perceptions are fair or not, there is no doubt that circumstances have certainly changed some teacher attitudes. At a Miami senior high school this spring, one social studies teacher asked his pupils whether their homework was completed. Half the students said no. The teacher recorded their answers in his gradebook but never bothered to collect the papers. Says the teacher, who has been in the profession for 15 years and has now become dispirited: "I'm not willing any more to take home 150 notebooks and grade them. I work from 7:30 a.m. to 2 p.m., and that's what I get paid for." A longtime teacher in a large suburban school outside Boston told *Time* it is common knowledge that some of her colleagues, anxious to preserve their jobs as enrollments dwindle, fail children simply to ensure hefty class size the next year.

The new doubts about teachers have led to a state-by-state demand from legislators and citizen groups that teachers take special examinations to prove they are competent, much like the student competency exams that have become a requirement in 38 states. Asks Indiana State Senator Joan Gubbins: "Shouldn't we first see if the teachers are competent before we expect the kids to be competent?"

With 41 million pupils, public school education is one of the nation's largest single government activities. Current expenditures (federal, state, and local) run to $95 billion. So vast and costly an educational system does not cheerfully react to criticism or adapt to change.

The push toward testing teacher competency, however, depends less on Washington than on state and local governments. One of the most instructive battles fought over the issue occurred in Mobile, Ala., and was led by conservative attorney Dan Alexander, president of the board of education. In 1978, after the board required competency testing of Mobile high school seniors, Alexander was besieged by angry parents, at least partly because 53% of the students who took the city's first competency exam flunked it. Recalls Alexander: "Parents came out of the woodwork saying, 'If you're going to crack down on my child, let me tell you about some of my children's teachers.'" One parent brought him a note sent home by a fifth-grade teacher with a master's degree, which read in part: "Scott is dropping in his studies he acts as if he don't Care. Scott want pass in his assignment at all, he a had a poem to learn and he fell to do it." Says Alexander: "I was shocked. I could not believe we had teachers who could not write a grammatically correct sentence. I took the complaints down to the superintendent, and what shocked me worse was that he wasn't shocked."

Alexander made the note public as the kickoff of a campaign for teacher testing. Says he: "Competency testing is probably a misnomer. You cannot test a teacher on whether he's competent, but you certainly can prove he's incompetent." The proposed exams for veteran teachers were blocked by Alexander's colleagues on the board. But they agreed that all new teachers should score at least 500 on the Educational Testing Service's 3¼-hr. National Teacher Examination (N.T.E.) which measures general knowledge, reading, writing and arithmetic. Only about half of the Mobile job applicants who took the N.T.E. in 1979 passed.

The American Federation of Teachers, which has 550,000 members, is opposed to testing experienced teachers, though it approves competency exams for new candidates. The much larger National Education Association is against any kind of competency testing for teachers, claiming teacher competency cannot be measured by written tests. Even so, some form of teacher testing has been approved in twelve states.[1] Proposals for teacher testing have been introduced in Colorado, Illinois, Iowa, Kansas, Missouri, New York, Vermont and Wisconsin, and a bill in Oklahoma is scheduled to be signed into law this week. Polls say the teacher-testing movement is supported by 85% of U.S. adults.

Thus far actual test scores of teacher applicants seem depressing. In Louisiana, for instance, only 53% passed in 1978, 63% last year. What about the ones who fail? Says Louisiana Certification Director Jacqueline Lewis: "Obviously they're moving out of state to teach in states where the tests are not required." The results of basic achievement tests taken by job applicants at Florida's Pinellas County school board (St. Petersburg, Clearwater) are not encouraging. Since 1976, the board has required teacher candidates to read at an advanced tenth-grade level and solve math problems at an eighth-grade level. Though all had their B.A. in hand, about one-third of the applicants (25% of the whites, 79% of the blacks) flunked Pinellas' test the first time they took it in 1979.

In 1900, when only 6% of U.S. children graduated from high school, secondary school teachers were looked up to as scholars of considerable learning. Public school teachers were essential to what was regarded as the proud advance of U.S. education. By 1930, 30% of American 17-year-olds were graduating from high school, and by the mid-1960s, graduates totaled 70%. The American public school was hailed for teaching citizenship and common sense to rich and poor, immigrant and native-born children, and for giving them a common democratic experience. "The public school was the true melting pot," William O. Douglas once wrote, "and the public school teacher was the leading architect of the new America that was being fashioned."

The academic effectiveness of the system was challenged in 1957, when the Soviet Union launched its Sputnik satellite. Almost overnight, it was perceived that American training was not competitive with that of the U.S.S.R. Public criticism and government funds began to converge on U.S. schools. By 1964, achievement scores in math and reading had risen to an alltime high. But in the '60s the number of students (and teachers too) was expanding tremendously as a result of the maturing crop of post-World War II babies. In the decade before 1969, the number of high school teachers almost doubled, from 575,000 to nearly 1 million. Writes Reading Expert Paul Copperman in *The Literary Hoax:* "The stage was set for an academic tragedy of historic proportions as the nation's high school faculty, about half of whom were young and immature, prepared to meet the largest generation of high school students in American history." To compound the problem, many teachers had been radicalized by the 1960s. They suspected that competition was immoral, grades undemocratic, and promotion based on merit and measurable accomplishment a likely way to discriminate against minorities and the poor. Ever since the mid-1960s, the average achievement of high school graduates has gone steadily downhill.

Ironically, the slide occurred at a time when teachers were getting far more training than ever before. In the early 1900s, few elementary school teachers went to college; most were trained at two-year normal schools. Now a bachelor's degree from college is a general requirement for teaching. Today's teaching incompetence reflects the lax standards in many of the educational programs at the 1,150 colleges around the country that train teachers. It also reflects on colleges generally, since teachers take more than half their courses in traditional departments like English, history and mathematics.

Research by W. Timothy Weaver, an associate professor of education at Boston University, seems to confirm a long-standing charge that one of the easiest U.S. college majors is education. Weaver found the high school seniors who planned to major in education well below the average for all college-bound seniors—34 points below average in verbal scores on the 1976 Scholastic Aptitude Test, 43 points below average in math. Teaching majors score lower in English than majors in almost every other field.

Evidence that many graduates of teacher-training programs cannot read, write or do sums adequately has led educators like Robert L. Egbert, president of the American Association of Colleges for Teacher Education, to urge higher standards on his colleagues. The National Council for Accreditation of Teacher Education has become warier about issuing its seal of approval, which is largely honorific, since state boards of education issue their own, often easy-going approval for teacher-training programs. Nevertheless, with an awakened interest in "consumer protection" for parents and pupils, the council denied accreditation to teacher-training programs at 31% of colleges reviewed in 1979, compared with 10% in 1973. Says Salem, Ore., School Superintendent William Kendrick: "For too long, we've believed that if you hold a teaching certificate you can do the job."

Many teachers favor rigorous teaching standards, including the use of compulsory minimum-competency tests—at least for candidates starting out in their careers. They are dismayed by the public's disapproval. Says Linda Kovaric, 32, a teacher at Olympic Continuation High School in Santa Monica, Calif.: "The administration tells you you're doing a crummy job, parents tell you you're doing a crummy job, kids even tell you you're doing a crummy job. A lot of teachers these days feel and look like soldiers who returned from Viet Nam. You see the same glazed look in their eyes."

Many teachers have come to see themselves as casualties in a losing battle for learning and order in an indulgent age. Society does not support them, though it expects them to compensate in the classroom for racial prejudice, economic inequality and parental indifference. Says *American School Board Journal* Managing Editor Jerome Cramer: "Schools are now asked to do what people used to ask God to do." The steady increase in the number of working mothers (35% work full time now) has sharply reduced family supervision of children and thrown many personal problems into the teacher's lap, while weakening support for the teacher's efforts. Says Thomas Anderson, 31, who plans to quit this month after teaching social studies for seven years in Clearwater, Fla.: "I know more about some of my kids than their mothers or fathers do."

A teacher's view, in short, of why teachers cannot teach is that teachers are not allowed to teach. "The teacher today is expected to be a mother, father, priest or rabbi, peacekeeper, police officer, playground monitor and lunchroom patrol," says David Imig, executive director of the American Association of Colleges for Teacher Education. "Over and above that, he's supposed to teach Johnny and Mary how to read." Adds Edith Shain, a veteran kindergarten teacher at the Hancock Park School in Los Angeles: "The teacher doesn't know who she has to please. She's not as autonomous as she once was."

In the past 15 years the number of teachers with 20 years or more experience has dropped by nearly half. Four out of ten claim they plan to quit before retirement. In 1965 more than half of America's teachers told polltakers they were happy in their work. Now barely a third say they would become teachers if they had to make the choice again.

For many teachers, whether to leave their profession is not seen as a question of choice, or economics, but as a matter of emotional necessity. The latest pedagogic phenomenon is something called "teacher burnout." It is a psychological condition, produced by stress, that can result in anything from acute loss of will to suicidal tendencies, ulcers, migraine, colitis, dizziness, even the inability to throw off chronic, and perhaps psychosomatic, colds.

This spring the first national conference on teacher burnout was held in New York City. Surprisingly, the syndrome seems nearly as common in small towns and well-off suburbs as in big cities. The National Education Association has already held more than 100 local workshops round the country to help teachers cope with the problem, which University of California Social Psychologist Ayala Pines defines as "physical, emotional and attitudinal exhaustion." Last March, Stress Consultant Marian Leibowitz held a burnout seminar in Edwardsville, Ill. (pop. 11,982). It drew a paying audience of 250 to a hall big enough for only 100.

According to Dr. Herbert Pardes, director of the National Institute of Mental Health, what emerges from the familiar litany of teacher complaints is that administrative headaches and even physical assaults on teachers can be psychologically less wounding than the frustrating fact that teachers feel unable to do enough that is constructive and rewarding in their classrooms. Whether it is blackboard jungle, red-tape jumble, a place of learning or a collective holding pen for the hapless young, the modern classroom, teachers claim, is out of teachers' control. Some reasons:

DISCIPLINE AND VIOLENCE

Last year 110,000 teachers, 5% of the U.S. total, reported they were attacked by students, an increase of 57% over 1977-78. Teachers believe administrators tend to duck the subject of violence in the schools to avoid adverse publicity. More than half the teachers assaulted feel that afterward authorities did not take adequate action. Today one in eight high school teachers says he "hesitates to confront students out of fear." One in every four reports that he has had personal property stolen at school.

Since the *Wood* vs. *Strickland* Supreme Court decision of 1975, which upheld the right to due process of students accused of troublemaking, the number of students expelled from school has dropped by about 30%. As always in a democracy, the problem of expulsion turns in part on the question of concern for the rights of the disruptive individual *vs.* the rights of classmates and of society. School officials argue that it is wiser and more humane to keep a violent or disruptive student in school than to turn him loose on the streets. But, says John Kotsakis of the Chicago Teachers Union, "schools are now being asked to be more tolerant of disruptive or criminal behavior than society." In a Washington, D.C., high school, a jealous boy tried to shoot his girlfriend in class. The boy was briefly suspended from school. No other action was taken. Says a teacher from that school: "These days if you order a student to the principal's office, he won't go. Hall monitors have to be called to drag him away."

STUDENT ATTITUDES TOWARD LEARNING

In a current hit song called *Another Brick in the Wall*, the rock group Pink Floyd brays: "We don't need no education." There is near unanimity among teachers that many students are defiantly uninterested in schoolwork. Says one West Coast teacher: "Tell me kids haven't changed since we were in high school, and I'll tell you you're living in a fantasy world." A New York panel investigated declining test scores and found that homework assignments had been cut nearly in half during the years from 1968 to 1977. Why? Often simply because students refuse to do them. Blame for the shift in student attitude has been assigned to such things as Watergate, the Viet Nam War, the Me culture. Also to television, which reduces attention span. Now there are 76 million TV homes in the U.S. *vs.* only 10 million in 1950. By age 18, the average American has spent an estimated 15,000 hours in front of the set, far more time than in school. Whatever the figures, teachers agree, television is a hard act to follow.

SHIFTING TIDES OF THEORY

Because it is American, American education dreams of panaceas—universal modern cures for the ancient pain of learning, easy ways to raise test scores and at the same time prepare the "whole child" for his role in society. Education has become a tormented field where armies of theorists clash, frequently using language that is unintelligible to the layman. Faddish theories sweep through the profession, changing standards, techniques, procedures. Often these changes dislocate students and teachers to little purpose. The New Math is an instructive example. Introduced in the early '60s without adequate tryout, and poorly understood by teachers and parents, the New Math eventually was used in more than half the nation's schools. The result: lowered basic skills and test scores in elementary math. Exotic features, like binary arithmetic, have since been dropped. Another trend is the "open classroom," with its many competing "learning centers," which can turn a class into a bullpen of babble. There was the look-say approach to reading (learning to read by recognizing a whole word), which for years displaced the more effective "phonics" (learning to read by sounding out syllables).

Pedagogues seeking a "science of education" are sometimes mere comic pinpricks in a teacher's side. For example, Ph.D. theses have been written on such topics as *Service in the High School Cafeteria, Student Posture* and *Public School Plumbing*. But many studies are hard on teacher morale. Sociologist James S. Coleman's celebrated 1966 survey of pupil achievement seemed glum news for teachers. That study argued that family background made almost all the difference, and that qualities of schools and teachers, good and bad, accounted "for only a small fraction of differences in pupil achievement." Later researchers, examining Coleman's work, found that pupils do seem to learn more when they receive more hours of instruction.

The sensible thing for any effective teacher would be to fend off such theories as best he can and go on teaching. As teachers are fond of saying, "Teaching occurs behind closed doors." But theory, some of it foolish and damaging, inexorably seeps under the doors and into the classrooms. For example, the sound idea that teachers should concentrate on whetting the interests of students and stirring creativity has been unsoundly used as an excuse to duck detailed schoolwork. Says Columbia's Teachers College Professor Diane Ravitch: "It is really putting things backward to say that if children feel good about themselves, then they will achieve. Instead, if children are learning and achieving, *then* they feel good about themselves." Ravitch believes U.S. education has suffered much from such pedagogic theories, and especially from the notion, which emerged from the social climate of the 1960s, that the pursuit of competency is "elitist and undemocratic."

TEXTBOOKS AND PAPERWORK

Teachers are consulted about textbooks but rarely decide what books are finally bought. The textbook business is a $1.3 billion a year industry. Books are ordered by editorial committees and updated at the pleasure of the publisher to sell in as many school systems as possible. Since the late 1960s, according to Reading Expert Copperman, publishers have found that if a textbook is to sell really well, it must be written at a level "two years below the grade for which it is intended."

Paperwork done by teachers and administrators for district, state and national agencies proliferates geometrically. Though it all may be necessary to some distant bureaucrat—a most unlikely circumstance—when teachers comply they tend to feel like spindling, folding and mutilating all the forms. Paperwork wastes an enormous amount of teaching time. In Atlanta, for example, fourth- and fifth-grade teachers must evaluate their students on 60 separate skills. The children must be rated on everything from whether they can express "written ideas clearly" to whether they can apply "scarcity, opportunity cost and resource allocation to local, national and global situations."

ADMINISTRATIVE HASSLES

School procedures, the size and quality of classes, the textbooks and time alloted to study are all affected by government demands, including desegregation of classes, integration of faculty, even federal food programs. One way or another, teachers are bureaucratically hammered at by public health officials (about vaccinations, ringworm, cavities, malnutrition), by social workers and insurance companies (about driver education and broken windows), by juvenile police, civil liberties lawyers, Justice Department lawyers, even divorce lawyers (about child custody).

MAINSTREAMING AS NIGHTMARE

Since the passage of Public Law 94-142 in 1975, it has been federal policy that all handicapped children, insofar as possible, be "mainstreamed," *i.e.*, educated in the same class with everyone else. The law is theoretically useful and just, as a means of avoiding unwarranted discrimination. But in practice it often puts an overwhelming strain on the teacher. "Mainstreaming is ludicrous," says Detroit Counselor Jeanne Latcham. "We have children whose needs are complicated: a child in the third grade who has already been in 16 schools, children who need love and attention and disrupt the classroom to get it. Ten percent of the students in Detroit's classrooms can't conform and can't learn. These children need a disproportionate amount of the teacher's time. It's a teacher's nightmare—she can't help them, but she never forgets them."

The tangle of teaching troubles is too complex to be easily unraveled. But one problem whose solution seems fairly straightforward is the matter of illiterate and uninformed teachers. Competency tests can—and should—be administered to screen out teachers, old as well as novice, who lack basic skills. Such screening would benefit pupils, but it would also put pressure on marginal colleges to flunk substandard students bound for a career in teaching. Indiana University Education Professor David Clark asks rhetorically: "Is it more important to make it easy for kids to reach professional level, or to have good teachers?" Pressure is also needed to ensure adequate funding for teacher training. As a typical example, at the University of Alabama last year total instructional cost for a student in a teacher-ed program was $648, in contrast to $2,304 for an engineering student.

In a classic 1960s study titled *The Miseducation of American Teachers*, James D. Koerner, now program officer at the Alfred P. Sloan Foundation, called for the opening of new paths to careers in teaching. At present a state certificate is required for public school teachers, who earn it by completing practice teaching and specialized education courses (such as philosophy of education and educational psychology). According to Koerner there is little evidence that this program of study improves teacher performance. Koerner calls for more intellectually demanding but more flexible requirements to make the field more attractive to talented people who lack specialized teaching credentials. A small step in this direction is a three-year-old pilot program run by the school board in Hanover, N.H. There, college graduates who want to teach are carefully screened for such qualities as imagination and love of children, as well as academic competency. After a year of probationary teaching, chosen candidates become certified teachers.

It has been argued that teaching needs to be more professional. But in some ways it is too professional now—too encrusted with useless requirements and too tangled in its own obscure professional jargon. The impenetrable language of educators has evolved into what Koerner calls "an artificial drive to create a profession." But it is more damaging to the country than the jargon of law, say, or even government, because it sabotages the use of clear writing and clear thinking by tens of thousands of teachers, and through them, hundreds of thousands of students.

Violence in schools has got to be dealt with effectively. A muscular and unprecedented step in the right direction may have just been taken in California. Over a six-year period, Los Angeles County schools lost an estimated $100 million as a result of school muggings, lawsuits, theft and vandalism while city and school officials ineffectually wrung their hands over jurisdictional problems. Last month the attorney general for the state of California sued, among others, the mayor of Los Angeles, the entire city council, the chief of police and the board of trustees of the Los Angeles Unified School District, demanding that authorities put together some coordinated program to punish the criminals and cut down on violence and theft.

A promising proposal was made by legislators in Pennsylvania last year. They introduced bills requiring that schools report all attacks on teachers to state authorities and that criminal penalties be stiffened for school offenses. Under one of the measures, carrying a gun or knife in school would be treated as a serious crime, and a student who assaulted a teacher would face up to seven years in jail.

Principals need to be more willing to manage their schools. When necessary, the resignation of bad teachers must be sought, even though union grievance procedures can be costly and time consuming. "Too many principals are afraid of grievances," says William Grimshaw, professor of political science at the Illinois Institute of Technology. More important, it should be easier to reward good teachers—if only with public recognition, which is rare at present. As Sylvia Schneirov, a third-grade teacher in Chicago, puts it: "The only praise you get is if your class is quiet and if your bulletin boards are ready when the superintendent comes—you better not have snowflakes on the board when you should have flowers."

Public praise for a job well done matters a great deal. Last year Raj Chopra, the Indian-born superintendent of schools in Council Bluffs, Iowa, raised Council Bluff's S.A.T. scores, which had slumped below national norms, by starting a systematic campaign to encourage "positive thinking" by—and about—Council Bluffs teachers. Says he: "We make them feel proud of their profession by emphasizing that what they do will have an impact on the country for years to come." On May 6, the city celebrated Teachers Day. Retailers, who had earlier been visited by a "teacher recognition task force," gave discounts to teachers that day.

Teaching children to read and write and do sums correctly is not so complicated a business as it is often made to seem. As Koerner puts it: "Almost any school can significantly improve its performance by the simple act of deciding to do so." Indeed, much of the trouble boils down to a failure of will, of old-fashioned teacherly "gumption" in the schools and outside them. As Marcia Fensin, a former teacher and mother of two daughters enrolled in Chicago's Joyce Kilmer Elementary School, says: "The teachers just don't care. They give busy work straight from the textbooks, and meanwhile our kids are not being motivated."

Ironically though, lack of care about education is also a favorite complaint of educators today. Echoing the view of many in the schools, President Lawrence Cremin of Columbia's Teachers College observes: "By and large, society gets what it deserves out of its school system. It gets what it expects. If you don't value things, you don't get them."

The evidence suggests that something so simple as caring can improve the schools. One of James Coleman's undisputed findings: all other things being equal, students achieve better in schools that have active Parent-Teacher Associations. PTAs can provide pressure to improve a teaching staff or school programs and facilities. More important, a widely supported PTA is the tangible sign of parental responsibility for education. Caring shows in other ways as well. Observes Cremin: "A number of studies indicate that certain kinds of schools are unusually effective. Whether the students are rich kids, poor kids, blacks, Hispanics or whites, these schools look very much alike on some criteria. The principal leads his teachers. The teachers become committed to teaching the basic skills. Expectations become high. Time is spent on classroom tasks, and a happy order pervades the school. Rules are widely known and quickly enforced. Parents are brought into the act and are supportive. In such schools, black kids learn, white kids learn, green kids learn."

Yet such is the dilemma of education today that even so clear-cut a matter as agreeing to establish very low minimum competency tests for teachers becomes a hot political issue, arousing fear that the tests will only serve as racial discrimination. Significantly, one of the most eloquent advocates of tough standards, and the man who speaks most probingly and practically about American education, its problems and possible salvation, is not an educator but a black leader, the Rev. Jesse Jackson. "Nobody can save us for us but us" is a Jackson slogan. He insists that parents sign a contract stating that they will get personally involved with school and require their children to do two hours of work a night, without benefit of television. "Many of us allow our children to eat junk," Jackson accuses, "watch junk, listen to junk, talk junk, play with junk, and then we're surprised when they come out to be social junkies." And again, "Tears will get you sympathy, but sweat will get you change." Ostensibly, he is exhorting black ghetto kids and their parents. But he could just as well be setting up a program for everyone, blacks and whites, middle-class parents and burnt-out teachers.

The salvation of the public schools lies, most of all, in just such individual dedication to learning, spread societywide. The schools are simply too big, too close to families and neighborhoods, and too diverse for the improvement of teaching to be ordered by a legislature, Governor, university or school superintendent. They do not need a social program as complex as, say, the Apollo space program, as the continued existence of good public schools throughout the nation shows. They need agreement by the many groups that shape them — parents, teachers, taxpayers, government — that teaching and good teachers are in trouble and need society's support. As to the historic issue, Thomas Jefferson put it well: "If a nation expects to be ignorant and free, in a state of civilization, it expects what never was and never will be."

NOTE

1. [Some form of teacher testing has been approved in] Alabama, Arizona, Arkansas, Florida, Georgia, Louisiana, Mississippi, North Carolina, South Carolina, Tennessee, Virginia, West Virginia.

The "White Flight" Controversy

Diane Ravitch

In the spring of 1975, James Coleman released the "preliminary results" of a new study concluding that school desegregation contributed to "white flight" from big cities and was fostering resegregation of urban districts. On the basis of his findings, Coleman maintained that whites were leaving both large and middle-sized cities with high proportions of blacks, and specifically that whites in big cities were fleeing integration, while whites in middle-sized cities were "not moving any faster from rapidly integrating cities than from others." In short, according to Coleman, "the flight from integration appears to be principally a large-city phenomenon."

In the most controversial passage of his study, Coleman argued:

> The extremely strong reactions of individual whites in moving their children out of large districts engaged in massive and rapid desegregation suggest that in the long run the policies that have been pursued will defeat the purpose of increasing overall contact among races in schools. . . . Thus a major policy implication of this analysis is that in an area such as school desegregation, which has important consequences for individuals and in which individuals retain control of some actions that can in the end defeat the policy, the courts are probably the worst instrument of social policy.

Coleman's study provoked bitter attacks from proponents of activist desegregation policies, such as Roy Wilkins and Kenneth Clark, not only because his findings were inimical to their cause, but because his "defection" seemed especially traitorous. After all, he had been the principal author of the Equal Education Opportunity Survey (known as the Coleman Report), which

Reprinted with permission of the author from *The Public Interest*, No. 51 (Spring 1978), pp. 135-149. © 1978 by National Affairs Inc.

had been authorized by Congress as part of the Civil Rights Act of 1964 and had served, since its publication in 1966, as the chief evidence of the beneficial effects of school desegregation. Coleman had also taken an outspoken public role as a leading scholarly advocate of school desegregation.

Coleman presented his paper (co-authored by Sara Kelly and John Moore of the Urban Institute) at a meeting of the American Educational Research Association on April 2, 1975, but it was not reported in *The New York Times* until June 7, 1975. (Some of Coleman's adversaries later attacked him for carrying his views to the press, but the delay in reporting the story indicates that he did not initiate the media attention.) Then, on July 11, 1975, Robert Reinhold of *The New York Times* reported that the 20 central-city districts in Coleman's study had not undergone court-ordered busing, and Coleman admitted that his views "went somewhat beyond the data." He acknowledged that he had not studied the effects of busing, since the cities under scrutiny had not been subject to court order, and he conceded that he had been "quite wrong" to have called the integration "massive" where it had occurred. But he nonetheless defended the overall implication of his work and continued to maintain that court-imposed desegregation exacerbated the rate of "white flight."

Mobilized by Coleman's well-publicized statements, scholars committed to desegregation lost no time in taking issue with his findings. On August 15, 1975, a "Symposium on School Desegregation and White Flight" was convened, funded by the National Institute of Education, co-sponsored by the Catholic University Center for National Policy Review and the Notre Dame Center for Civil Rights, and hosted by the Brookings Institution. Though Coleman was a participant, the papers that emerged from the symposium consisted entirely of rebuttals of his position. Later, Gregg Jackson, of the United States Commission on Civil Rights, criticized both Coleman's data and his methodology in two articles, a technical version in *Educational Researcher* (November 1975) and a popular version in *Phi Delta Kappan* (December 1975). Coleman's claim that desegregation accelerated "white flight" was vigorously denounced by Robert Green, of Michigan State University, and Thomas Pettigrew, of Harvard University, first at a press conference called by the NAACP, and then in jointly written articles in *Phi Delta Kappan* (February 1976) and in *Harvard Educational Review* (February 1976). Green and Pettigrew charged that Coleman had been selective in his choice of school districts and that their own reanalysis of districts with more than 75,000 pupils revealed no correlation between the degree of desegregation and the rate of "white flight."

There were three major criticisms of Coleman's study: that his conclusions were invalid because he did not look at enough districts and because the districts he did examine had not undergone court-ordered desegregation; that "white flight" from central cities is a long-term phenomenon predating school desegregation; and that desegregation does not cause "white flight" since the same level of "white flight" can be observed in big cities whether or not they have enacted desegregation plans. The policy implication of these criticisms is that framers of desegregation plans need not be concerned about the impact of "white flight," because desegregation does not cause greater numbers of whites to leave than would have left anyway. Green and Pettigrew state this directly:

> *While extensive desegregation may hasten the while flight phenomenon, particularly in the largest nonmetropolitan districts in the South, the effect, if it obtains at all, may only be temporarily during the first year of desegregation, and then only for those families which have already made plans to move.*

The counterargument against Coleman was strengthened during the summer of 1975 by another new study of the effects of desegregation on "white flight," written by Christine Rossell, an assistant professor of political science at Boston University. Her paper, presented to the American Political Science Association in September 1975 and published in *Political Science Quarterly* (Winter 1975), sought to establish definitively that school desegregation causes "little or no significant white flight, even when it is court ordered and implemented in large cities." Gary Orfield, editor of the papers from the August symposium on "white flight" (and also an author of one of the rebuttals to Coleman), called Rossell's study "particularly impressive," and Robert Green described it as "the most serious challenge to the Coleman position." And indeed, Rossell sought not only to refute Coleman's arguments but to prove that desegregation had little or no impact on "white flight," and that "white flight" was, at most, a temporary and minimal occurrence.

Rossell collected data from 86 school districts and grouped them by the degree to which students had been reassigned for purposes of school integration. She came to the conclusion that of the 10 districts with the highest degree of desegregation, only two (Pasadena and Pontiac) experienced any significant "white flight," but it was "minimal (about a 3-percent increase over the previous trend) and temporary." The whole group of cities with the highest amount of desegregation showed "a negligible increase of about 1 percent from the previous trend":

> *The important phenomenon here is that any loss of whites occurs before school opens in the first year of the plan. After that, white flight stabilizes to a rate slightly better than the pre-desegregation period. Therefore, white flight, if it occurs at all, occurs not from the problems experienced during the first year of desegregation, but from the fear of problems. In other words, if whites leave, it is typically not because they participated in the plan and did not like it, but because they refused to participate at all.*

Busing did not cause "white flight," she held, since she found "no significant increase in white flight in Northern school districts that desegregated under court order." Where Coleman had asserted that "white flight" was greatest in large districts undergoing rapid desegregation, Rossell disagreed:

> *The two large school districts, San Francisco and Denver, that engaged in such massive and rapid desegregation show no significant white flight. Nor do most of the other large school districts that implemented lesser degrees of school desegregation (Seattle; Milwaukee; Kansas City, Mo.; Indianapolis; Baltimore; Philadelphia; Los Angeles; and Chicago). Thus the data of the present study contradict almost every claim Coleman has made regarding school desegregation and white flight.*

Indeed, according to Rossell, mandatory city-wide school desegregation may be the best means to insure racial stability:

> *While almost all school districts (with the exception of Berkeley, California) are still experiencing white flight, it is quite encouraging that by the second and third year after desegregation, the school districts engaging in massive and rapid desegregation have a rate of white flight that is lower than their rate in the predesegregation period and lower than that of any other group [of cities in the study], including those that did not implement any desegregation at all. This is a heartening phenomenon and may mean that school desegregation and the educational innovation that typically accompanies it when it is city wide, could impede the increasing ghettoization of American cities.*

Thus, in Rossell's view, not only is school desegregation *not* a cause of "white flight," it may actually be the *remedy* for whatever minimal "white flight" occurs.

But if Rossell is right, how could a distinguished scholar like James Coleman have become so concerned about a relatively insignificant problem? Why had the media accepted the idea that "white flight" was of large proportions, when it was no more than one or two percent of white pupils each year? Conversely, how did Rossell come to the conclusion that "white flight" was minimal and of little or no significance?

To understand Rossell's optimistic conclusions, it is necessary to follow her method of calculating the rate of "white flight." She measured the effect of desegregation on "white flight" by observing changes in the percentage of white pupils enrolled in public schools before and after the major desegregation plan in each city, for as many years as data were available, with 1972-73 the final year of the study. If a district was 58-percent white one year, then dropped to 56-percent white and then to 53-percent white, Rossell would say that the district lost 2 percent the first year, 3 percent the second, and so on. For example, Table 1 presents five of the cities she analyzed, all in her "high desegregation" group. Thus, Rossell represents the decline in percentage white in Pasadena before desegregation with the following figures: -2.7, -1.5, -1.9, -2.1, -2.0, -2.4. A desegregation plan was adopted in 1970, and in that year

Table 1
Change in percentage of white students in "high desegregation" cities (Rossell's calculations)

	Percentage of pupils reassigned	Years before plan date							Plan date		Years after plan date			
		7	6	5	4	3	2	1			1	2	3	4
Pasadena[1]	98.48%	71.6%	68.9%	67.4%	65.5%	63.4%	61.4%	59.0%	1970	54.8%	50.3%	47.8%	—	—
Pontiac[1]	83.47	74.7	73.4	72.4	69.4	66.3	64.6	62.2	1971	56.8	56.4	—	—	—
Berkeley	57.72	—	—	54.0	51.8	49.6	50.3	48.7	1968	46.5	45.9	45.1	45.2%	46.1%
San Francisco[1]	42.49	—	45.3	42.4	41.2	41.2	37.1	36.9	1971	33.9	31.8	—	—	—
Denver[1]	24.64	—	—	70.4	69.1	67.7	66.2	65.6	1969	64.1	61.7	60.3	58.3	—

[1]Court-ordered desegregation.
Source: Paper presented by Rossell before the American Politicanl Science Association (September 1975).

Table 2
Racial change in Pasadena public schools

Year	Total number of pupils	Whites		Minorities		White loss	
		Number of pupils	Percentage of total	Number of pupils	Percentage of total	Number of pupils	Percentage of 1968 number
1968	31,259	19,201	61.4%	12,058	38.6%	—	—
1972	26,225	12,523	47.8	13,702	52.2	6,678	34.8%

Source: Author's calculations.

the figure representing white decline was −4.2; in the next two years, the figures were −4.5 and −2.5. In San Francisco, where a "massive and rapid" court-ordered busing plan was implemented in 1971, before desegregation the figures were −2.9, −1.2, 0, −4.1, −.2; after desegregation, they were −3.0 and −2.1. (Rossell obtained these figures by subtracting the percentage white in any given year from the percentage white in the previous year.) As noted earlier, Rossell argued that none of the cities in her study except Pasadena and Pontiac experienced any significant "white flight," and even in those two cities it was minimal and temporary. Indeed, since her method of comparing percentages yields such small figures to represent the declining proportions of white pupils each year, "white flight" appears to be a sorely overdramatized issue.

Unhappily, this is not the case. Rossell has selected a statistical method that will show small declines even in the face of large absolute movements. Consider, for example, a school district with 250,000 pupils, 200,000 whites (80 percent of the total) and 50,000 blacks (20 percent of the total). If 40,000 white pupils were to leave the district in a single year, it would then have 160,000 whites (76.2 percent of the total) and 50,000 blacks (23.8 percent of the total). Rossell would say that the change in the percentage white was −3.8, that is, a drop of 3.8 *percentage points. But what has actually happened is that 20 percent of the white pupils have left the district* (since 40,000 is 20 percent of 200,000). It is precisely Rossell's method of calculating "white flight" by subtracting percentages that leads her to her conclusions. In Pasadena, for example, Rossell's tables show a decline in percentage white from 61.4 percent in 1968 to 47.8 percent in 1972, a drop of 13.6 points. But the absolute numbers of whites in the Pasadena school system declined by 34.8 percent, while the absolute number of minorities rose slightly (see Table 2).

Since Rossell maintains that "white flight" rarely occurs after desegregation, it is worth nothing that the Pasadena school district continued to lose white pupils: By 1976-77, its total enrollment was 25,718, and its white population had declined to 9,839, a loss of 48.8 percent of the number of whites enrolled in 1968 and of 21.4 percent of whites enrolled in 1972.

Rossell explains why she preferred to compare percentages rather than absolute numbers:

> Coleman . . . *measures loss in white enrollment in a way that may tend to exaggerate white flight in some cities. He compares the raw figures on white enrollment in the previous year and then claims white flight if the latter is lower than the former. Yet one can easily predict cases where due to job layoffs, factory closings, etc., both whites and blacks leave a city at a faster rate than before, but blacks leave at a higher rate. Although this would result in the percentage black decreasing and the percentage white increasing, Coleman would still call this white flight, even though it might more properly be called "black flight." In the final analysis, the most important variable for policy purposes is the percentage white, not the number white.*

However, this criticism applies not to anyone using absolute numbers, which clearly reveal any joint fluctuation of racial groups, but to the researcher using only percentages, which can mask substantial changes in enrollments. In other words, Rossell is criticizing her own technique. For example, when black enrollment is growing while white enrollment is fairly stable, as it was in Boston during the 1960's, the method of comparing percentages gives an impression of "white flight" where none exists.

The best way to avoid the choice between percentages and absolute numbers is to supply both. When both are presented for the four other districts used by Rossell (in Table 1), a very different picture emerges, as evident from Table 3. Only in Berkeley, a small atypical university town that initiated its own desegregation plan, not under court order, was the white pupil loss truly insignificant. San Francisco, which Rossell maintains had "no significant white flight," lost one third of its white pupils during the period of her study. Furthermore, subsequent events in San Francisco and Denver (the two largest urban districts with massive court-ordered desegregation) do not sustain her hypothesis that "white flight" rarely occurs after the implementation of major desegregation plans. A court order was enacted in San Francisco in 1971; the number of white pupils in public schools there declined from 26,067 in 1972 to 14,958 in 1976, a loss of 42.6 percent of white enrollment in only four years. Nor did Denver, where a city-wide plan was imposed in 1974, maintain its white enrollment: Its 53,412 white pupils in 1972 declined to 36,539 in 1976, a loss of nearly a third of the white pupils in four years. In September 1977, Denver's white pupils declined by another 3,000 to 47.0 percent of the Denver system, having dropped from a majority of 65.6 percent in 1968 and 58.3 percent in 1972. Any statistical method that declares these demographic shifts "insignificant" is, at the very least, not very useful.

The use of Rossell's statistical method in the case of Boston, that maelstrom of desegregation woes, is so at variance with common knowledge as to throw social science into disrepute. Rossell released the following statement to the press in December 1975:

> Much has been made of the claim that school desegregation in Boston (Phase I in the Fall of 1974 and Phase II in the Fall of 1975) has caused massive white flight. The accompanying graph and table indicate that the decline in the percentage white enrolled in the public schools is part of a trend that began at least as early as 1964 and probably earlier. While the implementation of school desegregation appears to have somewhat accelerated this trend, a projection of the former trend indicates that Boston would have been a majority non-white system, even if it had not desegregated, by the fall of 1976. Therefore, desegregation is only responsible for accelerating by one year, the trend toward a majority non-white school system.

This statement was accompanied by Table 4.

But consider the actual figures, which are shown in Table 5. The absolute

Table 3
Racial change in "high desegregation" cities

City	Year	Total number of pupils	Whites		Minorities		White loss	
			Number of pupils	Percentage of total	Number of pupils	Percentage of total	Number of pupils	Percentage of 1968 number
Pontiac	1968	23,832	15,789	66.3%	8,043	33.7%	—	—
	1972	21,141	11,929	56.4	9,212	43.6	3,860	24.4%
Berkeley	1968	16,204	7,535	46.5	8,669	53.5	—	—
	1972	15,213	7,017	46.1	8,196	53.9	518	6.9
San Francisco	1968	94,154	38,824	41.2	55,330	58.8	—	—
	1972	81,970	26,067	31.8	55,903	68.2	12,757	32.9
Denver	1968	96,577	63,398	65.6	33,179	34.4	—	—
	1972	91,616	53,412	58.3	38,204	41.7	9,986	15.8

Source: Author's calculations.

Table 4
"Percentage white in Boston public schools, 1964-1975" (Rossell's calculations)

1964	1965	1966	1967	1968	1969	1970	1971	1972	1973	1974	(Estimated) 1975
75.6	74.2	73.9	72.4	68.5	66.0	64.1	61.5	59.6	57.2	52.3	47.8

Source: Press release by Rossell (December 1975).

figures reveal that white enrollment dropped by 7,418 (10.7 percent) from 1964 until 1970, an average loss of 1.8 percent annually. However, the loss in white pupils from 1970 through 1976 was 27,421 (44 percent), four times the rate of the previous six years. "White flight" was significantly higher during the implementation of the desegregation plan, and there is simply no way of knowing whether those who left had already been planning to go. It is possible to argue that the 1974-1975 desegregation of Boston's public schools was necessary and correct regardless of the number of whites who left the system. But it is indefensible to argue, against the evidence, that the desegregation plan caused only a one-year acceleration in the transition to a majority non-white school system.

We have inspected Rossell's case against Coleman in detail because it illustrates some of the issues involved in the debate. But the argument concerns more than the proper presentation of the data on declining white enrollments. Coleman also used econometric models to attempt to determine the extent to which desegregation as such was leading to declining white enrollments. These models could take into account the effect of whether a city was Southern or not, whether it had nearby high-percentage-white suburbs, and whether a trend independent of desegregation was reducing white enrollment (suburban movement or other factors). On these matters, the debate is too technical to summarize easily.

One of the issues was the proper measure of desegregation. Coleman argued that, independent of the specific causes (e.g., a court order) leading to it, an increase in the degree to which whites are exposed to blacks seemed, under certain circumstances, to reduce the number of whites. Ultimately, Coleman's model required some important qualifications. The increase in the amount of "white flight" that occurred with an increase in desegregation was particularly marked in larger cities, in cities with a large black school population, and in cities with adjacent school districts with a high proportion of white students. Coleman's conclusions, supported by mathematical models, also seem to conform to common sense and experience. His models have been modified, attacked, and retested, but the general conclusions still hold. After reanalyzing the data and taking into account various criticisms made of Coleman, Charles Clotfelter has concluded:

> The estimates in the current paper of the effect of desegregation — measured by hypothetical changes in exposure rates — support the view that desegregation has a strong overall effect on white enrollments in the largest school districts. Within these large districts, however, desegregation is a significant stimulus of white losses only in districts where blacks make up more than 7 percent of students. . . . For smaller districts, response to desegregation appears to be less intense. . . .

By attempting to deny the long-term significance of "white flight" and by refusing to acknowledge the impact of court-ordered busing on white pupil

Table 5
Enrollment in the Boston public schools, 1964-1976

Year	Total number of pupils	Whites Number of pupils	Whites Percentage of total	Minorities Number of pupils	Minorities Percentage of total	White loss Number of pupils	White loss Percentage of number in previous year
1964	91,800	69,400	75.6%	22,400	24.4%	—	—
1965	93,055	69,046	74.2	24,009	25.8	359	0.5%
1966	92,127	68,082	73.9	24,045	26.1	964	1.4
1967	92,441	66,927	72.4	25,512	27.6	1,155	1.7
1968	94,174	64,509	68.5	29,665	31.5	2,418	3.6
1969	94,885	62,624	66.0	32,261	34.0	1,885	2.9
1970	96,696	61,982	64.1	34,714	35.9	642	1.0
1971	96,400	59,286	61.5	37,114	38.5	2,696	4.3
1972	96,239	57,358	59.6	38,881	40.4	1,928	3.3
1973	93,647	53,593	57.2	40,054	42.8	3,765	6.6
1974	85,826	44,937	52.4	40,889	47.6	8,656	16.2
1975	76,461	36,243	47.4	40,218	52.6	8,694	19.3
1976	76,889	34,561	45.0	43,328	55.0	1,682	4.6

Source: Author's calculations.

losses, Coleman's critics have confused and confounded the analysis of desegregation policy. Worse yet, the issue has been unfairly politicized by the charge
that those who worry about the relationship between desegregation and "white
flight" are subverting the civil rights organizations. In view of the rate of white
exodus from the public schools of Boston, Denver, and San Francisco, as well
as the projected declines in Los Angeles after the implementation of busing, it is
impossible to contend that court-ordered racial assignment does not accelerate
"white flight" in large cities. It is not a contradiction to recognize that cities
where there has been no court-ordered busing have also experienced significant
"white flight" (though in no city has the rate of "white flight" been as great in a
single year as it was in Boston in 1974 and again in 1975). No matter how many
qualifications are attached to Coleman's methodology or research design, his
central concern about the diminishing number of whites in urban schools
remains valid.

This conclusion should not be misunderstood. Even if it were clearly
proved that desegregation causes "white flight," it would still be imperative to
eliminate unconstitutional racial discrimination. Certainly, no one—least of
all, Coleman—would propose maintaining racially segregated schools as a
way of inducing whites to remain in city schools. Coleman's question, raised
not in defense of segregation but about the long-range utility of system-wide
racial balance plans, was whether court-ordered busing makes desegregation
harder to achieve by hastening the departure of whites from city schools.
"White flight," in cities under court order and in cities not under court order, is
a real problem; it will not be solved by denying its existence or seriousness.

Table 6 demonstrates the extent of racial change in the 29 biggest cities in
the United States from 1968 to 1976. (This list is of *big-city school districts*, not
districts that have been made large by court order for purposes of integration.)
All have had desegregation controversies, but only a few have court-ordered
racial balance plans. *Of the 29 biggest city school districts in the nation, only
eight still have a white majority:* Milwaukee, Jacksonville, Columbus, Indianapolis, San Diego, Seattle, Nashville, and Pittsburgh. And three of these eight
are fast approaching the 50-percent mark (Milwaukee, Indianapolis, and
Pittsburgh). During this eight-year period, the following districts made the
transition from majority white to majority non-white: Los Angeles, Houston,
Miami, Dallas, Denver, Boston, Cincinnati, and Kansas City.

It seems unlikely that we will ever know with any degree of certainty
whether whites (and some middle-class blacks) are leaving the city because of
concern about desegregation or crime or poor services or racial tensions or the
quality of life or for some other reason or combination of reasons. But if it is
impossible to measure the precise impact of school desegregation on "white
flight," it is equally insupportable to claim that there is no effect whatever.
Court-ordered busing may or may not be the primary stimulus of white
withdrawal from city schools, but it is verly likely a contributing factor—and,
at least in Boston, an important contributing factor. Just as it is impossible to

Table 6
Racial change in urban public schools, 1968-1976

City	Year	Total number of pupils	Whites Number of pupils	Whites Percentage of total	Minorities[2] Number of pupils	Minorities[2] Percentage of total	White loss Number of pupils	White loss Percentage 1968 number	Total loss Number of pupils	Total loss Percentage of 1968 number
New York City	1968	1,063,787	467,365	43.9%	596,422	56.1%	139,300	29.8%	(+13,403)	(+1.3%)
	1976	1,077,190	328,065	30.5	749,125	69.5				
Los Angeles	1968	653,549	350,909	53.7	302,640	46.3	131,550	37.5	60,618	9.3
	1976	592,931	219,359	37.0	373,572	63.0				
Chicago	1968	582,274	219,478	37.7	362,796	62.3	88,693	40.4	58,053	10.0
	1976	524,221	130,785	25.0	393,436	75.0				
Houston	1968	246,098	131,099	53.3	114,999	46.7	59,305	45.2	36,073	14.7
	1976	210,025	71,794	34.2	138,231	65.8				
Detroit	1968	296,097	116,250	39.3	179,847	60.7	71,636	61.6	56,883	19.2
	1976	239,214	44,614	18.7	194,600	81.3				
Philadelphia	1968	282,617	109,512	38.7	173,105	61.3	27,502	25.1	24,675	8.7
	1976	257,942	82,010	31.8	175,932	68.2				
Miami	1968	232,465	135,598	58.3	96,867	41.7	37,236	27.5	(+7,529)	(+3.2)
	1976	239,994	98,362	41.0	141,632	59.0				
Baltimore	1968	192,171	66,997	34.9	125,174	65.1	28,005	41.8	32,050	16.7
	1976	160,121	38,992	24.4	121,129	75.6				
Dallas	1968	159,924	97,888	61.2	62,036	38.8	44,880	45.8	20,844	13.0
	1976	139,080	53,008	38.1	86,072	61.9				
Cleveland	1968	156,054	66,324	42.5	89,730	57.5	19,941	30.1	33,348	21.4
	1976	122,706	46,383	37.8	76,323	62.2				
Washington, D.C.	1968	148,725	8,280	5.6	140,445	94.4	3,796	45.8	22,138	14.9
	1976	126,587	4,484	3.5	122,103	96.5				
Milwaukee	1968	130,445	95,161	73.0	35,284	27.0	33,423	35.1	20,880	16.0
	1976	109,565	61,738	56.3	47,827	43.7				
Memphis	1968	125,813	58,271	46.3	67,542	53.7	24,423	41.9	8,317	6.6
	1976	117,496	33,848	28.8	83,648	71.2				
Jacksonville	1968	122,637	87,999	71.8	34,638	28.2	14,269	16.2	11,930	9.7
	1976	110,707	73,730	66.6	36,977	33.4				

City	Year									
St. Louis	1968	42,174	115,582	36.5	73,408	63.5	18,664	45.0	34,090	29.5
	1976	23,210	81,492	28.5	58,282	71.5				
New Orleans	1968	34,673	110,783	31.3	76,110	68.7	16,740	48.3	17,419	15.7
	1976	17,933	93,364	19.2	75,431	80.8				
Columbus, Ohio	1968	81,655	110,699	73.8	29,044	26.2	16,998	20.8	14,327	12.9
	1976	64,657	96,372	67.1	31,715	32.9				
Indianapolis	1968	72,010	108,587	66.3	36,577	33.7	26,823	37.2	26,585	24.5
	1976	45,187	82,002	55.1	36,815	44.9				
Atlanta	1968	42,506	111,227	38.2	68,721	61.8	33,275	78.3	28,747	25.8
	1976	9,231	82,480	11.2	73,199	88.8				
San Diego	1968	98,163	128,414	76.1	30,751	23.9	18,010	18.3	7,491	5.8
	1976	80,153	121,423	66.0	41,270	34.0				
Denver	1968	63,398	96,577	65.6	33,179	34.4	26,859	42.4	21,340	22.1
	1976	36,539	75,237	48.6	38,698	51.4				
Boston	1968	64,500	94,174	68.5	29,674	31.5	29,939	46.4	17,285	18.4
	1976	34,561	76,889	45.0	42,328	55.0				
San Francisco	1968	38,824	94,154	41.2	55,330	58.8	23,866	61.5	28,899	30.7
	1976	14,958	65,255	22.9	50,297	77.1				
Seattle	1968	77,293	94,025	82.2	16,732	17.8	35,670	46.1	32,206	34.3
	1976	41,623	61,819	67.3	20,196	32.7				
Nashville	1968	71,039	93,720	75.8	22,681	24.2	16,517	23.3	15,722	16.8
	1976	54,522	77,998	69.9	23,476	30.1				
Cincinnati	1968	49,231	86,807	56.7	37,576	43.3	18,534	37.6	21,172	24.4
	1976	30,697	65,635	46.8	34,938	53.2				
San Antonio	1968	21,310	79,353	26.9	58,043	73.1	11,348	53.3	13,641	17.2
	1976	9,962	65,712	15.1	55,750	84.9				
Pittsburgh	1968	46,005	76,628	60.3	30,263	39.7	14,051	30.5	17,606	23.0
	1976	31,954	59,022	54.1	27,068	45.9				
Kansas City	1968	39,510	74,202	53.2	34,692	46.8	21,950	44.4	23,155	31.2
	1976	17,560	51,047	34.4	33,487	65.6				

[1] Two big cities—Phoenix and San Jose—are not included because both have numerous districts not coextensive with the city's boundaries. Both are predominantly white.

[2] Includes blacks, Hispanics, Asians, and American Indians.

Source: Prepared by the author for a conference by the National Institute of Education and the Hudson Institute (September 15-16, 1977).

determine whether it is the direct cause, it is equally impossible to prove that it has no bearing at all on family decisions to remove children from urban schools.

Behind the controversy over Coleman's findings is a struggle over the future direction of policy. Coleman is urging a cautious and deliberate approach that takes into account the possibility of "white flight" and resegregation. His views, furthermore, support the idea that court remedies should be specific, rather than broad and system-wide.

Coleman's critics are committed to racial balancing of pupil populations as the best, most demonstrable assurance of full integration. The integration forces may not have won every court battle, but they have succeeded in popularizing the notion that every black school, regardless of the reason for its racial concentration, is a segregated school, the result of official discrimination rather than affinity or choice. In the aftermath of the Supreme Court's 1974 Detroit decision, which limited urban-suburban busing, integration advocates, in many instances, have had to confine their demands for busing to individual school districts. In our largest cities, this is not a solution likely to satisfy anyone for very long: "Success" in most big cities will mean a school system in which every school is predominantly non-white, and from which white pupils continue to leave every year. Unless "white flight" is stopped or reversed, racial balancing within cities will very likely produce the phenomenon of resegregation between city and suburb that Coleman has warned about.

The inadequacy of racial balancing within big-city school districts is likely to generate new pressures for metropolitan-area school integration. This is a proposal long favored by the United States Civil Rights Commission and civil rights groups, and it is already in effect in several smaller cities and counties. How such a proposal might be implemented in a city school district with a quarter-million, a half-million, or a million pupils is uncertain, as are the educational implications. What is predictable, however, is the political reaction: To date, no metropolitan region has voluntarily adopted a full city-suburban merger for school integration, and opposition can be anticipated from suburban districts (whose residents include many who fled the city schools), state legislatures (where urban interests are a minority), and Congress (which regularly passes ineffective busing curbs). Nothing less than a reversal of the Supreme Court's 1974 Detroit decision could produce the enforcement mechanism to impose metropolitan-area integration on a large scale. For now, at least, that is not in the offing.

But if racial balancing is of limited practicality because of the diminishing number of white pupils in most big cities, and if metropolitan cross-busing is of limited applicability because of the Supreme Court's 1974 ruling, what then? Few urban districts have had the capacity to look or plan beyond the latest political or fiscal crisis, but clearly some fresh synthesis is needed to restore a sense of direction to urban education. Atlanta is one city that offers hope of a new approach. Its schools are 90-percent black, and its professional leadership is predominantly black. At the instigation of the local NAACP (which defied the national NAACP), a deal was struck in court to forego busing in exchange for jobs and black control of the system. Now the system is intent on demonstrating that the schools can be made to work.

The Atlanta schools are stressing the kind of curriculum and values that will enable black children (and white children) to succeed in the mainstream of American life; this means an early emphasis on basic skills, taught in an orderly atmosphere in which achievement and hard work are rewarded. Atlanta has decided to build a new high school, and remarkably, it will be a selective, admission-by-academic-examination school, possibly the first new such school anywhere in the country for many years.

Meanwhile, the American Civil Liberties Union is pressing a court suit to compel the merger of the Atlanta school district and the surrounding white suburban districts, in order to make blacks a minority within a predominantly white metropolitan district; not surprisingly, the Atlanta district has shown no interest in surrendering its independence. The theory of Atlanta's educational leaders is that equal educational opportunity can be achieved through quality education. If they are right, and if they can create the kind of productive, effective schools that all parents want, their system could become a showplace for urban American schools and a magnet pulling back the children of those who fled the city during the past two decades. Andrew Young, while he was Atlanta's Congressman, predicted in a newspaper interview in 1975 that Atlanta's schools would ultimately prove to be better than the suburban schools, both because of their clear and purposeful educational approach and because of the city's considerable cultural resources, which no suburban shopping mall can match. Imagine that: "white flight" *to* the city, resulting not from coercion or condescension, but from an earnest search for good public schools.

Discussion Questions

1. What is your assessment of college education departments and the kinds of students they attract?

2. As recent high school graduates, how do you react to charges that you are less well educated than those who graduated twenty or thirty years ago?

3. How do you respond to the following question raised by Diane Ravitch: "But if racial balancing is of limited practicality because of the diminishing number of white pupils in most big cities, and if metropolitan cross-busing is of limited applicability because of the Supreme Court's 1974 ruling, what then?"

4. What is your reaction to Ravitch's premise (above) concerning "white flight"?

INDEX